N°	Nom	Classe	Date
	Khang Anh Le		
	(The Rock)		
	L3K		
	T.S.O.B'S		

OH HELL YEAH!

Titles available from Malvern Language Guides

GCSE French - Your Vocabulary Guide
GCSE French - Your Speaking Test Guide
French Grammar - Your Guide
Your French Dictionary

Standard Grade French (Scotland) - Your Vocabulary Guide
Common Entrance 13+ - Your French Guide

GCSE German - Your Vocabulary Guide
GCSE German - Your Speaking Test Guide
German Grammar - Your Guide
Your German Dictionary (autumn 96)

GCSE Spanish - Your Vocabulary Guide
GCSE Spanish - Your Speaking Test Guide
Spanish Grammar - Your Guide

GCSE Italian - Your Vocabulary Guide
GCSE Italian - Your Speaking Test Guide
Italian Grammar - Your Guide

Key Stage 3 French - Your Guide
Key Stage 3 German - Your Guide
Key Stage 3 Spanish - Your Guide

Mon Echange Scolaire
Mein Austausch
Mi Intercambio Escolar
Ma Visite en France

French - English, English - French

Your

FRENCH

Dictionary

Val Levick
Glenise Radford
Alasdair McKeane

ACKNOWLEDGEMENTS

We are grateful to Anne, Mick and John for editorial, moral, typographical and technical support, to Claire, Jonathan, John, Andrew and James for their tolerance of the whole process of writing and publishing this book, and to Paul Garner, Lisa Jefferson, Eleanor Palmer and Becky Sears for proof-reading and other editorial work.

Published by Malvern Language Guides
PO Box 76
Malvern
WR14 2YP

Tel: 01684 893756 (for price enquiries only)
01684 577433 (for other enquiries)

Further copies can be obtained by completing the order form at the back of the book.

Typeset by Malvern Language Guides

Printed by Aldine Press Ltd
Barnards Green Road
Malvern
WR14 3NB
Tel: 01684 562786

ISBN: 1 898219 41 9

CONTENTS

La France

Dunkerque
Calais
Boulogne
Lille
Cherbourg
Dieppe
Amiens
Le Havre
Rouen
La Seine
Reims
PARIS
Nancy
Strasbourg
Brest
St Malo
Le Rhun
Rennes
Le Mans
Orléans
Tours
La Loire
Dijon
Nantes
Poitiers
La Rochelle
Limoges
Clermont-Ferrand
Lyon
Grenoble
Bordeaux
LE MASSIF CENTRAL
Le Rhône
LES ALPES
La Garonne
Avignon
Nice
Biarritz
Toulouse
Montpellier
Marseille
Lourdes
Toulon
LES PYRENEES

LES PAYS FRANCOPHONES

l'Algérie *f*
la Belgique
le Bénin (ex Dahomey)
le Burkina Faso (ex Upper Volta)
le Burundi
le Cambodge (le Kampuchéa)
le Cameroun
le Canada
les Comores *fpl*
la Côte d'Ivoire
la République de Dijbouti
la France
le Gabon
la Guinée
l'île d'Haïti *f*
le Liban
le Luxembourg
l'île de Madagascar *f*
le Mali
le Maroc
l'île Maurice *f*
la Mauritanie
le Niger
la République Centrafricaine
le Ruanda
le Sénégal
les Seychelles *fpl*
la Suisse
le Tchad
le Togo

la Tunisie
le Vietnam
le Zaïre

la Guadeloupe - DOM
French overseas département in the Caribbean

la Martinique - DOM
French overseas département south of Guadeloupe

la Guyane - DOM
French overseas département between Surinam and Brazil

l'île de la Réunion *f* - DOM
French overseas département in the Indian Ocean

les îles de St-Pierre et Miquelon *fpl* - DOM
French islands off Newfoundland

Terres Australes et Antartiques *fpl* - TOM
French islands in the Antartic and Australasian area. Scientific base

la Nouvelle Calédonie - TOM
French overseas territory in the Pacific, to the east of Australia

la Polynésie française - TOM
French overseas territory in the Pacific

Wallis et Futuna - TOM
French islands in the Pacific

DOM: - les départements d'outre-mer
These areas are administratively part of France and are represented in the French parliament.
TOM: - les territoires d'outre mer
These areas are administered by France, but are not represented in the French parliament.

HOW TO USE A DICTIONARY

All learners of a foreign language will find knowing how to use a dictionary a really useful skill. From 1998 onwards dictionaries will be permitted in some parts of the GCSE exam, so it is sensible to learn how to look up words and to understand the abbreviations.

Alphabetical order

Dictionaries are arranged in alphabetical order. So all words beginning with the letter *a* come before all those beginning with the letter *b*, and so on. Within the section for each letter, the same applies. So the words which start with the letters *ab* come before those starting *ac*, and so on. In the same way, words starting *aba* come before those starting *abb*. If you are not totally sure of your alphabet, write it on a bookmark which you keep with your dictionary.

In French, accents over letters (*é, è, ê*) do not affect the alphabetical order.

Abbreviations

All dictionaries contain abbreviations for convenience. However, they are only convenient if you know what they mean! In this dictionary there are reminders of the most frequent abbreviations at the foot of each page. The full list of abbreviations we have used is given on page vii.

Looking up a French word

When you look up a **French** word, it is possible that you may find a number of English translations given, listed with the most common first. You will then need to work out which meaning is most likely in the context.

You may find that a word is not listed. This may mean that it is a past participle, or some other part of an irregular verb. Check the irregular verb table on page 208.

Adjectives

In French, adjectives change their spelling to agree with their noun.

Adjectives with the same form in both masculine and feminine, or adjectives which just add **-e** in the feminine are shown in one form only in this dictionary:

>   Example: **red** – rouge *adj*
>   **big** – grand *adj*

Adjectives with a more complicated feminine form are shown in both forms:

>   Example: **happy** – heureux, heureuse *adj*

Adjectives which for some reason do not change their spelling are marked as invariable: *adj inv*

Example: **smart** – (fashionable) chic *adj inv*

Plural forms of adjectives are mentioned only when they are unusual.

Example: **uneven** – inégal (*mpl* inégaux)

Nouns

Nouns are identified as masculine or feminine.

Example: **boy** – garçon *nm*
                  girl – fille *nf*

Some nouns can be either masculine or feminine. These are shown separately if they are spelled differently, or once only if the noun is the same in both genders.

Example: **customer** – client *nm*, cliente *nf*
                  pupil – élève *nmf*

Verbs

Verbs are classified as regular (*v reg*), regular with variations (*v reg* †), reflexive (*v refl*) or irregular (*v irreg* §)

Regular verbs are verbs which belong to the **-er**, **-ir** or **-re** groups:

Example: regard**er**, fin**ir**, répond**re**

These are identified as *v reg*.

Regular verbs with variations are **-er** verbs which broadly follow the regular pattern with some variations:

Example: man**ger**, commen**cer**, envo**yer**

These are identified as *v reg* †. Look at pages 232-233 for help with these verbs.

Irregular verbs are verbs which just have to be learned individually:

Example: devoir, pouvoir, voir

These are identified as *v irreg* §. Look in the verb table on pages 208-226 for help with these verbs.

Reflexive verbs are verbs with an extra pronoun:

Example: se laver*

They are identified as *v refl* if they are regular, as *v refl* † if they are **-er** verbs with variations and as *v refl* § if they are irregular.

Remember that ***** is the symbol used to show that a verb takes **être** in the perfect and other compound tenses.

You will not find every irregular reflexive verb listed in the verb table. If you cannot find the one you want, look it up without **se** or **s'**.

Looking up an English word

When you look up an **English** word to find the French equivalent, it is important to know if you are looking for an adjective, a noun, a verb, an adverb, etc. (Adjectives, adverbs, nouns and verbs are all identified in both parts of the dictionary. See pages viii-xii if you are unsure of any of these terms.) When you have found the French word, look that up in the French-English section. You should get the same English word you started with in the English-French section, or a word which means the same in the same situation.

In the English-French section of the dictionary, words which could be misleading have an explanation in brackets to clarify the meaning.

    Example: **square** – (in town) place *nf*

                      square – (on paper) case *nf*

                      square – (shape) carré *adj*

What else is in the dictionary?

There is a **table of irregular French verbs** at the end of the dictionary. If a verb has the § symbol after it, you will find it in the verb table on pages 208-226. To save space some verbs are not written out in full. So the entry for *revenir* will refer you to *venir*, which behaves in exactly the same way.

There is information about **how to write letters**, both formal and informal, on pages 236-239.

There is a **list of instructions** in French which you might see in text books and in examinations, together with translations of these instructions. These will be found on pages 240-244.

This dictionary also contains **simple explanations of grammatical terms**, with examples on pages viii-xii, and a reminder of **simple grammar points** on pages 227-235.

LIST OF ABBREVIATIONS

§	see verb table (pages 208-226)
†	**-er** verb with variations (pages 232-233)
*	verb takes *être* in perfect tense (page 234)
‡	word beginning with h which does not require the word before it to be abbreviated: le hibou, la haie, se hâter, de haute taille
adj	adjective
adv	adverb
art	article
coll	colloquial
conj	conjunction
def	definite
dem adj	demonstrative adjective (page 228)
dem pron	demonstrative pronoun
excl	exclamation
indef	indefinite
inv	invariable
neg	negative
nf	noun, feminine singular
nfpl	noun, feminine plural
nm	noun, masculine singular
nmf	noun which can be either masculine or feminine
nmpl	noun, masculine plural
pers pron	personal pronoun
pl	plural
poss adj	possessive adjective
pp	past participle
pref	prefix: mi-, demi-
prep	preposition
pron	pronoun
qqch	quelque chose
qqn	quelqu'un
rel pron	relative pronoun
sing	singular
sl	slang
s.o.	someone
sthg	something
v irreg §	verb, irregular; details in the verb table (pages 208-226)
v refl	verb, reflexive (page 231)
v reg	verb, regular (pages 229-230)
v reg †	verb, regular with variations (pages 232-233)

GRAMMATICAL TERMS EXPLAINED

adj   **Adjectives (les adjectifs)**

These are words which describe or tell you more about a noun.
There are many kinds of adjectives:
       Example: **big** – grand *adj*
                            green – vert *adj*
                            intelligent – intelligent *adj*
                            French – français *adj*
                            this – ce *adj*
but they all serve to give extra information about their noun.

adv   **Adverbs (les adverbes)**

These are words which are added to a verb, adjective or another adverb to tell you
how, when, where a thing was done:
       Example: **quickly** – rapidement *adv*
                            soon – bientôt *adv*
                            there – là *adv*

art   **Articles (les articles)**

There are two kinds of articles mentioned in this dictionary:
    def art   **Definite (l'article défini)**   **the** – le, la, les
    indef art   **Indefinite (l'article indéfini)**   **a, an, some** – un, une, des

coll   **Colloquial (familier)**

These are words used in spoken French but they are perhaps not always suitable for
written French.

conj   **Conjunctions (les conjonctions)**

These are words used to join sentences and clauses:
       Example: **and** – et *conj*
                            but – mais *conj*

excl   **Exclamations (les exclamations)**

These are phrases and words often used with an exclamation mark:
       Example: **help!** – au secours! *excl*

inv   **Invariable (invariable)**

These nouns or adjectives do not change their spelling for feminine or plural.

neg   **Negative (négatif)**

This identifies words such as *not* ne...pas, *nothing* ne...rien, *never* ne...jamais.

nm, nf, nmf   **Nouns (les noms)**

These are names of people, places and things. There are two genders in French: masculine **le/un** and feminine **la/une.** All nouns fit into one or other of these categories.

> Example: **boy** – garçon *nm*
> **girl** – fille *nf*

Some nouns can be either feminine or masculine:

> Example: **pupil** – élève *nmf*

pp   **Past Participles (les participes passés)**

These are parts of a verb used with an **auxiliary verb** *avoir* or *être* to form the **Perfect (Passé Composé)** and other compound tenses.
In English they often end in **-en, -ed** or **-t**:

> *given*   *looked*   *bought*

In French they often end in **-é, -i, -u, -s** or **-t**:

> donné   fini   répondu   pris   conduit

There are times when they agree (change their spelling).
Past participles are to be found in the **passé composé** columns in the verb table on pages 208-226.

poss adj   **Possessive Adjectives (les adjectifs possessifs)**

These adjectives show ownership:

> Example: **my**   mon, ma, mes

pref   **Prefix (préfixe)**

A prefix is a group of letters added, sometimes with a hyphen, to the beginning of a word to alter its meaning:

> Example: **happy** – heureux *adj*
> **unhappy** – **mal**heureux *adj*
> **hour** – heure *nf*
> **half hour** – **demi**-heure *nf*

prep   **Prepositions (les prepositions)**

These are words placed in front of nouns and pronouns to show position and other relationships:

Example: **in** – dans *prep*

                        before – avant *prep*

pron   **Pronouns (les pronoms)**

Pronouns are short words used to stand in the place of a noun to avoid repeating it or to give emphasis:

Example: **her, it** – la *pron*

dem pron   **Demonstrative Pronouns (les pronoms démonstratifs)**

These words are used to establish contrast between two things or people:

Example   **this one** – celui-ci *dem pron*

pers pron   **Personal Pronouns (les pronoms personnels)**

This is the general name given to subject, direct object, reflexive pronouns:

Example: **he** – il *pers pron*

                        him – le *pers pron*

                        himself – se *pers pron*

rel pron   **Relative Pronouns (les pronoms relatifs)**

These are words which join two phrases or ideas which are linked by meaning:

Example: **which** – qui, que *rel pron*

                        The book **which** *is on the table is mine*

                        Le livre **qui** est sur la table est à moi

sing, pl   **Singular, Plural (singulier, pluriel)**

Nouns and adjectives can be singular or plural:

Example: **boy** – garçon *nm*

                        holidays – vacances *nfpl*

sl   **Slang (l'argot)**

These words and phrases are heard in spoken French. They should only be used with care! Do not use them in written French.

Example: **lousy** – infect *adj sl*, moche *adj sl*

v reg, v irreg, v refl   **Verbs (les verbes)**

A verb will tell you the actions and events in a sentence.

   Example: *I am playing* football   **Je joue** au football

The form of the verb which is listed in this dictionary and verb table is called the infinitive. It means "to".....

   Example: regarder – *to look at, to watch*

The final two letters of the infinitive are important. They tell you to which group or conjugation the verb belongs.

v reg   **Regular Verbs (les verbes reguliers)**

There are three main regular families (conjugations) in French:

   -er   travailler – to work *v reg*
   -ir   finir – to finish *v reg*
   -re   répondre – to answer *v reg*

Many verbs belong to one of these groups and they are identified as *v reg* in the dictionary.

v reg †

Some of the **-er** verbs have variations in their spelling in the present tense:

   Example: manger – *v reg* † je mange nous mangeons
            commencer – *v reg* † je commence nous commençons

These verbs are identified as *v reg* † and more information about them will be found on pages 232-233.

v irreg §   **Irregular Verbs (les verbes irreguliers)**

These verbs, which do not follow one of the three patterns, are set out for you in the verb table on pages 208-226. They are verbs which are frequently used and which you **must** know. They are listed as *v irreg* §.

   Example: **laugh** – rire *v irreg* §

          be able to – pouvoir *v irreg* §

          come – venir* *v irreg* §

* is the symbol used to show that a verb takes **être** in the perfect and other compound tenses.

v refl   **Reflexive Verbs (les verbes pronominaux)**

These are verbs which have an extra pronoun:

      Example: *I wash myself*   Je **me** lave

                        she gets dressed   elle **s'**habille

They will always take *être* in the compound tenses and are marked with a *.

They are frequently regular **-er** verbs and are just marked *v refl*:

      Example: **wash o.s.** − se laver* *v refl*

Those which are **-er** with variations are marked *v refl* †:

      Example: **get up** − se lever *v refl* †

The common ones which are irregular are marked *v refl* § and are in the verb table:

      Example :   **sit down** − s'asseoir* *v refl* §

If you do not find the verb in its reflexive form in the table, try looking for it without the **se** or **s'**:

      Example: **get angry** − se mettre* en colère *v refl* §

Here you will have to look up **mettre** in the verb table.

You must also remember to use the correct reflexive pronoun.

A

a – *see avoir* § has
  elle a –she has
  il a – he has
  il y a – there is, there are
  on a – we have, you have, one has
à – *prep* to, at, in
  à la, à l', aux – to the, at the
  à bientôt – *adv* see you soon
  à bord de – on board
  à carreaux – *adj* checked
  à cause de – because of
  à ce moment-là – at that moment
  à ce soir – see you this evening
  à cinq francs – costing five francs
  à cinq minutes d'ici – 5 minutes from here
  à côté de – *adv* beside, next to
  à demain – *adv* see you tomorrow
  à dix kilomètres de – 10 km from
  à droite – on the right, to the right
  à emporter – to take away
  à gauche – on the left
  à haute voix – aloud
  à l'appareil – (on the phone) speaking
  à l'est – in the east
  à l'étage – upstairs
  à l'étranger – abroad
  à l'extérieur – outside
  à l'heure – on time
  à l'ouest – in the west
  à la campagne – in the country
  à la mer – at the sea
  à la montagne – in the mountains
  à la radio – on the radio
  à la tienne – cheers!
  à la vôtre – cheers!
  à Londres – in London
  à louer – for hire
  à moi – to me, mine, my
  à mon avis – in my opinion

  à Noël – at Christmas
  à Pâques – at Easter
  à part – beside, apart from
  à partir de – from
  à peine – hardly
  à peu près – more or less, scarcely
  à pied – on foot
  à point – medium (steak)
  à propos (de) – about, concerning
  à proximité de – near to
  à quel point – how much, to what extent
  à quelle heure? – at what time?
  à samedi – see you Saturday
  à souhait – to perfection
  à ta santé – cheers!
  à table! – *excl* the meal is ready!
  à tout à l'heure – see you later
  à toute vitesse – at top speed
  à vos souhaits! – bless you!
  à votre avis – in your opinion
  à votre santé! – cheers!
abandonner – *v reg* to give up
abbaye – *nf* abbey
abbé – *nm* priest, abbot
abeille – *nf* bee
abîmé – *adj* damaged, spoiled
abîmer – *v reg* to spoil, ruin
abonnement – *nm* subscription
aborder – *v reg* to approach
aboyer – *v reg* † to bark
abri – *nm* shelter
  à l'abri (de) – sheltered (from)
abricot – *nm* apricot
absent – *adj* absent
absolu – *adj* absolute
absolument – *adv* absolutely
accélérer – *v reg* † to accelerate
accent – *nm* accent
  accent aigu – acute accent (é)

accent circonflexe – circumflex accent (ê)

accent grave – grave accent (è)

accepter – *v reg* to accept

  accepter de – to agree to

accès – *nm* access, way in

  accès aux quais – "to the trains"

  accès interdit – no entry

accessible – *adj* approachable, affordable

accessoire – *nm* accessory, prop

accident – *nm* accident

  accident de train – train crash

  accident d'avion – plane crash

  par accident – by accident

accidenté – *adj* bumpy, uneven, injured

acclamation – *nf* acclaim

accompagnateur – *nm* tour leader

accompagnatrice – *nf* tour leader

accompagner – *v reg* to go with

  accompagné de – accompanied by

accord – *nm* agreement

accorder – *v reg* to grant, award

  faire accorder un verbe – *v irreg* § to make a verb agree

accrocher – *v reg* to hang up

accueillant – *adj* welcoming, friendly

accueillir – *v irreg* § to welcome

accuser – *v reg* to accuse

  accuser réception de – to acknowledge receipt of

achat – *nm* purchase

  faire des achats – *v irreg* § to go shopping

acheter – *v reg* † to buy

acier – *nm* steel

acrobate – *nmf* acrobat

acte – *nm* act (in play), action

acteur – *nm* actor (film)

actif, active – *adj* active

activité – *nf* activity

actrice – *nf* actress (film)

actualité – *nf* current events

actualités – *nfpl* news (at the cinema)

actuel, actuelle – *adj* present, current

  à l'heure actuelle – at the present time

actuellement – *adv* at the moment, currently

addition – *nf* bill

adhérent – *nm* member (club, etc)

adieu – goodbye

adjectif – *nm* adjective

administration – *nf* government, administration

admirer – *v reg* to admire

admissible – *adj* acceptable, eligible

adolescent(e) – *nmf* adolescent, teenager

adopté – *adj* adopted

adorable – *adj* delightful

adorer – *v reg* to love

adouci – *adj* softened, mellowed

s'adoucir* – *v refl* to become mild

adresse – *nf* address

adresser – *v reg* to address (letter, remark)

  s'adresser à* – *v refl* to speak to, apply to, contact

adulte – *adj* adult, grown up

adulte – *nmf* adult

adverbe – *nm* adverb

adversaire – *nmf* opponent

aérobic – *nm* aerobics

aérogare – *nf* airport buildings, air terminal (in city)

aéroglisseur – *nm* hovercraft

aéroport – *nm* airport

aérospatiale – *nf* aerospace industry, science of aerospace

affaire – *nf* business transaction, matter, problem

affaires – *nfpl* business

  une femme d'affaires – *nf* business woman

---

nm - noun masculine	*nmpl* - noun masculine plural	*adj* - adjective	*conj* - conjunction
nf - noun feminine	*nfpl* - noun feminine plural	*adv* - adverb	*pron* - pronoun

un homme d'affaires – *nm*
business man
affaires – *nfpl* belongings, things
affamé – *adj* starving, starved
affectueux, affectueuse – *adj*
affectionate
affiche – *nf* notice, poster
affirmer – *v reg* to state
affluence – *nf* crowds
affolé – *adj* terrified
affreux, affreuse – *adj* awful, ugly
affrontement – *nm* confrontation
afin de – *prep* in order to
africain – *adj* African
Afrique – *nf* Africa
Afrique du Sud – South Africa
agacer – *v reg* † to annoy
ça m'agace – that gets on my
nerves
âge – *nm* age
âgé – *adj* aged
âgé de six ans – six years old
être âgé – *v irreg* § to be old,
elderly
agence – *nf* agency
agence de renseignements –
information office
agence de voyages – travel
agency
agence immobilière – estate
agent
agenda – *nm* diary
agenouillé – *adj* kneeling
s'agenouiller* – *v refl* to kneel
agent – *nm* agent, official
agent de police – *nm* policeman
agglomération – *nf* urban area
agile – *adj* nimble, agile
agir – *v reg* to act
il s'agit de – it is about
agneau – *nm* lamb
agrafe – *nf* staple

agrafeuse – *nf* stapler
agrandir – *v reg* to increase, enlarge
agréable – *adj* pleasant
agréablement – *adv* pleasantly
agréer – *v reg* to accept
agresser – *v reg* to attack
agressif, agressive – *adj* aggressive
agricole – *adj* agricultural
agriculteur – *nm* farmer
ai – *see avoir* § have
j'ai … ans – I am … years old
aide – *nf* help
aider – *v reg* to help
aïe! – *excl* ouch! ow!
aigre – *adj* sour
aigu, aiguë – *adj* acute, sharp
accent aigu – acute accent (é)
aiguille – *nf* needle, (clock) hand
ail – *nm* garlic
aile – *nf* wing
ailier – *nm* winger
ailier droit, gauche – right, left
winger
ailleurs – *adv* somewhere else
d'ailleurs – moreover
aimable – *adj* friendly
aimer – *v reg* to like
beaucoup aimer – to like a lot
bien aimer – to like
j'aimerais – I would like
mieux aimer – to prefer
aîné – *adj* elder
ainsi – *adv* in this way, thus
ainsi que – as well as
air – *nm* air
avoir l'air de –
v irreg § to seem to
aire de jeu – *nf* adventure playground
aire de pique-nique – *nf* picnic area
aire de repos – *nf* rest area
aise – *nf* satisfaction

être à l'aise – *v irreg* § to feel at ease

mal à l'aise – ill at ease

aisé – *adj* easy, well-off

ajouter – *v reg* to add

ajuster – *v reg* to adjust

alarme – *nf* alarm

alcool – *nm* alcohol

alentours – *nmpl* surroundings

aux alentours de Paris – in the Paris area

Algérie – *nf* Algeria

algérien, algérienne – *adj* Algerian

Algérien(ne) – *nmf* Algerian person

aliment – *nm* food

alimentation – *nf* food, diet

alimentation générale – grocer's

alimenter – *v reg* to feed

allais – *see aller* § used to go

allait – *see aller* § used to go

si on allait? – shall we go?

allé – *pp aller* § went, have gone

allée – *nf* avenue, drive

Allemagne – *nf* Germany

allemand – *adj* German

allemand – *nm* German (language)

Allemand(e) – *nmf* German person

aller* – *v irreg* § to go

aller à – to go to

aller à la pêche – to go fishing

aller au lit – to go to bed

aller chercher – to go and get, fetch

aller faire – *v irreg* § to be going to do

aller voir – to go and see, visit (people)

bien aller – to be well

mal aller – to be ill

mieux aller – to be better

pour aller à...? – what is the way to?...

s'en aller* – *v refl* § to go away

aller-retour – *nm* return ticket

aller simple – *nm* single ticket

allez – *see aller v irreg* § go

allez! – *excl* come on!

allez tout droit – go straight on

allez-vous-en! – *excl* go away!

allez-y! – *excl* go on, go ahead!

alliance – *nf* wedding ring

allô! – *excl* hello! (on the phone)

allocation – *nf* allowance, benefit

allons – *see aller v irreg* § go

allonger – *v reg* † to lengthen

s'allonger* – *v refl* † to lie down

allons-y – let's go

allumer – *v reg* to light, switch on

allumer la radio – to switch on the radio

allumer les phares – to switch on headlights

allumette – *nf* match(stick)

allure – *nf* look, speed, walk

alors – *adv* then

alors que – whilst

et alors? – so what?

les Alpes – *nfpl* the Alps

alpin – *adj* alpine

alpinisme – *nm* mountain climbing

alpiniste – *nmf* mountaineer

alto – *nm* viola, alto

amande – *nf* almond

ambassade – *nf* embassy

ambiance – *nf* atmosphere

ambitieux – *adj* ambitious

ambulance – *nf* ambulance

ambulant – *adj* travelling

âme – *nf* soul

amélioration – *nf* improvement

améliorer – *v reg* to improve

aménagé – *adj* fitted, converted

aménagement – *nm* improvement (home)

---

aménager – *v reg* † to fit out, convert
amende – *nf* fine (punishment)
amener – *v reg* † to bring (someone)
amer, amère – *adj* bitter
américain – *adj* American
Américain(e) – *nmf* American
Amérique – *nf* America
  Amérique du Nord – North America
  Amérique du Sud – South America
ami – *nm* friend (male)
  petit ami – boy friend
amical – *adj* friendly
  amicalement – with best wishes from (letter)
amie – *nf* friend (female)
  petite amie – girlfriend
amitié – *nf* friendship
  amitiés – love from (letter)
amour – *nm* love
amoureux, amoureuse (de) – *adj* in love (with)
amplifier – *v reg* to amplify
ampoule – *nf* light bulb
amusant – *adj* amusing
amuser – *v reg* to amuse
  s'amuser* – *v refl* to have a good time
  amuse-toi bien! – have a good time!
  amusez-vous bien! – have a good time!
an – *nm* year
  en l'an 1789 – in 1789
  le nouvel an – New Year's Day
  trois fois par an – three times a year
analphabétisme – *nm* illiteracy
ananas – *nm* pineapple
ancêtre – *nmf* ancestor
ancien, ancienne – *adj* old, ex-
ancre – *nf* anchor

âne – *nm* donkey
anéantir – *v reg* to destroy, wipe out
ange – *nm* angel
angine – *nf* tonsillitis
  avoir une angine – *v irreg* § to have a sore throat
anglais – *adj* English
anglais – *nm* English (language)
Anglais(e) – *nmf* English person
Angleterre – *nf* England
anglophone – *adj* English speaking
angoisse – *nf* anguish, dread, fear
animal – *nm* animal
  animal domestique – pet
  animal sauvage – wild animal
animateur – *nm* organiser (male)
animatrice – *nf* organiser (female)
animaux – *nmpl* animals
animé – *adj* lively
  dessin animé – *nm* cartoon
anneau – *nm* ring
année – *nf* year
  année scolaire – school year
  bonne année! – Happy New Year!
  l'année dernière – last year
  l'année prochaine – next year
anniversaire – *nm* birthday
  bon anniversaire! – Happy Birthday!
  cadeau d'anniversaire – *nm* birthday present
  carte d'anniversaire – *nf* birthday card
annonce – *nf* advert
  petites annonces – *nfpl* classified, small ads
annoncer – *v reg* † to announce, forecast
annuaire – *nm* telephone directory
annuel, annuelle – *adj* annual, yearly
annuler – *v reg* to cancel
anorak – *nm* anorak

---

prep - preposition	*v reg* - verb regular	*v refl* - verb reflexive	§ - see verb tables
pp - past participle	*v irreg* - verb irregular	† - see verb information	* - takes être

antenne – *nf* aerial
  antenne parabolique – satellite dish
  être à l'antenne – *v irreg* § to be on the air
antibiotique – *nm* antibiotic
antillais – *adj* West Indian
Antillais(e) – *nmf* West Indian person
Antilles – *nfpl* West Indies
antiquaire – *nmf* antique dealer
antique – *adj* ancient
antiseptique – *nm* antiseptic
anxiété – *nf* anxiety
anxieux, anxieuse – *adj* worried
août – *nm* August
apercevoir – *v irreg* § to see, make out
  s'apercevoir* de – *v refl* § to notice
apéritif – *nm* aperitif, pre-meal drink
apparaître – *v irreg* § to appear, seem
appareil – *nm* appliance, machinery
appareil – *nm coll* phone
  il est à l'appareil – he's on the phone
appareil-photo – *nm* camera
apparence – *nf* appearance, aspect
appartement – *nm* flat
appartenir à – *v irreg* § to belong to
  cela m'appartient – that is mine
appel – *nm* call
  faire l'appel – *v irreg* § to call the register
appeler – *v reg* † to call
  appeler police-secours – to dial 999
  s'appeler* – *v refl* † to be called
  je m'appelle... – my name is...
appellation – *nf* name, classification
appétissant – *adj* appetizing
appétit – *nm* appetite
  bon appétit – enjoy your meal

applaudir – *v reg* to applaud
appliquer – *v reg* to apply
apporter – *v reg* to bring (something)
apprécier – *v reg* to appreciate
apprendre – *v irreg* § to learn
  apprendre à faire – to learn to do
apprenti(e) – *nmf* apprentice
apprentissage – *nm* apprenticeship
approche – *nf* approach
  à mon approche – as I came up
approcher – *v reg* to put near to
  s'approcher de* – *v refl* to go near to, approach
approprié – *adj* appropriate, suitable
approuver – *v reg* to approve of
appuyer – *v reg* † to support
  appuyer sur – to press on
  s'appuyer* sur – *v refl* † to lean on
après – *prep* after
  après avoir fini – after finishing, after having finished
  d'après – according to
  après tout – after all
après-demain – *adv* the day after tomorrow
après-midi – *nm inv* afternoon
araignée – *nf* spider
arbitre – *nm* referee
arbre – *nm* tree
  arbre de Noël – Christmas tree
  arbre fruitier – fruit tree
  arbre généalogique – family tree
arc – *nm* bow, arch
  arc en ciel – rainbow
  tir à l'arc – *nm* archery
archéologie – *nf* archaeology
archéologue – *nmf* archaeologist
architecte – *nmf* architect
argent – *nm* money, silver
  argent de poche – pocket money
argot – *nm* slang
arithmétique – *nf* arithmetic

arme – *nf* weapon
armée – *nf* army
  armée de l'air – air force
armoire – *nf* wardrobe
aromatisé – *adj* flavoured
arracher – *v reg* to snatch, pull up/out
arranger – *v reg* † to arrange, organise
  s'arranger* – *v refl* † to manage, get better, improve
arrêt – *nm* stop
  arrêt d'autobus – bus stop
  arrêt de 3 minutes – a 3-minute stop
arrêter – *v reg* to stop, arrest
  arrêter de faire quelque chose – to stop doing something
  s'arrêter* (de) – *v refl* to stop (o.s.)
  s'arrêter* de fumer – to stop smoking
arrhes – *nfpl* deposit
arrière – *nm* back, rear (vehicle)
  à l'arrière de – at the back (of)
  à l'arrière plan – in the background
  en arrière – backwards, behind
arrière – *nm* back (footballer)
arrivée – *nf* arrival
arriver* – *v reg* to arrive, happen
  ça m'est arrivé – that happened to me
arrondissement – *nm* district of city
arroser – *v reg* to water, spray
art – *nm* art, artistry
  les arts de la scène – *nmpl* performing arts
  étudier l'art dramatique – *v reg* to do drama
artichaut – *nm* artichoke
article – *nm* article, item
artificiel, artificielle – *adj* artificial
artisan – *nm* craftsman

artisanat – *nm* craft industry
artiste – *nmf* artist
as – *nm* ace
as – *see avoir* § have
ascenseur – *nm* lift
asiatique – *adj* Asian
Asie – *nf* Asia
asile – *nm* refuge, home (for aged)
aspirateur – *nm* vacuum cleaner
aspirer – *v reg* to breathe in
aspirine – *nf* aspirin
assassiner – *v reg* to murder
assemblée – *nf* meeting
assembler – *v reg* to assemble
s'asseoir* – *v refl* § to sit down
  asseyez-vous! – sit down! (plural)
  assieds-toi! – sit down! (singular)
assez – *adv* enough, fairly, quite, rather
  assez de – enough of
  j'en ai assez – I've had enough
assiette – *nf* plate
  assiette anglaise – mixed cold meats
assis, assise – *pp* seated, sitting down
assister à – *v reg* to be present at
associer – *v reg* to associate
assurance – *nf* insurance
assurer – *v reg* to assure, insure
  s'assurer de* – *v refl* to make sure of
asthme – *nm* asthma
astronaute – *nmf* astronaut
astronomie – *nf* astronomy
astuce – *nf* clever trick, shrewdness
atelier – *nm* workshop, studio
athlète – *nmf* athlete
athlétisme – *nm* athletics
  faire de l'athlétisme – *v irreg* § to do athletics
Atlantique – *nm* Atlantic Ocean
atmosphère – *nf* atmosphere

| *prep* - preposition | *v reg* - verb regular | *v refl* - verb reflexive | § - see verb tables |
| *pp* - past participle | *v irreg* - verb irregular | † - see verb information | * - takes être |

atout – *nm* trump, advantage
attacher – *v reg* to fasten, attach
  être attaché à – *v irreg* § to be attached to
attaquer – *v reg* to attack
atteindre – *v irreg* § to reach
attendre – *v reg* to wait (for)
attentat – *nm* attack
attention – *nf* attention, care
  attention! – look out!
  avec attention – carefully
  faire attention (à) – *v irreg* § to pay attention (to)
atterrir – *v reg* to land (plane)
atterrissage – *nm* landing (plane)
attestation du médecin – *nf* doctor's certificate
attirer – *v reg* to attract, draw
attraper – *v reg* to catch (fish, etc)
au (= à + le) – *prep* to the, at the
  au bord de la mer – by the sea
  au bout de – at the end of
  au cinéma – at the cinema
  au début – at the start
  au-dessous – below, under
  au-dessus de – above, on top of
  au feu! – fire!
  au fond de – at the bottom of
  au lieu de – instead of
  au milieu de – in the middle of
  au mois de – in the month of
  au mois de juin – in June
  au nom de – in the name of
  au nord (de) – in the north (of)
  au revoir! – goodbye!
  au rez-de-chaussée – downstairs, on the ground floor
  au secours! – help!
  au sud – in the south
auberge – *nf* inn
  auberge de jeunesse – youth hostel
aubergiste – *nmf* innkeeper, warden

aucun, aucune – *adj* not any, no
audace – *nf* daring, boldness
audacieux, audacieuse – *adj* bold
auditeur – *nm* listener
auditoire – *nm* audience
auditrice – *nf* listener
augmentation – *nf* increase
augmenter – *v reg* to increase
aujourd'hui – *adv* today
aumône – *nf* charity
auparavant – *adv* earlier, previously
auprès de – *prep* with, next to
aura – *see avoir* § will have
aurait – would have
  il y aurait – there would be
aussi – *adv* also, as well, too
  aussi ... que – as ... as
aussi – *conj* therefore, so
aussitôt – *adv* straight away
  aussitôt que – as soon as
Australie – *nf* Australia
australien, australienne – *adj* Australian
autant – *adv* the same
  autant de – as much/many, so much/many
  autant que – as much as
auteur – *nm* author
authentique – *adj* genuine
auto – *nf* car
autobus – *nm* bus
autocar – *nm* coach
autocollant – *nm* sticker
auto-école – *nf* driving school
automne – *nm* autumn
  en automne – in autumn
automobiliste – *nmf* motorist
autonome – *adj* independent
autorisation – *nf* permission
autoritaire – *adj* bossy
autorités – *nfpl* authorities
autoroute – *nf* motorway

---

nm - noun masculine   *nmpl* - noun masculine plural   *adj* - adjective   *conj* - conjunction
nf - noun feminine   *nfpl* - noun feminine plural   *adv* - adverb   *pron* - pronoun

autoroute à péage – toll motorway

auto-stop – *nm* hitch-hiking
  faire de l'auto-stop – *v irreg* § to go hitch-hiking

autour – *adv* around

autour de – *prep* around, round about
  tout autour – all around

autre – *adj* other, different
  autre part – somewhere else
  l'autre jour – the other day

autre – *pron* another
  d'autres – others
  les autres – the others
  personne d'autre – no-one else
  quelque chose d'autre – something else
  quelqu'un d'autre – someone else
  un autre jour – another day

autrefois – *adv* in the past

autrement – *adv* differently, otherwise

Autriche – *nf* Austria

autrichien, autrichienne – *adj* Austrian

aux (=à + les) – *prep* to the, at the

avait – *see avoir* § used to have
  il y avait – there was, were

avaler – *v reg* to swallow

avancement – *nm* promotion

avancer – *v reg* † to bring, go forward
  s'avancer* – *v refl* † to move forward

en avance – *adv* early
  ma montre est en avance – my watch is fast

avant – *prep* before
  avant de – + *infin* before ...ing
  avant de partir – before leaving
  avant hier – the day before yesterday
  avant peu – before long
  avant tout – above all

avantage – *nm* advantage

avantageux, avantageuse – *adj* advantageous

avare – *adj* mean, miserly

avec – *prep* with
  avec plaisir – with pleasure
  avec succès – with success
  et avec ça? – anything else?

avenir – *nm* future
  à l'avenir – from now on, in future

aventure – *nf* adventure
  film d'aventure – *nm* adventure film
  roman d'aventure – *nm* adventure story

aventureux, aventureuse – *adj* adventurous

avenue – *nf* avenue

averse – *nf* shower, downpour

avertir – *v reg* to warn

avertissement – *nm* warning

aveugle – *adj* blind

avez – *see avoir* § have

aviation – *nf* flying

avion – *nm* aeroplane

aviron – *nm* oar

avis – *nm* opinion
  à mon avis – in my opinion
  changer d'avis – *v reg* † to change one's mind

avocat – *nm* avocado pear

avocat(e) – *nmf* lawyer

avoir – *v irreg* § to have
  avoir besoin de – to need
  avoir chaud – to be warm
  avoir dix ans – to be 10 years old
  avoir du mal à – to have difficulty in
  avoir envie de – to wish to
  avoir faim – to be hungry
  avoir froid – to be cold
  avoir honte (de) – to be ashamed (of)

---

avoir horreur de – to hate
avoir l'air – to seem
avoir le droit de – to have the right to
avoir le temps de – to have time to
avoir lieu – to take place
avoir mal à la gorge – to have a sore throat
avoir mal à la jambe – to have a bad leg
avoir mal à la tête – to have a headache
avoir mal au bras – to have a bad arm
avoir mal au cœur – to feel sick

avoir mal au ventre – to have stomach ache
avoir mal aux dents – to have toothache
avoir peur – to be afraid
avoir raison – to be right
avoir soif – to be thirsty
avoir sommeil – to be sleepy
avoir tort – to be wrong
avoir un rhume – to have a cold
avouer – *v reg* to confess
avril – *nm* April
  poisson d'avril – *nm* April fool
ayez – *see avoir* § have

B

babyfoot – *nm* table football
bac – *nm* A level, GNVQ equivalent
bac – *nm* basin, ferry boat
  bac à vaisselle – washing up sink
baccalauréat – *nm* examination (see bac)
badge – *nm* badge (sew-on, stick-on)
badminton – *nm* badminton
bagages – *nmpl* luggage
bagarre – *nf* fight
bagnole – *nf sl* old car, banger
bague – *nf* ring
baguette – *nf* stick of bread
baie – *nf* bay
baignade – *nf* bathing
  baignade interdite – no bathing
se baigner* – *v refl* to bathe, swim
baignoire – *nf* bath (tub)
bâiller – *v reg* to yawn
bain – *nm* bath, swim
  prendre un bain – *v irreg* § to have a bath

baisse – *nf* fall, drop
baisser – *v reg* to fall (temperature), to lower
bal – *nm* dance, ball
balade – *nf coll* walk
se balader* – *v refl coll* to go for a walk
baladeur – *nm* personal stereo
balai – *nm* broom
balance – *nf* scales
  Balance – *nf* Libra
  être (de) la Balance – *v irreg* § to be (a) Libra
balancer – *v reg* † to swing
balançoire – *nf* swing
balayer – *v reg* † to sweep
balcon – *nm* balcony
baleine – *nf* whale
ball-trap – *nm* clay pigeon shooting
balle – *nf* bullet, small ball
  balle de tennis – tennis ball
ballon – *nm* (foot)ball, balloon

---

nm - noun masculine	*nmpl* - noun masculine plural	*adj* - adjective	*conj* - conjunction
nf - noun feminine	*nfpl* - noun feminine plural	*adv* - adverb	*pron* - pronoun

banal – *adj* common, trite
banane – *nf* banana
  sac banane – *nm* bumbag
banc – *nm* seat, bench
bande – *nf* group of people, tape
  bande dessinée – cartoon strip
Bangladesh – *nm* Bangladesh
  du Bangladesh – *adj* Bangladeshi
  habitant(e) du Bangladesh –
  nmf Bangladeshi person
banlieue – *nf* suburb
  de banlieue – suburban
  en banlieue – in the suburbs
bannière – *nf* banner
banque – *nf* bank
banquette – *nf* car seat, bench
banquier – *nm* banker
baptême – *nm* baptism, christening
bar – *nm* bar
barbe – *nf* beard
  barbe à papa – candyfloss
barbecue – *nm* barbecue
barbu – *adj* bearded
barque – *nf* small boat
barrage – *nm* dam, weir
barrette – *nf* (hair)slide
barrière – *nf* fence, gate
bas, basse – *adj* low
  à marée basse – at low tide
bas – *nm* foot (hill) bottom (page)
  en bas – downstairs
bas – *nm* stocking
basculer – *v reg* to topple, fall over
base – *nf* base, foot, root
  base de données – database
  à base de – based on
  de base – basic
basket – *nm* basketball
baskets – *nmpl* trainers
basse-cour – *nf* farmyard
bassin – *nm* bowl
basson – *nm* bassoon

bataille – *nf* battle
bateau – *nm* boat
  bateau à moteur – motor boat
  bateau à rames – rowing boat
bâtiment – *nm* building
bâtir – *v reg* to build
batterie – *nf* battery
  batterie de cuisine – kitchen
  equipment
batterie – *nf* drum kit
batteur – *nm* drummer
battre – *v reg* to beat
  battre des mains – to clap
  battre les cartes – to shuffle cards
  se battre* – *v refl* to fight
bavard – *adj* talkative
bavarder – *v reg* to chat
BD – *nf* cartoon
beau – *adj m* handsome, fine
beaucoup – *adv* a lot
  beaucoup de – a lot of, many
  beaucoup plus – much more
  pas beaucoup de – not many
beau-fils – *nm* stepson
beau-frère – *nm* brother-in-law
beau-père – *nm* father-in-law,
  stepfather
beauté – *nf* beauty
beaux-arts – *nmpl* fine arts
beaux-parents – *nmpl* parents-in-law
bébé – *nm* baby (both sexes)
bec – *nm* beak
  flûte à bec – *nf* recorder
beignet – *nm* doughnut, fritter
bel (beau) – *adj m sing before vowel*
  handsome, fine
belge – *adj* Belgian
Belge – *nmf* Belgian person
Belgique – *nf* Belgium
bélier – *nm* ram
  Bélier – *nm* Aries
  être (du) Bélier – *v irreg* § to be
  (an) Aries

belle – *adj f* beautiful, lovely
belle-fille – *nf* daughter-in-law, stepdaughter
belle-mère – *nf* mother-in-law, stepmother
belle-sœur – *nf* sister-in-law
bénéficier – *v reg* to gain, benefit
BEPC – (brevet d'études du premier cycle) *nm* exam for 15 year olds
berger – *nm* shepherd
  berger allemand – Alsatian dog
berlingot – *nm* boiled sweet, carton
besoin – *nm* need
  avoir besoin de – *v irreg* § to need
bétail – *nm* cattle
bête – *adj* stupid, silly, foolish
bête – *nf* animal, insect
bêtise – *nf* silly mistake, stupid remark
  faire une bêtise – *v irreg* § to do something silly
béton – *nm* concrete
beurre – *nm* butter
bibliothécaire – *nmf* librarian
bibliothèque – *nf* book case, library
bicolore – *adj* two-tone
bicyclette – *nf* bicycle
bidet – *nm* bidet
bidon – *nm* can, tin
  bidonville – *nm* shantytown
bien – *adv* good, well
  bien! – good!
  bien cuit – *adj* well cooked
  bien entendu – of course
  bien payé – well paid
  bien que – although
  bien sûr – of course
bien – *nm* good
  le bien public – the public good
bien-être – *nm* well-being
biens – *nmpl* possessions
bientôt (à) – *adv* see you soon!
bienvenu – *adj* welcome

  soyez le bienvenu! – welcome!
  vous êtes la bienvenue! – welcome!
bière – *nf* beer
bifteck – *nm* beefsteak
bijou – *nm* jewel
bijouterie – *nf* jeweller's shop
bilan – *nm* result, consequences, outcome, assessment
bilingue – *adj* bilingual
bille – *nf* marble (toy), ball bearing
billet – *nm* ticket, banknote
  billet aller-retour – return ticket
  billet de banque – banknote
  billet de 100 francs – a 100 franc note
  billet simple – single ticket
biologie – *nf* biology
biscotte – *nf* pre-toasted bread
biscuit – *nm* biscuit
bise – *nf* kiss
bison – *nm* bison
  bison futé – holiday route logo
bisou – *nm* kiss
  bisous – love from
bizarre – *adj* odd
blague – *nf* joke
blanc, blanche – *adj* white
blé – *nm* corn
blessé – *adj* injured
blesser – *v reg* to injure
  se blesser* – *v refl* to get injured
blessure – *nf* injury
bleu – *nm* bruise
bleu – *adj* blue
  bleu ciel – *adj inv* sky blue
  bleu clair – *adj inv* light blue
  bleu marine – *adj inv* navy blue
  bleu roi – *adj inv* royal blue
bleu de travail – *nm* overalls
bloc-notes – *nm* notepad
bloc sanitaire – *nm* toilet block
blond – *adj* fair

---

bloquer – *v reg* to jam, wedge
  bloquer les freins – to jam on the brakes
  être bloqué – *v irreg* § to be stuck
blouse – *nf* overall, smock, blouse
blouson – *nm* blouson jacket
blue-jean – *nm* pair of jeans
bobine – *nf* reel
body – *nm* leotard
bœuf – *nm* beef, bullock
bof! – *excl* so what, oh well!
boire – *v irreg* § to drink
  boire un coup – to have a drink
bois – *nm* wood
  en bois – made of wood, wooden
bois – *see boire* § drink
boisson – *nf* drink
  boisson chaude – hot drink
  boisson froide – cold drink
  boissons pilotes – price list of drinks in café
boit – *see boire* § drink(s)
boîte – *nf* box
boîte aux lettres – *nf* letter box
boivent – *see boire* § drink
bol – *nm* bowl
bombe – *nf* bomb, aerosol, riding hat
  alerte à la bombe – *nf* bomb scare
bon – *nm* coupon, form, voucher
  bon de commande – order form
bon (bonne) – *adj* good
  bon anniversaire! – happy birthday!
  bon appétit! – enjoy your meal!
  bon courage! – good luck!
  bon marché – *adj inv* cheap
  bon séjour! – enjoy your stay!
  bon voyage! – have a good trip!
  bon week-end! – have a good weekend!
bonbon – *nm* sweet

bonde – *nf* plug (bath)
bondir – *v reg* to leap, jump
bonheur – *nm* happiness
bonhomme – *nm coll* chap, bloke
  bonhomme de neige – snowman
bonjour – good morning, hello
bonne (bon) – *adj* good
  bonne année! – Happy New Year!
  bonne chance! – good luck!
  bonne fête! – happy name day!
  bonne journée! – have a nice day!
  bonne nuit! – goodnight!
  bonne soirée! – have a nice evening!
  de bonne heure – early
  de bonne humeur – in a good mood
bon sens – *nm* common sense
bonsoir – good evening
bonté – *nf* goodness, kindness
bord – *nm* edge, side, bank
  bord du trottoir – kerb
  au bord de la mer – at the seaside
  au bord de la rivière – on the river bank
bosse – *nf* bump
  avoir la bosse de – *v irreg* § to have a flair for
bosser – *v reg sl* to swot, slave away
botte – *nf* boot, bunch of flowers, vegetables
  botte de radis – bunch of radishes
bouche – *nf* mouth
bouchée – *nf* mouthful
boucher – *v reg* to block, put cork in
boucher, bouchère – *nmf* butcher
boucherie – *nf* butcher's shop
bouchon – *nm* cork, traffic jam
  ça bouchonne – there's heavy traffic
boucle – *nf* buckle, loop
boucle d'oreille – *nf* ear ring
bouclé – *adj* curly

---

prep - preposition   *v reg* - verb regular   *v refl* - verb reflexive   § - see verb tables
pp - past participle   *v irreg* - verb irregular   † - see verb information   * - takes être

boucler – *v reg* to fasten, buckle
bouder – *v reg* to sulk
boue – *nf* mud, silt
bouée – *nf* rubber ring
  bouée de sauvetage – lifebelt
boueux, boueuse – *adj* muddy
bouger – *v reg* † to move
bougie – *nf* candle
bouillir – *v irreg* § to boil, be boiling
  faire bouillir de l'eau – *v irreg* §
  to boil water
bouilloire – *nf* kettle
boulanger, boulangère – *nmf* baker
boulangerie – *nf* baker's shop
boule – *nf* bowl, ball
  jouer aux boules – *v reg* to play
  bowls
  mettre quelqu'un en boule – *v*
  irreg § *coll* to annoy s.o.
boulevard – *nm* boulevard, wide road
bouleversé – *adj* overcome with
  emotion, devastated, upset
boulot – *nm coll* work
boum – *nf* party
bouquet – *nm* bunch of flowers
bouquin – *nm sl* book
bouquiniste – *nm* secondhand
  bookseller
bourdon – *nm* bumble bee
bourdonner – *v reg* to hum, buzz
bourg – *nm* village, small country
  town
bourrer – *v reg* to fill, stuff
bourse – *nf* purse
  Bourse – Stock Exchange
bousculer – *v reg* to jostle
boussole – *nf* compass
bout – *nm* end
  au bout de la rue – at the end of
  the street
  au bout d'un mois – after a month
  être à bout de souffle – *v irreg* §
  to be out of breath

bouteille – *nf* bottle
  bouteille de gaz – gas cylinder
  bouteille de vin – bottle of wine
boutique – *nf* small shop
  boutique hors taxes – duty free
  shop
bouton – *nm* button, switch, zit
boxe – *nf* boxing
bracelet – *nm* armband, bracelet
branche – *nf* branch, bough
branché – *adj* fashionable, "in"
branchement – *nm* connection, hook-
  up (campsite)
brancher – *v reg* to plug in
bras – *nm* arm
brasserie – *nf* café, bar, pub
brave – *adj* fine, decent, brave
bravo! – well done!
bref, brève – *adj* short, brief
Bretagne – *nf* Brittany
  Grande Bretagne – Great Britain
bretelle – *nf* link road, strap
  bretelles – *nfpl* braces
breton, bretonne – *adj* Breton
brève – *adj f* short, brief
brevet – *nm* certificate
bricolage – *nm* odd jobs, DIY
bricoler – *v reg* to do odd jobs, potter
bride – *nf* bridle
brièvement – *adv* briefly
brillant – *adj* shining, brilliant
briller – *v reg* to shine
brin – *nm* blade (grass), twig
brique – *nf* brick, bar (soap), carton
  (juice), *sl* 10,000 francs
  en brique – brick built
briquet – *nm* cigarette lighter
briser – *v reg* to break, smash
britannique – *adj* British
Britannique – *nmf* British person
broche – *nf* brooch, spit, pin
brochette – *nf* kebab

---

nm - noun masculine	*nmpl* - noun masculine plural	*adj* - adjective	*conj* - conjunction
nf - noun feminine	*nfpl* - noun feminine plural	*adv* - adverb	*pron* - pronoun

brochure – *nf* booklet, brochure
broder – *v reg* to embroider
bronzé – *adj* tanned
bronzer – *v reg* to tan
  se bronzer* – *v refl* to sunbathe, tan
brosse – *nf* brush, paintbrush
  brosse à dents – toothbrush
brosser – *v reg* to brush
  se brosser* – *v refl* to brush one's clothes
  se brosser* les cheveux – to brush one's hair
  se brosser* les dents – to clean one's teeth
brouette – *nf* wheelbarrow
brouillard – *nm* fog
  il y a du brouillard – it is foggy
brouillé – *adj* jumbled
brouillon – *adj* muddled, untidy
  cahier de brouillon – *nm* rough book
bruine – *nf* drizzle
bruit – *nm* noise
brûler – *v reg* to burn
  brûler un feu rouge – to jump a red light
  brûler un stop – to ignore a stop sign
se brûler* – *v refl* to burn o.s.
  se brûler* les doigts – to burn one's fingers
brûlure – *nf* burn
brume – *nf* mist
brumeux, brumeuse – *adj* misty
brun, brune – *adj* brown
brusque – *adj* sudden
brusquement – *adv* suddenly
brut – *adj* dry (champagne), rough
brutal – *adj* violent

brutalement – *adv* violently
Bruxelles – Brussels
  chou de Bruxelles – *nm* Brussels sprout
bruyant – *adj* noisy
bu – *pp boire* § drunk
bûche – *nf* log
  Bûche de Noël – Yule log
buffet – *nm* buffet, sideboard
buisson – *nm* bush
  faire l'école buissonnière – *v irreg* § to play truant
bulle – *nf* bubble, speech balloon
bulletin – *nm* report
  bulletin d'information – news bulletin
  bulletin météo(rologique) – weather forecast
  bulletin scolaire – school report
bureau – *nm* desk, office, study
  bureau d'accueil – reception desk
  bureau de change – currency exchange office
  bureau de poste – post office
  bureau de renseignements – information office
  bureau de tabac – tobacconist's
  bureau de tourisme – tourist office
  bureau des objets trouvés – lost property office
bus – *nm* bus
but – *nm* goal, aim, purpose
  marquer un but – *v reg* to score a goal
buté – *adj* stubborn
buvait – *see boire* § used to drink
buvez – *see boire* § drink
buvette – *nf* refreshment bar
buvons – *see boire* § drink

C

ça – *pron* that
  ça alors! – you don't say!
  ça dépend – that depends
  ça fait dix francs en tout – that comes to ten francs
  ça fait trois semaines qu'il est parti – it's three weeks since he left
  ça m'est égal – I don't mind
  ça ne fait rien – it doesn't matter
  ça ne sert à rien – that's no use
  ça s'écrit comment? – how do you spell that?
  ça suffit – that's enough
  ça va? – how are things?
  ça va – OK, that's OK
  ça va mieux – that's better
  ça y est – that's it
cabine téléphonique – *nf* phone box
cabinet – *nm* cabinet, surgery, study
  cabinet de consultation – surgery
  cabinet de débarras – junk room
  cabinet de toilette – washing facilities
  cabinet de travail – study (room)
  cabinets – *nmpl* toilets
câble – *nm* cable
  avoir le câble – *v irreg* § to have cable TV
cacahuète – *nf* peanut
cacao – *nm* cocoa
cacher – *v reg* to hide
  se cacher* – *v refl* to hide o. s.
cache-cache – *nm* hide and seek
cachet – *nm* tablet
cachette – *nf* hiding place
cadeau – *nm* present
  cadeau d'anniversaire – birthday present

cadeau de Noël – Christmas present
cadet, cadette – *adj* younger, youngest
cadre – *nm* frame, context, executive
café – *nm* black coffee, café
  café crème – white coffee
  café express – espresso coffee
  café filtre – filter coffee
café-tabac – *nm* tobacconist's
cafetière – *nf* coffee pot
cahier – *nm* exercise book
  cahier de brouillon – rough book
caisse – *nf* cash desk
caissier, caissière – *nmf* cashier
calcul – *nm* sum, arithmetic
  être fort en calcul – *v irreg* § to be good at arithmetic
calculatrice – *nf* calculator
calculer – *v reg* to calculate
calculette – *nf* calculator
caleçon – *nm* underpants, leggings
  caleçon de bain – bathing trunks
calme – *adj* calm, quiet
calmer – *v reg* to calm s.o. down
  se calmer* – *v refl* to calm o.s. down
calendrier – *nm* calendar
camarade – *nmf* friend
cambrioler – *v reg* to break in
cambrioleur – *nm* burglar
camembert – *nm* camembert cheese, pie chart
caméra – *nf* cine camera
caméscope – *nm* camcorder
camion – *nm* lorry
camionnette – *nf* van
camionneur – *nm* lorry driver
campagne – *nf* countryside
  à la campagne – in the country

---

nm - noun masculine	*nmpl* - noun masculine plural	*adj* - adjective	*conj* - conjunction
nf - noun feminine	*nfpl* - noun feminine plural	*adv* - adverb	*pron* - pronoun

camper – *v reg* to camp
campeur – *nm* camper
camping – *nm* campsite, camping
   faire du camping – *v irreg* §
   to go camping
camping car – *nm* camper, motor
home
Canada – *nm* Canada
Canadien(ne) – *nmf* Canadian person
canadien, canadienne – *adj*
canadian
canadienne – *nf* open canoe, ridge
tent
Canal + – *nm* French subscription TV
channel
canapé – *nm* sofa, canapé
canard – *nm* duck
canari – *nm* canary
cancer – *nm* cancer
   Cancer – *nm* Cancer
   être (du) Cancer – *v irreg* § to be
   (a) Cancer
candidat(e) – *nmf* candidate
caniche – *nm* poodle
canif – *nm* pocket knife
canne – *nf* walking stick, cane
   canne à pêche – fishing rod
canoë – *nm* canoe
   faire du canoë – *v irreg* § to canoe
cantine – *nf* canteen
caoutchouc – *nm* rubber
capable – *adj* capable
capitaine – *nm* captain
capital – *adj* capital
capitale – *nf* capital city
capot – *nm* bonnet (car)
Capricorne – *nm* Capricorn
   être (du) Capricorne – *v irreg* §
   to be (a) Capricorn
car – *conj* for, because
car – *nm* coach (= bus)
caractère – *nm* character

avoir bon caractère – *v irreg* §
to be good tempered
avoir mauvais caractère –
v irreg § to be bad tempered
carafe – *nf* glass jug, decanter
caraïbe – *adj* Caribbean
   les Caraïbes – the Caribbean
carambolage – *nm* multiple crash
caravane – *nf* caravan
carburant – *nm* fuel
carnet – *nm* notebook
   carnet de tickets – book of tickets
   (bus, metro)
   carnet de camping – camping
   carnet
   carnet de chèques – cheque book
   carnet de timbres – book of
   stamps
carotte – *nf* carrot
carré – *adj* square
   mètre carré – *nm* square metre
carré – *nm* square
carreau – *nm* tile, windowpane,
diamond (cards)
   à carreaux – checked
carrefour – *nm* crossroads
carrément – *adv* frankly, bluntly
carrière – *nf* career, quarry
carte – *nf* card, map, menu
   carte à mémoire – smart card
   carte bancaire – banker's card
   carte bleue® – major French
   credit card
   carte d'abonnement – season
   ticket
   carte d'adhérent – member's card
   carte de crédit – credit card
   carte d'identité – identity card
   carte postale – postcard
   carte routière – map
   carte verte – green card
carton – *nm* cardboard ox
cas – *nm* case, situation

au cas où – in case
en cas d'urgence – in an
  emergency
en tout cas – anyway
le cas échéant – if need be
case – *nf* square, box (on paper)
casier – *nm* pigeon hole, locker
casque – *nm* helmet
cassé – *adj* broken
casser – *v reg* to break
  se casser* la jambe – *v refl*
  to break one's leg
casse-croûte – *nm* snack
casse-pieds – *nmf inv coll* a nuisance,
  a pain
casserole – *nf* saucepan
cassette – *nf* cassette
cassis – *nm* blackcurrant
cassoulet – *nm* stew
catastrophe – *nf* disaster
cathédrale – *nf* cathedral
catholique – *adj* Catholic
cauchemar – *nm* nightmare
cause – *nf* cause, reason
  à cause de – because of
causer – *v reg* to chat, cause
  causer un accident – to cause an
  accident
caution – *nf* deposit
cave – *nf* cellar
caverne – *nf* cave
CD – *nm* compact disc
CDI – (centre de documentation et
  d'information) *nm* library
ce, cet, cette, ces – *dem adj* this,
  these
c'est – it is, he is, she is
  c'est à dire – that is to say
  c'est combien? – how much is it?
  c'est tout – that's all
  c'était – it was
ceci – *dem pron* this
céder – *v reg* † to give in, give way

cédérom – *nm* CD ROM
CEDEX – company post box
cédille – *nf* cedilla (ç)
CEE – *abbr* EEC
ceinture – *nf* belt
  ceinture de sauvetage – life belt
  ceinture de sécurité – seat belt
cela – *dem pron* that one
célèbre – *adj* famous
céleri – *nm* celery
célibataire – *adj* single
célibataire – *nmf* single person
celui, celle, ceux, celles – *dem pron*
  the one, the ones
  celui de – the one belonging to
  celui qui – the one who
cendrier – *nm* ashtray
cent – *adj* hundred
  faire les cent pas – *v irreg* § to
  pace up and down
centaine – *nf* about a hundred
  plusieurs centaines de gens –
  several hundred people
  une centaine d'élèves – about
  100 pupils
centième – *adj* hundredth
centime – *nm* centime
centimètre – *nm* centimetre
centre – *nm* centre, heart
  centre commercial – shopping
  centre
  centre hospitalier – hospital
  complex
  centre sportif – sports centre
  centre-ville – town centre
  en plein centre de la ville –
  right in the town centre
cependant – *conj* however
ce qui, ce que – what
cercle – *nm* ring, circle, club
céréale – *nf* cereal
cerf-volant – *nm* kite
cerise – *nf* cherry

---

nm - noun masculine   *nmpl* - noun masculine plural   *adj* - adjective   *conj* - conjunction
nf - noun feminine   *nfpl* - noun feminine plural   *adv* - adverb   *pron* - pronoun

certain – *adj* certain, sure

certainement – *adv* of course

certifier – *v reg* to assure, guarantee

cerveau – *nm* brain, mind, intelligence

cervelle – *nf* brain, brains

CES – (collège d'enseignement secondaire) *nm* secondary school (11-15)

cesser – *v reg* to stop, cease

CET – (collège d'enseignement technique) *nm* technical college

ceux – *dem pron see celui* the ones

chacun, chacune – *indef pron* each one, every one

chagrin – *nm* sorrow

chahuter – *v reg* to play up, mess around (in class)

chaîne – *nf* chain, channel (TV)

  chaîne compacte – music centre

  chaîne Hi-Fi – Hi-Fi system

  chaîne-stéréo – stereo

chaise – *nf* chair

  chaise longue – couch, sun bed

chaleur – *nf* heat

chaleureux, chaleureuse – *adj* warm, friendly

chambre – *nf* bedroom

  chambre à deux lits – room with twin beds

  chambre à un lit – single room

  chambre avec un grand lit – room with a double bed

  chambre de familiale – family room

  chambre d'hôte – B & B

  chambre pour deux personnes – double room

chameau – *nm* camel

champ – *nm* field

champagne – *nm* champagne

Champagne – *nf* Champagne (region)

champignon – *nm* mushroom

champion(ne) – *nmf* champion

championnat – *nm* championship

chance – *nf* luck

  avec un peu de chance – with a bit of luck

  avoir de la chance – *v irreg* § to be lucky

change – *nm* exchange

changement – *nm* change, alteration

  changement d'horaire – timetable change

changer – *v reg* † to change

  changer de chaîne – to change channels, channel hop

  changer de l'argent – to change money

chanson – *nf* song

chanter – *v reg* to sing

chanteur – *nm* singer

chanteuse – *nf* singer

chapeau – *nm* hat

chapitre – *nm* chapter

chaque – *adj* each

  chaque fois – each time

charbon – *nm* coal

charcuterie – *nf* pork butcher's, cooked meats, delicatessen

charcutier, charcutière – *nmf* pork butcher

chargé – *adj* loaded, laden

charger – *v reg* † to load, put s.o. in charge of

chariot – *nm* (supermarket) trolley

charmant – *adj* charming

chasse – *nf* hunt, hunting

  aller* à la chasse – *v irreg* § to go hunting

chasser – *v reg* to hunt, chase

chat – *nm* cat

châtain – *adj inv* chestnut, brown

château – *nm* castle, stately home

chaton – *nm* kitten

chatouiller – *v reg* to tickle

---

chatte – *nf* cat

chaud – *adj* hot, warm
  il fait chaud – it is warm (weather)
  j'ai chaud – I am hot

chauffage – *nm* heating
  chauffage central – central
  heating

chauffe-eau – *nm* water heater

chauffeur – *nm* driver

chaussée – *nf* roadway
  chaussée déformée – bumpy road

chausser – *v reg* to put shoes on s.o.
  se chausser* – *v refl* to put one's
  shoes on

chaussette – *nf* sock

chaussure – *nf* shoe

chaussures de football – *nfpl*
  football boots
  chaussures de marche – hiking
  boots
  chaussures de ski – ski boots
  chaussures de sport – trainers

chauve – *adj* bald

chef – *nm* cook, boss

chemin – *nm* path, road, way
  chemin de fer – railway

cheminée – *nf* fire-place, hearth,
  chimney

chemise – *nf* shirt
  chemise de nuit – nightdress,
  nightshirt

chemisier – *nm* blouse

chêne – *nm* oak tree

chèque – *nm* cheque
  chèque de voyage – travellers'
  cheque

cher, chère – *adj* dear, expensive
  pas très cher – not very expensive
  pas trop cher – not too expensive

chercher – *v reg* to look for
  aller chercher* quelqu'un –
  v irreg § to go and fetch someone

cheval – *nm* horse

monter* à cheval – *v reg* to ride

chevaux – *nmpl* horses

cheveux – *nmpl* hair

cheville – *nf* ankle

chèvre – *nf* goat

chez – *prep* at the home of
  chez moi – at my house, home

chic – *adj inv* smart

chien – *nm* dog

chiffre – *nm* figure, number

chimie – *nf* chemistry

Chine – *nf* China

Chinois(e) – *nmf* Chinese person

chinois – *adj* Chinese

chiot – *nm* puppy

chips – *nmpl* crisps

chirurgien – *nm* surgeon

choc – *nm* crash, shock, impact

chocolat – *nm* chocolate
  chocolat chaud – hot chocolate

choisir – *v reg* to choose

choix – *nm* choice, selection
  avoir l'embarras du choix –
  v irreg § to be spoiled for choice

chômage – *nm* unemployment
  être au chômage – *v irreg* § to be
  on dole

chômeur – *nm* unemployed man

chômeuse – *nf* unemployed woman

choquer – *v reg* to shock

chorale – *nf* choir

chose – *nf* thing

chou – *nm* (*pl* choux) cabbage
  chou de Bruxelles – sprout

chouette – *adj.coll* great

chou-fleur – *nm* (*pl* choux-fleurs)
  cauliflower

chrétien, chrétienne – *adj* Christian

chuchoter – *v reg* to whisper

chute – *nf* fall
  chute d'eau – waterfall

ci – *adv* here

---

cidre – *nm* cider
ciel – *nm* sky
cinéma – *nm* cinema
cinq – *adj* five
cinquantaine – *nf* about fifty
cinquante – *adj inv* fifty
cinquantième – *adj* fiftieth
cinquième – *adj* fifth
   être en cinquième – *v irreg* § to be in Year 8
cintre – *nm* coat hanger
circonflexe – *adj* circumflex
   accent circonflexe – circumflex accent (ê)
circuit – *nm* tour
circulation – *nf* traffic
circuler – *v reg* to move about
cirque – *nm* circus
ciseaux – *nmpl* scissors
citer – *v reg* to mention
citron – *nm* lemon
   citron pressé – freshly squeezed lemon juice
clair – *adj* light (colour), clear
clairement – *adv* clearly
claquer – *v reg* to slam (door)
clarinette – *nf* clarinet
clarté – *nf* light, clarity
classe – *nf* class
   salle de classe – *nf* classroom
classer – *v reg* to file, classify
classeur – *nm* folder, ring binder
classique – *adj* classical
clavicule – *nf* shoulder blade
clavier – *nm* keyboard
clé – *nf* key, spanner
   clé de voiture – car key
client(e) – *nmf* customer
clignotant – *nm* indicator (car)
clignoter – *v reg* to flicker, blink,
   clignoter des yeux – to blink
climat – *nm* climate

climatisation – *nf* air conditioning
climatisé – *adj* air conditioned
clinique – *nf* clinic
clochard – *nm* down and out, tramp
cloche – *nf* bell
clou – *nm* nail (for wood)
clown – *nm* clown
   faire le clown – *v irreg* § to play the fool
club – *nm* club
   club des jeunes – youth club
cobaye – *nm* guinea-pig
Coca-cola® – *nm* coca-cola®
cocher – *v reg* to tick
cochon – *nm* pig
cochon d'Inde – *nm* guinea-pig
cochonnerie – *nf* dirty trick
code – *nm* code
   code de la route – highway code
   code postal – post code
   rouler en code – *v reg* to drive with dipped headlights
cœur – *nm* heart
coffre – *nm* boot of car
cogner – *v reg* to bump
   se cogner* – *v refl* to bump o.s.
se coiffer* – *v refl* to do one's hair
coiffeur, coiffeuse – *nmf* hairdresser
coiffure – *nf* hairstyle
coin – *nm* corner, area
   au coin de la rue – on the street corner
   au coin du feu – by the fire
   vous êtes du coin? – do you live locally?
coincer – *v reg* † to jam, be stuck
col – *nm* collar, pass (mountain)
colère – *nf* anger
   être en colère – *v irreg* § to be angry
   se mettre* en colère – *v refl* § to get angry

---

prep - preposition	*v reg* - verb regular	*v refl* - verb reflexive	§ - see verb tables
pp - past participle	*v irreg* - verb irregular	† - see verb information	* - takes être

colis – *nm* parcel
collant – *nm* pair of tights, leotard
colle – *nf* glue
collection – *nf* collection
collectionner – *v reg* to collect (stamps, etc)
collège – *nm* secondary school, college
collègue – *nmf* colleague
coller – *v reg* to glue, stick
collier – *nm* necklace
colline – *nf* hill
collision – *nf* collision
  entrer* en collision avec – *v reg* to collide with
colonie de vacances – *nf* summer camp
colorer – *v reg* to colour
combien (de) – *adv* how much, how many
  tous les combiens? – how often?
  combien de temps? – how long?
comédie – *nf* comedy (stage)
comédien – *nm* comedian, actor (stage)
comédienne – *nf* comedienne, actress (stage)
comestible – *adj* edible
comique – *adj* funny
commande – *nf* order
commander – *v reg* to order
comme – *conj* as, how
  comme ci, comme ça – so-so
  comme si – as if
commencer – *v reg* † to begin
comment – *adv* how
  comment allez-vous? – how are you?
  comment est ...? – what is ...like?
  comment vas-tu? – how are you?
commerçant(e) – *nmf* shopkeeper, market trader
commerce – *nm* business, trade

commerces – *nmpl* shops
commissariat de police – *nm* police station
commission – *nf* commission, errand, message
  faire des commissions – *v irreg* § to do the shopping
commode – *adj* easy, handy, convenient
commode – *nf* chest of drawers
commun – *adj* common, joint
  transports en commun – *nmpl* public transport
communauté – *nf* community
  Communauté Européenne – European Community
compagnie – *nf* company
compagnon – *nm* companion
comparaison – *nf* comparison
comparer – *v reg* to compare
compartiment – *nm* compartment
compétition – *nf* competition
complet – *adj* full (car park), no vacancies (hotel, B&B)
  pain complet – *nm* wholemeal bread
complet – *nm* suit
complètement – *adv* completely
compléter – *v reg* † to complete
complice – *nmf* accomplice
compliqué – *adj* complicated
composer – *v reg* to form, set up
  composer le numéro – to dial
composter un billet – *v reg* to date-punch a ticket
composteur de billets – *nm* date stamp machine
comprendre – *v irreg* § to understand
comprimé – *nm* tablet, pill
compris – *pp comprendre* § understood
compris – *adj* included, contained

c'est compris – it's agreed

service compris – service included

comptable – *nmf* accountant

compte – *nm* account, number

  en fin de compte – in the final analysis

compter – *v reg* to count

compteur – *nm* meter

  compteur de vitesse – speedometer

comptine – *nf* nursery rhyme

comptoir – *nm* counter

concerner – *v reg* to concern

concert – *nm* concert

concierge – *nmf* caretaker

concombre – *nm* cucumber

concours – *nm* competition, exam

concurrent(e) – *nmf* competitor, candidate

conducteur – *nm* driver

conductrice – *nf* driver

conduire – *v irreg* § to drive

conférence – *nf* lecture

confiance – *nf* confidence

confirmer – *v reg* to confirm

confiserie – *nf* sweet shop

confiture – *nf* jam

confort – *nm* comfort

confortable – *adj* comfortable

confus – *adj* confused, embarrassed

congé – *nm* time off, leave

  congé de mi-trimestre – half term holiday

congélateur – *nm* freezer

connaissance – *nf* knowledge, consciousness

connaître – *v irreg* § to know

connu – *pp connaître* § known

  bien connu – well known

consacrer – *v reg* to devote

conseil – *nm* piece of advice

conseiller – *v reg* to advise

consigne – *nf* left luggage office

consonne – *nf* consonant

constat – *nm* statement

constater – *v reg* to declare

construire – *v irreg* § to build

consulat – *nm* consulate

consulter – *v reg* to consult

contacter – *v reg* to contact

conte – *nm* story

  conte de fées – fairy tale

contenir – *v irreg* § to hold, take

content – *adj* pleased, happy

contenu – *nm* contents

contigu, contiguë – *adj* adjoining, next to

continent – *nm* continent

continuer – *v reg* to continue

contraire – *nm* opposite

  au contraire – on the contrary

contre – *prep* against

contrôler – *v reg* to examine, check, monitor

contrôleur – *nm* inspector (tickets)

convaincu – *adj* convinced

convenable – *adj* suitable, convenient

convenu – *adj* agreed

coordonnées – *nfpl* personal details

copain – *nm* friend (male)

copier – *v reg* to copy

copine – *nf* friend (female)

coq – *nm* cockerel

  coq au vin – chicken in red wine

coquelicot – *nm* poppy

coquillage – *nm* shell, shellfish

corbeille – *nf* basket

corde – *nf* rope, string, cord

cordonnerie – *nf* shoe repair shop

cornichon – *nm* gherkin

Cornouailles – *nfpl* Cornwall

corps – *nm* body

correct – *adj* correct

---

correspondance – *nf* connection (train), correspondence

correspondant – *nm* penfriend (male)

correspondante – *nf* penfriend (female)

correspondre – *v reg* to write to

corrigé – *nm* corrections

corriger – *v reg* † to correct

Corse – *nf* Corsica

corse – *adj* Corsican

corsé – *adj* full bodied, full flavoured

costaud – *adj* sturdy, stocky

costume – *nm* man's suit, (national) costume

côte – *nf* slope, hillside, coast, rib
    Côte d'Azur – the French Riviera
    côte de porc – pork chop

côté – *nm* side, aspect
    à côté de – beside
    de chaque côté – on each side, both sides
    de l'autre côté – on the other side

côtelette – *nf* chop, cutlet

coton – *nm* cotton
    coton hydrophile – cotton wool

cou – *nm* neck

couche – *nf* layer, coat (paint), nappy

coucher – *v reg* to put to bed
    se coucher* – *v refl* to go to bed

coucher de soleil – *nm* sunset

couchette – *nf* couchette, sleeper

coude – *nm* elbow

coudre – *v irreg* § to sew

couette – *nf* duvet, quilt

couler – *v reg* to flow

couleur – *nf* colour

couloir – *nm* corridor

coup – *nm* blow, knock, stroke
    coup de feu – shot
    coup de fil – phone call
    coup de foudre – love at first sight

coup de main – a helping hand

coup d'œil – glance

coup de pied – kick

coup de poing – punch

coup de pouce – nudge

coup de soleil – sun burn

coup de téléphone – phone call

coup de tonnerre – clap of thunder

coup de vent – gust of wind

coupable – *adj* guilty

couper – *v reg* to cut
    se couper* le doigt – *v refl* to cut one's finger

cour – *nf* playground, yard, court

courage – *nm* courage, drive

courageux, courageuse – *adj* brave

couramment – *adv* fluently

courant – *adj* everyday, ordinary

courant – *nm* current (water, electric)
    être au courant de – *v irreg* § to know about sthg

coureur, coureuse – *nmf* runner

courir – *v irreg* § to run

couronne – *nf* crown

courrier – *nm* post, mail

cours – *nm* lesson (school)
    cours du change – rate of exchange
    cours particulier – private tuition
    cours préparatoire – reception class
    cours privé – private school

course – *nf* race, running, errand
    faire des courses – *v irreg* § to go shopping

court – *adj* short

court – *nm* tennis court

couru – *pp courir* § ran

cousin(e) – *nmf* cousin

coussin – *nm* cushion

cousu – *pp coudre* § sewn

couteau – *nm* knife

---

coûter – *v reg* to cost
coûteux, coûteuse – *adj* expensive
couture – *nf* needlework
couvert – *adj* cloudy
couvert – *nm* table place, cover charge
  mettre le couvert – *v irreg* § to lay the table
couverture – *nf* blanket
couvrir – *v irreg* § to cover
crabe – *nm* crab
craie – *nf* chalk
craindre – *v irreg* § to fear
cravate – *nf* tie
crawl – *nm* front crawl
crayon – *nm* pencil
  crayon de couleur – coloured pencil
  crayon optique – light pen
crèche – *nf* day nursery, crib
crème – *nf* cream
  crème anglaise – custard
  crème Chantilly – whipped cream with sugar
  crème solaire – sun cream
crémerie – *nf* dairy
crêpe – *nf* pancake
crêperie – *nf* restaurant serving pancakes
creuser – *v reg* to dig
creux, creuse – *adj* hollow
crevaison – *nf* puncture
crevé – *adj* punctured, *sl* knackered
crever – *v reg* † to burst
crevette – *nf* shrimp
cricket – *nm* cricket (sport)
crier – *v reg* to shout
crise – *nf* fit, attack, crisis
  crise cardiaque – heart attack
critique – *nf* criticism, complaint
critiquer – *v reg* to criticise
croire – *v irreg* § to believe

croiser – *v reg* to cross, meet
croisière – *nf* cruise
croissant – *nm* crescent
  Croissant Rouge – Red Crescent
croix – *nf* cross
  Croix Rouge – Red Cross
croque-madame – *nm* toasted cheese sandwich with chicken
croque-monsieur – *nm* toasted cheese and ham sandwich
croquer – *v reg* to munch, bite into
croûte – *nf* crust, pastry
  casse-croûte – *nm* snack
cru – *pp croire* believed
cru – *adj* raw, uncooked
crudités – *nfpl* chopped raw vegetables
cruel, cruelle – *adj* cruel
cueillir – *v irreg* § to pick
cuillère – *nf* spoon
  cuillère à café – teaspoon
cuillerée – *nf* spoonful
  cuillerée à café – teaspoonful
  cuillerée à soupe – tablespoonful
cuir – *nm* leather
cuire, faire cuire – *v irreg* § to cook
cuisine – *nf* cookery, kitchen
cuisinier, cuisinière – *nmf* cook
cuisinière à gaz – *nf* gas cooker
cuisinière électrique – *nf* electric cooker
cuisse – *nf* thigh
  cuisses de grenouilles – *nfpl* frogs' legs
cuit – *adj* cooked
  bien cuit – well-cooked
cuivre – *nm* copper
cultiver – *v reg* to cultivate, grow
curieux, curieuse – *adj* curious, strange
curseur – *nm* cursor
cyclisme – *nm* cycling

faire du cyclisme – *v irreg* § to
  cycle

cycliste – *nmf* cyclist

D

d' – *abbr see de*
d'abord – *adv* first, first of all
d'accord! – OK, agreed!
dactylo – *nf* typist
dalle – *nf* paving stone
dame – *nf* lady
  Dames – Ladies' toilets
  jeu de dames – *nm* draughts
Danemark – *nm* Denmark
  au Danemark – in Denmark
danger – *nm* danger
  en cas de danger – in case of
    emergency
  être en danger – *v irreg* § to be in
    danger
dangereux – *adj* dangerous
danois – *adj* Danish
Danois(e) – *nmf* Dane
dans – *prep* in
  dans ce cas – in this case
  dans le Devon – in Devon
danser – *v reg* to dance
danseur – *nm* dancer (male)
danseuse – *nf* dancer (female)
date – *nf* date
  date de naissance – date of birth
d'avance – early
  arriver* avec 5 minutes
    d'avance – *v reg* to arrive 5
    minutes early
davantage – *adv* more
de – *prep* from, of
  de bonne heure – early
  de grand confort – very
    comfortable

de grand luxe – luxurious
de grand standing – posh,
  prestigious
de la part de – on behalf of
de l'autre côté – on the other side,
  on the other hand
de luxe – luxurious
de nuit – by night, of the night
de quelle couleur? – what
  colour?
de retour – back
de rien – don't mention it, you're
  welcome
de temps en temps – from time to
  time
débarquer – *v reg* to disembark
débarras – *nm* junk room
débarrasser – *v reg* to clear
  se débarrasser* de – *v refl* to get
    rid of
débat – *nm* debate
déborder – *v reg* to overflow
déboucher – *v reg* to uncork, emerge,
  flow into sea (river)
debout – *adv* standing up
débrouillard – *adj coll* smart,
  resourceful, crafty
se débrouiller* – *v refl* to manage,
  get by
début – *nm* beginning
débutant(e) – *nmf* novice, beginner
décalage horaire – *nm* time
  difference
décaler – *v reg* to stagger
décapsuleur – *nm* bottle opener
décédé – *adj* dead

décembre – *nm* December
déception – *nf* disappointment
décevant – *adj* disappointing
déchets – *nmpl* rubbish
déchiffrer – *v reg* to decipher
déchiré – *adj* torn
déchirer – *v reg* to tear
décider (de) – *v reg* to decide to
  se décider à* – *v refl* to make up
  one's mind
décision – *nf* decision
déclarer – *v reg* to declare
décoller – *v reg* to take off (aircraft),
  peel off (stickers)
décontracté – *adj* relaxed
décorer – *v reg* to decorate
découper – *v reg* to cut
découragé – *adj* discouraged
découvert – *pp découvrir* discovered
découvert – *adj* open, uncovered
  à découvert – overdrawn
découverte – *nf* discovery
découvrir – *v irreg* § to discover
décrire – *v irreg* § to describe
décrocher – *v reg* to take down, unhook
  décrocher le combiné – to lift
  the handset
déçu – *pp décevoir* disappointed
dedans – *adv* inside
défaut – *nm* defect, fault
défavorable – *adj* unfavourable
défendre – *v reg* to forbid, defend
défendu – *adj* forbidden
défense d'entrer – no entry
  défense de fumer – no smoking
  défense de stationner – no
  parking
défi – *nm* challenge
défilé – *nm* procession, parade
  défilé du 14 juillet – Bastille Day
  procession
défiler – *v reg* to parade, file past

faire défiler un programme –
  v irreg § to scroll a program
défini – *adj* definite, precise
déformer – *v reg* to bend, deform
  chaussée déformée – *nf* uneven
  road
défrayer – *v reg* to pay expenses
dégâts – *nmpl* damage
dégoûtant – *adj* disgusting
dégoûté – *adj* disgusted, fed up
degré – *nm* degree (temperature)
dégueulasse – *adj sl* disgusting,
  lousy, foul
dégustation – *nf* tasting (wine etc)
déguster – *v reg* to taste
dehors – *adv* outside
  en dehors de – apart from, outside
déjà – *adv* already
déjeuner – *v reg* to have lunch
déjeuner – *nm* lunch
  petit déjeuner – breakfast
délabré – *adj* dilapidated, tumbledown
délai – *nm* delay, time limit
délavé – *adj* faded
délicat – *adj* delicate
délicieux, délicieuse – *adj* delicious
déluge – *nm* flood
demain – *adv* tomorrow
  à demain – see you tomorrow
  à partir de demain – from
  tomorrow onwards
  demain matin – tomorrow
  morning
  demain soir – tomorrow evening
demande – *nf* request, claim, demand
demander – *v reg* to ask (for)
  demander à quelqu'un de
  faire quelque chose – to ask s.o.
  to do sthg
  demander des renseignements
  – to ask for information
démarche – *nf* way of walking

---

démarrer – *v reg* to start (vehicle)
déménager – *v reg* to move house
demeure – *nf* residence
demeurer – *v reg* to live
demi – *adj* half
  demi-frère – *nm* half-brother
  demi-heure – *nf* half an hour
  demi-pension – *nf* half board
  demi-sœur – *nf* half-sister
  demi-tarif – *nm* half-price
dent – *nf* tooth
dentelle – *nf* lace
dentifrice – *nm* toothpaste
dentiste – *nmf* dentist
dépannage – *nm* repair
  voiture de dépannage – *nf* breakdown lorry
dépanner – *v reg* to repair, help s.o.
départ – *nm* departure
département – *nm* administrative department (=county)
dépasser – *v reg* to overtake, exceed (speed limit)
dépêcher – *v reg* to despatch, send
  se dépêcher* – *v refl* to hurry
  dépêche-toi! – *imp* hurry up!
  dépêchez-vous! – *imp* hurry up!
dépendre – *v reg* to depend, be dependant upon
  ça dépend de... – it depends upon
dépenser – *v reg* to spend
déplacer – *v reg* † to move
  se déplacer* – *v refl* † to travel, move
dépliant – *nm* leaflet, brochure
déplier – *v reg* to unfold
déposer – *v reg* to put sthg down
déprimé – *adj* depressed
depuis – *prep* since
  depuis quand apprends-tu le français? – how long have you been learning French?
déranger – *v reg* † to disturb, bother

dériveur – *nm* sailing dinghy
dernier, dernière – *adj* last, latest, bottom
  au dernier étage – on the top floor
dernier, dernière – *nmf* the last, latest one
dérobé – *adj* hidden, stolen
dérober – *v reg* to steal
dérouler – *v reg* to unwind
  se dérouler* – *v refl* to take place
derrière – *prep* behind
des (= de + les) – *art* some, of the
des (pl of un/une) – *art* some
dès – *prep* from
  dès le début – from the beginning
  dès que – as soon as
désagréable – *adj* disagreable
désapprouver – *v reg* to disapprove (of)
désastre – *nm* disaster
désastreux, désastreuse – *adj* disastrous
désavantage – *nm* disadvantage
descendre* – *v reg* to come down, go down
  descendre* à pied – to walk down
  descendre* dans un hôtel – to stay at a hotel
  descendre* de voiture – to get out of the car
  descendre* du car – to get off the coach
  descendre l'escalier – to go down stairs *(with avoir)*
  descendre les valises – to bring down cases *(with avoir)*
descente – *nf* descent
description – *nf* description
désert – *nm* desert
désespéré – *adj* in despair, desperate
désespoir – *nm* despair

déshabiller – *v reg* to undress
  se déshabiller* – *v refl* to get
  undressed
désigner – *v reg* to indicate
  désigner du doigt – to point out
désintéressé – *adj* unselfish
désir – *nm* wish, desire
désirer – *v reg* to want
désobéir – *v reg* to disobey
désolé(e) – *adj* distressed
  je suis désolé(e) – I'm very sorry
désordre – *nm* disorder, muddle
  en désordre – untidy
désorienté – *adj* bewildered,
  confused
désormais – *adv* in future
dessert – *nm* dessert, pudding
dessin – *nm* drawing, design, pattern
  dessin animé – cartoon
  dessin industriel – engineering
  drawing
dessinateur, dessinatrice – *nmf*
  designer, draughtsman
dessiner – *v reg* to draw
dessous – *nm* underside
dessous – *adv* underneath
  au-dessous (de) – underneath,
  below
  en dessous – under, below
  par-dessous – underneath
dessus – *nm* top
  avoir le dessus – *v irreg* § to have
  the upper hand
dessus – *adv* above
  au-dessus (de) – above, over,
  on top
  par-dessus – over (the top of)
destination – *nf* destination
destiné (à) – *adj* intended (for)
détacher – *v reg* to untie, loosen
  se détacher* de – *v refl* to turn
  away from
détail – *nm* detail, description

prix de détail – *nm* retail price
vendre au détail – *v reg* to retail,
  sell individually
détecteur – *nm* detector
  détecteur de fumée – smoke
  detector
détendre – *v reg* to slacken
  se détendre* – *v refl* to relax
détendu – *adj* relaxed
détente – *nf* relaxation
déterminer – *v reg* to determine,
  decide
détester – *v reg* to hate
détour – *nm* bend, curve, detour
détresse – *nf* distress
détruire – *v irreg* § to destroy
dette – *nf* debt
deux – *adj* two
  deux fois – twice
  deux-points – *nm* colon (:)
  deux-temps – *nm* two-stroke
  (engine)
  tous les deux – both
  toutes les deux – both
deuxième – *adj* second
  deuxième classe – second class
devant – *prep* in front of
devant – *nm* front
développement – *nm* development
développer – *v reg* to develop, grow
devenir* – *v irreg* § to become
  qu'est-il devenu? – what has
  become of him?
déverser – *v reg* to pour out
déviation – *nf* diversion, alternative
  route
deviner – *v reg* to guess
devise – *nf* motto, slogan, currency
devoir – *nm* duty
  devoir de math – maths
  homework
devoir[1] – *v irreg* § to owe

prep - preposition	*v reg* - verb regular	*v refl* - verb reflexive	§ - see verb tables
pp - past participle	*v irreg* - verb irregular	† - see verb information	* - takes être

je vous dois combien? – how much do I owe you?

devoir[2] – *v irreg* § to have to, must
 elle doit partir – she has to go

devoirs – *nmpl* homework, prep

devra – *see devoir* § will have to

devrait – should, ought to

d'habitude – usually, as a rule

diable – *nm* devil

diabolo menthe – *nm* mint and lemonade

dialogue – *nm* conversation

diapositive – *nf* slide, transparency

dictionnaire – *nm* dictionary

Dieu – *nm* God

différence – *nf* difference

différent – *adj* different

difficile – *adj* difficult

difficilement – *adv* with difficulty

difficulté – *nf* difficulty

digérer – *v reg* † to digest

digne – *adj* worthy, dignified

dimanche – *nm* Sunday
 dimanche de Pâques – Easter Sunday

diminuer – *v reg* to reduce

diminution – *nf* reduction

dinde – *nf* turkey

dîner – *v reg* to have dinner

dîner – *nm* dinner, evening meal

dingue – *adj sl* crazy

diplôme – *nm* diploma, certificate

dire – *v irreg* § to say, tell
 cela va sans dire – that goes without saying
 cela vous dit de sortir? – do you fancy going out?
 c'est à dire – that is to say
 pour ainsi dire – so to speak
 que veut dire...? – what does... mean?

se dire* – *v refl* § to say to oneself, to claim to be
 comment se dit ... en français? – how do you say ... in French?

direct – *adj* direct, straight
 train direct – *nm* through train, express
 émission en direct – *nf* live broadcast

directement – *adv* directly

directeur – *nm* male primary headteacher, director

direction – *nf* direction

directrice – *nf* female primary head teacher, director

diriger – *v reg* † to direct
 se diriger vers* – *v refl* † to approach, go towards

dis – *see dire* § say

discothèque – *nf* disco

discours – *nm* talk, speech

discuter – *v reg* to discuss

disparaître – *v irreg* § to disappear

disparu – *pp disparaître* § disappeared

disponible – *adj* available

disposé – *adj* arranged

disputer – *v reg* to fight, play (match)
 se disputer* – *v refl* to quarrel

disque – *nm* disc, disk, record (music)
 disque compact – CD
 disque de stationnement – parking disc
 disque dur – hard disk
 disque optique compact – CD-ROM

disquette – *nf* floppy disk, diskette

dissimuler – *v reg* to conceal, hide

dissiper – *v reg* to clear (fog)

dissoudre – *v irreg* § to dissolve

distance – *nf* distance
 à deux ans de distance – within 2 years

---

nm - noun masculine   *nmpl* - noun masculine plural   *adj* - adjective   *conj* - conjunction
nf - noun feminine   *nfpl* - noun feminine plural   *adv* - adverb   *pron* - pronoun

à une distance de 500 mètres – 500 metres away

distraction – *nf* entertainment, absent mindedness

distrait – *adj* absent-minded

distribuer – *v reg* to give out
distribuer le courrier – to deliver the post

distributeur – *nm* agent, machine
distributeur automatique – slot machine
distributeur de billets – ticket machine, cash dispenser

dit – *see dire* § says, said

divers – *adj* various, varied

divertissement – *nm* recreation, amusement

diviser – *v reg* to divide

divorcé – *adj* divorced

divorcer – *v reg* † to get a divorce

dix – *adj* ten
dix sur dix – ten out of ten

dixième – *adj* tenth

dixième – *nmf* a tenth
être le/la dixième de la classe – *v irreg* § to be tenth in the class

dix-huit – *adj* eighteen

dix-neuf – *adj* nineteen

dix-sept – *adj* seventeen
au dix-septième siècle – in the 17th century

dizaine – *nf* (about) ten

docteur – *nm* doctor

documentaire – *nm* documentary

documentaliste – *nmf* librarian, researcher

documentation – *nf* documentation

doigt – *nm* finger
doigt de pied – toe

dois – *see devoir* § must, have to, owe

doit – *see devoir* § must, have to, owe

doivent – *see devoir* § must, have to, owe

DOM – (département d'outre-mer) *nm inv* French département overseas

domaine – *nm* property, domain

domestique – *adj* domestic
animal domestique – *nm* pet

domicile – *nm* home, address (on form)

dommage – *nm* damage, injury
c'est dommage – it is a pity
quel dommage! – what a pity!

don – *nm* gift, talent
avoir un don pour – *v irreg* § to have a gift for

donc – *conj* so, therefore

donjon – *nm* dungeon

donnée – *nf* data

donner – *v reg* to give
donner à manger au chat – to feed the cat
donner à quelqu'un – to give to someone
donner sur – to open on to

dont – *rel pron* whose, of which

dormir – *v irreg* § to sleep

dortoir – *nm* dormitory

dos – *nm* back

dose – *nf* dose, amount

dossier – *nm* file, dossier
dossier scolaire – school record

d'où? – from where?
d'où viens-tu? – where do you come from?

douane – *nf* customs

douanier – *nm* customs officer

double – *adj* double

doublé – *adj* lined (clothing)

doubler – *v reg* to overtake

douce – *adj see doux* mild, gentle, sweet

doucement – *adv* gently

douceur – *nf* gentleness, softness

douche – *nf* shower

doué – *adj* gifted

---

prep - preposition	*v reg* - verb regular
pp - past participle	*v irreg* - verb irregular

v refl - verb reflexive	§ - see verb tables
† - see verb information	* - takes être

douleur – *nf* pain

doute – *nm* doubt, uncertainty

  douter (de) – *v reg* to doubt, question

  se douter de* – *v refl* to suspect

douteux, douteuse – *adj* uncertain, doubtful

Douvres – Dover

doux, douce – *adj* mild, sweet, gentle

douzaine – *nf* dozen

douze – *adj* twelve

douzième – *adj* twelfth

dramatique – *adj* dramatic

  étudier l'art dramatique – *v reg* to do drama

drame – *nm* drama

drap – *nm* sheet

drapeau – *nm* flag

dresser – *v reg* raise, draw up

  dresser la tente – to pitch the tent

  dresser un animal – to train an animal

  se dresser* – *v refl* to stand up straight

drogue – *nf* drug

se droguer* – *v refl* to take drugs

droguerie – *nf* hardware shop

droit, droite – *adj* right, straight

allez tout droit – go straight on

droite – *nf* right

  à droite – on the right

  prenez la première à droite – take the first on the right

  rouler à droite – *v reg* to drive on the right

droit – *nm* right, law

  faire son droit – *v irreg* § to study law

  les droits de l'homme – *nmpl* human rights

drôle – *adj* funny

drôlement – *adv* amusingly

  il fait drôlement froid – it's awfully cold

du (= de + le) – *art* some

dû – *pp devoir* § obliged to

dur – *adj* hard

  travailler dur – *v reg* to work hard

durée – *nf* length, duration

durement – *adv* harshly, severely

durer – *v reg* to last

dut – *see devoir* § was obliged to, had to

dynamique – *adj* dynamic

E

eau – *nf* water
  eau chaude – hot water
  eau de vie – brandy
  eau froide – cold water
  eau minérale – mineral water
  eau non potable – non-drinking water
  eau potable – drinking water
ébahi – *adj* dumbfounded
éblouissant – *adj* dazzling
écart – *nm* gap
  à l'écart – out of the way
échange – *nm* exchange
échanger – *v reg* † to change, exchange, swop
échapper à – *v reg* to escape
  s'échapper* de – *v refl* to escape from
écharpe – *nf* scarf
échauffement – *nm* warm up
échauffer – *v reg* to warm up (sport)
échecs – *nmpl* chess
  jouer aux échecs – *v reg* to play chess
échelle – *nf* ladder, scale
échouer – *v reg* to fail
  s'échouer* – *v refl* to run aground
éclair – *nm* flash of lightning
éclaircie – *nf* bright period
éclater – *v reg* to burst
  éclater de rire – to burst out laughing
école – *nf* school
  école maternelle – nursery school
  école primaire – primary school
  école privée – private school
écolier – *nm* schoolboy
écolière – *nf* schoolgirl
écologie – *nf* ecology
écologiste – *nmf* ecologist

économe – *adj* careful with money
économie – *nf* economics, economy
économies – *nfpl* savings
  faire des économies – *v irreg* § to save up
économiser – *v reg* to economise, conserve
écossais – *adj* Scottish
Écossais(e) – *nmf* Scotsman, Scotswoman
Écosse – *nf* Scotland
écouter – *v reg* to listen (to)
écouteurs – *nmpl* headphones
écran – *nm* screen
écraser – *v reg* to run over, crush
  s'écraser* – *v refl* to crash (car)
écrémé – *adj* skimmed (milk)
s'écrier* – *v refl* to exclaim
écrire – *v irreg* § to write
  ça s'écrit comment? – how do you spell that?
écriture – *nf* handwriting
écrivain – *nm* writer
s'écrouler* – *v refl* to fall down, crumble
écume – *nf* foam, froth
écureuil – *nm* squirrel
écurie – *nf* stable
édifice – *nm* building
Edimbourg – Edinburgh
éditer – *v reg* to edit
éducatif, éducative – *adj* educational
éducation – *nf* education
  éducation physique – PE
  éducation religieuse – RE
effacer – *v reg* † to erase, delete
effectif – *nm* size, strength
effectif, effective – *adj* actual, effective, real

---

prep - preposition	*v reg* - verb regular	*v refl* - verb reflexive	§ - see verb tables
pp - past participle	*v irreg* - verb irregular	† - see verb information	* - takes être

effectivement – *adv* actually, really
effectuer – *v reg* to carry out, make
effet – *nm* effect, impression
  en effet – indeed
efficace – *adj* effective
effort – *nm* effort
  faire un effort – *v irreg* § to make
  an effort
effrayé – *adj* frightened
effrayer – *v reg* † to frighten
effroyable – *adj* horrifying
égal – *adj* equal
  ça m'est égal – I don't mind
également – *adv* equally, evenly
égalité – *nf* equality
égard – *nm* consideration
égarer – *v reg* to mislead, mislay
  s'égarer* – *v refl* to get lost
égaux – *adj mpl* equal
église – *nf* church
égoïste – *adj* selfish
élan – *nm* vigour, spirit
élargir – *v reg* widen
électricien – *nm* electrician
électricité – *nf* electricity
électrique – *adj* electric(al)
électronique – *nf* electronics
électrophone – *nm* record player
élégant – *adj* elegant
éléphant – *nm* elephant
élève – *nmf* pupil
élevé – *adj* high, elevated
  bien élevé – well brought up
élever – *v reg* † to bring up, rear
  s'élever* – *v refl* † to rise up
éleveur – *nm* stockbreeder
elle – *pron f* she, it
elle-même – *pron f* herself, itself
elles – *pron fpl* they
elles-mêmes – *pron f* themselves
éloigné – *adj* far away, remote

éloigner – *v reg* to move, take away
  (object)
  s'éloigner* – *v refl* to go, move away
emballage – *nm* package, packing
  papier d'emballage – *nm* wrapping
  paper
emballer – *v reg* to pack
embarquer – *v reg* to embark
embarras – *nm* trouble, embarrassment
  avoir l'embarras du choix –
  v irreg § to be spoiled for choice
embêtant – *adj* annoying, awkward
embêter – *v reg* to bother, annoy
embouteillage – *nm* traffic jam
embrasser – *v reg* to kiss
embrayage – *nm* clutch
émission – *nf* programme (TV or radio)
emmener – *v reg* † to take
s'emparer de* – *v refl* to take hold
  of
empêcher – *v reg* to stop, prevent
emplacement – *nm* site, pitch
emploi – *nm* job
emploi du temps – *nm* timetable
employé(e) – *nmf* employee
employer – *v reg* † to use, employ
employeur, employeuse – *nmf*
  employer
emporter – *v reg* to take away
  plats à emporter – *nmpl* take-
  away meals
emprunter (à) – *v reg* to borrow (from)
EMT – (éducation manuelle et technique)
  nf CDT
ému – *adj* moved, touched, excited
en – *prep & pron* in, of it, of them,
  some
  en anglais – in English
  en arrière – backwards
  en autobus – by bus
  en automne – in autumn
  en avant – forwards

---

nm - noun masculine	*nmpl* - noun masculine plural	*adj* - adjective	*conj* - conjunction
nf - noun feminine	*nfpl* - noun feminine plural	*adv* - adverb	*pron* - pronoun

en avoir besoin – *v irreg* § to need

en avoir marre – *v irreg* § *coll* to be fed up with

en banlieue – in the suburbs

en bas – downstairs, below

en béton – made of concrete

en bois – made of wood

en bon état – in good condition

en brique – built of brick

en car – by coach

en colère – angry

en coton – made of cotton

en cuir – made of leather

en désordre – in a mess

en-dessous de – under, below

en direction de – going to

en face de – opposite

en forme – on form, fit

en France – in France

en général – usually

en haut – upstairs, above

en laine – made of wool

en mauvais état – in poor condition

en même temps que – at the same time as

en métal – made of metal

en moyenne – on average

en panne – out of order

en plastique – made of plastic

en plein air – in the open air

en plein soleil – in full sunshine

en provenance de – coming from

en retard – late

en sus – in addition

en tête – in the lead

en train de – in the process of

en ville – in town

en voiture – by car

enchanté – *adj* delighted

enchanté(e) de vous connaître – pleased to meet you

encombré – *adj* cluttered, obstructed

encore – *adv* again, more, still

encore une fois – one more time

endormi – *adj* asleep

s'endormir* – *v refl* § to fall asleep

endroit – *nm* place

endurance – *nf* stamina, endurance

énergie – *nf* energy

énervé – *adj* irritated, nervous

énerver – *v reg* to annoy, irritate

ça m'énerve – that gets on my nerves

s'énerver* – *v refl* to get worked up

enfance – *nf* childhood

enfant – *nmf* child

enfer – *nm* hell

enfermer – *v reg* to shut in

s'enfermer* – *v refl* to shut oneself away

enfiler – *v reg* to slip into, put on

enfin – *adv* at last, finally

enflé – *adj* swollen

enfoncer – *v reg* † to drive in, put in (a nail, etc)

s'enfoncer* dans – *v refl* † to plunge, sink into

engager – *v reg* † to involve, enter (competition)

s'engager* à – *v refl* † to promise to

engrais – *nm* fertiliser, manure

enjamber – *v reg* to step over

enlever – *v reg* † to remove

ennemi – *nm* enemy

ennui – *nm* boredom, worry, problem

avoir des ennuis avec – *v irreg* § to have problems with

ennuyer – *v reg* † to bore, worry

s'ennuyer* – *v refl* † to be bored

ennuyeux, ennuyeuse – *adj* boring

énorme – *adj* enormous

énormément – *adv* tremendously

enquête – *nf* enquiry, survey

enragé – *adj* keen, fanatical, angry

enregistrer – *v reg* to record

---

prep - preposition	*v reg* - verb regular	*v refl* - verb reflexive	§ - see verb tables
pp - past participle	*v irreg* - verb irregular	† - see verb information	* - takes être

enrhumé – *adj* with a cold
enseigne – *nf* shop sign
enseignant(e) – *nmf* teacher
enseignement – *nm* teaching
enseigner – *v reg* to teach
ensemble – *adv* together
ensemble – *nm* set, group
enseveli – *adj* swallowed up, buried
ensoleillé – *adj* sunny
ensuite – *adv* afterwards, next, then
entendre – *v reg* to hear
  s'entendre* – *v refl* to agree, get on with
  entendu – *adj* agreed
  bien entendu – of course
entente – *nf* agreement, harmony
enterrer – *v reg* to bury
entêté – *adj* stubborn
enthousiasme – *nm* enthusiasm
entier, entière – *adj* complete, whole
entièrement – *adv* entirely
entorse – *nf* sprain
entouré de – *adj* surrounded by
entraîner – *v reg* to pull, lead, drag
  s'entraîner* – *v refl* to train
entraîneur – *nm* trainer (coach)
entre – *prep* between
  entre amis – among friends
  entre nous – between you and me
entrecôte – *nf* entrecôte steak, rib steak
entrée – *nf* entrance
  entrée gratuite – no charge for entrance
  entrée interdite – no entry
  entrée libre – browsers welcome
  entrée payante – there is an entrance charge
  billet d'entrée – *nm* entrance ticket
entreprise – *nf* firm, business
entrer* – *v reg* to go in

il entre dans la maison – he goes into the house
entretenir – *v irreg* § to maintain, support
  s'entretenir* avec – *v refl* § to speak to
entretien – *nm* maintenance, interview, discussion
envahir – *v reg* to invade
enveloppe – *nf* envelope
envelopper – *v reg* to wrap up, surround
envers – *prep* towards
envers – *nm* wrong side, back
  à l'envers – inside out
envie – *nf* desire, wish, envy
  avoir envie de – *v irreg* § to want to
environ – *adv* about
environs – *nmpl* surroundings, neighbourhood
environnement – *nm* environment
envol – *nm* take-off (plane)
s'envoler* – *v refl* to fly away, take off
envoyer – *v reg* † to send
épais, épaisse – *adj* thick
épaisseur – *nf* thickness
épargner – *v reg* to save, spare
épatant – *adj* splendid
épaule – *nf* shoulder
  épaule d'agneau – shoulder of lamb
épée – *nf* sword
épeler – *v reg* † to spell
éperdu – *adj* distraught, frantic
épice – *nf* spice
épicerie – *nf* grocer's shop
épicier, épicière – *nmf* grocer
épinards – *nmpl* spinach
épingle – *nf* pin
éplucher – *v reg* to peel
éponge – *nf* sponge
époque – *nf* time, era

épouse – *nf* wife
épouser – *v reg* to marry
épouvantable – *adj* terrible, appalling
épouvante – *nf* terror, fear
  film d'épouvante – *nm* horror film
  roman d'épouvante – *nm* horror story
époux – *nm* husband
époux – *nmpl* married couple
épreuve – *nf* test,
  épreuve écrite – written test
  épreuve orale – oral test
éprouver – *v reg* to feel, experience
EPS – (éducation physique et sportive) *nf* PE
épuisant – *adj* exhausting
épuisé – *adj* exhausted, tired out
équipe – *nf* team
équipement – *nm* equipment
équitation – *nf* horse riding
  faire de l'équitation – *v irreg* § to go horse riding
équivalent – *adj* equivalent
errer – *v reg* to wander
erreur – *nf* mistake
es – *see être* § are
escalade – *nf* climbing
escalier – *nm* staircase
  escalier de secours – fire escape
  escalier roulant – escalator
escargot – *nm* snail
espace – *nm* space
Espagne – *nf* Spain
espagnol – *adj* Spanish
espagnol – *nm* Spanish (language)
Espagnol(e) – *nmf* Spaniard
espèce – *nf* species, type
  versement en espèces – *nm* payment in cash
espérance – *nf* hope

espérance de vie – life expectancy
espérer – *v reg* † to hope
espion, espionne – *nmf* spy
espionnage – *nm* spying
  film d'espionnage – *nm* spy film
  roman d'espionnage – *nm* spy story
espoir – *nm* hope
  dans l'espoir de vous voir bientôt – hoping to see you soon
esprit – *nm* mind, spirit, wit
  esprit d'équipe – team spirit
essai – *nm* attempt, test, try
essayer – *v reg* † to try (on)
essence – *nf* petrol
  essence sans plomb – unleaded petrol
essentiel, essentielle – *adj* essential
essoreuse – *nf* spin dryer
essoufflé – *adj* out of breath
essuie-glace – *nm* windscreen wiper
essuie-mains – *nm* hand towel
essuyer – *v reg* † to wipe, clean
est – *see être* § is
est – *nm* east
  à l'est – in the east
  à l'est de – to the east of
estime – *nf* respect, regard
estimer – *v reg* to value, estimate
estival – *adj* summer
estivant(e) – *nmf* summer visitor, holiday-maker
estomac – *nm* stomach
  avoir mal à l'estomac – *v irreg* § to have a stomach ache
et – *conj* and
étable – *nf* stable
établir – *v reg* to set up
établissement – *nm* establishment
  établissement scolaire – school
étage – *nm* floor, storey

---

prep - preposition	*v reg* - verb regular	*v refl* - verb reflexive	§ - see verb tables
pp - past participle	*v irreg* - verb irregular	† - see verb information	* - takes être

à l'étage supérieur – on the next
floor up
au dernier étage – on the top floor
au premier étage – on the first floor
étagère – *nf* shelf
était – *see être* § was
étalage – *nm* display, shop window
étaler – *v reg* to spread out, roll out
étang – *nm* pond
étape – *nf* stage (of a race)
état – *nm* state, condition
Etats-Unis – *nmpl* USA
aux Etats-Unis – in the USA
été – *pp être* been
été – *nm* summer
en été – in summer
éteindre – *v irreg* § to extinguish, put
out, turn off (light)
éteindre les phares – to turn off
the headlights
étendu – *adj* extensive, spread out
étendue – *nf* expanse, area
éternuer – *v reg* to sneeze
êtes – *see être* § are
étincelle – *nf* spark
étiquette – *nf* label
étoffe – *nf* material
étoile – *nf* star
étonnant – *adj* surprising
étonné – *adj* amazed
étonner – *v reg* to astonish
être étonné – *v irreg* § to be
amazed
étouffer – *v reg* to stifle
étrange – *adj* strange, peculiar
étranger – *nm* foreigner, stranger
à l'étranger – abroad
étrangère – *nf* foreigner, stranger
être – *v irreg* § to be
être à l'affiche – to be advertised
être admis à l'hôpital – to be
admitted to hospital

être au courant – to know about
sth
être bien dans sa peau – to be at
ease with oneself
être collé – to have a detention
être de retour – to be back
être enrhumé – to have a cold
être en vacances – to be on
holiday
être recalé – to fail an exam
être reçu à un examen – to pass
an exam
être en... – to be in Year...
être en sixième – to be in Year 7
être en cinquième – to be in
Year 8
être en quatrième – to be in
Year 9
être en troisième – to be in Year 10
être en seconde – to be in Year 11
être en première – to be in Year 12
être en terminale – to be in Year 13
étroit – *adj* narrow, tight
étude – *nf* study (education)
faire ses études – *v irreg* § to
study
études – *nfpl* studies
études ménagères – home
economics
étudiant(e) – *nmf* student
étudier – *v reg* to study
étui – *nm* case
eurochèque – *nm* Eurocheque
Europe – *nf* Europe
européen, européenne – *adj*
European
Européen(ne) – *nmf* European
person
eu – *pp avoir* § had
eux – *pron* they, them
s'évader* – *v refl* to escape
s'évanouir* – *v refl* to faint, vanish
événement – *nm* event

éventuellement – *adv* possibly

évidemment – *adv* of course, obviously

évident – *adj* obvious

évier – *nm* sink

éviter – *v reg* to avoid

évoluer – *v reg* to develop, evolve

évolution – *nf* evolution

exact – *adj* exact, accurate

exactement – *adv* exactly, precisely

examen – *nm* examination

examinateur, examinatrice – *nmf* examiner

examiner – *v reg* to examine

excellent – *adj* excellent

excepté – *adj* apart from

exception – *nf* exception

à l'exception de – with the exception of

exceptionnellement – *adv* exceptionally, as a favour

excès – *nm* surplus, excess

s'exclamer* – *v refl* to exclaim

excursion – *nf* excursion, trip

excuse – *nf* excuse

faire des excuses – *v irreg* § to apologise

excuser – *v reg* to forgive, excuse

s'excuser* de – *v refl* to apologise for

excusez-moi – excuse me

exemple – *nm* example

par exemple – for example

s'exercer* – *v refl* † to practise (music)

exercice – *nm* exercise

exiger – *v reg* † to demand

exister – *v reg* to exist

il existe – there is, there are

expérience – *nf* experience, experiment

experimenté – *adj* experienced

expert – *nm* expert, consultant

expert-comptable – chartered accountant

explication – *nf* explanation

expliquer – *v reg* to explain

explorateur – *nm* explorer

exposer – *v reg* to exhibit

exposition – *nf* exhibition

exprès – *adv* on purpose

venir* exprès – *v irreg* § to come specially

express – *nm* fast train

café express – *nm* espresso coffee

exprimer – *v reg* to express

extérieur – *adj* exterior, outer

extérieur – *nm* outside

à l'extérieur – outside

externe – *nmf* day pupil

extrait – *nm* extract

extrait de naissance – birth certificate

extraordinaire – *adj* extraordinary

extrêmement – *adv* extremely

F

fable – *nf* story
fabrique – *nf* factory
fabriquer – *v reg* to manufacture
face à – *prep* facing
en face de – *prep* opposite
fâché – *adj* angry
fâcher – *v reg* to make angry
  se fâcher* – *v refl* to get angry
fâcheux, fâcheuse – *adj* annoying
facile – *adj* easy
facilement – *adv* easily
facilité – *nf* ability, easiness
  avoir la facilité de – *v irreg* § to
  have the opportunity to
faciliter – *v reg* to make easier
façon – *nf* manner, way, fashion
façonner – *v reg* to make, fashion
facteur – *nm* postman
factrice – *nf* postwoman
facture – *nf* bill
facultatif, facultative – *adj* optional
faculté – *nf* faculty
  faculté des lettres – faculty of
  arts
  faculté des sciences – faculty of
  sciences
faible – *adj* weak
faiblesse – *nf* weakness
faillir – *v reg* almost, nearly to do
something
  il a failli tomber – he nearly fell
faim – *nf* hunger
  j'ai faim – I am hungry
faire – *v irreg* § to do, make
  faire attention – to be careful, pay
  attention
  faire beau – to be warm, fine
  (weather)
  faire chaud – to be warm, hot

faire de l'auto-stop – to hitch-hike
faire de l'équitation – to go horseriding
faire de la natation – to swim
faire de la peinture – to paint
faire de la planche à voile – to go windsurfing
faire de la voile – to go sailing
faire des achats – to go shopping
faire des commissions – to go shopping
faire des courses – to do the shopping
faire des économies – to save up
faire des photos – to take photos
faire des progrès – to make progress
faire des promenades – to go walking
faire des sports nautiques – to do water sports
faire du babysitting – to do babysitting
faire du bricolage – to do odd jobs, DIY
faire du camping – to go camping
faire du crawl – to do front crawl
faire du cyclisme – to cycle
faire du jardinage – to do the gardening
faire du judo – to do judo
faire du lèche-vitrines – to go window shopping
faire du ménage – to do the housework
faire du patin à roulettes – to roller skate
faire du repassage – to do the ironing

faire du ski – to ski

faire du ski nautique – to water-ski

faire du stop – to hitch-hike

faire froid – to be cold

faire faillite – to go bankrupt

faire l'appel – to call the register

faire la connaissance de – to get to know

faire la cuisine – to cook

faire la grasse matinée – to have a lie in

faire la lessive – to do the washing

faire la navette – to commute

faire la vaisselle – to do the washing up

faire le lit – to make the bed

faire le plein – to fill up with petrol, diesel

faire les valises – to pack

faire les vendanges – to pick grapes

faire nettoyer – to have something cleaned

faire partie de – to belong to

faire réparer – to have something repaired

faire ses devoirs – to do one's homework

faire une demande – to make an application

faire une erreur – to make a mistake

faire une expérience – to do an experiment

faire une partie de tennis – to play a game of tennis

faire une promenade – to go for a walk

faire une promenade à vélo – to go for a bike ride

faire une promenade en bateau – to go boating

faire une randonnée – to hike, go for a (long) walk

faire visiter quelqu'un – to show someone round

se faire* mal – *v refl* § to hurt oneself

fait – *see faire* § does, makes

falaise – *nf* cliff

il a fallu – *see falloir* § it was necessary

il fallait – *see falloir* § it was necessary

falloir – *v irreg* § to have to

familial – *adj* of the family

famille – *nf* family

fantastique – *adj* fantastic, great

fantôme – *nm* ghost

farci – *adj* stuffed
   des tomates farcies – *nfpl* stuffed tomatoes

farine – *nf* flour

fatigant – *adj* tiring

fatigué – *adj* tired

il faudra – *see falloir* § it will be necessary

il faudrait – it would be necessary, you ought

fausse – *adj f* wrong, false

il faut – *see falloir* § it is necessary, you must

faute – *nf* fault

fauteuil – *nm* armchair

faux, fausse – *adj* wrong, false

favori, favorite – *adj* favourite

fax – *nm* fax (message)

félicitations! – *excl* Congratulations!

féliciter – *v reg* to congratulate

femelle – *nf* female

féminin, féminine – *adj* feminine

femme – *nf* woman, wife
   femme au foyer – housewife
   femme d'affaires – businesswoman

prep - preposition	*v reg* - verb regular	*v refl* - verb reflexive	§ - see verb tables
pp - past participle	*v irreg* - verb irregular	† - see verb information	* - takes être

femme de chambre –
chambermaid
femme de ménage – cleaning
lady
fendre – *v reg* to split
fenêtre – *nf* window
fente – *nf* crack, slot
fer – *nm* iron
fer à repasser – iron
fera – *see faire* § will do, make
ferait – would do, make
jour férié – *nm* public holiday
ferme – *nf* farm
fermé – *adj* closed
fermer – *v reg* to close, shut
fermer à clef – to lock
fermer le robinet – to turn off the
tap
fermeture – *nf* closing (action), (time)
fermeture annuelle – annual
closure
à la fermeture – at closing time
fermier, fermière – *nmf* farmer
féroce – *adj* fierce
ferry – *nm* ferry
festivités – *nfpl* festivities
fête – *nf* feast, holiday, name day
fête des Mères – Mothers' day
fête foraine – fun fair
Fête nationale – national holiday
(14th July)
fête des Rois – Twelfth Night
fêter – *v reg* to celebrate
feu – *nm* fire
feu arrière – rear light
feu d'artifice – firework (display)
feu de camp – camp-fire
feu de joie – bonfire
feu rouge – red traffic light
avez-vous du feu? – have you got
a light?
feuille – *nf* leaf, page, sheet of paper
feuilleter – *v reg* to glance through

feuilleton – *nm* serial "soap"
feutre – *nm* felt tip pen
feux – *nmpl* traffic lights
février – *nm* February
fiançailles – *nfpl* engagement
fiancé – *adj* engaged
fiancé(e) – *nmf* fiancé(e)
ficelle – *nf* string
fiche – *nf* official form
fichier – *nm* file (computer)
fidèle – *adj* faithful
fier, fière – *adj* proud
se fier* à – *v refl* to trust
fièvre – *nf* fever, high temperature
avoir de la fièvre – *v irreg* § to
have a temperature
figure – *nf* face
fil – *nm* thread, yarn
file – *nf* line
en file indienne – in single file
filer – *v reg* to go away, spin
filer à l'anglaise – to take French
leave, run away
filet – *nm* fillet steak
filet – *nm* net
fille – *nf* girl, daughter
fillette – *nf* little girl
film – *nm* film
film à succès – blockbuster
film d'amour – love film
film d'aventure – adventure film
film comique – comic film
film doublé – dubbed film
film d'épouvante – horror film
film d'horreur – horror film
film de science-fiction – science
fiction film
film en version originale – film
with original soundtrack
film policier – detective film
fils – *nm* son
fin – *nf* end

---

nm - noun masculine   *nmpl* - noun masculine plural   *adj* - adjective   *conj* - conjunction
nf - noun feminine   *nfpl* - noun feminine plural   *adv* - adverb   *pron* - pronoun

à la fin – finally
à la fin du mois – at the end of the month
en fin de compte – in the end
en fin de journée – at the end of the day
fin – *adj* fine, slender
final – *adj* final
finale – *nf* finals (sports)
finir – *v reg* to finish
finlandais – *adj* Finnish
Finlandais(e) – *nmf* Finnish person
Finlande – *nf* Finland
fit – *see faire* § did, made
fixe – *adj* steady, fixed
à heure fixe – at set times
menu à prix fixe – *nm* set menu
fixer – *v reg* to fix, set
à l'heure fixée – at the agreed time
flacon – *nm* small bottle
flamber – *v reg* to burn, blaze, singe
flamme – *nf* flame
flanc – *nm* side
flâner – *v reg* to stroll
flaque d'eau – *nf* puddle
flash – *nm* flash (gun)
flèche – *nf* arrow
fléchir – *v reg* to bend
fleur – *nf* flower
fleuve – *nm* river
flic – *nm coll* cop, policeman
flots – *nmpl* waves (sea)
flotte – *nf sl* water
flotter – *v reg* to float
flou – *adj* vague, blurred
flûte – *nf* flute
flûte à bec – recorder
foi – *nf* faith
être de bonne foi – *v irreg* § to be sincere
foie – *nm* liver

foire – *nf* fair
fois – *nf* time, occasion
chaque fois – each time
quatre fois quatre font seize – $4 \times 4 = 16$
trois fois par an – three times a year
fol, folle – *see fou* mad
foncé – *adj* dark (colour)
fonctionnaire – *nmf* civil servant
fonctionner – *v reg* to work, function
fond – *nm* back, bottom
au fond de – at the bottom, back of
au fond – basically, in fact
dans le fond – basically, in fact
fondre – *v reg* to thaw, melt
fondu – *adj* melted
font – *see faire* § make, do
foot – *nm* football
football – *nm* football
jouer au football – *v reg* to play football
joueur de football – *nm* football player
terrain de football – *nm* football pitch
footballeur – *nm* football player
forêt – *nf* forest
formater – *v reg* to format
formation – *nf* training
formation professionelle – vocational training
forme – *nf* form, shape
être en forme – *v irreg* § to be fit
former – *v reg* to form, create
se former* – *v refl* to form, develop
formidable – *adj* great, terrific
formulaire – *nm* form
formule – *nf* formula, phrase
fort – *adj* strong
être fort(e) en – *v irreg* § to be good at
fossé – *nm* ditch

---

prep - preposition   *v reg* - verb regular   *v refl* - verb reflexive   § - see verb tables
pp - past participle   *v irreg* - verb irregular   † - see verb information   * - takes être

fou, fol, folle – *adj* mad

foudre – *nf* lightning

fouiller – *v reg* to search

foulard – *nm* scarf

foule – *nf* crowd

se fouler* la cheville – *v refl* to sprain one's ankle

four – *nm* oven

    four à micro-ondes – microwave

fourchette – *nf* fork

fournir – *v reg* to provide, supply

fourrure – *nf* fur

foyer – *nm* home, hostel, hall

    foyer des élèves – pupils' common room

    foyer des jeunes – youth club

FR2 (France 2) – 2nd channel on French TV

FR3 (France 3) – 3rd channel on French TV

fragile – *adj* weak, fragile, delicate

frais, fraîche – *adj* cool, fresh

frais – *nmpl* expenses

fraise – *nf* strawberry

framboise – *nf* raspberry

franc – *nm* franc

franc, franche – *adj* frank

français – *adj* French

français – *nm* French (language)

Français(e) – *nmf* French person

France – *nf* France

France 2 – 2nd channel on French TV

France 3 – 3rd channel on French TV

franche – *adj f* frank

franchement – *adv* frankly

francophone – *adj* French-speaking

frange – *nf* fringe

frappant – *adj* striking

frapper – *v reg* to knock

    frapper à la porte – to knock on the door

frapper du pied – to stamp one's foot

frein – *nm* brake

freiner – *v reg* to brake

fréquenté – *adj* busy

fréquenter – *v reg* to attend, go out with, be with, associate with

frère – *nm* brother

frigidaire – *nm* fridge

frigo – *nm coll* fridge

frisé – *adj* curly

frissonner – *v reg* to shudder, shiver

frites – *nfpl* chips

    steak-frites – *nm* steak and chips

froid – *adj* cold

    avoir froid – *v irreg* § to be cold

    il fait froid – it is cold

    j'ai froid – I'm cold

fromage – *nm* cheese

    fromage de chèvre – goat's cheese

    fromage frais – soft white cheese

froncer les sourcils – *v reg* † to frown

front – *nm* forehead

frontière – *nf* border (country)

fruit – *nm* fruit

fruits de mer – *nmpl* seafood, shellfish

fuir – *v irreg* § to flee

fuite – *nf* flight, escape, leak

fumée – *nf* smoke

fumer – *v reg* to smoke

fumeur – *nm* smoker

    fumeur, non-fumeur – smoking, non smoking (area)

furet – *nm* ferret

furieux, furieuse – *adj* furious

fusil – *nm* rifle, gun

fut – *see* être § was

futur – *adj* future

G

gâcher – *v reg* to waste, spoil
gagner – *v reg* to win
gai, gaie – *adj* happy, cheerful
gaîment – *adv* cheerfully
galant – *adj* gallant, courteous
galerie – *nf* gallery, roof-rack
Pays de Galles – *nm* Wales
gallois – *adj* Welsh
gallois – *nm* Welsh (language)
Gallois(e) – *nmf* Welsh person
gamin(e) – *nmf* kid, child
gamin – *adj* mischievous, childish
gant – *nm* glove
   gant de toilette – flannel
garage – *nm* garage
garagiste – *nm* garage owner
garantir – *v reg* to guarantee
garçon – *nm* boy
   garçon de café – waiter
garder – *v reg* to keep, look after
   garder un bon souvenir de – to have a happy memory of
gardien – *nm* warden, guardian, caretaker
   gardien de but – goalkeeper
gare – *nf* station
   gare marchandises – goods station
   gare maritime – ferry terminal
   gare routière – coach station
   gare SNCF – railway station
garer – *v reg* to park
garnir – *v reg* to fit out with, fill
gas-oil – *nm* diesel
gaspiller – *v reg* to waste, squander
gâteau – *nm* cake
   gâteau d'anniversaire – birthday cake
gâter – *v reg* to spoil
gauche – *adj* left, awkward

gauche – *nf* left
   à gauche de – on the left of
   à la gauche – on the left
gaufre – *nf* waffle
gaz – *nm* gas
gazeux, gazeuse – *adj* fizzy, carbonated
gazole – *nm* diesel
gazon – *nm* lawn
gelé – *adj* frozen
gelée – *nf* frost, jelly
geler – *v reg* † to freeze
   il gèle – it is freezing
Gémeaux – *nmpl* Gemini
   être (des) Gémeaux – *v irreg* § to be (a) Gemini
gémir – *v reg* to groan
gênant – *adj* embarrassing
gendarme – *nm* policeman (village, small town)
gendarmerie – *nf* police station
gendre – *nm* son-in-law
gêné – *adj* embarrassed, short of money
gêner – *v reg* to bother, put out
général – *adj* general
   en général – in general
généralement – *adv* usually
généreux, généreuse – *adj* generous
Genève – Geneva
génial – *adj* fantastic, great
genou – *nm* knee
genre – *nm* type, kind
gens – *nmpl* people
gentil, gentille – *adj* kind
gentillesse – *nf* kindness
gentiment – *adv* kindly, nicely
géographie – *nf* geography
géologie – *nf* geology
gérant(e) – *nmf* manager

---

prep - preposition   *v reg* - verb regular   *v refl* - verb reflexive   § - see verb tables
pp - past participle   *v irreg* - verb irregular   † - see verb information   * - takes être

gerbille – *nf* gerbil
geste – *nm* gesture
gifle – *nf* slap on the face
gigot – *nm* leg of lamb
gilet – *nm* waistcoat
gingembre – *nm* ginger (spice)
gîte – *nm* gite, holiday cottage
givre – *nm* frost
glace – *nf* ice, ice-cream
  glace à la vanille – vanilla ice cream
  glace au chocolat – chocolate ice cream
glace – *nf* mirror, window (car)
glacé – *adj* frozen, iced
glacer – *v reg* † to freeze
glacial – *adj* icy
glaciaux – *adj mpl* icy
glaçon – *nm* ice cube
glissant – *adj* slippery
glisser – *v reg* to slip, slide
gloire – *nf* glory, praise
goéland – *nm* sea gull
golf – *nm* golf
  jouer au golf – *v reg* to play golf
golfe – *nm* gulf, bay
  Golfe de Gascogne – Bay of Biscay
gomme – *nf* rubber
gonflé – *adj* swollen
gonflement – *nm* swelling
gonfler – *v reg* to inflate, pump up
  être gonflé – *v irreg* § *coll* to have a nerve
gorge – *nf* throat
gorgée – *nf* mouthful
gosse – *nmf sl* kid, child
gourmand – *adj* greedy
gourmet – *nm* gourmet
goût – *nm* taste
goûter – *nm* afternoon tea, snack
goûter – *v reg* to taste

goutte – *nf* drop (liquid)
gouvernement – *nm* government
grâce – *nf* grace
  grâce à – thanks to
grain – *nm* grain
  grain de poussière – speck of dust
graine – *nf* seed
grammaire – *nf* grammar
gramme – *nm* gram
grand – *adj* big, great, tall
  grand ensemble – *nm* block of flats
  grand magasin – *nm* department store
  grande surface – *nf* hypermarket
  grandes vacances – *nfpl* summer holidays
Grande-Bretagne – *nf* GB
grandeur – *nf* size, dimension
grandir – *v reg* to grow, increase
grand-mère – *nf* grandmother
grand-père – *nm* grandfather
grands-parents – *nmpl* grandparents
grange – *nf* barn
grappe de raisin – *nf* bunch of grapes
gras, grasse – *adj* fat
  faire la grasse matinée – *v irreg* § to have a lie-in
gratis – *adv* free
gratte-ciel – *nm* skyscraper
gratter – *v reg* to scratch
gratuit – *adj* free
grave – *adj* serious
  accent grave – *nm* grave accent (è)
  ce n'est pas grave – it's not serious
grec, grecque – *adj* Greek
Grec, Grecque – *nmf* Greek person
Grèce – *nf* Greece
grêle – *nf* hail
  il grêle – it is hailing

---

nm - noun masculine   *nmpl* - noun masculine plural   *adj* - adjective   *conj* - conjunction
nf - noun feminine   *nfpl* - noun feminine plural   *adv* - adverb   *pron* - pronoun

grelotter – *v reg* to shiver
grenier – *nm* loft
grenouille – *nf* frog
grève – *nf* strike
  être en grève – *v irreg* § to be on strike
  faire la grève – *v irreg* § to strike
gréviste – *nmf* striker
griffe – *nf* claw
griffer – *v reg* to scratch
grillade – *nf* (meat) grill
grille – *nf* railings
grimper – *v reg* to climb
grincer – *v reg* † to creak, grate
grippe – *nf* flu
  j'ai la grippe – I've got flu
gris – *adj* grey
  il fait gris – it is a dull day
grogner – *v reg* to grumble, moan
grommeler – *v reg* † to mutter
gronder – *v reg* to scold

gros, grosse – *adj* big, fat
groupe – *nm* group
se grouper* – *v refl* to group together
guêpe – *nf* wasp
guère – *adv* hardly
guérir – *v reg* to heal, cure
guerre – *nf* war
  guerre civile – civil war
guichet – *nm* ticket office
guide – *nm* guide
guillemets – *nmpl* speech marks
  entre guillemets – in inverted commas
guitare – *nf* guitar
  jouer de la guitare – *v reg* to play the guitar
gymnase – *nm* gymnasium
gymnastique – *nf* gymnastics
  faire de la gymnastique – *v irreg* § to do gymnastics

H

habile – *adj* clever, skilled
habilement – *adv* skilfully
habiller – *v reg* to dress
  s'habiller* – *v refl* to get dressed
habit – *nm* outfit
habitant – *nm* inhabitant, occupier
habiter – *v reg* to live
  Où habites-tu? – Where do you live?
  J'habite Londres – I live in London
habitude – *nf* habit, custom
  comme d'habitude – as usual
  d'habitude – usually
habituel, habituelle – *adj* usual, customary
s'habituer* à – *v refl* to get used to
‡**hacher** – *v reg* to chop, mince

bifteck haché – *nm* minced beef
hachis parmentier – *nm* shepherd's pie
‡**haie** – *nf* hedge
‡**haine** – *nf* hatred
‡**hâlé** – *adj* sun-tanned
haleine – *nf* breath
  hors d'haleine – out of breath
‡**haleter** – *v reg* † to puff, pant
‡**halte** – *nf* pause, stop
‡**hamburger** – *nm* hamburger
‡**hamster** – *nm* hamster
‡**hanche** – *nf* hip (body)
‡**handball** – *nm* handball
‡**handicapé** – *adj* handicapped
‡**harceler** – *v reg* † to harass, pester

---

prep - preposition	*v reg* - verb regular	*v refl* - verb reflexive	§ - see verb tables
pp - past participle	*v irreg* - verb irregular	† - see verb information	* - takes être

‡hardi – *adj* bold

‡hareng – *nm* herring

‡haricot – *nm* bean
  ‡haricot vert – French bean, green bean

‡hasard – *nm* chance, hazard
  par hasard – by chance, accidentally

‡hâte – *nf* haste
  ‡à la hâte – in a hurry

‡hâter – *v reg* to hasten
  ‡se hâter* – *v refl* to hurry

‡haut – *adj* high, loud
  à haute voix – loudly
  à marée haute – high tide
  de haute taille – tall
  haut les mains! – hands up!
  parler haut – *v reg* to speak loudly

‡haut – *nm* top
  dans le haut – at the top
  du haut de – from the top of
  en haut de – at the top of

‡hauteur – *nf* height

‡haut-parleur – *nm* loudspeaker

‡le Havre – le Havre
  il arrive au Havre – he arrives at le Havre

hebdomadaire – *adj* weekly

hébergement – *nm* accommodation, lodging

héberger – *v reg* to accommodate

hein? – *excl* eh?, what?

hélas! – *excl* alas!

hélicoptère – *nm* helicopter

héliport – *nm* heliport

herbe – *nf* grass
  mauvaises herbes – *nfpl* weeds

‡hérisson – *nm* hedgehog

héroïne – *nf* heroine

héroïne – *nf* heroin

héroïque – *adj* heroic

‡héros – *nm* hero

hésiter – *v reg* to hesitate

heure – *nf* hour, class
  à l'heure – on time
  à tout à l'heure – see you later!
  c'est l'heure – it is time
  heure d'affluence – rush hour
  heure d'anglais – English lesson
  heure d'été – summer time
  heure(s) de pointe – rush hour
  heure du déjeuner – lunch hour
  ma montre est à l'heure – my watch is right
  24 heures sur 24 – round the clock
  tout à l'heure – a short while ago

heureusement – *adv* fortunately

heureux, heureuse – *adj* happy

‡heurter – *v reg* to knock, bump into
  ‡se heurter* à – *v refl* to bump into

‡hibou – *nm* owl

hier – *adv* yesterday

‡hi-fi – *adj inv* hi-fi

‡hi-fi – *nf inv* hi-fi

hindou – *adj* Hindu

Hindou(e) – *nmf* Hindu person

hirondelle – *nf* swallow

histoire – *nf* history, story
  histoire ancienne – ancient history
  histoire moderne – modern history
  c'est une drôle d'histoire – it's a strange story
  je ne veux pas d'histoires – I don't want any bother

histoire-géo – *nf* humanities

historique – *adj* historic

hiver – *nm* winter
  sports d'hiver – *nmpl* winter sports

HLM – (habitation à loyer modéré) *nf* council flat, housing association flat

‡hocher (la tête) – *v reg* to shake, nod (head)

---

‡**hockey** – *nm* hockey
‡**hollandais** – *adj* Dutch
‡**Hollandais(e)** – *nmf* Dutch person
‡**Hollande** – *nf* Holland
homme – *nm* man, mankind
  homme d'affaires – businessman
  homme de science – scientist
  homme politique – politician
  Hommes – Men's toilets
honnête – *adj* honest
honneur – *nm* honour
honorable – *adj* decent, creditable, worthy
‡**honte** – *nf* shame
  avoir honte (de) – *v irreg* § to be ashamed (of)
‡**honteux, honteuse** – *adj* shameful
hôpital – *nm* hospital
hôpitaux – *nmpl* hospital
‡**hoquet** – *nm* hiccup
  avoir le hoquet – *v irreg* § to have hiccups
horaire – *nm* timetable
horizon – *nm* horizon
  à l'horizon – on the horizon
horloge – *nf* (large public) clock
horreur – *nf* horror
  avoir horreur de – *v irreg* § to hate, detest
  quelle horreur – how dreadful, awful
‡**hors** – *prep* except for, apart from
  hors de – outside
  hors d'haleine – out of breath
  hors d'œuvre – *nm* starter
  hors saison – out of season
  hors-taxe – duty-free

hospitalité – *nf* hospitality
hôtel – *nm* hotel
  hôtel de ville – town hall
hôtesse de l'air – *nf* air hostess
houligan – *nm* hooligan
‡**housse** – *nf* duvet cover
‡**houx** – *nm* holly
hovercraft – *nm* hovercraft
huile – *nf* oil
  huile d'olive – olive oil
  peinture à l'huile – *nf* oil painting
‡**huit** – *adj* eight
  dimanche en huit – a week on Sunday
‡**huitième** – *adj* eighth
huître – *nf* oyster
humain – *adj* human
  des êtres humains – *nmpl* human beings
humeur – *nf* mood, temper
  être de bonne humeur – *v irreg* § to be in a good mood
  être de mauvaise humeur – *v irreg* § to be in a bad mood
humide – *adj* damp, wet
humour – *nm* humour
  avoir beaucoup d'humour – *v irreg* § to have a good sense of humour
‡**hurler** – *v reg* to howl
‡**hutte** – *nf* hut
hydroptère – *nm* hydrofoil
hymne national – *nm* national anthem
hypermarché – *nm* hypermarket

---

prep - preposition   *v reg* - verb regular   *v refl* - verb reflexive   § - see verb tables
pp - past participle   *v irreg* - verb irregular   † - see verb information   * - takes être

I

ici – *adv* here
  d'ici demain – by tomorrow
  il est d'ici – he is local
  loin d'ici – far away
  près d'ici – nearby, near here
idéal – *adj* ideal
idéal – *nm* the ideal thing, ideal
idée – *nf* idea
  bonne idée! – good idea!
identifier – *v reg* to identify
identité – *nf* identity
  carte d'identité – *nf* identity card
  pièce d'identité – *nf* means of
   identification, ID
idiot – *adj* stupid, idiotic
ignoble – *adj* disgraceful, vile
ignoré – *adj* unknown
ignorer – *v reg* not to know, be
  unaware of
  il ignore le problème – he does
   not know the problem
il – *pers pron* he, it
île – *nf* island
  les îles Anglo-Normandes – *nfpl*
   the Channel Islands
  les îles Britanniques – *nfpl* the
   British Isles
il faut – *see falloir* § it is necessary
illimité – *adj* unlimited
illisible – *adj* illegible
illumination – *nf* floodlight, lighting
illuminer – *v reg* to light up
illustration – *nf* illustration
illustre – *adj* famous
illustré – *nm* magazine
îlot – *nm* island, block of houses
ils – *pers pron* they
il s'agit de – it's a question of
il y a – there is, there are
  il n'y a pas (de) – there is(are) not

il y a combien de temps? – how
  long ago?
il y a six mois – six months ago
il y aura – *see avoir* § there will be
il y aurait – there would be
il y avait – *see avoir* § there was,
  there were
image – *nf* picture
imaginaire – *adj* imaginary
imagination – *nf* imagination
imaginer – *v reg* to imagine
imbattable – *adj* unbeatable
imbécile – *adj* idiotic
imbécile – *nmf* idiot
immatriculation – *nf* registration (car)
  numéro d'immatriculation –
   nm registration number
immatriculer – *v reg* to register (car)
immédiat – *adj* immediate
immédiatement – *adv* immediately
immense – *adj* huge, immense
immeuble – *nm* building, block of flats
immigré(e) – *nmf* immigrant
immobile – *adj* still, motionless
immobilier – *nm* property, real estate
  agence immobilière – *nf* estate
   agent's office
immobilité – *nf* stillness
immuable – *adj* unchanging
impair – *adj* odd (not even)
imparfait – *adj* imperfect
imparfait – *nm* imperfect tense
impasse – *nf* cul de sac, dead end
impatience – *nf* impatience, intolerance
impatient – *adj* impatient
impatienter – *v reg* to irritate, annoy s.o.
  s'impatienter* – *v refl* to get
   impatient
impeccable – *adj* perfect
imper – *nm* raincoat

---

nm - noun masculine	*nmpl* - noun masculine plural	*adj* - adjective	*conj* - conjunction
nf - noun feminine	*nfpl* - noun feminine plural	*adv* - adverb	*pron* - pronoun

imperméable – *nm* raincoat
impoli – *adj* impolite, rude
important – *adj* important
importer – *v reg* to be important, to matter
  n'importe comment – anyhow
  n'importe où – anywhere
  n'importe quand – anytime
  n'importe quel(le) – any
  n'importe qui – anyone
  n'importe quoi – anything
  qu'importe? – what does it matter?
imposer – *v reg* to lay down conditions, set a date
impossibilité – *nf* impossibility
impossible – *adj* impossible
impôt – *nm* tax
imprécis – *adj* unclear
impressionnant – *adj* impressive
impressionner – *v reg* to impress
imprévu – *adj* unexpected
imprimante – *nf* printer
  imprimante à jet d'encre – ink jet printer
  imprimante à laser – laser printer
imprimé – *adj* printed
imprimer – *v reg* to print
impropre – *adj* incorrect
imprudent – *adj* careless, foolish
impuissant – *adj* powerless, helpless
inaccoutumé – *adj* unaccustomed
inadmissible – *adj* out of the question, inadmissible
inattendu – *adj* unexpected
inaugurer – *v reg* to open, inaugurate
incapable – *adj* incapable, useless
incendie – *nm* fire (unplanned!)
  incendie de forêt – forest fire
inciter – *v reg* to encourage, incite
incliné – *adj* sloping
incliner – *v reg* to slope, tilt, lean

inclus – *adj* enclosed, including
inconnu – *adj* unknown
inconnu(e) – *nmf* stranger
inconvénient – *nm* drawback, disadvantage
incroyable – *adj* incredible
Inde – *nf* India
indécis – *adj* undecided
indépendant – *adj* independent
indéterminé – *adj* vague
indicateur – *nm* departure board, guide
  poteau indicateur – *nm* signpost
indicatif, indicative – *adj* indicative
indicatif de région – *nm* dialling code
indication – *nf* clue, information, instruction
indien, indienne – *adj* Indian
Indien(ne) – *nmf* Indian person
indigestion – *nf* indigestion
indigne – *adj* unworthy
indiquer – *v reg* to indicate, show
indispensable – *adj* essential, vital
individu – *nm* individual
individuel, individuelle – *adj* individual
industrialisé – *adj* industrialised
industrie – *nf* industry
industriel, industrielle – *adj* industrial
inégal – *adj* unequal, uneven (ground) note: *mpl inégaux* unequal
infect – *adj* disgusting
inférieur – *adj* lower
infiniment – *adv* infinitely
infinitif – *nm* infinitive
infirmerie – *nf* infirmary, sick bay
infirmier, infirmière – *nmf* nurse, matron
informaticien(ne) – *nmf* computer scientist, operator
information – *nf* piece of information
informations – *nfpl* news

informatique – *nf* computer science, IT

informatiser – *v reg* to computerise

informer – *v reg* to inform

  s'informer* de – *v refl* to enquire about

infraction – *nf* offence

ingénieur – *nm* engineer

ingrat – *adj* ungrateful

injure – *nf* insult

injuste – *adj* unjust

inondation – *nf* flood

inoubliable – *adj* unforgettable

inquiet, inquiète – *adj* anxious

inquiéter – *v reg* † to worry, upset s.o.

  s'inquiéter* – *v refl* † to be worried

inscription – *nf* registration, entry

inscrire – *v irreg* § to write down, enrol s.o.

  s'inscrire* – *v refl* § to enrol, put one's name down

insecte – *nm* insect

insensé – *adj* mad, foolish

insolation – *nf* sun-stroke

insoluble – *adj* insoluble

insonorisation – *nf* soundproofing

inspecteur – *nm* inspector

inspirer – *v reg* to inspire

installations – *nfpl* fittings, equipment

installer – *v reg* to install

  s'installer* – *v refl* to settle (down), move in

instant – *nm* moment, instant

instituteur – *nm* primary school teacher (male)

institutrice – *nf* primary school teacher (female)

instruction – *nf* education

  instruction civique – civics, social studies, PSE

  instruction religieuse – RE, RS

instruire – *v irreg* § to educate, teach

instrument – *nm* instrument

insuffisant – *adj* insufficient, inadequate, not enough

insulter – *v reg* to insult

insupportable – *adj* unbearable, dreadful

intégral – *adj* complete

intelligence – *nf* intelligence, understanding

intelligent – *adj* intelligent

intendant – *nm* bursar, finance officer

intention – *nf* intention

interdire – *v irreg* § to forbid

interdit – *adj* not allowed, forbidden

intéressant – *adj* interesting, good value (of prices)

  un prix intéressant – *nm* a bargain

intéresser – *v reg* to interest s.o.

  s'intéresser* à – *v refl* to be interested in

intérêt – *nm* interest

  avoir tout intérêt à – *v irreg* § to be well advised to do sth

intérieur – *nm* inside

interminable – *adj* endless

internat – *nm* boarding school

international – *adj* international

Internet – *nm* Internet

interpréter – *v reg* † to interpret

interroger – *v reg* † to question

interrompre – *v irreg* § to interrupt

interviewer – *v reg* to interview

intime – *adj* private, close, intimate

s'intituler* – *v refl* to be entitled, called, have the title

introduire – *v irreg* § to introduce

inutile – *adj* useless

inventer – *v reg* to invent

inverse – *nm* opposite

  à l'inverse – conversely

invitation – *nf* invitation

---

nm - noun masculine	*nmpl* - noun masculine plural	*adj* - adjective	*conj* - conjunction
nf - noun feminine	*nfpl* - noun feminine plural	*adv* - adverb	*pron* - pronoun

inviter – *v reg* to invite
ira – *see aller** § will go
irait – would go
irlandais – *adj* Irish
Irlandais(e) – *nmf* Irish person
Irlande – *nf* Ireland
   Irlande du Nord – Northern Ireland
irrité – *adj* angry, irritated
islamique – *adj* Islamic
islandais – *adj* Icelandic
Islande – *nf* Iceland

isolation – *nf* insulation
isolé – *adj* isolated, insulated
issue – *nf* way out
   voie sans issue – *nf* dead end
Italie – *nf* Italy
italien, italienne – *adj* Italian
italien – *nm* Italian (language)
Italien(ne) – *nmf* Italian person
itinéraire – *nm* route, itinerary
ivre – *adj* drunk

J

j' – *pers pron* I
j'ai – *see avoir* § I have
   j'ai chaud – I am hot
   j'ai faim – I am hungry
   j'ai froid – I am cold
   j'ai honte – I am ashamed
   j'ai peur (de) – I'm afraid (of)
   j'ai raison – I am right
   j'ai soif – I am thirsty
   j'ai tort – I am wrong
   j'en ai marre – *coll* I'm fed up
   j'en ai ras le bol – *coll* I'm fed up
jaloux, jalouse – *adj* jealous
jamaïquain – *adj* Jamaican
Jamaïque – *nf* Jamaica
jamais – *adv* never
   à jamais – for ever
jambe – *nf* leg
jambon – *nm* ham
janvier – *nm* January
Japon – *nm* Japan
japonnais – *adj* Japanese
Japonnais(e) – *nmf* Japanese person
jardin – *nm* garden
   jardin des plantes – botanical garden

   jardin potager – vegetable garden
   jardin public – park
   jardin zoologique – zoo
jardinage – *nm* gardening
jardinier, jardinière – *nmf* gardener
jaune – *adj* yellow
jazz – *nm* jazz
je, j' – *pers pron* I
jean – *nm* pair of jeans
je m'excuse – I'm sorry
j'en ai marre – *coll* I'm fed up
je ne sais pas – I don't know
je veux bien – I like
je voudrais – I would like
jet – *nm* jet (plane), throw (ball)
   jet d'eau – fountain
jetée – *nf* pier, jetty
jeter – *v reg* † to throw
jeton – *nm* token
jeu – *nm* game
   jeu concours – quiz
   jeu d'arcade – arcade game
   jeu de billard – snooker
   jeu d'échecs – chess set
   jeu de mots – pun

jeu de société – board game
jeu électronique – computer game
jeu vidéo – video game
jeudi – *nm* Thursday
jeune – *adj* young
jeune – *nmf* teenager
jeune femme – *nf* young woman
jeune fille – *nf* girl
jeune génération – *nf* younger
generation
jeune homme – *nm* young man
jeune personne – *nf* young person
jeunes mariés – *nmpl* newly weds
jeunesse – *nf* youth, young people
jogging – *nm* jogging, track suit
faire du jogging – *v irreg* § to go
jogging
joie – *nf* joy
joindre – *v irreg* § to join
joli – *adj* pretty
jongleur, jongleuse – *nmf* juggler
jonquille – *nf* daffodil
joue – *nf* cheek (face)
jouer – *v reg* to play
jouer au billard – to play snooker
jouer au football – to play
football
jouer aux échecs, aux cartes –
to play chess, cards
jouer du piano, de la guitare –
to play the piano, guitar
jouet – *nm* toy
joueur, joueuse – *nmf* player
jour – *nm* day
jour de congé – day off
jour de l'An – New Year's Day
jour des Rois – Twelfth Night,
Epiphany

jour férié – public holiday
jour J – D-day
jour ouvrable – working day
quinze jours – a fortnight
journal – *nm* newspaper
journalier, journalière – *adj* daily
journaliste – *nmf* journalist
journaliste sportif – sports
correspondant
journaux – *nmpl* newspapers
journée – *nf* day
toute la journée – all day long
Joyeux Noël! – *excl* Happy Christmas!
judo – *nm* judo
faire du judo – *v irreg* § to do
judo
juge – *nm* judge
juger – *v reg* † to judge
juif, juive – *adj* Jewish
juillet – *nm* July
juin – *nm* June
jumeaux – *nmpl* twins (boys, mixed)
jumelage – *nm* town twinning
jumelles – *nfpl* twins (girls),
binoculars
jupe – *nf* skirt
jus – *nm* juice
jus de fruit – fruit juice
jusque – *prep* until
jusqu'à – as far as
jusqu'à dimanche – until Sunday
jusqu'à la maison – as far as the
house
du matin jusqu'au soir – from
morning to evening
juste – *adj* exact, fair, tight, in tune
justement – *adv* exactly

K

karaté – *nm* karate
kart – *nm* kart
karting – *nm* go-carting
  faire du karting – *v irreg* §
  to go-cart
kilogramme –*nm* kilogram
kilomètre – *nm* kilometre

à dix kilomètres de –
  10 kilometres from
kiosque – *nm* kiosk, stall
kiwi – *nm* kiwi fruit
klaxonner – *v reg* to blow the (car)
horn

L

l' – *art, pers pron* the, it, her, him
la – *art, pers pron* the, it, her
là – *adv* there
  là-bas – over there
  là-dedans – inside
  là-haut – upstairs
  passez par là – go that way
laboratoire – *nm* laboratory
laborieux, laborieuse – *adj* hard,
laborious
lac – *nm* lake
lâche – *adj* cowardly, weak, feeble
lâche – *nmf* coward
lâcher – *v reg* to release
laid – *adj* ugly
laideur – *nf* ugliness
laine – *nf* wool
  en laine – woollen
laisse – *nf* lead (dog)
  tenir un chien en laisse – *v irreg* §
  to keep a dog on the lead
laisser – *v reg* to let, leave
  laisser tomber – to drop
lait – *nm* milk
laitue – *nf* lettuce
lame – *nf* blade
lampe – *nf* lamp
  lampe de poche – torch

  lampe électrique – torch
lancer – *v reg* † to throw
langue – *nf* tongue, language
  langue écrite – the written word
  langue étrangère – foreign language
  langue maternelle – mother
  tongue
  langue parlée – the spoken
  language
  langues modernes – *nfpl* modern
  languages
lanterne – *nf* lantern
lapin – *nm* rabbit
laquelle – *pron* which
large – *adj* broad
largement – *adv* widely
largeur – *nf* width
  en largeur – across
larme – *nf* tear
las, lasse – *adj* tired, weary
lassitude – *nf* weariness
latin – *nm* Latin
lavabo – *nm* wash basin
lavage automatique – *nm* car wash
lave-auto – *nm* car wash
lave-linge – *nm* washing machine
laver – *v reg* to wash

---

prep - preposition	*v reg* - verb regular	*v refl* - verb reflexive	§ - see verb tables
pp - past participle	*v irreg* - verb irregular	† - see verb information	* - takes être

machine à laver – *nf* washing machine

se laver* – *v refl* to wash o.s.
  se laver* la tête – to wash one's hair
  se laver* les dents – to clean one's teeth

laverie – *nf* laundrette

lave-vaisselle – *nm* dishwasher

le – *art, pers pron* the, it, him

lécher – *v reg* † to lick
  faire du lèche-vitrines – *v irreg* § to window shop

leçon – *nf* lesson

lecteur – *nm* reader
  lecteur de disquettes – disk drive

lectrice – *nf* reader

lecture – *nf* reading

légende – *nf* caption

léger, légère – *adj* light

légèrement – *adv* lightly

légume – *nm* vegetable

le Havre – le Havre
  il arrive au Havre – he arrives at le Havre

le long de – *prep* along

lendemain – *nm* next day
  le lendemain matin – the next morning

lent – *adj* slow

lentement – *adv* slowly

lentilles – *nfpl* contact lenses

lequel, lesquels, laquelle, lesquelles – *pron* which

les – *art, pron* the, them

lessive – *nf* washing (clothes), washing powder
  faire la lessive – *v irreg* § to do the washing

leste – *adj* agile, nimble

lettre – *nf* letter
  lettre majuscule – capital letter
  lettre miniscule – small letter

lettre recommandée – recorded letter

leur – *pron* to them

leur, leurs – *poss adj* their

levée du courrier – *nf* postal collection

lever – *v reg* † to lift up
  se lever* – *v refl* † to get up

lever du soleil – *nm* sunrise

lèvre – *nf* lip

lézarde – *nf* crack

liberté – *nf* freedom

librairie – *nf* bookshop

libre – *adj* free

libre-service – *nm* self-service shop, restaurant

licence – *nf* degree, permit

lien – *nm* link, connection

lier – *v reg* to bind, tie up

lieu – *nm* place
  lieu de naissance – place of birth
  avoir lieu – *v irreg* § to take place
  en premier lieu – in the first place, firstly

ligne – *nf* line, route
  à la ligne – new paragraph
  ligne blanche – white line (on road)
  ligne d'autobus – bus service
  prenez la ligne numéro 3 – catch the number 3 bus

lime – *nf* file

limite – *nf* limit
  à la limite – ultimately

limiter – *v reg* to limit, restrict

limonade – *nf* lemonade

linge – *nm* linen

lion – *nm* lion
  Lion – Leo
  être (du) Lion – *v irreg* § to be (a) Leo

liquide – *adj* liquid
  argent liquide – *nm* cash

---

nm - noun masculine	*nmpl* - noun masculine plural
nf - noun feminine	*nfpl* - noun feminine plural

adj - adjective	*conj* - conjunction
adv - adverb	*pron* - pronoun

lire – *v irreg* § to read
lis – *see lire* § read
lisse – *adj* smooth
liste – *nf* list
lit – *nm* bed
  lit de camp – camp bed
  lit de deux personnes – double bed
  lit d'une personne – single bed
  aller au lit – *v irreg* § to go to bed
literie – *nf* bedding
litre – *nm* litre
littérature – *nf* literature
littoral – *nm* coast
livraison – *nf* delivery
livre – *nf* pound weight (500 gr)
livre – *nm* book
  livre de poche – paperback
  livre scolaire – school book
livrer – *v reg* to deliver
livre sterling – *nf* pound sterling
livret – *nm* booklet
  livret de famille – family record book
local – *adj* local
locataire – *nmf* tenant, lodger
location – *nf* renting, hiring
  location de vélos – cycle hire
  location de voitures – car hire
locaux – *nmpl* offices
logement – *nm* accommodation
loger – *v reg* † to live, lodge
logiciel – *nm* software, computer program
  logiciel de jeu – game software
  acheter un logiciel – *v reg* † to buy software
logis – *nm* home
loi – *nf* law
loin – *adv* far away
  c'est loin? – is it far?
  loin de – far from
  plus loin – further

loisir – *nm* free time, leisure
Londres – London
long, longue – *adj* long
  le long de – along
longer – *v reg* † to go along, border
longtemps – *adv* a long time
longueur – *nf* length
lors de – *adv* at the time of
lorsque – *conj* when
lot – *nm* prize
  le gros lot – *nm* the jackpot
loterie – *nf* lottery, raffle
lotissement – *nm* housing estate
loto – *nm* bingo, French National lottery
louche – *adj* shady, untrustworthy
louer[1] – *v reg* to hire, rent
  à louer – for hire, to let
louer[2] – *v reg* to praise
loup – *nm* wolf
  à pas de loup – stealthily
louper – *v reg coll* to miss train, fail exam
lourd – *adj* heavy
  il fait lourd – it is sultry
lourdement – *adv* heavily
lourdeur – *nf* heaviness
loutre – *nf* otter
loyer – *nm* rent (*see* HLM)
lu – *pp lire* § read
lueur – *nf* gleam
lui – *pron* to him, her, for him, her
luisant – *adj* gleaming
lumière – *nf* light
lundi – *nm* Monday
lune – *nf* moon
lunettes – *nfpl* spectacles
  lunettes de soleil – sunglasses
  lunettes protectives – goggles
lut – *see lire* § read
lutte – *nf* struggle
lutter – *v reg* to struggle

luxe – *nm* wealth, luxury
  de grand luxe – de luxe model
  voiture de luxe – *nf* luxury car
Luxembourg – *nm* Luxembourg
luxembourgeois – *adj* from
  Luxembourg
Luxembourgeois(e) – *nmf*
  inhabitant of Luxembourg

lycée – *nm* sixth form college
  lycée technique – technical
  college
lycéen(ne) – *nmf* student at lycée
lys – *nm* lily

M

m' – *pers pron* me
ma (mon, mes) – *poss adj* my
mâcher – *v reg* to chew
machin – *nm* whatsit, gadget,
  thingummyjig
machinal – *adj* mechanical, automatic
machinalement – *adv* automatically
machine – *nf* machine
  machine à coudre – sewing
  machine
  machine à laver – washing
  machine
  machine à sous – slot machine
mâchoire – *nf* jaw
maçon – *nm* builder
maçonnerie – *nf* brickwork
Madame – *nf* Mrs, Ms, Madam
Mademoiselle – *nf* Miss
magasin – *nm* shop
  magasin d'alimentation
  générale – general store
  courir les magasins – *v irreg* §
  to go round the shops
magazine – *nm* magazine
  magazine d'actualités – current
  affairs magazine
  magazine de luxe – glossy
  magazine
  magazine hebdomadaire –
  weekly magazine

  magazine mensuel – monthly
  magazine
maghrébin(e), – *adj* from North
  Africa
magicien – *nm* magician
magie – *nf* magic
magnétique – *adj* magnetic
magnétophone – *nm* tape recorder
magnétoscope – *nm* video recorder,
  VCR
  enregistrer au magnétoscope –
  v reg to video
magnifique – *adj* wonderful
mai – *nm* May
maigre – *adj* thin
maigrir – *v reg* to slim, get thin
maillot – *nm* vest, leotard
  maillot de bain – swimsuit
  maillot jaune – leader's jersey
  (Tour de France)
main – *nf* hand
  main courante – handrail
  main-d'œuvre – *nf* manpower,
  labour
  fait à la main – *adj* handmade
  donner un coup de main à –
  v reg to give s.o. a hand
  serrer la main à – *v reg* to shake
  hands with
maintenant – *adv* now

---

nm - noun masculine	*nmpl* - noun masculine plural	*adj* - adjective	*conj* - conjunction
nf - noun feminine	*nfpl* - noun feminine plural	*adv* - adverb	*pron* - pronoun

maintenir – *v irreg* § to maintain, support
maire – *nm* mayor
mairie – *nf* town hall
mais – *conj* but
maïs – *nm* maize, sweetcorn
maison – *nf* house
  maison des jeunes – youth club
  maison individuelle – detached house
  maison jumelle – semi-detached house
  maison mitoyenne – semi-detached house
  rentrer* à la maison – *v reg* to go home
  rester* à la maison – *v reg* to stay at home
maître – *nm* master
  maître nageur – swimming instructor
  maître-sauveteur – lifeguard
maîtresse – *nf* mistress
  maîtresse de maison – hostess
maîtriser – *v reg* to control
  se maîtriser* – *v refl* to control oneself
majesté – *nf* majesty
majestueux, majestueuse – *adj* majestic
majeur – *adj* major, over 18
majuscule – *adj* capital
  en majuscules – in capital letters
mal – *adv* badly
mal – *nm* evil, wrong, pain
  mal au cœur – sickness
  mal au ventre – stomach ache
  mal aux dents – toothache
  mal de mer – sea sickness
  mal payé – *adj* badly paid
  avoir du mal à – *v irreg* § to have difficulty
malade – *adj* ill

malade – *nmf* patient, sick person
maladie – *nf* illness
maladroit – *adj* clumsy, awkward
malaise – *nm* discomfort, sickness
malchance – *nf* bad luck
malchanceux, malchanceuse – *adj* unlucky
mâle – *adj nm* male
malentendu – *nm* misunderstanding
malfaiteur – *nm* criminal
malgré – *prep* in spite of
malheureux, malheureuse – *adj* unhappy, unfortunate
malhonnête – *adj* dishonest
malin, maligne – *adj* malicious, shrewd
malle – *nf* trunk (large case)
maltais – *adj* Maltese
Malte – *nf* Malta
maltraiter – *v reg* to ill-treat
maman – *nf* mummy
mamie – *nf* granny
manche – *nf* sleeve
  La Manche – English Channel
manche – *nm* handle
mandat d'arrêt – *nm* warrant for arrest
mandat postal – *nm* postal order
manège – *nm* roundabout, riding school
manette – *nf* joystick (computer)
manger – *v reg* † to eat
mangue – *nf* mango
manière – *nf* way, manner
manifestation – *nf* demonstration
manifester – *v reg* to demonstrate
mannequin – *nm* model, dummy
manque – *nm* lack of
  quel manque de chance! – what bad luck!
manqué – *adj* failed, spoiled, wasted
manquer – *v reg* to lack, miss, fail

je lui manque – he misses me
il me manque – I miss him
mansarde – *nf* attic
manteau – *nm* coat
manuel, manuelle – *adj* manual
manuel (scolaire) – *nm* text book
maquereau – *nm* mackerel
maquette – *nf* scale model
maquillage – *nm* make-up
se maquiller* – *v refl* to put on
make-up
maraîchage – *nm* market gardening
maraîcher – *nm* market gardener
marais – *nm* marsh
marbre – *nm* marble
marchand – *nm* shopkeeper
  marchand de chaussures – shoe
seller
  marchand de fromages – cheese
seller
  marchand de fruits – fruitseller
  marchand de journaux –
newsagent
  marchand de légumes –
greengrocer
marchandise – *nf* merchandise
marche – *nf* walking, step
  attention à la marche – mind the
step
  marche arrière – reverse
marché – *nm* market
  marché aux puces – flea market
  Marché Commun – Common
Market
  marché couvert – covered market
  marché en plein air – open air
market
  marché noir – black market
marcher – *v reg* to work, function,
walk
mardi – *nm* Tuesday
  Mardi gras – Shrove Tuesday
mare – *nf* pond

marée – *nf* tide
  marée basse – low tide
  marée haute – high tide
  marée noire – oil slick
mari – *nm* husband
mariage – *nm* marriage
  mariage civil – registry office
wedding
  mariage religieux – church wedding
marié – *adj* married
marié – *nm* bridegroom
mariée – *nf* bride
marier – *v reg* to marry
  se marier* avec – *v refl* to get
married
marin – *nm* sailor
marine – *nf* navy
  bleu marine – *adj inv* navy blue
marmite – *nf* cooking pot
Maroc – *nm* Morocco
marocain – *adj* Moroccan
marque – *nf* make, brand name
  tenir la marque – *v irreg* § to
keep the score
marquer – *v reg* to mark
  marquer un but – to score a goal
  marquer un point – to score a
point
marrant – *adj coll* funny
en avoir marre – *v irreg* § *coll* to be
fed up
  j'en ai marre – *coll* I'm fed up
(with it)
marron – *adj inv* chestnut, brown
mars – *nm* March
marteau – *nm* hammer
marteler – *v reg* † to hammer
masculin – *adj* masculine
masse – *nf* mass
  masse de nuages – bank of clouds
match – *nm* match
  match à domicile – home game

---

match à l'extérieur – away game
match aller – first leg
match nul – draw
match retour – second leg
matelas – *nm* mattress
  matelas pneumatique – air bed
matelot – *nm* sailor
matériaux – *nmpl* materials,
  components
matériel – *nm* equipment
  matériel de camping – camping
  equipment
maternel, maternelle – *adj* motherly
  école maternelle – *nf* nursery
  school
mathématiques – *nfpl* mathematics
  maths – maths
matière – *nf* subject (school), material
matin – *nm* morning
matinal – *adj* morning
matinée – *nf* morning, afternoon
  performance
  faire la grasse matinée – *v irreg*
  § to have a lie in
mauvais – *adj* bad
  le mauvais numéro – wrong
  number
  un mauvais moment – bad time
  un mauvais quart d'heure – bad
  time
mauvaise herbe – *nf* weed
me – *pron* me, to me, for me, myself
mec – *nm sl* bloke, guy, chap
  mon mec – *coll* my boyfriend
mécanicien – *nm* mechanic
mécanicienne – *nf* mechanic
méchant – *adj* naughty, spiteful
  chien méchant – beware of the dog
mécontent – *adj* annoyed, discontented
médaille – *nf* medal
  médaille olympique – Olympic
  medal
médecin – *nm* doctor

médecine – *nf* medicine (science)
  médecine douce – alternative
  medicine
médicament – *nm* medicine
  (treatment)
Méditerranée – *nf* Mediterranean
méfiance – *nf* suspicion, distrust
méfiant – *adj* suspicious
se méfier* de – *v refl* to mistrust
meilleur – *adj* better
  meilleurs vœux – best wishes
mélange – *nm* mixture, mix
mélanger – *v reg* † to mix, blend
mêlée – *nf* scuffle, scrum (rugby)
mêler – *v reg* to mix, shuffle (cards)
melon – *nm* melon
  chapeau melon – *nm* bowler hat
membre – *nm* member, limb
même – *adj* same, very, actual
  moi-même – *pron* myself
  toi-même – *pron* yourself
  lui-même – *pron* himself
  elle-même – *pron* herself
  soi-même – *pron* oneself
  nous-mêmes – *pron* ourselves
  vous-même(s) – *pron* yourselves
  eux-mêmes – *mpl pron* themselves
  elles-mêmes – *fpl pron* themselves
même – *adv* even
mémoire – *nf* memory
menace – *nf* threat
menacer – *v reg* † to threaten
ménage – *nm* housekeeping, housework
  faire du ménage – *v irreg* § to do
  housework
  femme de ménage – *nf* cleaning
  lady
ménager, ménagère – *adj* domestic,
  of the home
mener – *v reg* † to lead
mensonge – *nm* lie, untruth
mensuel, mensuelle – *adj* monthly
mensurations – *nfpl* measurements

---

prep - preposition	*v reg* - verb regular	*v refl* - verb reflexive	§ - see verb tables
pp - past participle	*v irreg* - verb irregular	† - see verb information	* - takes être

menteur, menteuse – *nmf* liar
menteur, menteuse – *adj* false,
untruthful
menthe – *nf* mint (herb)
mentir – *v irreg* § to tell lies
menton – *nm* chin
menu – *nm* menu
menu – *adj* thin
mer – *nf* sea
  à la mer – at the seaside
  mer du Nord – North Sea
  mer Méditerranée – Mediterranean
  Sea
  mer Morte – Dead Sea
merci – *excl* thank you
  merci beaucoup – thank you very
  much
mercredi – *nm* Wednesday
merde – *coll* damn
mère – *nf* mother
  mère aubergiste – warden (youth
  hostel)
  mère de famille – housewife,
  mother
merguez – *nf* spicy sausage
mérite – *nm* merit, worth
mériter – *v reg* to deserve, merit
merle – *nm* blackbird
merveilleux, merveilleuse – *adj*
marvellous
mes (mon, ma) – *adj poss* my
Mesdames – *nfpl* Ladies
Mesdemoiselles – *nfpl* young ladies
messe – *nf* Mass
Messieurs – *nmpl* Gentlemen
mesure – *nf* measurement
  sur mesure – made to measure
mesurer – *v reg* to measure, calculate
métal – *nm* metal
  métaux précieux – *nmpl* precious
  metals
métallique – *adj* metallic, of metal

météo – *nf* weather forecast
  météo marine – shipping report
méthode – *nf* method
métier – *nm* occupation, profession,
trade
  il est boulanger de son métier
  – he is a baker by trade
mètre – *nm* metre
  mètre carré – square metre
métro – *nm* underground
  station de métro – *nf* tube station
mettre – *v irreg* § to put, put on
  mettre dans le bon ordre – to
  put in the right order
  mettre de côté – to put aside
  mettre en marche – to start up
  mettre le couvert – to set the
  table
  mettre le réveil – to set the alarm
  mettre une croix – to mark with a
  cross
  mettre une lettre à la poste –
  to post a letter
se mettre* à – *v refl* § to start to
  se mettre* d'accord – to agree
  se mettre* en colère – to get
  angry
  se mettre* en route – to set out
  se mettre* en short – to put on a
  pair of shorts
meuble – *nm* (piece of) furniture
  meubles – *nmpl* furniture
meublé – *adj* furnished
meubler – *v reg* to furnish
meurtre – *nm* murder
meurtrier, meurtrière – *nmf*
murderer
mi- – *pref* half
  à mi-chemin – half way
  à mi-voix – in an undertone
  mi-clos – *adj* half-closed
  travailler à mi-temps – *v reg* to
  work part time

---

micro – *nm* microphone

micro-onde – *nf* microwave
  four à micro-ondes – *nm* microwave oven

micro-ordinateur – *nm* microcomputer

midi – *nm* midday, lunch time
  demain midi – tomorrow lunch time
  Midi – *nm* South of France
  midi cinq – five past twelve
  midi et demi – half past twelve
  midi et quart – quarter past twelve
  midi moins le quart – quarter to twelve
  repas de midi – *nm* lunch, midday meal

miel – *nm* honey

miette – *nf* crumb

mieux – *adv* better
  au mieux – at, for the best
  de mieux en mieux – better and better
  tant mieux – all the better, so much the better

mignon, mignonne – *adj* nice, pretty, sweet

mil – *adj inv* thousand (on legal documents)

milieu – *nm* middle, environment
  au milieu de – in the middle of
  milieu naturel – natural environment

militaire – *nm* soldier

mille – *adj inv* thousand
  cinq mille – five thousand

milliard – *nm* thousand million
  cinq milliards de francs – five thousand million francs

millier – *nm* thousand
  par milliers – in thousands

million – *nm* million
  cinq millions de dollars – five million dollars

minable – *adj* useless, pathetic

mince – *adj* thin

mince! – *excl* bother! drat!

mine – *nf* expression
  avoir bonne mine – *v irreg* § to look well
  avoir mauvaise mine – *v irreg* § to look ill

mineur – *adj* minor, under 18

mineur – *nm* miner, minor

mini-jupe – *nf* mini-skirt

minoritaire – *adj* minority
  groupe minoritaire – *nm* minority group

minuit – *nm* midnight
  minuit et demi – half past midnight

minuscule – *adj* tiny

minuscule – *nf* small letter

minute – *nf* minute
  à la minute – there and then, on the spot

miroir – *nm* mirror

mis – *see mettre* § put

misérable – *adj* wretched, miserable

misère – *nm* poverty

mit – *see mettre* § put

mi-temps – *nf* half time (sport)

mixte – *adj* mixed

MJC – (maison des jeunes et de la culture) *nf* youth community centre

MLF – (mouvement de la libération des femmes) *nm* Women's Lib

Mlle – (Mademoiselle) Miss

Mme – (Madame) Mrs, Ms

mobilier – *nm* furniture

mobylette – *nf* moped

moche – *adj sl* rotten, ugly, lousy

mode – *nf* fashion
  suivre la mode – *v irreg* § to be fashionable

mode – *nm* method

mode de gouvernement – form of government
mode d'emploi – instructions for use
modèle – *nm* model, design
modelisme – *nm* model-making
modéré – *adj* moderate
modeste – *adj* humble, not very well off, modest
modifier – *v reg* to change, modify
mœurs – *nfpl* customs, habits
moi – *pron* me, to me
à moi – mine
donnez-moi un kilo de poires – give me a kilo of pears
moi-même – myself
plus grand que moi – bigger than me
moineau – *nm* sparrow
moins – *adv* less
à moins que – unless
moins cher – less expensive
moins de – less than
moins grand que – smaller than
moins le quart – quarter to
moins – *prep* less, minus
dix moins six font quatre – 10 - 6 = 4
il fait moins dix degrés – it is minus 10ºC
mois – *nm* month
au mois d'avril – in April
au mois de mai – in May
dans un mois – in a month's time
par mois – per month
moitié – *nf* half
la moitié du temps – half the time
moitié anglais, moitié gallois – half English, half Welsh
mol, molle – (see mou) *adj* soft
môme – *nmf sl* brat, kid
moment – *nm* moment
mon (ma, mes) – *adj poss* my

monde – *nm* world
Tiers Monde – *nm* Third World
il y a du monde – there are a lot of people
tout le monde – everybody
mondial – *adj* world
la deuxième guerre mondiale – the second world war
mon Dieu! – *excl* my goodness!
moniteur – *nm* instructor
monitrice – *nf* instructor
monnaie – *nf* change, currency
avez-vous de la monnaie? – have you any change?
Monsieur – Mr, Sir
monsieur l'agent – "officer"
monsieur – *nm* gentleman, man
montagne – *nf* mountain
à la montagne – in, to the mountains
montant – *nm* total
montant – *adj* rising
monter* – *v reg* to climb, get into
monter* à cheval – to ride
monter* dans le train – to get on the train
montgolfière – *nf* hot air balloon
montre – *nf* (wrist)watch
montrer – *v reg* to show
se montrer* – *v refl* to turn out to be
monument – *nm* monument
moquer – *v reg* to mock
se moquer* de – *v refl* to make fun of
je m'en moque – I couldn't care less
moquette – *nf* fitted carpet
morceau – *nm* piece
morceau de pain – piece of bread
mordre – *v reg* to bite
morne – *adj* gloomy, dismal
morsure – *nf* bite

nm - noun masculine   *nmpl* - noun masculine plural   *adj* - adjective   *conj* - conjunction
nf - noun feminine   *nfpl* - noun feminine plural   *adv* - adverb   *pron* - pronoun

mort – *pp mourir* § dead
  mort de fatigue – dead tired
mort – *nf* death
morue – *nf* cod
mosquée – *nf* mosque
mot – *nm* word, message
  mot de passe – password
  le mot juste – the right word
  mots croisés – *nmpl* crossword
  puzzle
motard – *nm* biker, motorcyclist
moteur – *nm* engine
motif – *nm* reason, motive, pattern
motivation – *nf* motive, motivation
motiver – *v reg* to justify, account for,
  motivate
moto – *nf* motorbike
motocycliste – *nmf* motorcyclist
mou, mol, molle – *adj* soft, loose, weak
mouche – *nf* fly
  prendre la mouche – *v irreg* § to
  take offence
se moucher* – *v refl* to blow one's nose
mouchoir – *nm* handkerchief
  mouchoir en papier – *nm* tissue
mouette – *nf* seagull
mouillé – *adj* wet
  se faire* mouiller – *v refl* § to get
  wet
moule – *nf* mussel
moulin – *nm* mill
  moulin à vent – windmill
mourir – *v irreg* § to die
mousse – *nf* foam
mousseux, mousseuse – *adj* frothy,
  sparkling (wine)
moustache – *nf* moustache
  moustaches – *nfpl* whiskers (cat,
  etc)
moustique – *nm* mosquito
moutarde – *nf* mustard
mouton – *nm* sheep, mutton

moutons – *nmpl* white horses (on
sea)
mouvement – *nm* movement, action
  mouvements de gymnastique –
  nmpl exercises
moyen – *nm* means
  moyen de transport – means of
  transport
moyen, moyenne – *adj* average
  avoir la moyenne – *v irreg* §
  to get average marks
  en moyenne – on average
muguet – *nm* lily of the valley
multicolore – *adj* multi-coloured
municipal – *adj* municipal, council-run
munir de – *v reg* to equip, provide with
  se munir* de – *v refl* to provide
  o.s. with
mur – *nm* wall
mûr – *adj* ripe, mature (person)
mûre – *nf* blackberry, bramble
muscle – *nm* muscle
musculaire – *adj* muscular
musée – *nm* museum
musicien(ne) – *nmf* musician
musique – *nf* music
  musique classique – classical music
  musique de fond – background
  music
  musique folklorique – folk music
  musique pop – pop music
  écouter de la musique – *v reg* to
  listen to music
musulman – *adj* Muslim
musulman(e) – *nmf* Muslim (person)
myope – *adj* short-sighted
myrtille – *nf* bilberry
mystère – *nm* mystery
mystérieux, mystérieuse – *adj*
mysterious
mythe – *nm* myth

N

n' – see ne

nage – *nf* swimming, stroke
   nage papillon – butterfly stroke
   nage sur le dos – backstroke
   être en nage – *v irreg* § to be
    dripping with sweat
   s'eloigner* à la nage – *v refl*
    to swim away

nager – *v reg* † to swim
   nager la brasse – to do
    breaststroke

naissance – *nf* birth

naître – *v irreg* § to be born

nana – *nf sl* chick, bird (girl)

nappe – *nf* table-cloth
   nappe de mazout – oil slick

natation – *nf* swimming

nation – *nf* nation
   Nations Unies – *nfpl* United
    Nations

national – *adj* national
   grève nationale – *nf* national strike
   route nationale – *nf* trunk road

nationalité – *nf* nationality

nationaux – *nmpl* nationals (people)

natte – *nf* plait

nature – *nf* nature, kind, sort

naturel – *nm* nature, disposition
   avoir bon naturel – *v irreg* §
    to have a happy nature

naturel, naturelle – *adj* natural

naturellement – *adv* naturally,
   of course

naufrage – *nm* shipwreck

nautique – *adj* nautical
   sports nautiques – *nfpl* water
    sports

nautisme – *nm* water sports

navette – *nf* shuttle

faire la navette – *v irreg* §
   to commute

naviguer sur Internet – *v reg*
   to surf the Internet

navire – *nm* ship

ne, n' – *neg adv*
   ne...aucun – not any, not one
   ne...guère – hardly
   ne...jamais – never
   ne...ni...ni – neither...nor
   ne...nulle part – nowhere
   ne...pas – not
   ne...personne – nobody
   ne...plus – no more, no longer
   ne...que – only
   ne...rien – nothing

né, née – *pp naître* § born

néanmoins – *adv* nevertheless

néant – *nm* nothingness, void

nécessaire – *adj* necessary

nécessité – *nf* necessity, need

néerlandais – *adj* Dutch

Néerlandais(e) – *nmf* Dutchman
   Dutchwoman

néfaste – *adj* harmful, unlucky

négatif, négative – *adj* negative

négatif – *nm* negative

négligé – *adj* neglected, careless

négliger – *v reg* † to neglect, pay no
   attention to, be careless

négoce – *nm* commerce, business

négociant(e) – *nmf* merchant

négocier – *v reg* to negotiate

neige – *nf* snow
   bonhomme de neige – *nm* snowman
   boule de neige – *nf* snowball

neiger – *v reg* † to snow

neigeux, neigeuse – *adj* snowy

nerf – *nm* nerve

---

nm - noun masculine	**nmpl** - noun masculine plural	**adj** - adjective	**conj** - conjunction
nf - noun feminine	**nfpl** - noun feminine plural	**adv** - adverb	**pron** - pronoun

vivre sur les nerfs – *v irreg* §
to live on one's nerves

nerveux, nerveuse – *adj* nervous, tense

n'est-ce pas – *adv* isn't it?, don't you? etc

net, nette – *adj* clean, tidy, distinct

nettement – *adv* clearly, sharply
il va nettement mieux – he is distinctly better

nettoyage – *nm* cleaning
nettoyage à sec – dry cleaning

nettoyer – *v reg* † to clean

neuf – *adj inv* nine

neuf, neuve – *adj* new, brand new

neutre – *adj* neutral, colourless

neuvième – *adj* ninth

neveu – *nm* nephew

nez – *nm* nose

ni...ni – *conj* neither ...nor

nid – *nm* nest

nièce – *nf* niece

nier – *v reg* to deny

n'importe comment – anyhow

n'importe où – anywhere

n'importe quand – anytime

n'importe quel(le) – any

n'importe qui – anybody

n'importe quoi – anything

niveau – *nm* level
au niveau – up to standard
niveau de vie – standard of living
passage à niveau – *nm* level crossing

noce – *nf* wedding

Noël – *nm* Christmas
à Noël – at Christmas
bûche de Noël – *nf* Yule log
cadeau de Noël – *nm* Christmas present
chant de Noël – *nm* carol
sapin de Noël – *nm* Christmas tree
veille de Noël – *nf* Christmas Eve

nœud – *nm* knot

noir – *adj* black
l'Afrique noire – black Africa
il fait noir – it is dark

noisette – *nf* hazelnut

noix – *nf* nut, walnut
noix de coco – coconut

nom – *nm* name, noun
au nom de – in the name of
nom commun – common noun
nom (de baptême) – Christian name
nom de famille – surname
nom propre – proper noun

nombre – *nm* number

nombreux, nombreuse – *adj* numerous, many

nommer – *v reg* to call, name, nominate

non – *neg, adv* no, non-, not
je crois que non – I don't think so
non-compris – not included
non-fumeur – non-smoking
non loin d'ici – not far from here, nearby
non plus – neither, not either
non seulement – not only

nord – *nm* north
nord-est – north east
nord-ouest – north west

normal – *adj* normal, usual

normalement – *adv* normally

Normandie – *nf* Normandy

Norvège – *nf* Norway

norvégien, norvégienne – *adj* Norwegian

nos (notre) – *adj poss* our

note – *nf* mark, grade, note (music)
avoir de bonnes notes – *v irreg* § to get good marks
avoir de mauvaises notes – *v irreg* § to get bad marks
demander la note – *v reg* to ask for the bill (in a hotel)

noter – *v reg* to write down

---

prep - preposition   *v reg* - verb regular   *v refl* - verb reflexive   § - see verb tables
pp - past participle   *v irreg* - verb irregular   † - see verb information   * - takes être

notre (nos) – *adj poss* our
nôtre(s), le, la, les – *pron* ours
noueux, noueuse – *adj* knotty
nouilles – *nfpl* noodles, pasta
nounours – *nm* teddy bear
nourrir – *v reg* to feed
nourriture – *nf* food
nous – *pron* we, to us, us
nouveau, nouvel, nouvelle – *adj* new
  de nouveau – again, once more
  nouveau-né – new-born
  Nouvel An – *nm* New Year
  Nouvel An juif – *nm* Jewish New
    Year
  Nouvelle Année – *nf* New Year
  Nouvelle Zélande – *nf* New
    Zealand
nouveauté – *nf* novelty
nouvelle – *nf* a piece of news, short
  story
  bonne nouvelle – good news
  mauvaise nouvelle – bad news
nouvelles – *nfpl* news
  avoir de ses nouvelles – *v irreg* §
    to have news of him/her
novembre – *nm* November
  le onze novembre – November 11th
se noyer* – *v refl* † to drown
nu, nue – *adj* bare, naked
  nu-pieds – *nmpl* sandals
  nu-tête – bare-headed

  pieds nus – barefoot
nuage – *nm* cloud
nuageux, nuageuse – *adj* cloudy
nucléaire – *nm* nuclear power
nuit – *nf* night
  au milieu de la nuit – in the
    middle of the night
  il fait nuit – it is dark
nul – *pron* no one, none
nul, nulle – *adj* no, useless
  être nul en géographie – *v irreg*
    § to be no good at Geography
  il est nul – he is useless
  match nul – *nm* a goalless draw
  nulle part – nowhere
numéro – *nm* number
  numéro de compte – account
    number
  numéro de télécopie – fax
    number
  numéro de téléphone – phone
    number
  numéro d'immatriculation –
    registration number (car)
  j'habite au numéro 3 – I live at
    number 3
numéroter – *v reg* to number
nuque – *nf* nape of the neck
nutritif, nutritive – *adj* nourishing
nylon – *nm* nylon
  en nylon – made of nylon

O

obédience – *nf* allegiance
obéir à – *v reg* to obey
obéissance – *nf* obedience
obéissant – *adj* obedient
objectif – *nm* camera lens, objective
   objectif à grand angle – wide angle lens
objectif, objective – *adj* objective
objet – *nm* object
   objets trouvés – *nmpl* lost property
   bureau des objets trouvés – *nm* lost property office
obligation – *nf* duty, obligation
obligatoire – *adj* obligatory, inevitable
obliger – *v reg* † to force, make compulsory
   être obligé de – *v irreg* § to be obliged to
oblitération – *nf* cancelling
   cachet d'oblitération – *nm* postmark
oblitérer – *v reg* † to cancel
obscur – *adj* dark, vague, obscure
obscurcir – *v reg* to obscure, cloud
   s'obscurcir* – *v refl* to grow dark
obscurité – *nf* darkness
obsèques – *nfpl* funeral
observateur, observatrice – *adj* observant
observateur, observatrice – *nmf* observer
observation – *nf* observation
observer – *v reg* to observe
   faire observer que – *v irreg* § to point out that
obstacle – *nm* obstacle, hurdle
   course d'obstacles – *nf* obstacle race

obstiné – *adj* obstinate
s'obstiner à* – *v refl* to insist, persist in
obtenir – *v irreg* § to obtain
occasion – *nf* opportunity, chance, occasion
   avoir l'occasion de – *v irreg* § to have the chance to
   d'occasion – second hand
occasionel, occasionelle – *adj* casual, occasional
occasionner – *v reg* to cause, bring about
occident – *nm* west
   l'Occident – the West
occidental – *adj* western
   occidentaux – *adj mpl* western
occupant – *nm* occupant
occupation – *nf* occupation
   grève avec occupation des locaux – *nf* sit down strike
occupé – *adj* occupied, busy
   être occupé – *v irreg* § to be busy
occuper – *v reg* to fill, take up
   s'occuper* de – *v refl* to deal with, look after
occurrence – *nf* instance, case of
OCDE – (Organisation de coopération et de développement économiques) *nf* OECD (Organisation for Economic Cooperation and Development)
océan – *nm* ocean
   Océan Atlantique – Atlantic Ocean
   Océan Pacifique – Pacific Ocean
océanaute – *nmf* deep-sea diver
octobre – *nm* October
odeur – *nf* smell
   mauvaise odeur – bad smell
   odeur de brûlé – smell of burning
   sans odeur – odourless

---

odieux, odieuse – *adj* hateful
odorat – *nm* sense of smell
  avoir l'odorat fin – *v irreg* § to have a keen sense of smell
œil – *nm* eye (*plural* yeux)
œuf – *nm* egg
  œuf à la coque – boiled egg
  œufs brouillés – *nmpl* scrambled egg
  œuf sur le plat – fried egg
œuvre – *nf* work, task, deed, work of art
offensant – *adj* insulting
offense – *nf* insult
  faire offense à – *v irreg* § to insult
offensé – *adj* hurt, insulted
offenser – *v reg* to offend, hurt
offensif, offensive – *adj* offensive
office – *nm* office
  office de publicité – advertising office
  office de tourisme – tourist office
office – *nm* church service, Mass
offre – *nf* offer, bid
offrir – *v irreg* § to give, offer
oie – *nf* goose
oignon – *nm* onion
oiseau – *nm* bird
oisif, oisive – *adj* idle
  vie oisive – *nf* life of leisure, idleness
olive – *nf* olive
olivier – *nm* olive tree
olympique – *adj* Olympic
ombragé – *adj* shaded, shady
ombre – *nf* shadow, shade
  à l'ombre – in the shade
  ombre à paupière – eye shadow
ombrelle – *nf* sunshade, parasol
omelette – *nf* omelette
  omelette aux champignons – mushroom omelette

omelette aux fines herbes – omelette with herbs
omnibus – *nm* stopping train
OMS – (Organisation mondiale de la Santé) *nf* WHO (World Health Organisation)
on – *pron* we, you, they, someone, people in general
oncle – *nm* uncle
onde – *nf* wave (frequency), airwave
ongle – *nm* nail (finger)
ont – *see avoir* § have
ONU – (Organisation des Nations Unies) *nf* UN, United Nations
onze – *adj inv* eleven
  le onze novembre – November 11th
onzième – *adj nmf* eleventh
opéra – *nm* opera
opérateur – *nm* operator
opération – *nf* operation, process
opératrice – *nf* operator
opiniâtre – *adj* stubborn, obstinate
opinion – *nf* opinion
  opinion publique – public opinion
opportun – *adj* timely
  en temps opportun – at the right time
opportunément – *adv* just at the right time
opposé – *adj* opposing, opposite
  en sens opposé – in the opposite direction
opposé – *nm* opposite, reverse
s'opposer* à – *v refl* to rebel against, oppose
opposition – *nf* opposition
  les partis de l'opposition – *nmpl* opposition parties
oppressant – *adj* oppressive
oppresser – *v reg* to weigh heavily on
opprimer – *v reg* to oppress
opter (pour) – *v reg* to choose, opt for

---

opticien, opticienne – *nmf* optician
optimiste – *adj* optimistic
optimiste – *nmf* optimist
or – *nm* gold
  or massif – solid gold
  en or – (made of) gold
orage – *nm* thunderstorm
  il y aura des orages – there will
  be thunderstorms
orageux, orageuse – *adj* stormy
orange – *nf* orange (fruit)
  orange pressée – freshly squeezed
  orange juice
orange – *nm* orange (colour)
orange – *adj* orange
orbital – *adj* orbital
orchestre – *nm* orchestra, band, stalls
  orchestre de chambre –
  chamber orchestra
  orchestre de cordes – string
  orchestra
  orchestre de jazz – jazz band
  à l'orchestre – in the stalls
ordinaire – *adj* ordinary, usual
ordinairement – *adv* usually
ordinal – *nm* ordinal number
ordinateur – *nm* computer
ordonnance – *nf* prescription,
organisation
ordonné – *adj* tidy, methodical
ordonner – *v reg* to arrange, order
ordre – *nm* order, command
  mettre en ordre – *v irreg* § to tidy
  par ordre alphabétique –
  in alphabetical order
  par ordre d'importance –
  in order of importance
ordures – *nfpl* rubbish
  ordures ménagères – household
  rubbish
oreille – *nf* ear
  avoir l'oreille fine – *v irreg* §
  to have a keen ear

  écouter de toutes ses oreilles –
  v reg to be all ears
oreiller – *nm* pillow
oreillons – *nmpl* mumps
orfèvre – *nm* silver, goldsmith
organigramme – *nm* flowchart
organique – *adj* organic
organisation – *nf* organisation, set up
organisé – *adj* organised
organiser – *v reg* to arrange, organise
organisme – *nm* body, organism
orgue – *nm* organ
orgueil – *nm* arrogance, pride
orgueilleux, orgueilleuse – *adj*
arrogant, proud
orient – *nm* east
  l'Extrême Orient – the Far East
  le Moyen Orient – the Middle East
oriental – *adj* eastern
orientation – *nf* training, advice
  orientation professionnelle –
  careers advice
orienter – *v reg* to position, direct,
advise
  s'orienter* – *v refl* to find one's
  bearings
originaire de – *adj* native to, born in
origine – *nf* origins
  à l'origine – in the beginning
ornement – *nm* ornament
orner – *v reg* to decorate
ornithologie – *nf* ornithology
orphelin, orpheline – *nmf* orphan
orphelinat – *nm* orphanage
orthographe – *nf* spelling
os – *nm* bone
  trempé jusqu'aux os – soaked to
  the skin
oser – *v reg* to dare
ostensible – *adj* conspicuous
ostentation – *nf* display, show
otage – *nm* hostage

OTAN – (Organisation du traité de l'Atlantique Nord) *nf* NATO

ôter – *v reg* to take off

  s'ôter* de – *v refl* to get out of

  ôte-toi de là! – get out of the way!

ou – *conj* or

où – *adv* where

oubli – *nm* forgetfulness, forgetting

oublier – *v reg* to forget

ouest – *nm* west

  à l'ouest – in the west, to the west of

ouest – *adj inv* western, of the west

ouf! – *excl* phew!

oui – *adv* yes

  je crois que oui – I think so

ouragan – *nm* hurricane

ours – *nm* bear

  ours blanc – polar bear

  ours en peluche – teddy bear

ourson – *nm* bear cub

outil – *nm* tool

outillage – *nm* tools

outragé – *adj* very offended

outrageux, outrageuse – *adj* outrageous

outre – *prep* as well as

  en outre – besides

les territoires d'outre-mer (TOM) – French overseas territories

outré – *adj* exaggerated, outraged

ouvert – *adj* open *see ouvrir* §

ouvertement – *adv* openly

ouverture – *nf* opening

  heures d'ouverture – *nfpl* opening hours

ouvrage – *nm* (piece of) work

  se mettre* à l'ouvrage – *v refl* § to start work

ouvre-boîte – *nm* tin opener

ouvre-bouteille – *nm* bottle opener

ouvreuse – *nf* usherette

ouvrier, ouvrière – *nmf* worker

ouvrier, ouvrière – *adj* working class

ouvrir – *v irreg* § to open, switch on

  ouvrir le robinet – to turn on the tap

s'ouvrir* – *v refl* § to open, undo

  la porte s'ouvre sur le jardin – the door opens on to the garden

ouvrit – see ouvrir § opened

ovale – *adj* oval

oxygène – *nm* oxygen

ozone – *nm* ozone

  couche d'ozone – *nf* ozone layer

P

pacifique – *adj* peaceful
pacifiste – *nmf* pacifist
pacte – *nm* pact
pagaie – *nf* paddle
page – *nf* page
paie – *nf* wages, pay
paiement – *nm* payment
paille – *nf* straw
pain – *nm* bread
  pain complet – wholemeal bread
  pain de mie – sandwich bread
  pain grillé – toast
pair – *adj* even (not odd)
paire – *nf* pair (of)
  paire de draps – a pair of sheets
paisible – *adj* peaceful, quiet
paix – *nf* peace
Pakistan – *nm* Pakistan
pakistanais – *adj* Pakistani
Pakistanais(e) – *nmf* Pakistani
person
palais – *nm* palace
pâle – *adj* pale
palier – *nm* landing
pâlir – *v reg* to turn pale
palmarès – *nm* prize list
palmier – *nm* palm tree
pamplemousse – *nm* grapefruit
pancarte – *nf* placard
panda géant – *nm* giant panda
panier – *nm* basket
panique – *nf* panic
panne – *nf* breakdown
  en panne d'essence – run out of
petrol
  être en panne – *v irreg* § to have
broken down
panneau – *nm* board, sign
panorama – *nm* view, panorama

pansement – *nm* dressing, plaster
pantalon – *nm* trousers (pair of)
pantoufle – *nf* slipper
papa – *nm* daddy
pape – *nm* Pope
papeterie – *nf* stationer's shop
papi – *nm* grandad
papier – *nm* paper
  papiers d'identité – *nmpl* papers
papillon – *nm* butterfly
  nœud papillon – *nm* bow tie
Pâque juive – *nf* Passover
Pâques – *nm* Easter
  à Pâques – at Easter
  joyeuses Pâques – *nfpl* Happy
Easter
paquet – *nm* package
par – *prep* by
  par avion – by air mail
  par deux – in twos
  par exemple – for example
  par ici – this way
  par jour – per day
  par-là – over there
  par la côte – via the coast
  par la fenêtre – out of the window
  par la suite – afterwards
  par le train – by train
  par mois – per month
  par personne – per person
  par semaine – per week
parachute – *nm* parachute
parachutisme – *nm* parachuting
paradis – *nm* heaven, paradise
paragraphe – *nm* paragraph
paraître – *v irreg* § to appear, seem
parapluie – *nm* umbrella
parasol – *nm* sunshade
parc – *nm* park

---

prep - preposition   *v reg* - verb regular   *v refl* - verb reflexive   § - see verb tables
pp - past participle   *v irreg* - verb irregular   † - see verb information   * - takes être

parc d'attractions – amusement park

parce que – *conj* because

par ci, par là – *adv* here and there

parcmètre – *nm* parking meter

parcourir – *v irreg* § to travel

parcours – *nm* distance

  parcours de santé – fitness circuit

par-delà – *prep* beyond

par-derrière – *prep* round the back of

par-dessous – *prep* underneath

par-dessus – *prep* above, over

pardessus – *nm* coat

pardon! – *excl* sorry!

pardonner – *v reg* to forgive

pare-brise – *nm* windscreen

pare-chocs – *nm inv* bumper

pareil, pareille – *adj* similar, same

parent – *nm* parent, relative

parenthèses – *nfpl* brackets

paresse – *nf* laziness

paresseux, paresseuse – *adj* lazy

parfait – *adj* perfect

parfaitement – *adj* perfectly

parfois – *adv* sometimes

parfum – *nm* flavour, perfume

parfumé – *adj* flavoured, sweet-smelling

parfumerie – *nf* perfume shop

pari – *nm* bet, wager

parier – *v reg* to bet

parisien, parisienne – *adj* Parisian

Parisien(ne) – *nmf* Parisian person

parking – *nm* car park, parking space

parlement – *nm* parliament

parler – *v reg* to speak, talk

parmi – *prep* among

parole – *nf* word, speech, song lyrics

part – *nf* part, portion, share

  à part – aside, except for

c'est de la part de qui? – who is speaking? (phone)

de ma part – on my behalf

prendre part à – *v irreg* § to take part in

partager – *v reg* † to share

partenaire – *nmf* partner

parterre – *nm* flower bed

parti – *nm* political party

participant(e) – *nmf* entrant, person taking part in

participer à – *v reg* to take part in

particularité – *nf* characteristic, feature

particulier, particulière – *adj* special, particular, peculiar

  en particulier – in particular, especially

partie – *nf* part

  partie de golf – a round of golf

  partie de tennis – game of tennis

partir* – *v irreg* § to leave, set off

  à partir de demain – from tomorrow

  partir* de – to leave from

  partir* en vacances – to go on holiday

partout – *adv* everywhere

parvenir* – *v irreg* § to reach, succeed

pas – *nm* step, footstep

  à pas de loup – stealthily

  au pas – at a walking pace

  faire un pas en arrière – *v irreg* § to step backwards

  faire un pas en avant – *v irreg* § to step forwards

  marcher d'un bon pas – *v reg* to walk briskly

  Pas de Calais – *nm* Straits of Dover

pas – *neg adv* not

  ne...pas – not

  ce n'est pas – it is not

  je ne suis pas – I am not

---

pas beaucoup – not much
pas cher – not expensive
pas de – no
pas de chance – no luck
pas du tout – not at all
pas encore – not yet
pas grand-chose – not very much
pas mal – not bad
pas mal de – quite a few
pas très cher – not very expensive
pas trop cher – not too expensive
passage – *nm* way, passage, passing
  passage à niveau – level crossing
  passage clouté – pedestrian
  crossing
  passage interdit – no entry
  passage pour piétons –
  pedestrian walkway
  passage protégé – right of way
  passage souterrain – subway
  être de passage – *v irreg* § to be
  passing through
passager, passagère – *nmf*
passenger
passant(e) – *nmf* passer-by
passé – *adj* past
  il est trois heures passées – it is
  past three o'clock
passé – *nm* past, past tense
passeport – *nm* passport
passer* – *v reg* to pass, pass by
  passer* à la caisse – to go to the
  cash desk
  passer* à la douane – to go through
  customs
  passer* à la télévision – to be on
  television
  par où est-il passé? – which way
  did he come?
passer – *v reg (with avoir)* to go
through, across
  passer la maison – to go past the
  house
  passer l'aspirateur – to vacuum

passer le permis – to take one's
  driving test
passer les vacances – to spend one's
  holiday
passer un examen – to take an exam
passer un film – to show a film
se passer* – *v refl* to happen
  qu'est-ce qui se passe? – what's
  going on?
se passer* de – *v refl* to do without
passerelle – *nf* gangway, bridge
passe-temps – *nm* hobby, pastime
passionnant – *adj* exciting,
fascinating
passionné(e) – *nmf* fan
  être passionné de – *v irreg* §
  to be keen on
pastèque – *nf* watermelon
pastille – *nf* throat pastille
pâte – *nf* pastry, paste
  pâte brisée – shortcrust pastry
  pâte dentifrice – toothpaste
  pâte feuilletée – flaky pastry
pâté – *nm* pâté
  pâté de campagne – farmhouse pâté
paternel, paternelle – *adj* fatherly
pâtes – *nfpl* pasta, noodles
patience – *nf* patience
patient – *adj* patient
patient(e) – *nmf* patient
patienter – *v reg* to wait
patin – *nm* skate
  patins à glace – *nmpl* ice skates
  patins à roulettes – *nmpl* roller
  skates
patiner – *v reg* to skate
patinoire – *nf* rink
pâtisserie – *nf* cake, pastry, cake shop
pâtissier, pâtissière – *nmf* pastry
cook
patrie – *nf* homeland
patron – *nm* manager, owner, boss
patron – *nm* pattern

---

prep - preposition   *v reg* - verb regular   *v refl* - verb reflexive   § - see verb tables
pp - past participle   *v irreg* - verb irregular   † - see verb information   * - takes être

patrouille – *nf* patrol
patte – *nf* paw, (animal) foot
pâturage – *nm* pasture, grazing
pause de midi – *nf* dinner hour
pauvre – *adj* poor
pauvreté – *nf* poverty
pavé – *nm* paving stone
pavillon – *nm* detached house
payable – *adj* payable, due
payant – *adj* where one must pay,
  not free
payer – *v reg* † to pay (for)
pays – *nm* country, region
  Pays Bas – *nmpl* Netherlands
  Pays de Galles – *nm* Wales
  pays développé – developed
    country
  pays d'origine – country of origin
  pays en voie de
    développement – developing
    country
  pays francophones – *nmpl*
    French speaking countries
paysage – *nm* countryside
paysan, paysanne – *nmf*
  countryman/woman farmer
PDG – (président directeur général)
  nm chairman (company)
péage – *nm* toll
peau – *nf* skin
pêche – *nf* fishing
  aller* à la pêche – *v irreg* § to go
    fishing
  canne à pêche – *nf* fishing rod
pêche – *nf* peach
  avoir la pêche – *v irreg* § *coll* to
    be on form
pêcher – *v reg* to fish
pécher – *v reg* † to sin
pêcheur – *nm* fisherman
peigne – *nm* comb
  se donner* un coup de peigne
    – *v refl* to comb one's hair

se peigner* – *v refl* to comb one's
  hair
peignoir – *nm* dressing gown
peindre – *v irreg* § to paint
peine – *nf* sadness, pain, trouble
  à peine – hardly, scarcely
  avoir de la peine à – *v irreg* §
    to have difficulty in
  ce n'est pas la peine! – don't
    bother! It's not worth it!
peintre – *nm* painter
peinture – *nf* painting, paint
  peinture fraîche – wet paint
peler – *v reg* † to peel
pèlerin – *nm* pilgrim
pèlerinage – *nm* pilgrimage
pelle – *nf* shovel, spade
pellicule – *nf* film (for camera)
pelote – *nf* pelota, ball (of wool)
peloton – *nm* squad, group of runners
  (in a race)
pelouse – *nf* lawn
penchant – *nm* liking for
  avoir un penchant pour qqch –
    v irreg § to have a liking for
    something
penché – *adj* slanting, sloping
pencher – *v reg* to tilt, lean
  se pencher* – *v refl* to lean over
pendant – *prep* during
pendant que – *conj* while
penderie – *nf* wardrobe
pendre – *v reg* to hang
pendule – *nf* clock (domestic)
pénétrer – *v reg* † to go into, enter
pénible – *adj* difficult, unpleasant
pensée – *nf* thought
penser – *v reg* to think
  penser à – to think about
  penser de – to think (have an
    opinion about)
pensif, pensive – *adj* thoughtful

pension – *nf* guest house, boarding school
  demi-pension – half board
  pension complète – full board
pensionnaire – *nmf* boarder
  demi-pensionnaire – *nmf* pupil taking school lunch
pensionnat – *nm* boarding school
pente – *nf* slope
  en pente – sloping
pépin – *nm* pip, seed
pépinière – *nf* nursery (plants, trees)
percer – *v reg* † to bore, pierce
percussion – *nf* percussion
  instrument de percussion – *nm* percussion instrument
percuter – *v reg* to strike, crash into
perdre – *v reg* to lose, waste
  perdre du temps – to waste time
  perdre le souffle – to get out of breath
  perdre son chemin – to lose one's way
  perdre un match – to lose a match
  se perdre* – *v refl* to get lost
perdu – *adj* lost, wasted, missed
père – *nm* father
  père aubergiste – warden (youth hostel)
  Père Noël – Father Christmas
perfectionnement – *nm* improvement
perfectionner – *v reg* to improve
  se perfectionner* en français – *v refl* to improve one's French
périmé – *adj* out of date, time-expired
période – *nf* period, intermission
  période de chaleur – heat wave
périphérique – *nm* ring road
périr – *v reg* to die, perish
permanence – *nf* study (room)
  être de permanence – *v irreg* § to be on call

permettre – *v irreg* § to allow
permis – *adj* permitted
permis – *nm* permit, licence
  permis de conduire – driving licence
permission – *nf* permission
perroquet – *nm* parrot
perruche – *nf* budgerigar
persil – *nm* parsley
personnage – *nm* character, individual
  personnage célèbre – celebrity
personne – *nf* person
  personne âgée – elderly person
  personne du troisième âge – senior citizen
  par personne – per person
personne – *pron* not anybody, nobody
  ne...personne – nobody
  presque personne – hardly anyone
personnel, personnelle – *adj* personal
personnel – *nm* staff
  faire partie du personnel – *v irreg* § to be on the staff
personnellement – *adv* personally
persuader – *v reg* to convince, persuade
perte – *nf* loss, ruin, waste
  perte d'énergie – energy loss
  à perte de vue – as far as the eye can see
pervenche – *nf* periwinkle, *coll* traffic warden (female)
pesant – *adj* heavy, weighty
peser – *v reg* † to weigh
pessimiste – *adj* pessimistic
peste – *nf* plague
P et T (Postes et Télécommunications) – Post Office
pétanque – *nf* game of bowls, boules
péter – *v reg coll* † to go bang, fart

---

pétillant – *adj* sparkling (drinks)
petit – *adj* little, small, young
　avec un petit effort – *nm* with a little effort
　mon petit frère – *nm* my little brother
　petit ami – *nm* boyfriend
　petit à petit – gradually, little by little
　petit déjeuner – *nm* breakfast
　petite amie – *nf* girlfriend
　petite annonce – *nf* small ad
　petite-fille – *nf* granddaughter
　petit-fils – *nm* grandson
　petit pain – *nm* bread roll
　petits-enfants – *nmpl* grandchildren
　petits pois – *nmpl* peas
pétrole – *nm* crude oil
pétrolier – *nm* oil tanker
peu – *adv* little, not much
　à peu près – almost, more or less
　de peu – slightly
　peu importe – it does not matter much
　peu intéressant – not very interesting
　peu nombreux – very few
　un peu de – a little of
peuple – *nm* people, nation
peuplier – *nm* poplar tree
peur – *nf* fear
　avoir peur – *v irreg* § to be afraid
peut-être – *adv* perhaps, maybe
peut-on? – *see pouvoir* § can one?
peut – *see pouvoir* § can
peuvent – *see pouvoir* § can
peux – *see pouvoir* § can
phare – *nm* headlight
　mettre les phares en code – *v irreg* § to dip headlights
　rouler en phares – *v reg* to drive on full headlights

phare – *nm* lighthouse
pharmacie – *nf* chemist's shop
pharmacien, pharmacienne – *nmf* chemist
photo – *nf* photo
　photo satellite – satellite photo
　prendre une photo – *v irreg* § to take a photo
photocopie – *nf* photocopy
photocopier – *v reg* to photocopy
photocopieuse – *nf* photocopier
photographe – *nmf* photographer
photographie – *nf* photography
photographier – *v reg* to photograph
　se faire* photographier – *v refl* § to have one's photo taken
phrase – *nf* phrase, sentence
physique – *nf* physics
physique – *nm* appearance, physique
physique – *adj* physical
piano – *nm* piano
　jouer du piano – *v reg* to play the piano
pichet – *nm* jug
pièce – *nf* coin, play, piece, room
　pièce de dix francs – ten franc coin
　pièce de rechange – spare part
　pièce de théâtre – play
　pièce d'identité – *nf* ID
　appartement de six pièces – *nm* a six roomed flat
　trois francs la pièce – three francs each
pied – *nm* foot
　aller* à pied – *v irreg* § to go on foot, walk
　aller* pieds nus – *v irreg* § to go barefoot
piège – *nm* trap
pierre – *nf* stone
　en pierre – built of stone
piéton – *nm* pedestrian

---

nm - noun masculine	*nmpl* - noun masculine plural
nf - noun feminine	*nfpl* - noun feminine plural

adj - adjective	*conj* - conjunction
adv - adverb	*pron* - pronoun

piéton, piétonne – *adj* pedestrian
  zone piétonne – *nf* pedestrian
  precinct
piger – *v reg* † *sl* to understand
pile – *nf* stack, pile, battery
  pile ou face? – heads or tails?
pilote – *nm* pilot
  pilote de ligne – airline pilot
pilule – *nf* pill
pincée – *nf* a pinch of
pincer – *v reg* † to pinch
pingouin – *nm* penguin
ping pong – *nm* ping pong, table tennis
pion – *nm* pawn (chess), supervisor
  (school)
pionnier – *nm* pioneer
piquant – *adj* savoury, spicy
pique-nique – *nm* picnic
  pique-niquer – *v reg* to picnic
piquer – *v reg* to sting, bite
  se faire* piquer – *v refl* § to have
  an injection, get stung
piquet – *nm* post, pole
piqûre – *nf* sting, bite, injection
pire – *adj* worse
pis – *adj* worse
  tant pis – too bad
piscine – *nf* swimming pool
pisser – *v reg coll* to urinate
pissoir – *nm coll* urinal
piste – *nf* track, ski-run
pitié – *nf* pity
pittoresque – *adj* picturesque
placard – *nm* cupboard
place – *nf* square, seat
  place du marché – market place
  réserver une place – *v reg* to book
  a seat
  rester* sur place – *v reg* to stay
  on the spot
placer – *v reg* † to put, place, set

se placer* – *v refl* † to take one's
  place
se placer* comme mécanicien
  – *v refl* † to get a job as a mechanic
plafond – *nm* ceiling
plage – *nf* beach
plaie – *nf* wound
plaindre – *v irreg* § to feel sorry for
  se plaindre* – *v refl* § to complain
plaire à – *v irreg* § to please
plaisanter – *v reg* to joke
plaisanterie – *nf* joke
plaisir – *nm* pleasure
  avec plaisir – with pleasure
plan – *nm* plan, map
  plan de la ville – town plan
planche – *nf* plank, board
  planche à repasser – ironing
  board
  planche à roulettes – skateboard
  planche à voile – sailboard
plancher – *nm* floor
planète – *nf* planet
plante – *nf* plant
planter – *v reg* to plant
plastique – *adj* plastic
  en plastique – (made of) plastic
plat – *adj* flat
plat – *nm* dish, course (meal)
  plat cuisiné – ready-cooked dish
  plat du jour – dish of the day
  plat principal – main dish
plateau – *nm* tray
plate-bande – *nf* flower bed
platine-laser – *nf* CD player
plâtre – *nm* plaster
plein – *adj* full
  en plein air – in the open air
  en pleine nuit – in the middle of the
  night
  faire le plein – *v irreg* § to fill up
  with petrol

---

prep - preposition	*v reg* - verb regular	*v refl* - verb reflexive	§ - see verb tables
pp - past participle	*v irreg* - verb irregular	† - see verb information	* - takes être

plein de – full of
plein tarif – full fare
pleurer – *v reg* to weep, cry
pleuvoir – *v irreg* § to rain
  il pleut – it is raining
  il pleut à verse – it is pouring
  il pleut des cordes – it's raining
  cats and dogs
  il pleuvait – it was raining
  il pleuvra – it will rain
  il a plu – it rained
pli – *nm* pleat, fold, crease
plier – *v reg* to fold
plomb – *nm* lead (metal)
  sans plomb – unleaded
plombage – *nm* filling
plombé – *adj* leaden (sky), filled
  (tooth)
plombier – *nm* plumber
plongée – *nf* diving
  plongée sous-marine – scuba
  diving
plonger – *v reg* † to dive
plu – *pp pleuvoir*, or *plaire* § rained or
  pleased
pluie – *nf* rain
plume – *nf* feather
plupart – *nf* most of, the majority
pluriel – *nm* plural
  au pluriel – in the plural
plus – *adv* more
  de plus en plus – more and more
  deux heures plus tôt – two hours
  earlier
  il est plus grand que moi – he is
  taller than I am
  il fait plus trois – it is +3°C
  il n'a plus rien dit – he did not
  say another word
  il n'en reste plus – there is no
  more left
  ne...plus – no more, no longer
  plus de – more than

plus...que – more ... than
  un peu plus – a little more
plusieurs – *adj* several
plus-que-parfait – *nm* pluperfect tense
plutôt – *adv* rather
  plutôt que – rather than
pluvieux, pluvieuse – *adj* rainy
pneu – *nm* tyre
  pneu à plat – flat tyre
  pneu crevé – punctured tyre
poche – *nf* pocket
  livre de poche – *nm* paperback
poêle – *nf* frying pan
poêle – *nm* stove
  poêle à bois – wood-burning stove
poésie – *nf* poetry
poète – *nm* poet
poids – *nm* weight
  perdre du poids – *v irreg* § to
  lose weight
  prendre du poids – *v irreg* § to put
  on weight
poids lourd – *nm* heavy lorry, HGV
poignée – *nf* handful, door handle
  poignée de main – handshake
poignet – *nm* wrist
poil – *nm* hair
  à poil – naked
poilu – *adj* hairy
poing – *nm* fist
point – *nm* point, place, spot
  point de départ – starting point
  point de repère – reference point,
  landmark
  point de vue – point of view
  point d'exclamation – exclamation
  mark (!)
  point d'interrogation – question
  mark (?)
  point (final) – full stop (.)
  point du jour – day break
  point noir – accident black spot
  point-virgule – semi-colon (;)

---

deux points – colon (:)
à point – medium (steak)
à quel point – to what extent
pointu – *adj* sharp, pointed
pointure – *nf* shoe size
poire – *nf* pear
poireau – *nm* leek
pois – *nm* pea
  à pois – spotted (fabric)
poison – *nm* poison
poisson – *nm* fish
  poisson d'avril – April fool
  poisson-rouge – goldfish
poissonnerie – *nf* fish shop
poissonnier – *nm* fishmonger
Poissons – *nmpl* Pisces
  être (des) Poissons – *v irreg* § to
  be (a) Pisces
poitrine – *nf* chest
poivre – *nm* pepper
poivron – *nm* pepper
  poivron rouge – red pepper
  poivron vert – green pepper
poli – *adj* polite
police – *nf* police
  agent de police – *nm* policeman
  police de la circulation – traffic
  police
  Police Nationale – Police force
  police-secours – police rescue
  service
police – *nf* policy
  police d'assurance – insurance
  policy
policier, policière – *adj* police,
  detective
  chien policier – *nm* police dog
  film policier – *nm* detective film
  roman policier – *nm* detective
  story
politesse – *nf* politeness
politique – *nf* politics, policy
pollen – *nm* pollen

pollué – *adj* polluted
pollution – *nf* pollution
polyvalent – *adj* multi-purpose
pomme – *nf* apple
pomme de terre – *nf* potato
pommes frites – *nfpl* French fries
pommier – *nm* apple tree
pompe – *nf* petrol pump
pompier – *nm* fireman
  pompiers – *nmpl* fire brigade
pompiste – *nm* petrol-pump attendant
ponctuation – *nf* punctuation
ponctuel, ponctuelle – *adj* punctual
poney – *nm* pony
pont – *nm* bridge
  faire le pont – *v irreg* § to take an
  extra day off near a weekend
populaire – *adj* popular
population – *nf* population
porc – *nm* pork, pig
port – *nm* harbour, port
  port de pêche – fishing port
  port de plaisance – yacht marina
  arriver* au port – *v reg* to dock
  sortir* du port – *v irreg* § to
  leave harbour
porte – *nf* door
  porte d'entrée – front door
  porte de secours – emergency exit
  sonner à la porte – *v reg* to ring
  the bell
porte-clés – *nm* key ring
portefeuille – *nm* wallet
porte-monnaie – *nm* purse
portée – *nf* range, reach
  à portée de main – within reach
porter – *v reg* to carry, wear
porteur – *nm* porter
portière – *nf* car, train door
portugais – *adj* Portuguese
Portugais(e) – *nmf* Portuguese person
Portugal – *nm* Portugal

---

au Portugal – in, to Portugal

pose – *nf* installation, exposure
  film de 36 poses – *nm* 36 exposure film

poser – *v reg* to put (down)
  poser une question – to ask a question

posséder – *v reg* † to own

possibilité – *nf* possibility

possible – *adj* possible

poste – *nf* post, Post Office
  employé(e) de la poste – *nmf* Post Office worker
  mettre une lettre à la poste – *v irreg* § to post a letter
  poste restante – post to be collected

poste – *nm* post, station, set, job
  poste de douane – customs post
  poste d'enseignant – teaching post
  poste de police – police station
  poste de secours – first aid station

poster – *v reg* to post

poster – *nm* poster

pot – *nm* pot, jar, mug, drink *sl*
  pot à bière – beer mug
  pot catalytique – catalytic converter
  pot d'échappement – exhaust pipe
  pot de confiture – jar of jam
  pot de fleurs – flowerpot
  prendre un pot – *v irreg* § to have a drink

potable – *adj* drinkable
  eau potable – drinking water
  non-potable – non drinking

potage – *nm* soup

poteau – *nm* post

poterie – *nf* pottery

poubelle – *nf* dustbin

pouce – *nm* thumb

poudre – *nf* powder

poule – *nf* hen

poulet – *nm* chicken
  poulet rôti – roast chicken

poumons – *nmpl* lungs

poupée – *nf* doll

pour – *prep* for, to, in order to
  pour cent – per cent
  pour le moment – for the moment
  pour que – so that
  le pour et le contre – the pros and cons
  partir* pour la France – *v irreg* § to leave for France

pourboire – *nm* tip

pourcentage – *nm* percentage

pourpre – *adj* crimson

pourquoi? – *adv, conj* why?

pourra – *see pouvoir* § will be able to

pourrait – might, could

pourri – *adj* bad, rotten

poursuite – *nf* chase, pursuit, race

poursuivre – *v irreg* § to chase, pursue, hunt

pourtant – *adv* yet, nevertheless, however

pourvu que – *conj* provided that

pousser – *v reg* to push, grow
  pousser un cri – to shout, scream

poussette – *nf* pushchair

poussez! – push!

poussière – *nf* dust

poussin – *nm* chick

pouvait – *see pouvoir* § was able to

pouvoir – *nm* power

pouvoir – *v irreg* § can, may, be able to

pouvez – *see pouvoir* § can

pouvons – *see pouvoir* § can

prairie – *nf* meadow

pratique – *adj* practical

pratiquer un sport – *v reg* to do a sport

pré – *nm* meadow

préau – *nm* playground shelter

---

nm - noun masculine	*nmpl* - noun masculine plural	*adj* - adjective	*conj* - conjunction
nf - noun feminine	*nfpl* - noun feminine plural	*adv* - adverb	*pron* - pronoun

précaution – *nf* caution, care, precaution

précédent – *adj* previous

précéder – *v reg* † to come before, be in front of

précieux, précieuse – *adj* valued, precious

précipitamment – *adv* hurriedly, hastily

se précipiter* – *v refl* to rush, hurry

précis – *adj* exact, precise, accurate
  à sept heures précises – at 7 o'clock sharp

précisément – *adv* exactly, clearly

préciser – *v reg* to make clear, specify

précoce – *adj* early

préfecture – *nf* county hall, police HQ

préférence – *nf* preference
  de préférence – preferably

préférer – *v reg* † to prefer
  préféré – *adj* preferred

préfet – *nm* prefect, chief of police

préfixe – *nm* prefix

préjugé – *nm* prejudice

premier, première – *adj* first
  arriver* en premier – *v reg* to arrive first
  au premier étage – on the first floor
  billet de première classe – *nm* first class ticket
  être en première – *v irreg* § to be in Year 12
  le premier avril – April Fools' Day
  la première fois – the first time
  Premier ministre – *nm* Prime Minister

premièrement – *adv* firstly

prenait – *see prendre* § took

prendra – *see prendre* § will take

prendrait – would take

prendre – *v irreg* § to take, catch, have
  prendre des dispositions – to make arrangements
  prendre des notes – to take notes
  prendre l'avion – to fly
  prendre le petit déjeuner – to have breakfast
  prendre le train – to catch the train
  prendre rendez-vous – to arrange to meet
  prendre un bain – to have a bath
  prendre une douche – to have a shower
  prendre une photo – to take a photo
  prenez la première à gauche – take the first on the left

prénom – *nm* first name

préoccupé – *adj* preoccupied

préoccuper – *v reg* to concern
  se préoccuper de* – *v refl* to be concerned with

préparatifs – *nmpl* preparations

préparatoire – *adj* preparatory

préparer – *v reg* to prepare

près (de) – *adv* close by, near (to)
  de près – from close by, closely
  regarder de près – *v reg* to look closely at

presbyte – *adj* long-sighted

prescrire – *v irreg* § to prescribe

présence – *nf* presence

présent – *adj* present

présent – *nm* present tense

présenter – *v reg* to present, introduce
  je vous présente mon frère – may I introduce my brother?
  se présenter* – *v refl* to introduce o.s.

préservatif – *nm* condom

presque – *adv* almost, nearly

---

prep - preposition   *v reg* - verb regular   *v refl* - verb reflexive   § - see verb tables
pp - past participle   *v irreg* - verb irregular   † - see verb information   * - takes être

presse – *nf* newspapers, press
pressé – *adj* hurried
  être pressé – *v irreg* § to be in a
  hurry
presser – *v reg* to squeeze, press
  se presser* – *v refl* to hurry
  citron pressé – *nm* freshly
  squeezed lemon juice
pression – *nf* pressure, draught beer
  une pression, s'il vous plaît –
  a draught beer, please
prêt – *adj* ready
  prêt-à-porter – ready to wear
prêter – *v reg* to lend
preuve – *nf* proof
prévenir – *v irreg* § to warn
prévision – *nf* forecast
prévoir – *v irreg* § to forecast, plan,
  provide for
prévu – *adj* agreed, planned
  comme prévu – as agreed
prier – *v reg* to ask, beg, pray
prière – *nf* prayer
  prière de ne pas... – please do not...
primaire – *adj* primary
  école primaire – *nf* primary school
prime – *nf* bonus, free gift
  prime de licenciement –
  redundancy payment
principal – *adj* principal, main
principal – *nm* principal
principe – *nm* principle
  en principe – in principle,
  theoretically
printemps – *nm* spring
  au printemps – in spring
priorité – *nf* priority, right of way
  vous n'avez pas la priorité –
  you do not have right of way
pris – *pp prendre* § taken
prise de courant – *nf* power point,
  plug
prison – *nf* prison

prisonnier – *nm* prisoner
prit – *see prendre* § took
privé – *adj* private
priver – *v reg* to deprive
  se priver* de – *v refl* to go without
prix – *nm* price, prize, race
  à tout prix – at all costs
  menu à prix fixe – *nm* set price
  menu
  Prix Nobel pour la paix – Nobel
  Peace Prize
probable – *adj* probable
problème – *nm* problem
prochain – *adj* next
  jeudi prochain – *nm* next
  Thursday
  l'année prochaine – *nf* next year
  la semaine prochaine – next week
proche – *adj* close
  la banque la plus proche –
  the nearest bank
producteur – *nm* producer
produire – *v irreg* § to produce
produit – *nm* product
  produit de beauté – cosmetic
  produits surgelés – *nmpl* frozen
  food
prof – *nmf* teacher
professeur – *nm* teacher
profession – *nf* profession, job, trade
profit – *nm* profit
profiter de – *v reg* to take advantage
  of
profond – *adj* deep
profondément – *adj* deeply
programme – *nm* programme,
  syllabus
programmeur, programmeuse –
  nmf programmer
progrès – *nm* progress
  faire des progrès – *v irreg* §
  to make progress
projet – *nm* plan, project

---

projets de vacances – *nmpl* holiday plans

quels sont vos projets pour le weekend? – what are your plans for the weekend?

prolonger – *v reg* † to extend, prolong

promenade – *nf* walk

promenade en bateau – boat trip

faire une promenade – *v irreg* § to go for a walk

promener – *v reg* † to take s.o. for a walk

promener le chien – to take the dog for a walk

se promener* – *v refl* † to go for a walk

promesse – *nf* promise

promettre – *v irreg* § to promise

promotion – *nf* special offer

en promotion – on special offer

pronom – *nm* pronoun

pronominal – *adj* reflexive

verbes pronominaux – *nmpl* reflexive verbs

propos – *nm* talk, remark, words

à propos de – about, concerning

proposer – *v reg* to propose

proposition – *nf* suggestion

propre – *adj* clean, own

ma propre voiture – my own car

une voiture propre – a clean car

propriétaire – *nmf* owner

propriété – *nf* property

protection – *nf* protection

protéger – *v reg* † to protect

protestant – *adj* Protestant

protester – *v reg* to protest

prouver – *v reg* to prove

provenance – *nf* origin

en provenance de – coming from

province – *nf* region, province

proviseur – *nm* head of a lycée

provisions – *nfpl* food

proximité – *nf* nearness

à proximité de – near to, close to

prudent – *adj* sensible, careful

soyez prudent(s)! – be careful!

prune – *nf* plum

pruneau – *nm* prune

pu – *pp pouvoir* § could, was able to

pub – *nf coll* advert

public, publique – *adj* public

publicité – *nf* advertising, publicity

publier – *v reg* to publish

puce – *nf* flea, micro-chip

puce électronique – microchip

puce mémoire – memory chip

jeu de puces – *nm* tiddlywinks

marché aux puces – *nm* flea market

puis – *adv* then, next

puis – *see pouvoir* § can, may

puis-je? – may I?

puisque – *conj* since, as

puissance – *nf* strength, power

puits – *nm* well (for water)

pull(over) – *nm* pullover

punaise – *nf* drawing pin

punir – *v reg* to punish

punk – *adj inv, nmf* punk

pur – *adj* pure, innocent, honourable

pustule – *nf* zit, spot

put – *see pouvoir* § could

PV – (procès-verbal) *nm* fixed penalty fine

pyjama – *nm* pair of pyjamas

Pyrénées – *nfpl* Pyrenees

Q

quai – *nm* platform
qualité – *nf* quality
  de bonne qualité – good quality
  de mauvaise qualité – poor
  quality
  de qualité supérieur – superior
  quality
  qualité de la vie – quality of life
quand – *conj, adv* when
  quand même – none the less, even
  though
quand? – *adv* when?
quant à – *adv* as for
  quant à moi – as for me
quantité – *nf* quantity
  une quantité de – a lot of
quarante – *adj* forty
quarante et un – *adj* forty-one
quart – *nm* quarter
  quart de siècle – quarter of a
  century
  quart d'heure – quarter of an hour
  une heure et quart – quarter past
  one
  une heure moins le quart –
  quarter to one
quartier – *nm* quarter, district
  les gens du quartier – *nmpl* local
  people
  vous êtes du quartier? – are you
  local?
quatorze – *adj* fourteen
  le quatorze juillet – July 14th
  Louis quatorze – Louis XIV
quatorzième – *adj* fourteenth
quatre – *adj* four
quatre-vingt-dix – *adj* ninety
quatre-vingt-onze – *adj* ninety-one
quatre-vingts – *adj* eighty
quatre-vingt-un – *adj* eighty-one

quatrième – *adj* fourth
que – *conj* that
  je vois qu'il part – I see that he is
  going
que – *pron* which, that
  le livre que j'ai acheté – the
  book which I bought
que? – *question* what?
  que dites-vous? – what did you
  say?
  qu'est-ce que...? – what...?
  qu'est-ce que c'est? – what is it?
  **qu'est-ce que c'est en
  français?** – what is it in French?
  qu'est-ce qu'il y a? – what is
  there?
  qu'est-ce qui...? – what...?
  que veut dire...? – what does ...
  mean?
Québec – Quebec
quel(s)?, quelle(s)? – *adj* what?,
which?
  quel dommage! – what a pity!
quelque, quelques – *adj* some
  quelque part – somewhere
  quelques idées – *nfpl* some ideas
quelque chose – *pron* something
  quelque chose de bon –
  something good
  quelque chose de mauvais –
  something bad
quelquefois – *adv* sometimes
quelques-uns, quelques-unes –
pron some, a few of
quelqu'un – *pron* somebody, anybody
  quelqu'un d'autre – someone
  else
querelle – *nf* dispute, quarrel
quereller – *v reg* to scold
  se quereller* – *v refl* to quarrel
question – *nf* question

---

nm - noun masculine	*nmpl* - noun masculine plural	*adj* - adjective	*conj* - conjunction
nf - noun feminine	*nfpl* - noun feminine plural	*adv* - adverb	*pron* - pronoun

il n'en est pas question – it's out of the question

poser une question – *v reg* to ask a question

question écrite – written question

question orale – oral question

questionner – *v reg* to question s.o.

queue – *nf* tail, queue

queue de cheval – pony tail

en queue de la classe – at the bottom of the class

faire la queue – *v irreg* § to queue

qui? – *question* who?

à qui est ce livre? – whose book is this?

qui entre? – who is coming in?

qui est-ce qui? – who?

qui – *pron* who, whom, which

le garçon qui arrive s'appelle Jacques – the boy who is arriving is called Jacques

quiche lorraine – *nf* egg and cheese flan

quiétude – *nf* tranquillity, peace

quincaillerie – *nf* hardware shop

quinzaine – *nf* about fifteen, fortnight

dans une quinzaine – in a fortnight

il y a une quinzaine – a fortnight ago

quinze – *adj* fifteen

quinze jours – a fortnight

tous les quinze jours – every two weeks

quinzième – *adj* fifteenth

quitter – *v reg* to leave

quoi? – *pron* what?

à quoi bon? – what's the use?

de quoi s'agit-il? – what is it about?

quoi de neuf? – what's new?

quoi encore? – what else?

quoi – *pron* what

as-tu de quoi manger? – have you anything to eat?

il n'a pas de quoi! – don't mention it!

quotidien – *nm* daily newspaper

quotidien, quotidienne – *adj* daily

la vie quotidienne – *nf* daily life

R

rabais – *nm* discount
rabattre – *v reg* to lower prices
raccommoder – *v reg* to mend
raccorder – *v reg* to connect, join
raccourcir – *v reg* to shorten, get shorter
raccrocher – *v reg* to hang up
race – *nf* race, breed
  race humaine – human race
racine – *nf* root
racisme – *nm* racism
raciste – *nmf, adj* racist
raconter – *v reg* to recount, tell
  raconter n'importe quoi – to talk rubbish
raconteur, raconteuse – *nmf* storyteller
radiateur – *nm* radiator
radiation – *nf* radiation
radio – *nf* radio
  radio libre – independent radio
  radio pirate – pirate radio
  passer* à la radio – *v reg* to be on the radio
radiocassette – *nf* radio cassette player
radis – *nm* radish
  botte de radis – *nf* bunch of radishes
rafale – *nf* gust of wind or rain
raffermir – *v reg* to strengthen, harden
raffiné – *adj* refined
raffinerie – *nf* refinery (oil)
rafraîchissant – *adj* refreshing
rage – *nf* anger, rabies
rager – *v reg* † to be angry, rage
rageur, rageuse – *adj* ill-tempered
raide – *adj* straight, stiff
raideur – *nf* hardness, stiffness
raisin – *nm* grapes

raison – *nf* reason
  avoir raison – *v irreg* § to be right
raisonnable – *adj* sensible, reasonable
raisonnement – *nm* reasoning, argument
raisonner – *v reg* to reason, argue
rajouter – *v reg* to add
rajuster – *v reg* to adjust
  se rajuster* – *v refl* to tidy o.s.
ralentir – *v reg* to slow down
  ralentir! – slow down now! (road sign)
râler – *v reg* to groan, moan, complain
rallonger – *v reg* † to lengthen
ramadan – *nm* Ramadan
ramassage – *nm* collection
  car de ramassage scolaire – *nm* school bus
rame – *nf* oar
ramener – *v reg* † to bring back
  ramener du pain – to fetch bread
ramer – *v reg* to row
rançon – *nf* ransom
rancune – *nf* grudge
rancunier, rancunière – *adj* spiteful
randonnée – *nf* long walk, hike
randonneur, randonneuse – *nmf* hiker
rang – *nm* row, rank
ranger – *v reg* † to tidy, put away
  ranger ses affaires – to tidy up
rapide – *adj* fast
rapide – *nm* express train
rapidement – *adv* quickly
rapidité – *nf* speed, swiftness
rappel – *nm* reminder, recall
rappeler – *v reg* † to ring back, remind

---

se rappeler* – *v refl* † to remember, recall

rapport – *nm* report, relationship

rapporter – *v reg* to bring back

rapproché – *adj* nearby, close

raquette – *nf* racket, bat

rare – *adj* rare, few

rarement – *adj* rarely

ras – *adj* close-cropped

j'en ai ras le bol – *coll* I'm fed up (with it)

raser – *v reg* to shave off

se raser* – *v refl* to shave, *coll* to get bored

rasoir – *nm* razor

rasoir électrique – electric razor

rassembler – *v reg* to gather together

rassurant – *adj* reassuring

rassurer – *v reg* to reassure

rat – *nm* rat

rater – *v reg* to miss (train etc)

rater un examen – to fail an exam

RATP – (Régie autonome des transports parisiens) *nf* Paris transport authority

rattraper – *v reg* to catch up with

ravi – *adj* delighted

ravir – *v reg* to delight

se raviser* – *v refl* to change one's mind

ravissant – *adj* beautiful, delightful

rayé – *adj* striped, lined

rayé de ma liste – crossed off my list

rayer – *v reg* to cross out

rayon – *nm* ray, shelf, department

rayon de disques – record department

rayon de soleil – ray of sunlight

rayon de vêtements – clothes department

rayonnant – *adj* radiant, beaming

rayure – *nf* stripe, scratch

à rayures – striped

réaction – *nf* reaction

réagir – *v reg* to react

réaliser – *v reg* to fulfil, carry out, realise

se réaliser* – *v refl* to come true, be achieved

réalité – *nf* reality, fact

rebelle – *adj* rebellious

rebellion – *nf* rebellion

rebondir – *v reg* to spring to life, get moving again, bounce

rebord – *nm* edge

rebord de la fenêtre – windowsill

récemment – *adv* recently

récent – *adj* recent

réception – *nf* reception

réceptionniste – *nmf* receptionist

recette – *nf* recipe, formula, takings

recevez – *see recevoir* § receive

recevoir – *v irreg* § to receive

recevoir des amis – to have friends round

réchauffer – *v reg* to warm up again, reheat

se réchauffer* – *v refl* to get warm

réchauffement de la température – *nm* rise in temperature

recherche – *nf* search, research

recherches – *nfpl* enquiries, investigations

recherché – *adj* much sought after, in demand

rechercher – *v reg* to look for, research

réciproquement – *adv* vice versa

récit – *nm* story, account

réclamation – *nf* complaint

réclamer – *v reg* to ask for, claim

reçois – *see recevoir* § receive

reçoit – *see recevoir* § receives

---

prep - preposition	*v reg* - verb regular	*v refl* - verb reflexive	§ - see verb tables
pp - past participle	*v irreg* - verb irregular	† - see verb information	* - takes être

reçoivent – *see recevoir* § receive
récolte – *nf* harvest
récolter – *v reg* to harvest
recommandé – *adj* recommended, registered
   lettre recommandée – *nf* registered letter
recommander – *v reg* to recommend
recommencer – *v reg* † to begin again
récompense – *nf* reward
   en récompense de – as reward for
reconnaissance – *nf* gratitude
reconnaissant – *adj* grateful
reconnaître – *v irreg* § to recognise
reconnu – *pp reconnaître* § accepted, recognised
recouvrir – *v irreg* § to cover, conceal
récréation – *nf* break
rectangulaire – *adj* rectangular
rectifier – *v reg* to put right, correct
reçu – *pp recevoir* § received
   être reçu – *v irreg* § to pass an exam
reculer – *v reg* to move back, reverse
récupérer – *v reg* † to pick up, collect, recover
rédaction – *nf* essay, editorial staff
redevance – *nf* tax, licence fee
rédiger – *v reg* † to write, compose
redoubler – *v reg* to increase, intensify
   redoubler une année – to repeat a year (at school)
redoutable – *adj* formidable, fearsome
redouter – *v reg* to dread
réduction – *nf* reduction
réduire – *v irreg* § to reduce
réduit – *adj* small scale, reduced
réel, réelle – *adj* real, significant
refaire – *v irreg* § to renew, redo
réfectoire – *nm* dining hall, canteen

réfléchi – *adj* well thought out
réfléchir – *v reg* to think, reflect
réflection – *nf* remark
reflet – *nm* reflection
réfrigérateur – *nm* fridge
refroidir – *v reg* to cool down
refugié(e) – *nmf* refugee
refus – *nm* refusal
refuser – *v reg* to refuse
regard – *nm* glance, look, expression
regarder – *v reg* to watch, to look at
régime – *nm* diet
   être au régime – *v irreg* § to be on a diet
région – *nf* region, area
règle – *nf* ruler, rule
   en règle – in order
   règles – *nfpl* period (menstrual)
règlement – *nm* regulation, settlement
régler – *v reg* † to settle, pay up
règne – *nm* reign, rule
régner – *v reg* † to rule, reign
regret – *nm* regret
regretter – *v reg* to regret
régularité – *nf* regularity, steadiness
régulier, régulière – *adj* regular, steady
rein – *nm* kidney (in body)
reine – *nf* queen
rejoindre – *v irreg* § to join
réjouir – *v reg* to delight
   se réjouir* – *v refl* to be delighted
relais – *nm* relay race
   relais routier – roadside restaurant
relatif, relative – *adj* relative, comparative
relier – *v reg* to join up, link, bind
religion – *nf* religion
religieux, religieuse – *adj* religious
   religieuse – *nf* cream choux bun
relire – *v irreg* § to re-read
reluire – *v irreg* § to shine, gleam

---

nm - noun masculine	*nmpl* - noun masculine plural	*adj* - adjective	*conj* - conjunction
nf - noun feminine	*nfpl* - noun feminine plural	*adv* - adverb	*pron* - pronoun

remarquer – *v reg* to notice
rembourser – *v reg* to refund, reimburse
remède – *nm* remedy
remédiable – *adj* curable
remerciement – *nm* thanks
remercier – *v reg* to thank
remettre – *v irreg* § to put back, restart
  se remettre* – *v refl* § to get better
remise – *nf* delivery, discount, reduction, shed
remords – *nm* remorse
remorque – *nf* trailer, tugboat
remorquer – *v reg* to tow
remplaçant(e) – *nmf* substitute, reserve
remplacement – *nm* replacement
remplacer – *v reg* † to replace
rempli – *adj* full
remplir – *v reg* to fill, fill in
  remplir une fiche/un formulaire – to fill in a form
remporter – *v reg* to take away again
remporter – *v reg* to win (prize, championship)
remuer – *v reg* to move
remunération – *nf* pay
renard – *nm* fox
rencontre – *nf* meeting
rencontrer – *v reg* to meet, bump into
rendez-vous – *nm* appointment
rendre – *v reg* to give back
  rendre visite à – to visit s.o.
  se rendre* – *v refl* to surrender
  se rendre* à – *v refl* to go to
  se rendre* compte – *v refl* to realise
renfermer – *v reg* to contain, hold, lock up
renforcer – *v reg* † to strengthen, reinforce

renommé – *adj* famous, renowned
renoncer à – *v reg* † to give up
renouveler – *v reg* † to renew
rénover – *v reg* to renovate
renseignement – *nm* information
renseigner – *v reg* to give information to
  se renseigner* – *v refl* to find out
rentrée – *nf* start of school year
rentrer* – *v reg* to come back
  rentrer* dans – to crash into
renverser – *v reg* to knock, turn over, spill
  se renverser* – *v refl* to overturn
renvoi – *nm* dismissal, expulsion
renvoyer – *v reg* † to dismiss, sack
répandu – *adj* widespead
réparateur – *nm* repair man, restorer
réparation – *nf* repair
réparer – *v reg* to repair
repartir* – *v irreg* § to set off again
repas – *nm* meal
  repas de midi – lunch
  aux heures de repas – at meal times
repasser – *v reg* to iron clothes, resit exam
repasser* – *v reg* to come/go again
répéter – *v reg* † to repeat
répétition – *nf* rehearsal
replier – *v reg* to fold
répliquer – *v reg* to reply
répondeur – *nm* answering machine
  répondeur téléphonique – *nm* (telephone) answering machine
répondre – *v reg* to reply, answer
réponse – *nf* answer
reportage – *nm* report, live commentary
se reposer* – *v refl* to rest
reprendre – *v irreg* § to take back
  reprendre haleine – to get one's breath back
représentant(e) – *nmf* representative

représentation – *nf* performance

représenter – *v reg* to show, represent

reproche – *nm* reproach, blame

reprocher – *v reg* to blame

RER – (Réseau express régional) *nm* Paris express metro system

réservation – *nf* reservation

réservé – *adj* reserved, booked

réserver – *v reg* to reserve

résidence – *nf* residence, residential flats

résister – *v reg* to resist, stand up to

résoudre – *v irreg* § to solve, decide on

respecter – *v reg* to respect

respirer – *v reg* to breathe (in)

responsabilité – *nf* responsibility

responsable – *nmf* organiser, leader

ressembler à – *v reg* to resemble, look like

ressentir – *v irreg* § to feel

restaurant – *nm* restaurant
     restaurant libre-service – self-service restaurant

reste – *nm* rest, remainder
     les restes – *nmpl* left-overs
     du reste – besides

rester* – *v reg* to stay

restituer – *v reg* to restore, give back

résultat – *nm* result

résumé – *nm* summary

rétablir – *v reg* to restore
     se rétablir* – *v refl* to get better

retard – *nm* delay
     en retard – late

retarder – *v reg* to delay, be slow (clock)

retenir – *v irreg* § to hold back

retenue – *nf* detention
     être en retenue – *v irreg* § to be in detention

retomber* – *v reg* to fall

retour – *nm* return
     bon retour! – have a safe journey home!
     de retour – back again, home

retourner – *v reg* (*with avoir*) to turn round, turn over

retourner* – *v reg* to return, go back

retraite – *nf* retreat

retraité(e) – *adj* retired

retrouver – *v reg* to find (again)
     se retrouver* – *v refl* to meet (again)

rétroviseur – *nm* driving mirror

réunion – *nf* meeting

réunir – *v reg* to gather, call together
     se réunir* – *v refl* to meet, get together

réussir – *v reg* to succeed
     réussir à un examen – to pass an exam

réussite – *nf* success

revanche – *nf* return match, revenge
     en revanche – on the other hand

rêve – *nm* dream

réveil – *nm* alarm clock
     radio-réveil – *nm* clock radio

se réveiller* – *v refl* to wake up

réveillon – *nm* Christmas Eve dinner, New Year's Eve party

révéler – *v reg* † to reveal

revenait – *see revenir** § was coming back

revendication – *nf* grievance, claim, demand

revenir* – *v irreg* § to come back
     je n'en reviens pas – I can't get over it

revenu – *pp revenir** § came back

revenu – *nm* income

rêver – *v reg* to dream

réverbère – *nm* street lamp

revient – *see revenir** § comes back

---

nm - noun masculine   *nmpl* - noun masculine plural   *adj* - adjective   *conj* - conjunction
nf - noun feminine   *nfpl* - noun feminine plural   *adv* - adverb   *pron* - pronoun

reviennent – *see revenir** § come back

revint – *see revenir** § came back

revoir – *v irreg* § to see again
  au revoir – goodbye

révolution – *nf* revolution
  Révolution française – French Revolution (1789)

revue – *nf* magazine

rez-de-chaussée – *nm* ground floor
  au rez-de-chaussée – on the ground floor

Rhin – *nm* Rhine

rhinocéros – *nm* rhinoceros

rhume – *nm* cold
  rhume des foins – hay fever
  attraper un rhume – *v reg* to catch cold

ri – *pp rire* § laughed

riait – *see rire* § was laughing

riant – *adj* cheerful

riche – *adj* rich

richesse – *nf* wealth

rideau – *nm* curtain

ridicule – *adj* ridiculous

rien – *pron* nothing
  de rien – you're welcome, don't mention it
  ne...rien – nothing
  rien d'autre – nothing else

rigoler – *v reg coll* to have a good time

rigolo, rigolote – *adj coll* funny

rira – *see rire* § will laugh

rirait – would laugh

rire – *v irreg* § to laugh

risque – *nm* risk

risquer – *v reg* to risk, be likely to
  elle risque de se perdre – she is likely to get lost

rit – *see rire* § laughs, laughed

rivière – *nf* river

riz – *nm* rice

robe – *nf* dress

robe de chambre – *nf* dressing gown

robinet – *nm* tap

robot de cuisine – *nm* food processor

robuste – *adj* tough

rocade – *nf* by-pass road

rock – *nm* rock music

rôder – *v reg* to prowl

rognon – *nm* kidney (on menu)

roi – *nm* king
  le jour des Rois – Twelfth Night

rollers in line – *nmpl* in-line skates

roman – *nm* novel, story
  roman d'aventure – adventure story
  roman d'épouvante – horror story
  roman de science fiction – science fiction novel
  roman d'espionnage – spy story
  roman policier – detective story

romancier, romancière – *nmf* novelist

rompre – *v irreg* § to break

rompu – *pp rompre* broken

rond – *adj* round

rondelle – *nf* slice (of salami)

rond-point – *nm* roundabout
  tournez à droite au rond-point – turn right at the roundabout

ronfler – *v reg* to snore

ronger – *v reg* † to gnaw

ronronner – *v reg* to purr

rosbif – *nm* roast beef, Englishman *sl*

rose – *adj* pink

rose – *nf* rose

rôti – *adj* roast(ed)

rôti – *nm* roast meat

roue – *nf* wheel
  roue arrière – back wheel
  roue avant – front wheel

---

prep - preposition	*v reg* - verb regular	*v refl* - verb reflexive	§ - see verb tables
pp - past participle	*v irreg* - verb irregular	† - see verb information	* - takes être

roue de secours – spare wheel

rouge – *adj* red

rouge à lèvres – *nm* lipstick

rouge-gorge – *nm* robin

rougeole – *nf* measles

rouillé – *adj* rusty

rouler – *v reg* to drive, move

  rouler à 80 km/h – to drive at 50 mph

  rouler au pas – to drive at walking pace

roulotte – *nf* caravan

route – *nf* road

  route à quatre voies – dual carriageway

  route départementale (D) – secondary road

  RN route nationale – *nf* trunk road, major road

  bonne route! – have a good journey!

  en route – on the way

sur la RN 137 – on the RN 137

routier – *nm* lorry driver

routier, routière – *adj* road

  gare routière – *nf* coach station

roux, rousse – *adj* red haired, auburn

Royaume-Uni – *nm* United Kingdom, UK

rude – *adj* rough

rue – *nf* road, street

rugby – *nm* rugby

  rugby à quinze – rugby union

  rugby à treize – rugby league

ruine – *nf* ruin

rural – *adj* country, rural

rusé – *adj* wily, sly

russe – *adj* Russian

Russe – *nmf* Russian person

Russie – *nf* Russia

rustique – *adj* rustic

rythme – *nm* rhythm

S

s' – *pron* himself, herself, oneself

sa (son, ses) – *poss adj* his, her, its

SA – (société anonyme) *nf* plc

sabbat – *nm* Sabbath

sable – *nm* sand

sablier – *nm* egg timer

sablonneux, sablonneuse – *adj* sandy

sabot – *nm* clog

sabre – *nm* sword

sac – *nm* bag

  sac à dos – rucksack

  sac à main – handbag

  sac à provisions – shopping bag

  sac banane – bum bag

sac de couchage – sleeping bag

sacoche – *nf* postman's bag

sacré – *adj* blessed, confounded

sacrifié – *adj* sacrificed

  prix sacrifiés – *nmpl* give-away prices, prices slashed

sacrifier – *v reg* to give up, sacrifice

safari – *nm* safari

safran – *nm* saffron

  riz au safran – *nm* saffron rice

sagace – *adj* shrewd

sagacité – *nf* shrewdness

sage – *adj* good, wise, well-behaved

sagement – *adj* sensibly

nm - noun masculine	*nmpl* - noun masculine plural	*adj* - adjective	*conj* - conjunction
nf - noun feminine	*nfpl* - noun feminine plural	*adv* - adverb	*pron* - pronoun

sagesse – *nf* good sense, wisdom
Sagittaire – *nm* Sagittarius
   être (du) Sagittaire – *v irreg* § to be (a) Sagittarius
saignant – *adj* rare (steak)
saigner – *v reg* to bleed
   elle saigne du nez – she has a nose bleed
sain – *adj* healthy
   sain et sauf – safe and sound
sainement – *adj* healthily
   manger sainement – to eat healthily
saint – *adj* holy
   vendredi saint – Good Friday
   la Saint Sylvestre – New Year's Eve
sais – *see savoir* § know how to, can
   je sais nager – I can swim
saisir – *v reg* to seize, take hold of
   saisir une occasion – to take an opportunity
saison – *nf* season
   en cette saison – at this time of year
   en haute saison – in high season
   en toutes saisons – all year round
   hors saison – low season
saisonnier, saisonnière – *adj* seasonal
sait – *see savoir* § knows how to, can
   elle sait écrire – she knows how to, can write
   il sait lire – he can read
salade – *nf* salad, lettuce
   salade composée – mixed salad
   salade de tomates – tomato salad
   salade verte – green salad
salaire – *nm* pay, salary
salarié – *adj* wage-earning
sale – *adj* dirty
salé – *adj* salty
salir – *v reg* to make dirty
salle – *nf* room, hall
   salle à manger – dining room

salle d'attente – waiting room
salle de bains – bathroom
salle de classe – classroom
salle de conférence – lecture room
salle de consultation – surgery
salle de jeux – games room
salle de musique – music room
salle de séjour – living-room
salle des professeurs – staff room
salle polyvalente – multi-purpose room
salon – *nm* lounge, sitting room
salubre – *adj* healthy
saluer – *v reg* to greet
salut – *nm* greeting, safety, salvation
   Salut! – Hi! Hello!
samedi – *nm* Saturday
   à samedi – see you on Saturday
SAMU – (service d'assistance médical d'urgence) *nm* mobile medical emergency unit
sandale – *nf* sandal
sandwich – *nm* sandwich
   sandwich au fromage – cheese sandwich
   sandwich au jambon – ham sandwich
sang – *nm* blood
sanglot – *nm* sob
sanitaire – *adj* health, sanitary
   bloc sanitaire – *nm* toilet block
sanitaires – *nmpl* toilet, bathroom
sans – *prep* without
   non sans peine – not without difficulty
   sans abri – homeless
   sans doute – without doubt
   sans interruption – without a break
   sans le sou – penniless
   sans plomb – lead-free
santé – *nf* health
   à ta, votre santé – Cheers!

être en bonne santé – *v irreg* §
to be in good health
être en mauvaise santé – *v irreg*
§ to be in poor health
sapeur-pompier – *nm* fireman
sapin – *nm* fir tree
  sapin de Noël – Christmas tree
sardine – *nf* sardine
satellite – *nm* satellite
  satellite de
  télécommunications –
  telecommunications satellite
  satellite espion – spy satellite
satisfaire – *v irreg* § to satisfy
satisfait – *adj* happy with, satisfied
sauce – *nf* sauce, gravy
  sauce vinaigrette – French salad
  dressing
saucisse – *nf* sausage
  saucisse de Francfort – frankfurter
saucisson (sec) – *nm* slicing sausage
sauf – *prep* except, except for, unless
sauf, sauve – *adj* unhurt, unharmed
  sain et sauf – safe and sound
saule – *nm* willow tree
saumon – *nm* salmon
saura – *see savoir* § will know
saurait – would know
saut – *nm* leap, jump
  saut à la perche – pole vault
  saut en hauteur – high jump
sauter – *v reg* to jump, leap
sauterelle – *nf* grasshopper
sauvage – *adj* wild
sauver – *v reg* to save
  se sauver* – *v refl* to run away
sauvetage – *nm* rescue
  canot de sauvetage – *nm* lifeboat
savait – *see savoir* § used to know
savant – *adj* learned, clever, skilful
savent – *see savoir* § know, can
savez – *see savoir* § know, can

savoir – *v irreg* § to know
  je sais ce que je dis – I know
  what I am saying
  je sais la réponse – I know the
  answer
  je sais lire – I can read
  je sais quoi faire – I know what to
  do
  on ne sait jamais! – you never
  know!
  savez-vous si...? – do you know
  whether, if...?
savon – *nm* soap
savons – *see savoir* § know
savoureux – *adj* tasty
scène – *nf* stage
  être en scène – *v irreg* § to be on
  stage
  mettre en scène – *v irreg* § to
  stage
schéma – *nm* diagram, sketch
scie – *nf* saw
science – *nf* science
  science économique – economics
  sciences naturelles – *nfpl*
  biology, natural sciences
  sciences physiques – *nfpl*
  physical sciences
science-fiction – *nf* science fiction
  film de science-fiction – *nm* sci-
  fi film
  livre de science-fiction – *nm* sci-
  fi story
scientifique – *adj* scientific
scolaire – *adj* school
  année scolaire – *nf* school year
  établissement scolaire – *nm*
  school
scolarisation – *nf* schooling
scolarité – *nf* schooling
  scolarité obligatoire –
  compulsory schooling
scooter – *nm* scooter

---

nm - noun masculine	*nmpl* - noun masculine plural	*adj* - adjective	*conj* - conjunction
nf - noun feminine	*nfpl* - noun feminine plural	*adv* - adverb	*pron* - pronoun

Scorpion – *nm* Scorpio
  être (du) Scorpion – *v irreg* § to be (a) Scorpio
scotch® – *nm* sticky tape, whisky
se, s' – *pron* himself, herself, oneself
séance – *nf* (film) showing, session
seau – *nm* bucket
sec, sèche – *adj* dry
sèche-cheveux – *nm* hair dryer
sèche-linge – *nm* dryer
sécher – *v reg* † to dry
  se sécher* les cheveux – *v refl* † to dry one's hair
sécheresse – *nf* drought
second, seconde – *adj* second
  être en seconde – *v irreg* § to be in Year 11
secondaire – *adj* secondary
secouer – *v reg* to shake
secours – *nm* help, assistance
  au secours! – help!
  premiers secours – *nmpl* first aid
  secours d'urgence – emergency aid
secousse – *nf* bump, jolt, tremor
secret, secrète – *adj* secret
secrétaire – *nmf* secretary
secteur – *nm* district, area, sector
  secteur privé – private sector
  secteur public – public sector
  secteur sauvegardé – conservation area
sécurisant – *adj* reassuring
sécurité – *nf* security
  se sentir* en sécurité – *v refl* § to feel safe
séduisant – *adj* attractive
sein – *nm* heart, middle, breast
seize – *adj* sixteen
seizième – *adj* sixteenth
séjour – *nm* stay, living room
  salle de séjour – *nf* living room

séjourner – *v reg* to stay
sel – *nm* salt
  sel fin – table salt
  sel marin – sea salt
  sels de bain – *nmpl* bath salts
selection – *nf* selection
selectionner – *v reg* to select, pick (team)
self – *nm* self-service restaurant
selle – *nf* saddle
selon – *prep* according to
semaine – *nf* week
  semaine dernière – last week
  semaine des quatre jeudis – a month of Sundays
  dans deux semaines – in two weeks' time
  en semaine – during the week
  la semaine prochaine – next week
semblable – *adj* alike, similar
semblant – *nm* appearance, semblance
  faire semblant de – *v irreg* § to pretend to
sembler – *v reg* to seem
il semble – *v impers* it seems
  il me semble que... – it seems to me that..., I think that
semelle – *nf* sole (shoe)
semer – *v reg* † to sow seed
sens – *nm* sense, meaning, direction
  sens de l'humour – sense of humour
  sens du rythme – sense of rhythm
  sens interdit – no entry
  sens unique – one way street
  en sens contraire – in the opposite direction
  en sens inverse – in the opposite direction
sensass – *adj sl* great, sensational
sensation – *nf* feeling, impression

---

prep - preposition   *v reg* - verb regular   *v refl* - verb reflexive   § - see verb tables
pp - past participle   *v irreg* - verb irregular   † - see verb information   * - takes être

sensationnel, sensationnelle – *adj* marvellous

sensé – *adj* sensible

sensible – *adj* sensitive

sentier – *nm* path

sentiment – *nm* feeling

sentir – *v irreg* § to smell, be aware of, feel

se sentir* – *v refl* § to feel, to be felt
  se sentir* bien – to feel well
  se sentir* mal – to feel ill

séparation – *nf* separation, parting

séparé – *adj* separated

séparément – *adv* separately

séparer – *v reg* to split, divide, pull off
  se séparer* de – *v refl* to part with, separate from

sept – *adj* seven

septembre – *nm* September

septième – *adj* seventh

série – *nf* set, class, series

sérieux, sérieuse – *adj* serious

serpent – *nm* snake

serpenter – *v reg* to wind (road)

sera – *see être* § will be

serait – would be

serre – *nf* greenhouse

serré – *adj* congested

serrer – *v reg* to squeeze, grip
  serrer la main à – to shake s.o. by the hand
  se serrer* la ceinture – *v refl* to tighten one's belt
  se serrer* la main – *v refl* to shake hands
  serrez à droite – keep to the right

serrure – *nf* lock

serveur – *nm* barman, waiter

serveuse – *nf* barmaid, waitress

service – *nm* duty, service

service d'assistance médical d'urgence – (SAMU) mobile medical emergency unit

service de garde – emergency services

service 15% (non) compris – 15% service (not) included

services sociaux – *nmpl* social services

premier service – first sitting

être de service – *v irreg* § to be on duty

serviette – *nf* serviette
  serviette de bain – towel
  serviette hygiénique – sanitary towel

servir – *v irreg* § to serve
  se servir* – *v refl* § to serve oneself
  se servir* de – *v refl* § to use

ses (son, sa) – *poss adj* his, her, its

seuil – *nm* threshold

seul, seule – *adj* alone, single, solitary

seulement – *adv* only

sévère – *adj* strict

shampooing – *nm* shampoo

short – *nm* pair of shorts

si – *conj* if
  s'il te plaît – please
  s'il vous plaît – please

si – *adv* yes
  mais si! – yes I am! oh yes, it is!

SIDA – (Syndrome Immuno-Déficitaire Acquis) *nm* AIDS

siècle – *nm* century
  au vingtième siècle – in the 20th century

siège – *nm* seat, head office

le sien, la sienne, les siens, les siennes – *pron* his, hers, its
  les siens – his, her family

siffler – *v reg* to whistle

sifflet – *nm* whistle

---

nm - noun masculine   *nmpl* - noun masculine plural   *adj* - adjective   *conj* - conjunction
nf - noun feminine   *nfpl* - noun feminine plural   *adv* - adverb   *pron* - pronoun

sigle – *nm* set of initials, acronym

signal – *nm* sign, signal
  signal de détresse – distress signal

signaler – *v reg* to indicate

signature – *nf* signature

signe – *nm* sign
  signe du zodiaque – sign of the zodiac

signer – *v reg* to sign

silence – *nm* silence

silencieusement – *adv* silently

silencieux, silencieuse – *adj* silent

silhouette – *nf* outline, silhouette

simple – *adj* simple, single
  billet simple – *nm* single ticket

simplement – *adv* simply

simplifier – *v reg* to simplify

sincère – *adj* sincere

sincèrement – *adv* sincerely

singe – *nm* monkey

singulier, singulière – *adj* remarkable
  au singulier – in the singular

sinon – *conj* except, other than, otherwise

sirop – *nm* syrup, squash
  sirop contre la toux – cough medicine

site – *nm* place of interest

sitôt – *adv* as soon as

situation – *nf* position, location, situation

situé à – *adj* situated (in, at)

situer – *v reg* to situate, locate
  se situer* – *v refl* to place o.s.

six – *adj* six

sixième – *adj* sixth
  être en sixième – *v irreg* § to be in year 7

ski – *nm* skiing, ski
  ski de fond – cross country skiing
  ski nautique – water skiing

faire du ski – *v irreg* § to go skiing

slip – *nm* underpants, pants, knickers

SMIC – (salaire minimum interprofessional de croissance) *nm* index-linked minimum wage

smicard(e) – *nmf* person earning minimum wage

SNCF – (Société nationale des chemins de fer français) French railways

snob – *adj* snobbish

sociable – *adj* sociable

social – *adj* social
  services sociaux – social services

société – *nf* company, society

sœur – *nf* sister

soi – *pron* oneself
  soi-disant – so-called
  soi-même – oneself

soie – *nf* silk

soif – *nf* thirst
  avoir soif – *v irreg* § to be thirsty

soigné – *adj* well cared for, well-groomed

soigner – *v reg* to care for

soigneusement – *adj* carefully

soin – *nm* care, tidiness

soins – *nmpl* care, treatment
  premiers soins – first aid

soir – *nm* evening
  à ce soir – see you this evening
  chaque soir – each, every evening
  du soir – p.m. (after 5 p.m.)
  hier soir – last night, yesterday evening
  repas du soir – *nm* evening meal
  tous les soirs – every evening

soirée – *nf* evening, party

sois – *see* être § be!
  sois sage – be good, behave yourself

soit – *adv* very well, so be it

soit ...soit – *conj* either ... or...

---

soit l'un ou soit l'autre – either one or the other

soixantaine – *nf* about sixty

  il a la soixantaine – he is in his sixties

soixante – *adj* sixty

  les années soixante – *nfpl* the sixties

soixante-dix – *adj* seventy

soixante et onze – *adj* seventy one

soixante et un – *adj* sixty one

soja – *nm* soya

sol – *nm* ground, soil

soldat – *nm* soldier

solde – *nm* (bank) balance

  en solde – in the sales

  soldes – *nmpl* the sales

solder – *v reg* to sell at sale price

sole – *nf* sole (fish)

soleil – *nm* sun

  coucher du soleil – *nm* sunset

  lever du soleil – *nm* sunrise

  rayon de soleil – *nm* ray of sunlight

solennel, solennelle – *adj* solemn

solide – *adj* sturdy, tough, solid

solitaire – *adj* lone, lonely

solliciter – *v reg* to appeal, seek

sollicitude – *nf* concern

solution – *nf* solution

sombre – *adj* dark

sommaire – *nm* summary

sommeil – *nm* sleep

  avoir sommeil – *v irreg* § to be sleepy

sommes – *see être* § are

sommet – *nm* summit, top

son (sa, ses) – *poss adj* his, her, its

son – *nm* sound

sondage – *nm* survey, opinion poll

songer – *v reg* † to think, dream

sonner – *v reg* to ring

sonnerie – *nf* bell

sonnette – *nf* bell

sonore – *adj* ringing, resonant

sont – *see être* § are

sort – *see sortir** § goes, comes out

sort – *nm* fate

sortable – *adj* presentable

sorte – *nf* type, sort, kind

  une sorte de – a kind of

sortie – *nf* way out, exit, outing

  sortie de secours – emergency exit

  sortie d'usine – factory gate

sortir – *v irreg* § to come, go out

  s'en sortir – *v refl* § to get out of a mess

sot, sotte – *adj* foolish, stupid

sottise – *nf* stupid remark, silly action

  dire des sottises – *v irreg* § to make stupid remarks

  faire une sottise – *v irreg* § to do something stupid

sou – *nm* small coin, penny

  des sous – *nmpl* cash

  je n'ai pas le sou – I'm broke

  sans le sou – penniless

souci – *nm* care, worry

se soucier de** – *v refl* to care about

soucoupe – *nf* saucer

soudain – *adj* sudden

soudain – *adv* suddenly

souffle – *nm* breath, breathing, puff of wind

souffler – *v reg* to blow

souffrant – *adj* unwell

souffrir – *v irreg* § to suffer

souhait – *nm* wish

  à souhait – to perfection

  à tes souhaits! – bless you!

souhaiter – *v reg* to wish

soulager – *v reg* † to soothe, relieve pain

soulever – *v reg* † to lift up, raise

---

soulier – *nm* shoe
souligner – *v reg* to underline
soumettre – *v irreg* § to submit to
soumis – *adj* submissive
soupçon – *nm* suspicion
soupçonner – *v reg* to suspect
soupe – *nf* soup
souper – *nm* supper
soupir – *nm* sigh
  pousser un soupir – *v reg* to sigh
soupirer – *v reg* to sigh
souple – *adj* athletic, supple
source – *nf* spring, source
sourcil – *nm* eyebrow
sourd – *adj* deaf
  sourd-muet – deaf and dumb
sourire – *nm* smile
sourire – *v irreg* § to smile
souris – *nf* mouse
sous – *prep* under
  sous-développé – under-developed
  sous la pluie – in the rain
  sous-marin – underwater
  sous terre – underground
sous-sol – *nm* basement
sous-titré – *adj* subtitled
sous-titres – *nmpl* subtitles
soutenir – *v irreg* § to support, hold up
  je soutiens Liverpool – I support Liverpool
souterrain – *adj* underground, subway
soutien – *nm* support
soutien-gorge – *nm* bra
souvenir – *nm* memory, souvenir
se souvenir* de – *v refl* § to remember
souvent – *adv* often
soyez – *see être* be
  soyez sage – be good, behave yourselves

SPA – (Société protectrice des animaux) *nf* animal protection organisation
spacieux, spacieuse – *adj* spacious
spaghetti – *nm* spaghetti
sparadrap – *nm* plaster, elastoplast®
spécial – *adj* special
spécialiste – *nmf* specialist
spécialité – *nf* speciality
  spécialités locales – *nfpl* local specialities
spécifier – *v reg* to specify
spectacle – *nm* entertainment, show, sight
spectaculaire – *adj* spectacular
spectateur – *nm* spectator
spectatrice – *nf* spectator
spéléologie – *nf* pot-holing
sport – *nm* sport
  sports d'équipe – *nmpl* team sports
  sports d'hiver – *nmpl* winter sports
sportif, sportive – *adj* athletic, keen on sports
stade – *nm* stadium
stage – *nm* course, training
stagiaire – *nmf* trainee
standard – *nm* switchboard (phone)
standardiste – *nmf* switchboard operator
station – *nf* resort, station
  station balnéaire – seaside resort
  station de métro – underground station
  station de taxis – taxi rank
  station-service – petrol station
stationnement – *nm* parking
  stationnement interdit – no parking
stationner – *v reg* to park, be parked
steak – *nm* steak
  steak haché – mince

---

stopper – *v reg* to stop, mend (garment)

store – *nm* roller blind

stressé – *adj* stressed out

stresser – *v reg* to cause stress

strict – *adj* strict

studieux, studieuse – *adj* studious

studio – *nm* bed sit

stupéfait – *adj* stunned, dumbfounded

stupéfiant – *nm* drug, narcotic

stupide – *adj* stupid

style – *nm* style
    style de vie – life style

styliste – *nmf* designer

stylo – *nm* pen
    stylo à bille – ball-point pen
    stylo à cartouche – cartridge pen
    stylo à encre – fountain pen

su – *pp savoir* § known

subir – *v reg* to undergo, be subject to

subit – *adj* sudden

submergé – *adj* flooded

subsister – *v reg* to survive

subvention – *nf* subsidy

subventionner – *v reg* to subsidise
    école subventionnée – *nf* grant aided school

succès – *nm* success

succéder – *v reg* † to follow, succeed
    se succéder * – *v refl* † to follow one another

sucer – *v reg* † to suck

sucette – *nf* lollipop

sucre – *nm* sugar

sucré – *adj* sweet

sucrier – *nm* sugar bowl

sud – *nm* south
    vent du sud – *nm* south wind
    sud-est – *nm* south-east
    sud-ouest – *nm* south-west

Suède – *nf* Sweden

suédois – *adj* Swedish

Suédois(e) – *nmf* Swedish person

suffire – *v irreg* § to be sufficient

suffisamment – *adv* sufficiently

suffisant – *adj* sufficient

suggérer – *v reg* † to suggest

suis[1] – *see être* § am

suis[2] – *see suivre* § follow

suisse – *adj* Swiss

Suisse – *nf* Switzerland

Suisse – *nmf* Swiss person

suite – *nf* series, outcome, continuation
    par suite de – as a result of

suivant – *adj* next, following

suivi – *adj* well-attended
    suivi de – followed by

suivre – *v irreg* § to follow
    se suivre* – *v refl* § to be in the right order

sujet – *nm* subject, topic
    au sujet de – about

super – *adj* terrific, great

super – *nm* 4-star leaded petrol
    super sans plomb – super unleaded petrol

superbe – *adj* glorious, magnificent

supérieur – *adj* upper, superior
    à l'étage supérieur – on the floor above

supermarché – *nm* supermarket

supplément – *nm* extra charge
    en supplément – extra

supplémentaire – *adj* additional, further

support – *nm* support, stand

supporter – *v reg* to hold up, bear, support

supposer – *v reg* to assume, suppose

supprimer – *v reg* to delete, remove, ban

sur – *prep* on, upon, by
    donner sur – *v reg* to look out on to
    neuf sur dix – nine out of ten

sûr – *adj* certain, sure, safe

surdose – *nf* overdose
  prendre une surdose – *v irreg* §
  to take an overdose

sur-le-champ – *adv* straightaway

sur le point de – on the point of,
  about to

sûreté – *nf* safety

Sûreté – *nf* French Criminal
  Investigation Dept

surf – *nm* surfing

surface – *nf* surface, area
  grande surface – hypermarket

surfer sur le Net – *v reg* to surf the
  Net

surgelé – *adj* deep frozen
  aliments surgelés – *nmpl* frozen
  foods

surlendemain – *nm* two days later

surmonter – *v reg* to overcome

surnommer – *v reg* to nickname

surprenant – *adj* surprising

surprendre – *v irreg* § to surprise,
  discover, catch out

surpris – *adj* surprised, amazed

surprise – *nf* surprise

surprise-partie – *nf* party

sursaut – *nm* jump, start

se réveiller* en sursaut – *v refl*
  to wake up with a start

sursauter – *v reg* to jump, start

surtout – *adv* above all, especially

surveillant(e) – *nmf* school
  supervisor

surveiller – *v reg* to supervise, keep
  an eye on

survenir – *v irreg* § to take place

survêtement – *nm* tracksuit

survivre – v irreg § to survive

en sus – *adv* in addition

suspendre – *v reg* to hang

suspendu – *adj* hanging

sut – *see savoir* § knew

svelte – *adj* slim, slender

SVP (s'il vous plaît) – *adv* please

sweat-shirt – *nm* sweatshirt

symbole – *nm* symbol

sympa – *adj inv sl* nice

sympathie – *nf* liking, friendship,
  warmth

sympathique – *adj* nice, pleasant

synagogue – *nf* synagogue

syndicat – *nm* union, association

syndicat d'initiative – *nm* tourist
  information office

système – *nm* system
  système de vie – way of life

T

ta (ton, tes) – *poss adj* your

tabac – *nm* tobacconist

table – *nf* table
  à table! – the meal is ready
  table basse – coffee table
  table de chevet – bedside table
  table des matières – contents
  quitter la table – *v reg* to leave the
  table

se mettre* à table – *v refl* § to sit
  down at the table

tableau – *nm* picture, scene, board
  tableau d'affichage – notice
  board
  tableau des départs– departure
  board
  tableau noir – blackboard

tablette – *nf* bar (of chocolate)

---

prep - preposition	*v reg* - verb regular	*v refl* - verb reflexive	§ - see verb tables
pp - past participle	*v irreg* - verb irregular	† - see verb information	* - takes être

tablier – *nm* apron

tache – *nf* stain
  tache d'encre – blot, ink stain

tâche – *nf* task

tacher – *v reg* to stain

tâcher de – *v reg* to try to

taie d'oreiller – *nf* pillowcase

taille – *nf* size (clothes)

taille – *nf* size, height, waist
  avoir une grande taille – *v irreg*
  § to be large
  de petite taille – small
  la taille 38 – size 38 (clothes size,
  English 10)

taille-crayon – *nm inv* pencil
sharpener

tailler – *v reg* to cut, prune

tailleur – *nm* lady's suit, tailor

se taire* – *v irreg* § to be silent
  tais-toi! – be quiet!
  taisez-vous! – be quiet!

talon – *nm* heel

tambour – *nm* drum

Tamise – *nf* Thames

tandis que – *conj* whereas, while

tant – *adv* so much, so many
  tant de – so much, so many
  tant mieux – so much the better,
  that's fine
  tant pis – never mind, tough!
  tant que – as much as

tante – *nf* aunt

tantôt...tantôt – *adv*
sometimes...sometimes

tapage – *nm* din, row

tapageur, tapageuse – *adj* rowdy

taper – *v reg* to hit
  taper à la machine – to type

tapis – *nm* carpet
  tapis à bagages – luggage
  carousel
  tapis roulant – conveyor belt

tapissé de – *adj* lined, covered with

tapisser – *v reg* to wallpaper

taquiner – *v reg* to tease

tard – *adv* late
  il est tard – it is late
  plus tard – later

tarder – *v reg* to delay

tardif, tardive – *adj* late, tardy

tardivement – *adv* belatedly

tarif – *nm* price list

tarte – *nf* tart, flan
  tarte à la framboise – raspberry
  tart
  tarte aux pommes – apple tart
  tarte maison – home-made tart,
  pie

tartine – *nf* piece of bread and butter

tartiner – *v reg* to spread (with butter,
jam, etc)

tas – *nm* heap, pile

tasse – *nf* cup
  tasse à thé – tea cup
  tasse de thé – cup of tea

taupe – *nf* mole

taureau – *nm* bull
  Taureau – Taurus
  être (du) Taureau – *v irreg* §
  to be (a) Taurus

taux de change – *nm* rate of exchange

taxe – *nf* tax
  TVA – (taxe à la valeur ajoutée)
  VAT

taxi – *nm* taxi

te – *pron* you, to you, yourself

technicien, technicienne – *nmf*
technician

technologie – *nf* technology

tee-shirt – *nm* T-shirt

teinture – *nf* colour, dye

teinturerie – *nf* dry cleaner's

tel, telle – *adj* such a, so

télégramme – *nm* telegram

téléjournal – *nm* TV news

téléphérique – *nm* ski lift

---

nm - noun masculine	*nmpl* - noun masculine plural	*adj* - adjective	*conj* - conjunction
nf - noun feminine	*nfpl* - noun feminine plural	*adv* - adverb	*pron* - pronoun

téléphone – *nm* telephone
téléphoner – *v reg* to phone
téléspectateur, téléspectatrice – *nmf* viewer
téléviseur – *nm* television set
télévision – *nf* television
  télévision cablée – cable TV
tellement – *adv* so
témoignage – *nm* evidence, personal account
témoin – *nm* witness
température – *nf* temperature
tempête – *nf* storm, high wind
temps – *nm* time, weather
  à mi-temps – part-time
  à temps – on time
  à temps partiel – part-time
  de temps en temps – from time to time
  il faisait un temps superbe – the weather was wonderful
  par mauvais temps – in bad weather
  temps libre – free time
tendre – *v reg* to hold out
tendre – *adj* tender
tendresse – *nf* tenderness
tendu – *adj* stretched out, straight
tenir – *v irreg* § to hold
  se tenir* – *v refl* § to stand
tennis – *nm* tennis
  tennis – *nfpl* a pair of trainers
  partie de tennis – *nf* a game of tennis
tentative – *nf* attempt
tente – *nf* tent
tenter – *v reg* to try, tempt
tenu – *pp tenir* § held
tenue – *nf* outfit
terminal – *adj* last, terminal
  en terminale – in year 13
terminer – *v reg* to finish, complete
  ça, c'est bien terminé! – that turned out well!
  se terminer* – *v refl* to end, finish

terne – *adj* colourless, lifeless, drab
terrain – *nm* ground, pitch, court
  terrain à bâtir – building plot
  terrain de camping – campsite
  terrain de sport – sports ground
terrasse – *nf* terrace, patio
  terrasse de café – café terrace
terre – *nf* land, earth
  la planète Terre – planet Earth
  jeter par terre – *v reg* † to throw something on the ground
terreur – *nf* terror
terrible – *adj* terrible, awful, fantastic
terrifier – *v reg* to terrify
terrine – *nf* pâté, dish
territoire – *nm* territory
terroriser – *v reg* to terrorise
terrorisme – *nm* terrorism
terroriste – *nmf* terrorist
tes (ton, ta) – *poss adj* your
tête – *nf* head, face
  avoir une tête frisée – *v irreg* § to have curly hair
  être tête nue – *v irreg* § to be bare-headed
  faire une drôle de tête – *v irreg* § to pull a face
têtu – *adj* obstinate
TF1 – (télévision française 1) *nf* French TV channel
TGV – (train à grande vitesse) *nm* high speed train
thé – *nm* tea
  thé à la menthe – mint tea
  thé au citron – lemon tea
  thé au lait – tea with milk
  thé nature – tea without milk
théâtre – *nm* theatre
  théâtre de marionnettes – puppet theatre
  faire du théâtre – *v irreg* § to act (on stage)
théière – *nf* teapot

---

prep - preposition   *v reg* - verb regular   *v refl* - verb reflexive   § - see verb tables
pp - past participle   *v irreg* - verb irregular   † - see verb information   * - takes être

thème – *nm* translation into a foreign language

thermomètre – *nm* thermometer

thon – *nm* tuna fish

ticket – *nm* ticket
  ticket de consigne – left luggage ticket
  ticket de métro – underground ticket
  ticket de quai – platform ticket

tiède – *adj* lukewarm, mild

le tien, la tienne, les tiens, les tiennes – *pron* yours, your own
  les tiens – your family

tiendra – *see tenir* § will hold

tiendrait –would hold

tiennent – *see tenir* § hold

tiens! – goodness!

tient – *see tenir* § holds

tiers – *adj* third, one third (fraction)
  le Tiers Monde – the Third World

tigre – *nm* tiger

timbales – *nfpl* timpani, drums

timbre – *nm* stamp, tone of voice
  timbre à deux franc – 2 franc stamp
  timbre-poste – postage stamp

timide – *adj* shy

tir – *nm* shooting
  tir à l'arc – archery

tirage – *nm* (lottery) draw, printing

tire-bouchon – *nm* corkscrew

tirer – *v reg* to pull, draw
  se tirer* – *v refl* to get out of

tiret – *nm* dash (punctuation) (-)

tiroir – *nm* drawer

tisane – *nf* herbal tea

tissage – *nm* weaving

tisser – *v reg* to weave

tissu – *nm* fabric, cloth

titre – *nm* title

toast – *nm* slice of toast

toboggan – *nm* toboggan, sledge

toi – *pron* you
  toi-même – yourself

toile – *nf* cloth, canvas
  toile d'araignée – spider's web

toilette – *nf* toilet
  toilette de mariée – wedding dress
  faire sa toilette – *v irreg* § to get ready

toilettes – *nfpl* toilets

toit – *nm* roof
  toit d'ardoise – slate roof
  toit de chaume – thatched roof

tolérer – *v reg* † to allow, tolerate

TOM – (territoires d'outre-mer) *nmpl* French overseas territories

tomate – *nf* tomato
  tomates farcies – *nfpl* stuffed tomatoes

tombeau – *nm* tomb

tomber* – *v reg* to fall
  tomber* en panne – to break down
  tomber* malade – to fall ill

ton (ta, tes) – *poss adj* your

ton – *nm* tone

tonalité – *nf* tone, sound (on phone)

tondre – *v reg* to clip, shear
  tondre la pelouse – to mow the lawn

tondu – *adj* short (hair), clipped

tongs – *nfpl* flip-flops

tonne – *nf* ton

tonneau – *nm* barrel

tonner – *v reg* to thunder

tonnerre – *nm* thunder

torchon – *nm* tea towel

tordre – *v reg* to twist
  se tordre* la cheville – *v refl* to twist an ankle

tort – *nm* fault
  avoir tort – *v irreg* § to be wrong

---

nm - noun masculine	*nmpl* - noun masculine plural	*adj* - adjective	*conj* - conjunction
nf - noun feminine	*nfpl* - noun feminine plural	*adv* - adverb	*pron* - pronoun

donner tort à – *v reg* to blame
tortue – *nf* tortoise
tortueux, tortueuse – *adj* twisting
tôt – *adv* early
  plus tôt – earlier
  se coucher* tôt – *v refl* to go to bed early
total – *nm* total
  faire le total – *v irreg* § to add up
totalement – *adv* totally
totalité – *nf* the whole, all of
touchant – *prep* concerning
touche – *nf* key (on keyboard)
toucher – *v reg* to touch, get money
  prière de ne pas toucher – please do not touch
  toucher ... francs par mois – to get ... francs per month
  toucher un chèque – to cash a cheque
  toucher un mandat – to cash a postal order
toujours – *adv* always, still
toupie – *nf* spinning top
tour – *nf* tower
  tour d'habitation – tower block
  Tour Eiffel – Eiffel Tower
tour – *nm* turn, tour
  Tour de France – Tour de France
  tour de taille – waist measurement
  à tour de rôle – in turn
  faire le tour du monde – *v irreg* § to go round the world
  faire un tour en ville – *v irreg* § to go round town
  jouer un tour à – *v reg* to play a trick on
tourisme – *nm* tourism
touriste – *nmf* tourist
tournant – *nm* bend, turning point
tourner – *v reg* to turn
  tourner un film – to make a film
tournesol – *nm* sunflower

tournevis – *nm* screwdriver
tournoi – *nm* tournament
  tournoi des cinq nations – Five Nations Championship (rugby)
tournoyer – *v reg* † to whirl round
Toussaint – *nf* All Saints' Day (November 1st)
tousser – *v reg* to cough
tout, toute, tous, toutes – *adj, pron* all
  tout le monde – everyone
  tout le temps – all the time
  tout neuf – brand new
  tout seul – alone
  toute la journée – all day
  toute l'année – all year round
  toute la nuit – all night
  tous les deux – both
  tous les jours – every day
  tous les 36 du mois – once in a blue moon
  dans tous les sens – in all directions
  toutes directions – all routes
  toutes les deux – both
  toutes les deux heures – every two hours
  toutes sortes de – all sorts of
  à tout à l'heure – see you later
  à toute vitesse – at top speed
  à toute heure – at any time
  tout à coup – suddenly
  tout à fait – quite, totally, completely
  tout à l'heure – shortly, recently
  tout de même – all the same
  tout de suite – at once
  tout droit – straight on
  tout en chantant – while singing
  tout près – very close
  tout va bien – all is well
  parler tout bas – *v reg* to speak in an undertone, quietly
toutefois – *adv* however
toux – *nf* cough
trac – *nm sl* nerves, stage fright

prep - preposition	*v reg* - verb regular	*v refl* - verb reflexive	§ - see verb tables
pp - past participle	*v irreg* - verb irregular	† - see verb information	* - takes être

tracasser – *v reg* to harass, bother
tracer – *v reg* † to draw, trace
tracteur – *nm* tractor
tradition – *nf* tradition
traditionnel, traditionnelle – *adj* traditional
traduction – *nf* translation
traduire – *v irreg* § to translate
trafic – *nm* traffic, trafficking
   trafic aérien – air traffic
tragique – *adj* tragic
trahir – *v reg* to betray
trahison – *nf* betrayal, treachery
train – *nm* train
   train à grande vitesse (TGV) – high speed train
   être en train de – *v irreg* § to be in the process of
traîner – *v reg* to pull, drag, lie around
   laisser traîner – *v reg* to leave ... lying around
trait d'union – *nm* hyphen (-)
traitement – *nm* treatment
   traitement de texte – word processing
traiter – *v reg* to treat
traître, traîtresse – *adj* treacherous
trajet – *nm* journey
trampoline – *nm* trampoline
   faire du trampoline – *v irreg* § to trampoline
tramway – *nm* tramway, tram
tranche – *nf* slice
trancher – *v reg* to slice
tranquille – *adj* peaceful, calm
tranquillement – *adv* peacefully, quietly
transférer – *v reg* † to transfer
transformer (en) – *v reg* to change (to), transform
transistor – *nm* transistor
transmettre – *v irreg* § to pass on, transmit

transmission – *nf* broadcast
transpirer – *v reg* to sweat
transport – *nm* transport
transports en commun – *nmpl* public transport
trapu – *adj* stocky
travail – *nm* work
travailler – *v reg* to work
travaux – *nmpl* roadworks, work in progress
   travaux d'aménagement – alterations
   travaux pratiques – lab work, practical work
travers – shortcoming, fault
   à travers – through
traversée – *nf* crossing
traverser – *v reg* to cross
traversin – *nm* bolster
trébucher – *v reg* to stumble
trèfle – *nm* clover, shamrock, clubs (cards)
treize – *adj* thirteen
treizième – *adj* thirteenth
tremblant – *adj* trembling, shaky
tremblement – *nm* shiver
   tremblement de terre – earthquake
trembler – *v reg* to shake, shiver
trempé – *adj* soaked
   trempé jusqu'aux os – wet through
tremper – *v reg* to dip, soak, drench
   se tremper* – *v refl* to have a quick dip
tremplin – *nm* diving board, springboard
trentaine – *nf* about thirty
trente – *adj* thirty
trentième – *adj* thirtieth
très – *adv* very
trésor – *nm* treasure
triangle – *nm* triangle
triangulaire – *adj* triangular
tri – *nm* selection, sorting out

---

nm - noun masculine   *nmpl* - noun masculine plural   *adj* - adjective   *conj* - conjunction
nf - noun feminine   *nfpl* - noun feminine plural   *adv* - adverb   *pron* - pronoun

faire le tri – *v irreg* § to sort out, select

tribunal – *nm* court

tricher – *v reg* to cheat

tricot – *nm* knitting, jumper

tricoter – *v reg* to knit

trier – *v reg* to select

trimestre – *nm* term

triomphe – *nm* victory, triumph

triompher – *v reg* to win

triste – *adj* sad

tristement – *adv* sadly

tristesse – *nf* sadness

trois – *adj* three
    coûter trois fois rien – *v reg* to cost very little

troisième – *adj* third
    personne du troisième âge – *nf* senior citizen

trombone – *nm* trombone

trompe – *nf* horn, elephant's trunk

tromper – *v reg* to deceive
    se tromper* – *v refl* to be mistaken

trompette – *nf* trumpet

tronc – *nm* (tree) trunk

trop – *adv* too, too much
    trop de monde – too many people
    j'ai dix francs de trop – I have 10 francs too much

trottoir – *nm* pavement
    trottoir roulant – moving walkway

trou – *nm* hole
    trou de serrure – keyhole

troublé – *adj* disturbed, worried

troupeau – *nm* flock, herd

trousse – *nf* pencil case
    trousse de maquillage – make-up bag

trouver – *v reg* to find

se trouver* – *v refl* to be (situated)
    bien se trouver* à Paris – to be happy in Paris
    York se trouve en Angleterre – York is in England

truc – *nm* thing, whatsit, way, tip

truite – *nf* trout

T-shirt – *nm* T-shirt

TSVP – (tournez, s'il vous plaît) PTO, turn over the page

tu – *pron* you
    t'as = tu as – *coll* you have

tube – *nm* tube, hit song

tué(e) – *nmf* person killed in accident

tuer – *v reg* to kill

Tunisie – *nf* Tunisia

tunisien, tunisienne – *adj* Tunisian

tunnel – *nm* tunnel
    tunnel sous la Manche – the Channel Tunnel

se tut – *see se taire** was silent

tuyau – *nm* pipe, tip *sl*, hint *sl*

se tutoyer* – *v refl* to use "tu" rather than "vous"

TVA – (taxe à la valeur ajoutée) *nf* VAT, value added tax

type – *nm* chap, bloke, type

typique – *adj* typical

U

UHT – (ultra haute température) *adj* UHT (heat treated)
ultérieur – *adj* subsequent
ultime – *adj* final
ultra- – *pref* extreme
un – *indef art* a, an, one (masculine)
une – *indef art* a, an, one (feminine)
uni – *adj* plain coloured, united
unifier – *v reg* to unify
uniforme – *nm* uniform
  uniforme scolaire – school uniform
union – *nf* association, union
  en union avec – in union with
  Union européenne – European Union
unique – *adj* only
  fille unique – *nf* only daughter
  fils unique – *nm* only son
unir – *v reg* to link, join up
  s'unir* – *v refl* to unite
unité – *nf* unit, unity
  prix de vente à l'unité – *nm* unit selling price, price per item
univers – *nm* universe, world
universel, universelle – *adj* universal
universitaire – *adj* academic, of the university

cité universitaire – *nf* halls of residence
université – *nf* university
urbain – *adj* urban
urgence – *nf* urgency
  salle des urgences – *nf* emergency department
  d'urgence – emergency
urgent – *adj* urgent
usage – *nm* custom, use
  c'est l'usage – it's the custom
usagé – *adj* worn, old, second hand
usager – *nm* user
  usager de la drogue – drug user
  usager de la route – road user
usé – *adj* worn out, exhausted
user – *v reg* to wear away, wear out
usine – *nf* factory, works
ustensile – *nm* tool, utensil
  ustensiles de jardinage – *nmpl* gardening tools
usuel, usuelle – *adj* every day
utile – *adj* useful
utilement – *adv* usefully
utilisateur, utilisatrice – *nmf* user
utiliser – *v reg* to use

V

va – *see aller*** § goes, is going
  ça va? – how are you?
vacance – *nf* vacancy
vacances – *nfpl* holidays
  vacances de Noël – Christmas holidays

vacances de Pâques – Easter holidays
grandes vacances – summer holidays
en vacances – on holiday
être en vacances – *v irreg* § to be on holiday

---

nm - noun masculine   nmpl - noun masculine plural   *adj* - adjective   *conj* - conjunction
nf - noun feminine   nfpl - noun feminine plural   *adv* - adverb   *pron* - pronoun

partir* en vacances – *v irreg* § to go on holiday

vacarme – *nm* din, loud noise

vaccin – *nm* vaccine

vache – *nf* cow

vague – *adj* indistinct, vague

vague – *nf* wave (sea)
  vague de chaleur – heatwave

vaincre – *v irreg* § to win, conquer

vaincu – *adj* beaten, defeated

vainqueur – *nm* victor, winner

vais – *see aller** § go, am going

vaisseau – *nm* ship, vessel

vaisselier – *nm* dresser, sideboard

vaisselle – *nf* crockery
  faire la vaisselle – *v irreg* § to do the washing up

valable – *adj* valid

valait – *see valoir* § was worth

valeur – *nf* value
  taxe à la valeur ajoutée – *nf* VAT

valider – *v reg* to validate, stamp

valise – *nf* suitcase
  faire les valises – *v irreg* § to pack (cases)

vallée – *nf* valley

vallon – *nm* valley (small)

valoir – *v irreg* § be worth

vandale – *nmf* vandal

vanille – *nf* vanilla
  glace à la vanille – *nf* vanilla ice cream

vanité – *nf* vanity, conceit

vaniteux, vaniteuse – *adj* vain, conceited

vanter – *v reg* to speak highly of
  se vanter* – *v refl* to boast

vapeur – *nf* steam, vapour, haze

variable – *adj* changeable, variable

varicelle – *nf* chicken pox

varié – *adj* varied

hors d'œuvres variés – *nmpl* selection of starters

varier – *v reg* to vary

vas – *see aller** go, are going

vase – *nf* mud, sludge

vase – *nm* flower vase

vaste – *adj* vast, immense

vaudra – *see valoir* § will be worth

vaudrait – would be worth

vaut – *see valoir* § is worth
  ça ne vaut pas la peine – it's not worth it

veau – *nm* calf, veal

vécu – *pp vivre* § lived

vécut – *see vivre* § lived

vedette – *nf* film star (both *m* and *f*)

végétarien(ne) – *adj* vegetarian

véhicule – *nm* vehicle

veille – *nf* wakefulness, day before
  la veille de Noël – Christmas Eve

veiller – *v reg* to keep watch

veilleuse – *nf* nightlight, sidelight

veine – *nf* vein, seam, inspiration
  avoir de la veine – *v irreg* § to be lucky

vélo – *nm* bike
  VTT – (vélo tout terrain) mountain bike

vélomoteur – *nm* motorized bike

velours – *nm* velvet

venait – *see venir* § used to come, was coming

vendange – *nf* grape harvest
  pendant les vendanges – during the grape picking

vendeur, vendeuse – *nmf* sales assistant

vendre – *v reg* to sell
  à vendre – for sale
  se vendre* à la douzaine – *v refl* to be sold by the dozen
  se vendre* à la pièce – to be sold individually

vendredi – *nm* Friday
  vendredi saint – Good Friday
venger – *v reg* † to avenge
  se venger* – *v refl* † to take revenge
venin – *nm* poison
venir* – *v irreg* § to come
  faire venir le médecin – *v irreg*
  § to send for the doctor
  venir* de faire – *v irreg* § to have
  just done
  je viens d'arriver – I have just
  arrived
  il venait de sortir – he had just
  gone out
vent – *nm* wind
  vent d'est – east wind
  vent d'ouest – west wind
  vent du nord – north wind
  vent du sud – south wind
vente – *nf* sale
  vente aux enchères – auction sale
  en vente – on sale
ventre – *nm* stomach
  avoir mal au ventre – *v irreg* § to
  have stomach ache
venu – *pp venir** § came, come
ver de terre – *nm* earthworm
verdure – *nf* greenery
verger – *nm* orchard
verglas – *nm* black ice (on road)
vérifier – *v reg* to check
  vérifier la pression des pneus –
  to check the tyre pressures
  vérifier le niveau d'eau –
  to check the water level
  vérifier le niveau d'huile –
  to check the oil level
véritable – *adj* real, genuine
vérité – *nf* truth
verra – *see voir* § will see
verrait – would see
verre – *nm* glass
verrou – *nm* bolt, lock

verrouiller – *v reg* to bolt, lock
vers – *prep* towards, about
  vers la droite – to the right
  vers la plage – to the beach
  vers midi – towards midday
vers – *nm* line (poetry)
Verseau – *nm* Aquarius
  être (du) Verseau – *v irreg* §
  to be (an) Aquarius
versement – *nm* payment, instalment
verser – *v reg* to pour out, pay
version – *nf* version, translation
  version française – French
  version
  en version originale – in the
  original version
verso – *nm* back (of piece of paper)
  voir au verso – see over
vert – *adj* green
  vert-foncé – dark green
  vert-pomme – apple green
  les Verts – *nmpl* the Greens (party)
vertige – *nm* dizziness, giddiness
veste – *nf* jacket
vestiaire – *nm* cloak-room, changing-
room
vestibule – *nm* hall
vestige – *nm* remnant, trace
veston – *nm* jacket
vêtement – *nm* article of clothing
  vêtements – *nmpl* clothes
  vêtements de dessous –
  underclothes
  vêtements de rechange – change
  of clothes
vétérinaire – *nm* veterinary surgeon
vêtu (de) – *adj* dressed (in)
veuf – *nm* widower
veuf, veuve – *adj* widowed
veuillez... – *from vouloir* please...
veulent – *see vouloir* § wish, want
veut – *see vouloir* § wishes, wants
  je veux bien – I'd love to

---

nm - noun masculine	*nmpl* - noun masculine plural	*adj* - adjective *conj* - conjunction
nf - noun feminine	*nfpl* - noun feminine plural	*adv* - adverb *pron* - pronoun

veuve – *nf* widow
vexer – *v reg* to hurt, upset, offend s.o.
  se vexer* – *v refl* to be hurt, upset, offended, get angry
viande – *nf* meat
victime – *nf* victim
victoire – *nf* victory
victorieux, victorieuse – *adj* victorious
vidange – *nf* oil change
vide – *adj* empty
vidéo – *adj* video
  caméra vidéo – *nf* video camera
  cassette vidéo – *nf* video cassette
  jeu vidéo – *nm* video game
vider – *v reg* to empty
vie – *nf* life
vieil – *adj m sing* old
  un vieil homme – an old man
vieille – *adj f sing* old
  une vieille maison – an old house
vieillesse – *nf* old age
vieillir – *v reg* to grow old
viendra – *see venir** § will come
viendrait – would come
viennent – *see venir** § come
vient – *see venir** § comes
Vierge – *nf* Virgo
  être (de la) Vierge – *v irreg* § to be (a) Virgo
vieux – *adj m sing* old
  le vieux monsieur – the old gentleman
  vieux-jeu – *adj* old fashioned
vif, vive – *adj* lively, keen
vigne – *nf* vine
vigneron – *nm* vine grower
vigoureux, vigoureuse – *adj* vigorous
vignoble – *nm* vineyard
vilain – *adj* ugly, nasty, bad
village – *nm* village

ville – *nf* town, city
  ville touristique – tourist centre
  au centre de la ville – in the town centre
  en ville – in town
vin – *nm* wine
  vin blanc – white wine
  vin cuit – fortified wine
  vin ordinaire – table wine
  vin rosé – rosé wine
  vin rouge – red wine
vinaigre – *nm* vinegar
vinaigrette – *nf* French dressing
vingt – *adj* twenty
vingtaine – *nf* about twenty, a score
vingt et unième – *adj* twenty first
vingtième – *adj* twentieth
  au vingtième siècle – in the 20th century
vint – *see venir** § came
violence – *nf* violence
violet, violette – *adj* purple
violon – *nm* violin
  jouer du violon – *v reg* to play the violin
virage – *nm* turn, bend
virer – *v reg* to turn, turn round
virgule – *nf* comma (,)
visage – *nm* face
vis-à-vis – *adv* face to face
visibilité – *nf* visibility
visible – *adj* obvious, clear, visible
visiblement – *adv* clearly, obviously
visite – *nf* visit
  visite guidée – guided tour
  visite scolaire – school trip
visiter – *v reg* to visit (a place)
  rendre visite à – *v reg* to visit (a person)
visiteur, visiteuse – *nmf* visitor
visuel, visuelle – *adj* visual
vit – *see voir* § saw

---

vite – *adv* quickly, fast

vitesse – *nf* speed, gear

  à toute vitesse – at top speed

vitre – *nf* (pane of) glass

vitrine – *nf* shop window

vivant – *adj* living, alive

vivre – *v irreg* § to live

vocabulaire – *nm* vocabulary

vociférer – *v reg* † to scream

vœu – *nm* wish

  meilleurs vœux – best wishes

voici – *prep* here is, here are

  voici un an – a year ago

voie – *nf* track, lane

  voie d'accès – access road

  voie ferrée – railway

voilà – *prep* there is, there are

voile – *nf* sail

voile – *nm* veil

voilier – *nm* sailing ship

voir – *v irreg* § to see

  se voir* – *v refl* § to show, happen, meet

voire – *adv* even

voisin – *adj* nearby, neighbouring

voisin(e) – *nmf* neighbour

voisinage – *nm* neighbourhood

voit – *see voir* § sees

voiture – *nf* car, railway carriage

  voiture de tourisme – private car

voix – *nf* voice

vol – *nm* flight, theft

  vol à voile – gliding

  vol libre – free fall parachuting

volaille – *nf* poultry

volant – *nm* steering wheel

  cerf volant – *nm* kite

voler – *v reg* to fly

voler (à) – *v reg* to steal (from)

volet – *nm* shutter

voleur – *nm* thief

volley-ball – *nm* volleyball

volonté – *nf* will, wish, goodwill

volontiers – *adv* gladly

voltigeur, voltigeuse – *nmf* acrobat

vomir – *v reg* to vomit

vont – *see aller** § go, are going

votre (vos) – *poss adj* your

(le, la) vôtre, les vôtres – *pron* yours, your own

  à la vôtre – your health

vos (votre) – *poss adj* your

voudra – *see vouloir* § will want to

voudrait – would want to

vouloir – *v irreg* § to want (to)

  vouloir dire – to mean

  vouloir faire – to want to do

  qu'est-ce que ça veut dire? – what does that mean?

voulu – *see vouloir* § wanted to

voulut – *see vouloir* § wanted to

vous – *pron* you, to you

  vous-même(s) – yourself

voûte – *nf* archway, vault

voyage – *nm* journey

voyager – *v reg* † to travel

  voyager en autobus – to travel by bus

  voyager en avion – to fly

  voyager en car – to travel by coach

  voyager en voiture – to travel by car

  voyager par le train – to travel by train

voyageur, voyageuse – *nmf* traveller, passenger

voyons – *see voir* § see

voyons! – let's see, come on now!

voyou – *nm* hooligan

vrai – *adj* true

vraiment – *adv* really

vu – *pp voir* § seen

vue – *nf* view, sight

vulgaire – *adj* common, vulgar

W

wagon – *nm* railway carriage
  wagon-lit – *nm* sleeper
  wagon-restaurant – *nm* dining car
waters – *nmpl* toilet

Où sont les waters? – Where are the toilets?
WC – *nmpl* toilet
weekend – *nm* weekend
western – *nm* western
whisky – *nm* whisky

X

xénophobe – *adj* xenophobe, nationalist
xérès – *nm* sherry

Y

y – *adv* there
y – *pron* of it, of them, some
  ça y est! – that's it!
  il s'y connaît – he's an expert
  il y a – there is, there are
  il y en a deux, papa – there are two of them, Dad

y compris –including
yacht – *nm* yacht
yaourt – *nm* yoghurt
yeux – *nmpl* eyes (*sing* œil)
yoga – *nm* yoga

Z

zèbre – *nm* zebra
zéro – *nm* nil, nothing, zero
zone – *nf* area, zone
  zone bleue – controlled parking zone

zone industrielle – industrial area
zone piétonne – pedestrian precinct
zoo – *nm* zoo
zut! – *excl* blow! blast!

A

a – un *indef art m*
a – une *indef art f*
abandon – abandonner *v reg*
abbey – abbaye *nf*
able to – capable de *adj*
  be able to – pouvoir *v irreg* §
aboard – à bord *adv*
about – à propos de, au sujet de, autour, environ
about – vers, au sujet de *prep*
  be about to do – être sur le point de *v irreg* §
above – dessus *adv*
above – au-dessus de, par-dessus *prep*
above all – surtout *adv*
abroad – à l'étranger *adv*
absence – absence *nf*
absent – absent *adj*
absent-minded – distrait *adj*
absolute – absolu *adj*
absolutely – absolument *adv*
absurd – absurde *adj*
accent – accent *nm*
accept – accepter *v reg*
acceptable – admissible *adj*
access – accès *nm*
  access road – route d'accès *nf*
accident – accident *nm*
  by accident – par hasard *adv*
acclaim – acclamation *nf*
accommodation – hébergement *nm*, logement *nm*
accompany – accompagner *v reg*, aller* avec *v irreg* §
  accompanied by – accompagné de
accomplice – complice *nmf*
according to – d'après, selon *prep*
account – (financial) compte *nm*
account – (story) récit *nm*

on account of – à cause de
accountant – comptable *nmf*
accurate – précis *adj*, exact *adj*
accuse – accuser *v reg*
ace – as *nm*
ache – douleur *nf*, mal *nm*
  my head aches – ma tête me fait mal
acrobat – acrobate *nmf*
across – à travers, en face *adv*
  go across – traverser *v reg*
act – agir *v reg*
  act – (on stage) faire du théâtre *v irreg* §, jouer *v reg*
  be in the act of – être en train de *v irreg* §
active – actif, active *adj*
activity – activité *nf*
actor – (film) acteur *nm*
actress – (film) actrice *nf*
acute – aigu, aiguë *adj*
  acute accent (é) – accent aigu *nm*
add – ajouter *v reg*
  add up – faire le total *v irreg* §
address – adresse *nf*
  address – adresser *v reg*, s'adresser* à *v refl*
adjective – adjectif *nm*
admire – admirer *v reg*
adolescent – adolescent *nm*, adolescente *nf*
adopt – adopter *v reg*
adopted – adopté *adj*, adoptif, adoptive *adj*
adore – adorer *v reg*
adult – adulte *adj*
adult – adulte *nmf*
advance – avancer *v reg* †
advantage – advantage *nm*

---

prep - preposition   *v reg* - verb regular   *v refl* - verb reflexive   § - see verb tables
pp - past participle   *v irreg* - verb irregular   † - see verb information   * - takes être

advantageous – avantageux,
  avantageuse *adj*
adventure – aventure *nf*
  adventure film – film d'aventure *nm*
  adventure story – roman
  d'aventure *nm*
advert – (TV) pub *nf*
advertisement – publicité *nf*,
  annonce *nf*
advertising – publicité *nf*
advice – conseils *nmpl*
  piece of advice – conseil *nm*
aerial – antenne *nf*
aerobics – aérobic *nm*
aeroplane – avion *nm*
aerosol – bombe *nf,* atomiseur *nm*
affectionate – affectueux, affectueuse
  adj
afford – avoir les moyens d'acheter
  v irreg §
(be) afraid (of) – avoir peur (de)
  v irreg §
Africa – Afrique *nf*
African – africain *adj*
after – après *prep*
after all – après tout *adv*
afternoon – après-midi *nm inv*
afterwards – après, ensuite,
  par la suite *adv*
again – encore, encore une fois,
  de nouveau *adv*
against – contre *prep*
age – âge *nm*
aged – âgé *adj*
  15 years of age – âgé de quinze ans
agency – agence *nf*
agent – agent *nm*
aggressive – agressif, agressive *adj*
ago – il y a *adv*
  a long time ago – il y a longtemps
  a fortnight ago – il y a une
  quinzaine
agreeable – agréable *adj*

agree – s'entendre*(avec) *v refl*, se
  mettre*d'accord (avec) *v refl* §, être
  d'accord *v irreg* §
agreed – convenu, entendu, prévu *adj*
agricultural – agricole *adj*
air – air *nm*
  air conditioned – climatisé *adj*
  air conditioning – climatisation *nf*
  air force – armée de l'air *nf*
  air hostess – hôtesse de l'air *nf*
  be on the air – être à l'antenne
    v irreg §
  by air mail – par avion
  in the open air – en plein air
airbed – matelas pneumatique *nm*
aircraft – avion *nm*
airport – aéroport *nm*
  airport building – aérogare *nf*
air sickness – mal de l'air *nm*
alarm clock – réveil *nm*
  set the alarm – mettre le réveil
    v irreg §
alas! – hélas! *excl*
alcohol – alcool *nm*
A level – baccalauréat *nm*
algebra – algèbre *nf*
Algeria – Algérie *nf*
Algerian – algérien, algérienne *adj*
Algerian person – Algérien *nm*,
  Algérienne *nf*
alive – vivant *adj*
all – tout, toute, tous, toutes *adj, pron*
  all included – tout compris
  all of us – nous tous
  all over – (everywhere) partout *adv*
  all over – (finished) fini *adj*
  all sorts of – toutes sortes de
  all the same – tout de même *adv*
  all the time – tout le temps
  all year round – toute l'année
allow – permettre *v irreg* §,
  tolérer *v reg* †, accorder *v reg*
allowance – allocation *nf*

---

nm - noun masculine	*nmpl* - noun masculine plural	*adj* - adjective	*conj* - conjunction
nf - noun feminine	*nfpl* - noun feminine plural	*adv* - adverb	*pron* - pronoun

almost – presque, à peu près *adv*
alone – seul *adj*
  alone – tout seul
along – le long de *prep*
aloud – à haute voix *adv*
alphabet – alphabet *nm*
Alps – les Alpes *nfpl*
already – déjà *adv*
alright! – d'accord, entendu! *excl*
also – aussi *adv*
alter - changer *v reg* †
altogether – complètement,
  tout à fait *adv*
always – toujours *adv*
am – suis *see* être *v irreg* §
a.m. – du matin
amazed – étonné *adj*, surpris *adj*
  be amazed – être étonné *v irreg* §
ambulance – ambulance *nf*
America – Amérique *nf*
American – américain *adj*
American – (person) Américain *nm*,
  Américaine *nf*
among – entre, parmi *prep*
  among friends – entre amis
amount – quantité *nf*, somme *nf*
amuse – amuser *v reg*
amusement – divertissement *nm*
amusement park – parc
  d'attractions *nm*
amusement arcade – galerie de
  jeux électroniques *nf*
amusing – amusant *adj*
an – un *indef art m*
an – une *indef art f*
ancient – ancien, ancienne,
  antique *adj*
ancient history – histoire ancienne
  nf
and – et *conj*
anger – colère *nf*, rage *nf*
angling – pêche à la ligne *nf*

go angling – pêcher à la ligne
  v reg
angry – en colère *adj*, enragé *adj*,
  fâché *adj*
  get angry – se mettre* en colère
  v irreg §, se fâcher* *v refl*
animal – animal *nm* (animaux *nmpl*),
  bête *nf*
ankle – cheville *nf*
  to sprain one's ankle – se
  fouler* la cheville *v refl*
anniversary – anniversaire *nm*
announce – annoncer *v reg* †
annoy – agacer *v reg* †, embêter,
  énerver *v reg*, ennuyer *v reg* †
annoying – embêtant *adj*, fâcheux,
  fâcheuse *adj*, ennuyeux,
  ennuyeuse *adj*
annual – annuel, annuelle *adj*
anorak – anorak *nm*
another – autre *pron*
answer – répondre *v reg*
answer – réponse *nf*
  right answer – la bonne réponse *nf*
answering machine – répondeur *nm*
anti- – anti- *pref*
antibiotic – antibiotique *nm*
antibiotic – antibiotique *adj*
antiseptic – antiseptique *nm*
antiseptic – antiseptique *adj*
anxious – inquiet, inquiète *adj*
any – n'importe quel(le) *pron*
  any – (some) du, de la, de l', des *art*
  any – (not) de, d'
  any – (every) tout *adj*
  anybody – quelqu'un, n'importe
  qui *pron*
  is there anyone there? – il y a
  quelqu'un?
  anyhow – de toute façon, en tout
  cas *adv*
  anyone – quelqu'un, n'importe qui
  pron

---

anything – n'importe quoi, quelque chose *pron*
anything else? – et avec ça?
anyway – en tout cas, de toute façon
anywhere – n'importe où *adv*
apartment – appartement *nm*
apart from – excepté, à part
aperitif – (pre-meal drink) apéritif *nm*
apologise – faire des excuses *v irreg* §
apologise for – s'excuser* de *v refl*
appalling – épouvantable *adj*
appear – apparaître *v irreg* §
appearance – apparence *nf,* apparition *nf*
appendicitis – appendicite *nf*
appetite – appétit *nm*
appetizing – appétissant *adj*
applause – applaudissement *nm*
apple – pomme *nf*
  apple tart – tarte aux pommes *nf*
  apple tree – pommier *nm*
appliance – appareil *nm*
apply to – s'adresser à* *v refl*
appointment – rendez-vous *nm*
appreciate – apprécier *v reg*
apprentice – apprenti *nm,* apprentie *nf*
apprenticeship – apprentissage *nm*
approach – approche *nf,* accès *nm*
approach – (person) aborder *v reg*
approach – s'approcher* de *v refl*
approachable – accessible *adj*
approachable – (person) abordable *adj*
approve of – approuver *v reg*
approximately – à peu près, environ *adv*
apricot – abricot *nm*
April – avril *nm*
  April fool – poisson d'avril *nm*
apron – tablier *nm*

arcade – (shops) galerie *nf*
archery – tir à l'arc *nm*
architect – architecte *nmf*
are – *see* être *v irreg* §
area – (district) quartier *nm*
area – région *nf,* zone *nf*
area – aire *nf*
  parking area – aire de parking *nf*
  picnic area – aire de pique-nique *nf*
  rest area – aire de repos *nf*
aren't – (are not) *see* être *v irreg* §
argue – se disputer* *v refl*
argument – discussion *nf,* dispute *nf*
arithmetic – arithmétique *nf*
arm – bras *nm*
armband – bracelet *nm,* brassard *nm*
armchair – fauteuil *nm*
army – armée *nf*
around – autour *adv*
  around – autour de *prep*
  around here – par ici
arrange – arranger *v reg* †
arrange – (a time, date) fixer *v reg*
  arrange to meet – prendre rendez-vous *v irreg* §
arrest – arrêter *v reg*
arrival – arrivée *nf*
arrive – arriver* *v reg*
arrow – flèche *nf*
art – dessin *nm,* art *nm*
art gallery – musée (des beaux arts) *nm,* galerie d'art *nf*
art school – école des beaux arts *nf*
artful – rusé *adj*
article – article *nm*
article of clothing – vêtement *nm*
artist – artiste *nmf*
as – (while) pendant que *conj*
  as – comme, puisque *conj*
  as agreed – comme prévu
  as ... as – aussi ... que *adv*

nm - noun masculine	*nmpl* - noun masculine plural	*adj* - adjective	*conj* - conjunction
nf - noun feminine	*nfpl* - noun feminine plural	*adv* - adverb	*pron* - pronoun

as far as – jusqu'à *prep*
as for me – quant à moi *prep*
as if – comme si *adv*
as much, as many – autant *adv*
as soon as – aussitôt que,
  dès que *conj*
as well – aussi *adv*
ashamed – honteux, honteuse *adj*
  be ashamed (of) – avoir honte
  (de) *v irreg* §
ashtray – cendrier *nm*
Asia – Asie *nf*
Asian – asiatique *adj*
aside from – à part, de côté *adv*
ask a question – poser une question
  v reg
ask for – demander *v reg*
  ask for information – demander
  des renseignements *v reg*
  ask s.o. to do sthg – demander à
  quelqu'un de faire quelque chose
  v reg
  ask for the bill – (restaurant)
  demander l'addition *v reg*
  ask for the bill – (hotel) demander
  la note *v reg*
ask – (invite) inviter *v reg*
ask about – se renseigner* sur *v refl*
asleep – endormi *adj*
  fall asleep – s'endormir* *v refl*
aspirin – aspirine *nf*
assembly – assemblée *nf*
assignment – (piece of work)
  devoir *nm*, tâche *nf*
assist – aider *v reg*
assistance – secours *nm*
assistant – (shop) vendeur *nm*,
  vendeuse *nf*
assure – assurer *v reg*
asthma – asthme *nm*
astonish – étonner *v reg*
at – à *prep*
  at last – enfin *adv*

at my house – chez moi
at once – tout de suite
at times – parfois
at the... – chez le...
at the bottom of the page –
  au bas de la page
at the end of – à la fin de
at the same time as – en même
  temps que
at top speed – à toute vitesse
ate – *see eat*
athlete – athlète *nmf*
athletic – sportif, sportive *adj*
athletics – athlétisme *nm*
Atlantic Ocean – Océan Atlantique
  nm
atmosphere – ambiance *nf*
attach – attacher *v reg*
attack – attentat *nm*
attack – attaquer *v reg*
attempt – tenter *v reg*
attend – assister à *v reg*, aller* à
  (school) *v irreg* §
attention – attention *nf*
attic – mansarde *nf*
attract – attirer *v reg*
attractive – beau, bel, belle *adj*
auburn – roux, rousse *adj*
August – août *nm*
aunt – tante *nf*
Australia – Australie *nf*
Austria – Autriche *nf*
Austrian – autrichien,
  autrichienne *adj*
author – auteur *nm*
authorities – autorités *nfpl*
automatic – automatique *adj*
automatically – machinalement *adv*
autumn – automne *nm*
  during autumn – pendant
  l'automne
  in autumn – en automne
available – disponible *adj*

---

prep - preposition	*v reg* - verb regular	*v refl* - verb reflexive	§ - see verb tables
pp - past participle	*v irreg* - verb irregular	† - see verb information	* - takes être

avenue – avenue *nf*
average – moyen, moyenne *adj*
avocado pear – avocat *nm*
avoid – éviter *v reg*
away – (not at school) absent
   away – (on holiday) en vacances
   be away – s'absenter* *v refl*
   go away – partir* *v irreg*

go away! – allez-vous-en!, va-t'en!
10 kilometres away – à une
   distance de dix kilomètres
away game – match à l'extérieur
   nm
awful – affreux, affreuse *adj*
awkward – embêtant *adj*

B

B & B – chambre d'hôte *nf*
baby – (both sexes) bébé *nm*
   go babysitting – faire du
   babysitting *v irreg* §
back – (returned) rentré *adj*
   back – (come) revenir* *v irreg* §
   back – (reverse a car) reculer *v reg*
back – fond *nm*
   at the back of – au fond de
back – (vehicle) arrière *nm*
back – (footballer) arrière *nm*
at the back of – à l'arrière de
back – (body) dos *nm*
back pack – sac à dos *nm*
backwards – en arrière *adv*
   go backwards and forwards –
   aller* et venir* *v irreg* §
bacon – bacon *nm*, lard *nm*
bad – mauvais *adj*, vilain *adj*
   too bad – tant pis *adv*
bad – (ill) malade *adj*
bad – (serious) grave *adj*
bad – (wicked) méchant *adj*
bad-tempered – de mauvaise
   humeur *adj*
badge – badge *nm*
badly – mal *adv*
badminton – badminton *nm*

bag – sac *nm*
baker – boulanger *nm*, boulangère *nf*
baker's shop – boulangerie *nf*
balcony – balcon *nm*
bald – chauve *adj*
ball – (football) ballon *nm*
ball – (golf, tennis) balle *nf*
ball-point pen – stylo à bille *nm*
balloon – ballon *nm*
banana – banane *nf*
band – orchestre *nm*
bang – coup *nm*
banger – (car) bagnole *nf*,
   guimbarde *nf sl*
banger – (firework) pétard *nm*
banger – (sausage) saucisse *nf*
Bangladesh – Bangladesh *nm*
Bangladeshi – du Bangladesh *adj*
Bangladeshi person – habitant du
   Bangladesh *nm*, habitante du
   Bangladesh *nf*
bank – (river) bord *nm*
bank – banque *nf*
banker's card – carte bancaire *nf*
bank holiday – jour férié *nm*
bank note – billet de banque *nm*
bar – (pub) bar *nm*
bar – (of chocolate) tablette *nf*

---

nm - noun masculine   *nmpl* - noun masculine plural   *adj* - adjective   *conj* - conjunction
nf - noun feminine   *nfpl* - noun feminine plural   *adv* - adverb   *pron* - pronoun

barbecue – barbecue *nm*
barber – coiffeur *nm*
bare – (empty) vide *adj*
bare – (not covered) nu, nue *adj*
barefoot – pieds nus
bare-headed – nu-tête
bargain – prix intéressant *nm*, occasion *nf*
barmaid – serveuse *nf*
barman – serveur *nm*
barn – grange *nf*
base – base *nf*
   based on – à base de, basé sur
basement – sous-sol *nm*
basically – au fond, dans le fond *adv*
basin – (wash) lavabo *nm*
basket – corbeille *nf*, panier *nm*
basketball – basket *nm*
bat – (table tennis, etc) raquette *nf*
bath – (tub) baignoire *nf*
bath – (wash) bain *nm*
   have a bath – prendre un bain *v irreg* §
bath salts – sels de bain *nmpl*
bathe – se baigner* *v refl*
bathing – baignade *nf*
bathing trunks – caleçon de bain *nm*, maillot de bain *nm*
bathroom – salle de bains *nf*
battery – (car) batterie *nf*
battery – (torch) pile *nf*
battle – bataille *nf*
bay – baie *nf*
be – être *v irreg* §
   be able to – pouvoir *v irreg* §
   be afraid – avoir peur *v irreg* §
   be amazed – être étonné* *v irreg* §
   be ashamed – avoir honte *v irreg* §
   be at – assister à *v reg*
   be aware of – se rendre compte* *v refl*
   be better – mieux aller* *v irreg* §

be bored – s'ennuyer* *v refl* †
be born – naître* *v irreg* §
be busy – être occupé *v irreg* §
be careful – être prudent *v irreg* §
be careful! – soyez prudent(s)!
be cold – (person) avoir froid *v irreg* §
be cold – (weather) faire froid *v irreg* §
be fine – (weather) faire beau *v irreg* §
be fit – être en forme *v irreg* §
be good at – être fort(e) en *v irreg* §
be hot – (person) avoir chaud *v irreg* §
be hot – (weather) faire chaud *v irreg* §
be hungry – avoir faim *v irreg* §
be ill – mal aller* *v irreg* §
be in a hurry – être pressé *v irreg* §
be in detention – être en retenue *v irreg* §
be interested in – s'intéresser* à *v refl*
be keen on – être passionné de *v irreg* §
be likely to – risquer *v reg*
be lucky – avoir de la chance *v irreg* §
be mistaken – se tromper* *v refl*
be obliged to – être obligé de *v irreg* §
be on stage – être en scène *v irreg* §
be on television – passer* à la télévision *v reg*
be on the radio – passer* à la radio *v reg*
be on the staff – faire partie du personnel *v irreg* §
be out of breath – être à bout de souffle *v irreg* §
be parked – stationner *v reg*

---

prep - preposition   *v reg* - verb regular   *v refl* - verb reflexive   § - see verb tables
pp - past participle   *v irreg* - verb irregular   † - see verb information   * - takes être

be quiet! – tais-toi! taisez-vous!
be right – avoir raison *v irreg* §
be situated – se trouver* *v refl*
be sleepy – avoir sommeil *v irreg* §
be sorry – regretter *v reg*
be thirsty – avoir soif *v irreg* §
be up – (out of bed) être levé
  v irreg §, être debout *v irreg* §
be well – bien aller* *v irreg* §
be warm – (weather) faire beau
  v irreg §
be worried – s'inquiéter* *v refl* †
be wrong – avoir tort *v irreg* §
beach – plage *nf*
  on the beach – sur la plage
bean – ‡haricot *nm*
bear – ours *nm*
beard – barbe *nf*
bearded – barbu *adj*
beat – battre *v reg*
beaten – battu *adj*, vaincu *adj*
beautiful – beau, bel, belle *adj*
beauty – beauté *nf*
because – parce que *conj*
because of – à cause de *prep*
become – devenir* *v irreg* §
bed – lit *nm*
  air bed – matelas pneumatique *nm*
  camp bed – lit de camp *nm*
  double bed – lit de deux personnes
  nm
  flower bed – parterre *nm*
  go to bed – se coucher* *v refl*
  make the bed – faire le lit
  v irreg §
  single bed – lit d'une personne *nm*
bedding – literie *nf*
bedroom – chambre *nf*
bedside table – table de chevet *nf*
bed-sit – studio *nm*
bedtime – heure du coucher *nf*
bee – abeille *nf*
beef – bœuf *nm*

beefburger – hamburger *nm*
beefsteak – bifteck *nm*
minced beef – bifteck haché *nm*
been – été *see* être *v irreg* §
beer – bière *nf*
before – (time) avant *prep*
before – (place) devant *prep*
  before leaving – avant de partir
  the day before yesterday –
  avant-hier
  the day before – veille *nf*
beg – demander *v reg*
begin – commencer *v reg* †
beginner – débutant *nm,* débutante *nf*
begin again – recommencer *v reg* †
beginning – début *nm*
  at the beginning – au début de
behave – se conduire* *v refl* §
behind – derrière *prep*
behind – (late) en retard
  leave behind – oublier *v reg*
Belgian – belge *adj*
Belgian person – Belge *nmf*
Belgium – Belgique *nf*
believe – croire *v irreg* §
  believed – cru *see croire v irreg* §
bell – (in church) cloche *nf*
bell – (on door) sonnette *nf*
bell – (in school) sonnerie *nf*
belong to – (be member of) être
  membre de *v irreg* §
belong to – (own) appartenir à
  v irreg §
belongings – (things) affaires *nfpl*
below – en bas, en dessous *adv*
belt – ceinture *nf*
  seat belt – ceinture de sécurité *nf*
bench – banc *nm*
bend – (in road) virage *nm*, tournant *nm*
bend over – se pencher* *v refl*
beneath – sous *prep*
benefit – allocation *nf*

beside – à part *adv*
besides – en plus de *prep*
best – le mieux *adv*
best – le meilleur, la meilleure *adj*
   best wishes – meilleurs vœux *nmpl*
   do one's best – faire de son mieux
    v irreg §
bet – parier *v reg*
better – meilleur *adj*, mieux *adv*
   be better – mieux aller* *v irreg* §
   get better – se remettre* *v refl* §
between – entre *prep*
   between you and me – entre
   nous
bicycle – bicyclette *nf*
bidet – bidet *nm*
big – grand *adj*, gros, grosse *adj*
bigger than – plus grand que
bike – vélo *nm*
   go for a bike ride – faire une
   promenade à bicyclette *v irreg* §
bike – faire de la bicyclette *v irreg* §
biker – motard *nm*
bikini – bikini *nm*
bilingual – bilingue *adj*
bill – (restaurant) addition *nf*
bin – poubelle *nf*
bingo – loto *nm*
biology – biologie *nf*, sciences
   naturelles *nfpl*
bird – oiseau *nm*
biro® – stylo à bille *nm*
birth – naissance *nf*
   birth certificate – extrait de
   naissance *nm*
   date of birth – date de naissance
   nf
birthday – anniversaire *nm*
   birthday cake – gâteau
   d'anniversaire *nm*
   birthday card – carte
   d'anniversaire *nf*

birthday present – cadeau
   d'anniversaire *nm*
biscuit – biscuit *nm*
bite – mordre *v reg*
bite – (mosquito) piqûre *nf*
bite – (insect) piquer *v reg*
bitter – amer, amère *adj*
black – noir *adj*
   black coffee – café *nm*
   black ice – verglas *nm*
blackberry – mûre *nf*
blackboard – tableau noir *nm*
blackcurrant – cassis *nm*
blame – accuser *v reg*, reprocher
   v reg, donner tort à *v reg*
blame – reproche *nm*
blanket – couverture *nf*
blast! – zut! *excl*
bless you! – à vos souhaits!
blind – (not seeing) aveugle *adj*
blind – (at window) store *nm*
blister – ampoule *nf*
block – bloc *nm*
   block of flats – immeuble *nm*
block – bloquer *v reg*
blockbuster – film à gros succès *nm*
bloke – mec *nm sl*, type *nm sl*
blonde – blond *adj*
blood – sang *nm*
blouse – chemisier *nm*, corsage *nm*
blouson jacket – blouson *nm*
blow – coup *nm*
blow – (wind) souffler *v reg*
blow one's nose – se moucher* *v refl*
blow the horn – (car) klaxonner
   v reg
blow up – (inflate) gonfler *v reg*
blow! – zut! *excl*
blue – bleu *adj*
   navy blue – bleu marine *adj inv*
board – panneau *nm*, tableau *nm*

board – pension *nf*
  full board – pension complète *nf*
  half board – demi-pension *nf*
board – (at school) être en pension *v irreg* §
board a ship – monter* à bord *v reg*
  on board – à bord
board game – jeu de societé *nm*
boarder – (school) pensionnaire *nmf*
boarding school – pensionnat *nm*, pension *nf*
boast – se vanter* *v refl*
boat – bateau *nm*
  boat trip – promenade en bateau *nf*
body – corps *nm*
boil water – faire bouillir de l'eau *v irreg* §
boil, be boiling – bouillir *v irreg* §
boiled egg – œuf à la coque *nm*
bold – audacieux, audacieuse *adj*
bomb – bombe *nf*
  bomb scare – alerte à la bombe *nf*
bone – os *nm*
bonfire – feu de joie *nm*
bonnet – (car) capot *nm*
book – livre *nm*
  sci-fi book – livre de science-fiction *nm*
book – carnet *nm*
  book of stamps – carnet de timbres *nm*
  book of tickets – (bus, metro) carnet de tickets *nm*
book a seat – réserver une place *v reg*
book case – bibliothèque *nf*
booked – réservé *adj*
  fully booked – complet *adj*
booking office – guichet *nm*
booklet – brochure *nf*, livret *nm*
bookshelf – rayon à livres *nm*, étagère *nf*
bookshop – librairie *nf*
boot (of car) – coffre *nm*

boot – botte *nf*, chaussure montante *nf*
  football boots – chaussures de football *nfpl*
  ski-boots – chaussures de ski *nfpl*
  walking boots – chaussures de marche *nfpl*
booze – beaucoup boire *v irreg* §
booze – alcool *nm*
border – (country) frontière *nf*
border – (flower) plate-bande *nf*, bordure *nf*
bore – ennuyer *v reg* †
  to be bored – s'ennuyer* *v refl* †
boredom – ennui *nm*
boring – ennuyeux, ennuyeuse *adj*
born – né, née *see naître v irreg* §
  be born – naître *v irreg* §
  born on ... – né, née, le...
borrow (from) – emprunter (à) *v reg*
boss – patron *nm*, chef *nm*
bossy – autoritaire *adj*
both – (tous) les deux, (toutes) les deux *pron*
bother – (annoy) embêter *v reg*
bother – (disturb) déranger *v reg* †
bottle – bouteille *nf*
bottle opener – décapsuleur *nm*, ouvre-bouteille *nm*
bottom of class – dernier, dernière *adj*
bottom – fond, bas *nm*
  at the bottom of the page – au bas de la page
  at the bottom of – au fond de
bought – acheté *see acheter v reg* †
bow – (archery) arc *nm*
bow tie – nœud papillon *nm*
bowl – (dish) bol *nm*
bowl – (cricket) lancer *v reg* †
bowling alley – bowling *nm*
bowls – boules *nfpl*
  play bowls – jouer aux boules *v reg*

---

nm - noun masculine   *nmpl* - noun masculine plural   *adj* - adjective   *conj* - conjunction
nf - noun feminine   *nfpl* - noun feminine plural   *adv* - adverb   *pron* - pronoun

box – boîte *nf*
box – boxer *v reg*
boxing – boxe *nf*
boy – garçon *nm*
boy friend – petit ami *nm*
bra – soutien-gorge *nm*
bracelet – bracelet *nm*
brackets – parenthèses *nfpl*
brain – cerveau *nm*
brake – frein *nm*
brake – freiner *v reg*
branch – branche *nf*
brand name – marque *nf*
brand new – neuf, neuve *adj*
brave – courageux, courageuse *adj*
bread – pain *nm*
bread and butter – tartine *nf*
break – briser *v reg*, casser *v reg*,
    rompre *v irreg* §
break one's leg – se casser* la
    jambe *v refl*
break down – tomber* en panne
    v reg
break in – cambrioler *v reg*
break – (between lessons) récréation
    nf
break up – (school) commencer les
    vacances *v reg* †
breakdown – panne *nf*
breakdown lorry – voiture de
    dépannage *nf*
breakfast – petit déjeuner *nm*
    have breakfast – prendre le petit
    déjeuner *v irreg* §
breath – haleine *nf*
    out of breath – hors d'haleine *adj*
breathe – respirer *v reg*
breed – race *nf*
Breton – breton, bretonne *adj*
brick – brique *nf*
brick – en brique *adj*
bricklayer – maçon *nm*
bride – mariée *nf*

bridegroom – marié *nm*
bridesmaid – demoiselle d'honneur
    nf
bridge – pont *nm*
brief – (short) bref, brève *adj*
briefcase – serviette *nf*
briefs – (underwear) slip *nm*
bright – (clever) intelligent *adj*
bright – (shining) brillant *adj*
bring – (someone) amener *v reg* †
bring – (something) apporter *v reg*
bring back – (person) ramener
    v reg †
bring back – (thing) rapporter *v reg*
bring up – (children) élever *v reg* †
British – britannique *adj*
British person – Britannique *nmf*
Brittany – Bretagne *nf*
broad – large *adj*
broadcast – transmission *nf*
broadcast – diffuser *v reg*
brochure – brochure *nf*, dépliant *nm*
broke – (without money) fauché *adj sl*
    I'm broke – je n'ai pas le sou
broken – cassé *adj*
broken down – en panne *adj*
broom – balai *nm*
brother – frère *nm*
brother-in-law – beau-frère *nm*
brown – brun, brune *adj*,
    marron *adj inv*
bruise – bleu *nm*
brush – brosser *v reg*
brush – brosse *nf*
    brush one's hair – se brosser* les
    cheveux *v refl*
Brussels – Bruxelles
    Brussels sprout – chou de
    Bruxelles *nm*
bucket – seau *nm*
budgerigar – perruche *nf*

---

buffet – buffet *nm*

build – bâtir *v reg*, construire *v irreg* §

builder – maçon *nm*

building – bâtiment *nm*

bull – taureau *nm*

bumbag – sac banane *nm*

bump – (swelling) bosse *nf*

bump – (knock) choc *nm*

bump into – ‡heurter *v reg*

   bump into – ‡se heurter* à *v refl*

bump into – (meet) rencontrer *v reg*

bump o.s. – se cogner* *v refl*

bumper – pare-chocs *nm inv*

bunch of flowers – bouquet *nm*

bunch of grapes – grappe de raisin *nf*

bunch of radishes – botte de radis *nf*

bungalow – bungalow *nm*

burglar – cambrioleur *nm*

burgle – cambrioler *v reg*

burn – brûlure *nf*

burn – brûler *v reg*

   burn o.s. – se brûler* *v refl*

   burn one's fingers – se brûler* les doigts *v refl*

burst – crever *v reg* †

burst out laughing – éclater de rire *v reg*

bus – autobus *nm*, bus *nm*

   catch the bus – prendre l'autobus *v irreg* §

bus service – ligne d'autobus *nf*

bus stop – arrêt d'autobus *nm*

bush – buisson *nm*

business – affaires *nfpl*, commerce *nm*

business man – homme d'affaires *nm*

business woman – femme d'affaires *nf*

busy – occupé *adj*

but – mais *conj*

butcher – boucher *nm*, bouchère *nf*

butcher's shop – boucherie *nf*

butter – beurre *nm*

butterfly – papillon *nm*

button – bouton *nm*

buy – acheter *v reg* †

   buy software – acheter un logiciel *v reg* †

by – par, en *prep*

   by bus – en autobus

   by car – en voiture

   by coach – en car

   by day – de jour

   by the day – à la journée

   by the hour – à l'heure

   by the kilo – au kilo

bypass – (road) rocade *nf*

---

nm - noun masculine	*nmpl* - noun masculine plural	*adj* - adjective	*conj* - conjunction
nf - noun feminine	*nfpl* - noun feminine plural	*adv* - adverb	*pron* - pronoun

C

cabbage – chou *nm* (*pl* choux)

cable – câble *nm*

  cable car – téléphérique *nm*

  cable TV – télévision cablée *nf*

café – café *nm*

café terrace – terrasse de café *nf*

cage – cage *nf*

cagoule – K-way® *nm*

cake – gâteau *nm*, pâtisserie *nf*

  cake shop – pâtisserie *nf*

  birthday cake – gâteau
    d'anniversaire *nm*

calculate – calculer *v reg*

calculator – calculatrice *nf*,
  calculette *nf*

calendar – calendrier *nm*

calf – veau *nm*

call – appel *nm*

call – appeler *v reg* †

  call – (phone) téléphoner à *v reg*,
    passer un coup de fil à *v reg*

  call the register – faire l'appel
    v irreg §

  be called – s'appeler* *v refl* †

call box – cabine téléphonique *nf*

call for – (friend) passer* prendre
  v reg

calm – calme *adj*

calm o.s. down – se calmer* *v refl*

camcorder – caméscope *nm*

came – *see venir v irreg* §

camel – chameau *nm*

camembert cheese – camembert *nm*

camera – appareil-photo *nm*

camp – camper *v reg*

  camp-fire – feu de camp *nm*

  camper – campeur *nm*

  camping carnet – carnet de
    camping *nm*

campsite – camping *nm*, terrain de
  camping *nm*

go camping – faire du camping
  v irreg §

can – (tin) boîte *nf*

  can-opener – ouvre-boîte(s) *nm*

can – (know how to) savoir *v irreg* §

can – (be able to) pouvoir *v irreg* §

  can I? – puis-je?

  I can't – je ne peux pas

Canada – Canada *nm*

Canadian – canadien, canadienne *adj*

Canadian person – Canadien *nm*,
  Canadienne *nm*

canary – canari *nm*

cancel – annuler *v reg*

cancer – cancer *nm*

candidate – candidat *nm*, candidate *nf*

candle – bougie *nf*

candy floss – barbe à papa *nf*

canoe – canoë *nm*

canoe – faire du canoë *v irreg* §

canteen – cantine *nf*, réfectoire *nm*

cap – casquette *nf*

capable – capable *adj*

capital – (city) capitale *nf*

capital letter – lettre majuscule *nf*

captain – capitaine *nm*

car –voiture *nf*, auto *nf*

  car ferry – ferry *nm*

  car hire – location de voitures *nf*

  car key – clé de voiture *nf*

  car park – parking *nm*

  car phone – téléphone de voiture
    nm

  car seat – banquette *nf*

  car wash – station de lavage *nf*,
    lave-auto *nm*

  by car – en voiture *nf*

caravan – caravane *nf*

---

prep - preposition	*v reg* - verb regular	*v refl* - verb reflexive	§ - see verb tables
pp - past participle	*v irreg* - verb irregular	† - see verb information	* - takes être

card – carte *nf*
  credit card – carte de crédit *nf*
  identity card – carte d'identité *nf*
  post card – carte postale *nf*
  play cards – jouer aux cartes *v reg*
care – attention *nf*
  care about – s'intéresser* à *v refl*
  care for – soigner *v reg*
career – carrière *nf*
  careers advice – orientation
  professionnelle *nf*
careful – prudent *adj*
  be careful – faire attention *v irreg* §
careful with money – économe *adj*
carefully – avec attention,
  soigneusement *adv*
careless – imprudent *adj*
caretaker – concierge *nmf*
carpet – tapis *nm*
carpet – (fitted) moquette *nf*
carrot – carotte *nf*
carry – porter *v reg*
carry on – continuer *v reg*
cartoon – (drawing) dessin *nm*
cartoon – (cinema) dessin animé *nm*
cartoon strip – BD *nf*, bande
  dessinée *nf*
case – cas *nm*
case – (luggage) valise *nf*
  pack the cases – faire les valises
  v irreg §
cash – (money) argent *nm*
  cash – (not a cheque) argent liquide
  nm
  cash a cheque – encaisser un
  chèque *v reg*
  cash desk – caisse *nf*
  go to the cash desk – passer* à la
  caisse *v reg*
  cash machine – (dispenser)
  distributeur de billets *nm*
cashier – caissier *nm*, caissière *nf*
cassette – cassette *nf*

video cassette – vidéo *nf*
cassette recorder – magnétophone *nm*
castle – château *nm*
cat – chat *nm*, chatte *nf*
catch – prendre *v irreg* §
  catch – (fish, etc) attraper *v reg*
  catch cold – attraper un rhume
  v reg
  catch the number three bus –
  prenez la ligne numéro trois
  catch up with – rattraper *v reg*
cathedral – cathédrale *nf*
Catholic – catholique *adj*
cauliflower – chou-fleur *nm*
  (*pl* choux-fleurs)
cause – cause *nf*, raison *nf*
  cause an accident – causer un
  accident *v reg*
  cause stress – stresser *v reg*
cave – caverne *nf*
CD – disque compact *nm*
CD player – platine-laser *nf*
CD ROM – cédérom *nm,* disque
  optique compact *nm*
CDT – EMT (éducation manuelle et
  technique) *nf*
cedilla (ç) – cédille *nf*
ceiling – plafond *nm*
celebrate – fêter *v reg*
celebration – fête *nf*
celebrity – personnage célèbre *nm*
celery – céleri *nm*
cellar – cave *nf*
cello – violoncelle *nm*
  play the cello – jouer du
  violoncelle *v reg*
centime – centime *nm*
centimetre – centimètre *nm*
central heating – chauffage central *nm*
centre – centre *nm*
century – siècle *nm*
cereal – céréale *nf*
certain – certain *adj*, sûr *adj*

---

nm - noun masculine	*nmpl* - noun masculine plural	*adj* - adjective	*conj* - conjunction
nf - noun feminine	*nfpl* - noun feminine plural	*adv* - adverb	*pron* - pronoun

certainly – bien sûr, certainement, volontiers *adv*
certificate – brevet *nm*
chair – (armchair) fauteuil *nm*
champagne – champagne *nm*
champion – champion *nm*, championne *nf*
championship – championnat *nm*
chance – occasion *nf*
chance – ‡hasard *nm*
  by chance – par hasard
change – changement *nm*
change of clothes – vêtements de rechange *nmpl*
change – (coins) monnaie *nf*
  have you any change? – avez-vous de la monnaie?
change – changer *v reg* †
change – (exchange) échanger *v reg* †
change – (alter) transformer (en) *v reg*
change clothes – changer de vêtements *v reg* †
change gear – changer de vitesse *v reg* †
change money – changer de l'argent *v reg* †
change one's mind – changer d'avis *v reg* †, se raviser* *v refl*
changeable – variable *adj*
changing-room – (sport) vestiaire *nm*
changing-room – (shop) cabine d'essayage *nf*
channel – (TV) chaîne *nf*
Channel Islands – îles Anglo-Normandes *nfpl*
Channel Tunnel – tunnel sous la Manche *nm*
  English Channel – Manche *nf*
chap – type *nm sl*, mec *nm sl*
chapter – chapitre *nm*
character – caractère *nm*
character – (drama) personnage *nm*
charge – prix *nm*

charge card – carte d'achat *nf*
charming – charmant *adj*
chase – chasser *v reg*, poursuivre *v irreg* §
chat – causer *v reg*, bavarder *v reg*
cheap – bon marché *adj inv*
cheat – tricher *v reg*
check – contrôler *v reg*, vérifier *v reg*
  check the oil level – vérifier le niveau d'huile *v reg*
  check tickets – contrôler les billets *v reg*
  check the tyre pressures – vérifier la pression des pneus *v reg*
  check the water level – vérifier le niveau d'eau *v reg*
checked – à carreaux *adj*
cheek – (face) joue *nf*
cheerful – gai, gaie *adj*
cheerfully – gaîment *adv*
cheese – fromage *nm*
  cheese sandwich – sandwich au fromage *nm*
chemist – pharmacien *nm*, pharmacienne *nf*
chemistry – chimie *nf*
chemist's shop – pharmacie *nf*
cheque – chèque *nm*
  cheque book – carnet de chèques *nm*
  cheque card – carte bancaire *nf*
  cash a cheque – toucher un chèque *v reg*
cherry – cerise *nf*
chess – échecs *nmpl*
  play chess – jouer aux échecs *v reg*
chest – (body) poitrine *nf*
chest – (box) coffre *nm*
chest of drawers – commode *nf*
chicken – poulet *nm*
chief – chef *nm*, patron *nm*
child – enfant *nmf*

only child – enfant unique *nmf*
childhood – enfance *nf*
child-minder – nourrice *nf*
chimney – cheminée *nf*
chin – menton *nm*
China – Chine *nf*
Chinese – chinois *adj*
Chinese person – Chinois *nm*, Chinoise *nf*
chip – (micro) puce *nf*
chips – frites *nfpl*
chocolate – chocolat *nm*
    chocolate ice cream – glace au chocolat *nf*
choice – choix *nm*
choir – chorale *nf*
choose – choisir *v reg*
Christian – chrétien, chrétienne *adj*
Christian name – prénom *nm*
Christmas – Noël *nm*
    at Christmas – à Noël
    Father Christmas – Père Noël *nm*
    Happy Christmas! – Joyeux Noël!
Christmas Eve – veille de Noël *nf*
Christmas holidays – vacances de Noël *nfpl*
Christmas present – cadeau de Noël *nm*
Christmas tree – arbre de Noël *nm*
church – église *nf*
cider – cidre *nm*
cinema – cinéma *nm*
circle – cercle *nm*
circumflex accent (ê) – accent circonflexe *nm*
circus – cirque *nm*
city – ville *nf*
civil servant – fonctionnaire *nmf*
clarinet – clarinette *nf*
    play the clarinet – jouer de la clarinette *v reg*

class – classe *nf*
classical – classique *adj*
    classical music – musique classique *nf*
classified (small) ads – petites annonces *nfpl*
classroom – salle de classe *nf*
clean – propre *adj*, net, nette *adj*
clean – (house) nettoyer *v reg* †
clean one's teeth – se brosser* les dents *v refl*, se laver* les dents *v refl*
cleaning – nettoyage *nm*
cleaning lady – femme de ménage *nf*
clear – (table) débarrasser *v reg*
clearly – clairement, nettement, précisément *adv*
clear up – (tidy) ranger *v reg* †
clever – intelligent *adj*
cliff – falaise *nf*
climb – grimper *v reg*
clinic – centre médical *nm*
cloak-room – vestiaire *nm*
clock – (domestic) pendule *nf*
clock – (large public) horloge *nf*
clock radio – radio-réveil *nm*
close – (near) proche *adj*
    close by – près (de) *adv*
close – (shut) fermer *v reg*
closed – fermé *adj*
cloth – tissu *nm*
clothes – vêtements *nmpl*
clothes department – rayon de vêtements *nm*
cloud – nuage *nm*
cloudy – nuageux, nuageuse *adj*
club – club *nm*
clutch – (car) embrayage *nm*
clutch – (hold) empoigner *v reg*, saisir *v reg*
coach – autocar *nm*
coach – (bus) car *nm*
coach station – gare routière *nf*
coast – côte *nf*

---

nm - noun masculine	*nmpl* - noun masculine plural	*adj* - adjective	*conj* - conjunction
nf - noun feminine	*nfpl* - noun feminine plural	*adv* - adverb	*pron* - pronoun

coat – manteau *nm*, pardessus *nm*

coat hanger – cintre *nm*

Coca cola® – coca-cola® *nm*

cocoa – cacao *nm*

code – code *nm*

coeducational – mixte *adj*

coffee – (black) café *nm*
  coffee with milk – café crème *nm*
  expresso coffee – café express *nm*
  filter coffee – café filtre *nm*

coffee pot – cafetière *nf*

coffee table – table basse *nf*

coin – pièce *nf*

cold – froid *adj*
  cold water – eau froide *nf*
  be cold – (person) avoir froid
  v irreg §
  be cold – (weather) faire froid
  v irreg §

cold – (illness) rhume *nm*
  catch cold – attraper un rhume
  v reg
  have a cold – être enrhumé
  v irreg §

collar – col *nm*

colleague – collègue *nmf*

collect – (pick up) récupérer *v reg* †

collect – (stamps, etc) collectionner
v reg

collection – collection *nf*

college – (sixth form) lycée *nm*

college – (technical) lycée technique
nm

collide with – entrer* en collision
avec *v reg*

collision – collision *nf*

colloquial – familier, familière *adj*

colon (:) – deux-points *nm*

colour – couleur *nf*

comb – peigne *nm*

comb one's hair – se peigner* *v refl*,
se donner* un coup de peigne *v refl*

come – venir* *v irreg* §, arriver* *v reg*

come back – rentrer* *v reg*,
revenir* *v irreg* §

come down – descendre* *v reg*

come in – entrer* *v reg*

come on! – allez!

come out – sortir* *v irreg* §

come up – monter* *v reg*

comfort – confort *nm*

comfortable – confortable *adj*

comic – comique *adj*

comic film – film comique *nm*

comic strip – bande dessinée *nf*

coming from – (train) en provenance
de

comma (,) – virgule *nf*

command – ordre *nm*

common – vulgaire *adj*

Common Market – Marché
Commun *nm*

common noun – nom commun *nm*

commute – faire la navette *v irreg* §

compact disc – CD *nm*

company – société *nf*

compare – comparer *v reg*

comparison – comparaison *nf*

competition – concours *nm*

competitor – concurrent *nm*,
concurrente *nf*

complain – râler *v reg coll*,
se plaindre* *v refl* §

complete – compléter *v reg* †

complete – entier, entière *adj*

complete – finir *v reg*, terminer *v reg*

completely – complètement *adv*

complicated – compliqué *adj*

compulsory – obligatoire *adj*

computer – ordinateur *nm*

computer game – jeu électronique
nm

computer operator – informaticien
nm, informaticienne *nf*

computer programmer –
programmeur *nm*, programmeuse *nf*

---

computer scientist – informaticien *nm*, informaticienne *nf*

computer studies – informatique *nf*

computerise – informatiser *v reg*

concern – concerner *v reg*
  be concerned with – s'occuper* de *v refl*

concerning – à propos de

concert – concert *nm*

concrete – béton *nm*

condition – état *nm*
  in good condition – en bon état
  in poor condition – en mauvais état

condom – préservatif *nm*

confirm – confirmer *v reg*

congratulate – féliciter *v reg*

congratulations! – félicitations!

connection – (train) correspondance *nf*

consequently – aussi *conj*

conservatory – véranda *nf*

construct – construire *v irreg* §

construction worker – ouvrier du bâtiment *nm*

consult – consulter *v reg*

contact – contacter *v reg*, s'adresser à* *v refl*

contact lenses – lentilles *nfpl*

contain – contenir *v irreg* §

contents – contenu *nm*

contents – (book) table des matières *nf*

contest – concours *nm*

continent – continent *nm*

continue – continuer *v reg*

convenient – commode *adj*, convenable *adj*, pratique *adj*

conversation – dialogue *nm*

convinced – convaincu *adj*

cook – cuisinier *nm*, cuisinière *nf*

cook – cuisiner *v reg*, faire la cuisine *v irreg* §

cook – chef *nm*

cooker – cuisinière *nf*

cookery – cuisine *nf*

cool – frais, fraîche *adj*

cope – se débrouiller* *v refl*

copy – copier *v reg*

cork – bouchon *nm*

corkscrew – tire-bouchon *nm*

corner – coin *nm*
  at the corner of – au coin de

cornet – (music) cornet *nm*

cornet – (ice cream) cornet de glace *nm*

Cornwall – Cornouailles *nfpl*

correct – correct *adj*

correct – corriger *v reg* †

corrections – corrigé *nm*

corridor – couloir *nm*

Corsica – Corse *nf*

cost – coûter *v reg*

cost – (price) prix *nm*

costing – qui coûte

cottage – petite maison de campagne *nf*

cottage – (thatched) chaumière *nf*

cotton – coton *nm*

cotton wool – coton hydrophile *nm*

couchette – couchette *nf*

cough – toux *nf*

cough – tousser *v reg*

cough medicine – sirop contre la toux *nm*

could – pourrait

could you – (polite request) voulez-vous?

could – (was able to) pouvait *see pouvoir* *v irreg* §

council flat – HLM (habitation à loyer modéré) *nf*

count – compter *v reg*

counter – (PO, bank) guichet *nm*

counter – (shop) comptoir *nm*

country – pays *nm*

nm - noun masculine	*nmpl* - noun masculine plural	*adj* - adjective	*conj* - conjunction
nf - noun feminine	*nfpl* - noun feminine plural	*adv* - adverb	*pron* - pronoun

country – (not town) campagne *nf*
  in the country – à la campagne
countryside – campagne *nf*
coupon – bon *nm*
courage – courage *nm*
course – stage *nm*
  of course – naturellement, bien sûr, bien entendu *adv*
court – (sport) terrain *nm*
court – (tennis) court *nm*
cousin – cousin *nm*, cousine *nf*
cover – couvrir *v irreg* §
covered (with) – couvert (de) *adj*
cow – vache *nf*
crab – crabe *nm*
craftsman – artisan *nm*
crafty – débrouillard, rusé *adj coll*
crash – (car) s'écraser* *v refl*
crash into – rentrer* dans *v reg*
crazy – fou, fol, folle *adj*
cream – crème *nf*
  sun cream – crème solaire *nf*
credit card – carte de crédit *nf*
crescent – croissant *nm*
cricket – (sport) cricket *nm*
crisps – chips *nmpl*
crockery – vaisselle *nf*
cross – (angry) en colère *adj*
cross – (go across) traverser *v reg*
cross country – cross *nm*
cross out – rayer *v reg*
crossing – (channel) traversée *nf*
crossing – (level) passage à niveau *nm*
crossing – (pedestrian) passage clouté *nm*
crossroads – carrefour *nm*
crossword – (puzzle) mots croisés *nmpl*

crowd – foule *nf*
cruel – cruel, cruelle *adj*
cruise – croisière *nf*
crush – écraser *v reg*
cry – (shout) crier *v reg*
cry – (weep) pleurer *v reg*
cucumber – concombre *nm*
cul de sac – impasse *nf*
cup – tasse *nf*
  cup of tea – tasse de thé *nf*
cupboard – placard *nm*
cup final – finale de la coupe *nf*
cup-tie – match de coupe *nm*
curious – curieux, curieuse *adj*
curly – bouclé *adj*, frisé *adj*
currency – monnaie *nf*
currency exchange office – bureau de change *nm*
current – actuel, actuelle *adj*
current – (electric) courant *nm*
curriculum – programme scolaire *nm*
cursor – curseur *nm*
curtain – rideau *nm*
cushion – coussin *nm*
custard – crème anglaise *nf*
custom – usage *nm*
customer – client *nm*, cliente *nf*
customs – douane *nf*
customs officer – douanier *nm*
cut – couper *v reg*
cut lawn – tondre la pelouse *v reg*
cut one's finger – se couper* le doigt *v refl*
cycle – faire du cyclisme *v irreg* §
cycle hire – location de vélos *nf*
cycling – cyclisme *nm*
cyclist – cycliste *nmf*

D

dad(dy) – papa *nm*

daily – journalier, journalière *adj*, quotidien, quotidienne *adj*

daily life – la vie quotidienne *nf*

daily paper – quotidien *nm*

dairy – crémerie *nf*

damage – dommage *nm*

damaged – abîmé *adj*

damp – humide *adj*

dance – bal *nm*

dance – danser *v reg*

dancer – danseur *nm*, danseuse *nf*

Dane – Danois *nm*, Danoise *nf*

Danish – danois *adj*

danger – danger *nm*

dangerous – dangereux, dangereuse *adj*

dare – oser *v reg*

dark – obscur *adj*

dark – (colour) foncé *adj inv*

dash (-) – (punctuation) tiret *nm*

data – donnée *nf*

database – base de données *nf*

date – date *nf*

  up to date – branché *adj*, moderne *adj*

date – (meeting) rendez-vous *nm*

date of birth – date de naissance *nf*

daughter – fille *nf*

daughter-in-law – belle-fille *nf*

day – jour *nm*, journée *nf*

  all day – toute la journée

  day after tomorrow – le surlendemain *nm*

  day before yesterday – avant-hier *adv*

  day off – jour de congé *nm*

  day pupil – externe *nmf*

  next day – le lendemain *nm*

  per day – par jour, à la journée

  the other day – l'autre jour *nm*

dead – décédé, mort *adj*

dead end – impasse *nf*

deaf – sourd *adj*

deaf and dumb – sourd-muet *adj*

dear – cher, chère *adj*

death – mort *nf*

deceive – tromper *v reg*

December – décembre *nm*

decide to – décider (de) *v reg*

decision – décision *nf*

deckchair – chaise longue *nf*

declare – déclarer *v reg*

decorate – décorer *v reg*

deep – profond *adj*

deep frozen – surgelé *adj*

deeply – profondément *adv*

defeated – vaincu *adj*

definite – défini *adj*

degree – (temperature) degré *nm*

degree – (university) licence *nf*

delay – délai *nm*, retard *nm*

delay – tarder *v reg*

delicate – délicat *adj*, fragile *adj*

delicatessen – charcuterie *nf*

delicious – délicieux, délicieuse *adj*

delighted – enchanté *adj*

deliver – livrer *v reg*

deliver the post – distribuer le courrier *v reg*

delivery – livraison *nf*

demand – exiger *v reg* †

demonstrate – manifester *v reg*

demonstration – manifestation *nf*

Denmark – Danemark *nm*

dentist – dentiste *nmf*

deny – nier *v reg*

department – rayon *nm*

---

department store – grand magasin *nm*
departure – départ *nm*
departure board – tableau des départs *nm*
depend – dépendre *v reg*
deposit – arrhes *nfpl*, caution *nf*
deposit – poser *v reg*, déposer *v reg*
depressed – déprimé *adj*
describe – décrire *v irreg* §
description – description *nf*
deserve – mériter *v reg*
design – modèle *nm*
designer – dessinateur *nm*, dessinatrice *nf*
designer – styliste *nmf*
desire – envie *nf*, désir *nm*
desire – désirer *v reg*, avoir envie de *v irreg* §
desk – bureau *nm*
desperate – désespéré *adj*
dessert – (pudding) dessert *nm*
destination – destination *nf*
detached house – maison individuelle *nf*, pavillon *nm*
detail – détail *nm*
detective – policier, policière *adj*
detective film – film policier *nm*
detective story – roman policier *nm*
detention – retenue *nf*
  be in detention – être en retenue *v irreg* §
develop – développer *v reg*
development – développement *nm*
diabetes – diabète *nm*
diabetic – diabétique *adj*
dial the number – composer le numéro *v reg*
dialling code – indicatif de région *nm*
diary – agenda *nm*
dictionary – dictionnaire *nm*
did – *see faire v irreg* §
die – mourir* *v irreg* §

diesel – gas-oil *nm*, gazole *nm*
diet – régime *nm*
  be on a diet – être au régime *v irreg* §
difference – différence *nf*
different – différent *adj*
different – autre *adj*
differently – autrement *adv*
difficult – difficile *adj*, pénible *adj*
difficulty – difficulté *nf*
  have difficulty – avoir du mal à *v irreg* §
dim – (stupid) stupide *adj*
din – vacarme *nm*
dinghy – (inflatable) canot pneumatique *nm*
dining car – wagon-restaurant *nm*
dining hall – réfectoire *nm*
dining room – salle à manger *nf*
dinner – (evening meal) dîner *nm*
dinner hour – (lunch time break) pause de midi *nf*
dinosaur – dinosaure *nm*
direct – direct *adj*
direction – direction *nf*, sens *nm*
  in the opposite direction – en sens contraire
  in all directions – dans tous les sens
directly – directement *adv*
dirty – sale *adj*
disadvantage – inconvénient *nm*
disagreable – désagréable *adj*
disappear – disparaître *v irreg* §
disappointed – déçu *adj*
disappointing – décevant *adj*
disaster – catastrophe *nf*, désastre *nm*
disastrous – désastreux, désastreuse *adj*
disc – disque *nm*
disco – discothèque *nf*
discount – rabais *nm*

---

discouraged – découragé *adj*
discover – découvrir *v irreg*
discuss – discuter *v reg*
discussion – discussion *nf*, débat *nm*
disgraceful – ignoble *adj*
disgusted – dégoûté *adj*
disgusting – dégoûtant *adj*, infect *adj*
dish – plat *nm*
  dish of the day – plat du jour *nm*
dishwasher – lave-vaisselle *nm*
disk – disquette *nf*
  disk drive – lecteur de disquettes
  nm
display – (in shop window) étalage *nm*
distance – distance *nf*
  in the distance – au loin *adv*
distant – lointain *adj*
distinct – net, nette *adj*
distressed – désolé *adj*
district – quartier *nm*, région *nf*
  district of city – arrondissement
  nm
disturb – déranger *v reg* †
dive – plonger *v reg* †
diversion – déviation *nf*
divide – diviser *v reg*
divorced – divorcé *adj*
DIY – faire du bricolage *v irreg* §,
  bricoler *v reg*
dizziness – vertige *nm*
do – faire *v irreg* §
  do athletics – faire de l'athlétisme
  v irreg §
  do drama – étudier l'art
  dramatique *v reg*
  do (an) experiment – faire une
  expérience *v irreg* §
  do gardening – faire du jardinage
  v irreg §
  do gymnastics – faire de la
  gymnastique *v irreg* §

do homework – faire des devoirs
  v irreg §
do housework – faire du ménage
  v irreg §
do ironing – faire du repassage
  v irreg §
do odd jobs – bricoler *v reg*, faire
  du bricolage *v irreg* §
do one's hair – se coiffer* *v refl*
do shopping – faire des commissions
  v irreg §, faire des courses *v irreg* §
do a sport – pratiquer un sport
  v reg
do (the) washing – faire la lessive
  v irreg §
do washing up – faire la vaisselle
  v irreg §
do water sports – faire des sports
  nautiques *v irreg* §
do well – se débrouiller* *v refl*
well done! – bravo!
do you see? – voyez-vous?
dock – arriver au port* *v reg*
doctor – docteur *nm*, médecin *nm*
doctor's certificate – attestation du
  médecin *nf*
documentary – documentaire *nm*
dog, bitch – chien *nm*, chienne *nf*
  beware of the dog – chien
  méchant
dole – (on the) au chômage *adj*
doll – poupée *nf*
domestic – domestique *adj*, ménager,
  ménagère *adj*
done – *see faire v irreg* §
don't you, doesn't he? – n'est-ce
  pas?
donkey – âne *nm*
door – porte *nf*
  knock on the door – frapper à la
  porte *v reg*
door – (car, train) portière *nf*
dormitory – dortoir *nm*

---

dose – (amount) dose *nf*

double – double *adj*

double bass – contrebasse *nf*

double decker – autobus à l'impériale *nm*

double room – chambre pour deux personnes *nf*

doubtful – douteux, douteuse *adj*

doughnut – beignet *nm*

Dover – Douvres

down – en bas *adj*

  lower down – plus bas

  come down, go down – descendre* *v reg*

  come, go downhill – descendre* *v reg*

downpour – averse *nf*

downstairs – en bas, au rez-de-chaussée *adv*

  go downstairs – descendre* en bas *v reg*

dozen – douzaine *nf*

drama – drame *nm*, l'art dramatique *nm*

  do drama – étudier l'art dramatique *v reg*

drat! – mince! *excl*

draughts – jeu de dames *nm*

draughtsman – dessinateur *nm*

draw – (lottery) tirage au sort *nm*

draw – (score) match nul *nm*

draw – (match) faire match nul *v irreg* §

draw – (picture) dessiner *v reg*

draw – (pull) tirer *v reg*

drawback – inconvénient *nm*

drawer – tiroir *nm*

drawing – dessin *nm*

dreadful – insupportable *adj*

dream – rêve *nm*

dream – rêver *v reg*, songer *v reg* †

dress – robe *nf*

dress o.s. – s'habiller* *v refl*

dressed (in) – vêtu (de) *adj*

dresser – vaisselier *nm*

dressing – (medical) pansement *nm*

dressing gown – robe de chambre *nf*

dressing table – coiffeuse *nf*

dress rehearsal – répétition générale *nf*

drink – boisson *nf*

drink – boire *v irreg* §

  have a drink – prendre un pot *v irreg sl* §

drinkable – potable *adj*

  drinking water – eau potable *nf*

drive – allée *nf*

drive – rouler *v reg*

drive – conduire *v irreg* §

driver – conducteur *nm*, conductrice *nf*

driving licence – permis de conduire *nm*

  take a driving test – passer son permis *v reg*

driving mirror – rétroviseur *nm*

drop – laisser tomber *v reg*

drown – se noyer* *v refl*

drug – (medical) médicament *nm*

drug – (narcotic) drogue *nf*, stupéfiant *nm*

  be on drugs – se droguer* *v refl*

drum kit – batterie *nf*

  play the drums – jouer de la batterie *v reg*

drunk – ivre *adj*

dry – sec, sèche *adj*

dry – sécher *v reg* †

dry cleaner's – teinturerie *nf*

dry cleaning – nettoyage à sec *nm*

dry one's hair – se sécher* les cheveux *v refl* †

dryer – sèche-linge *nm*, séchoir *nm*

duck – canard *nm*

dumb – muet, muette *adj*

dumbfounded – stupéfait *adj*

---

duration – durée *nf*
during – pendant *prep*
dust – poussière *nf*
dustbin – poubelle *nf*
Dutch – ‡hollandais *adj*,
   néerlandais *adj*

Dutch person – ‡Hollandais *nm*,
   Hollandaise *nf*
Dutchman, Dutchwoman –
   Néerlandais *nm*, Néerlandaise *nf*
duty-free – hors-taxe *adj*
duvet – couette *nf*
duvet cover – ‡housse *nf*

E

each – chaque *adj*
   each time – chaque fois *nf*
each one – chacun,
   chacune *indef pron*
ear – oreille *nf*
   earache – mal à l'oreille *nm*
   earring – boucle d'oreille *nf*
earlier – plus tôt *adv*
earlier – auparavant *adv*
early – tôt, de bonne heure *adv*
early – (for appointment) en avance
   adv
earn – gagner *v reg*
earth – terre *nf*
earthquake – tremblement de terre
   nm
easily – facilement *adv*
east – est *nm*
Easter – Pâques *nm*
   at Easter – à Pâques
   Easter egg – œuf de Pâques *nm*
   Easter holidays – vacances de
   Pâques *nfpl*
easy – facile *adj*
eat – manger *v reg* †
ecologist – écologiste *nmf*
ecology – écologie *nf*
economics – sciences économiques
   nfpl
economise – économiser *v reg*

edge – bord *nm*
   on the edge of – au bord de
edible – comestible *adj*
Edinburgh – Edimbourg
education – éducation *nf*, instruction
   nf
educational – éducatif, éducative *adj*
effective – effectif, effective *adj*,
   efficace *adj*
effort – effort *nm*
egg – œuf *nm*
   boiled egg – œuf à la coque *nm*
   hard boiled egg – œuf dur *nm*
   fried egg – œuf sur le plat *nm*
   scrambled egg – œufs brouillés
   nmpl
eh? – hein? *excl*
eight – ‡huit *adj*
eighteen – dix-huit *adj*
eighth – ‡huitième *adj*
eighty – quatre-vingts *adj*
eighty-one – quatre-vingt-un *adj*
either ... or... – soit ...soit *conj*
elastoplast® – sparadrap *nm*
elbow – coude *nm*
elder – aîné *adj*
elderly – âgé *adj*
eldest – aîné *adj*
electric cooker – cuisinière
   électrique *nf*

---

nm - noun masculine	*nmpl* - noun masculine plural	*adj* - adjective *conj* - conjunction
nf - noun feminine	*nfpl* - noun feminine plural	*adv* - adverb *pron* - pronoun

electric razor – rasoir électrique *nm*
electric(al) – électrique *adj*
electrician – électricien *nm*
electricity – électricité *nf*
electronics – électronique *nf*
elegant – élégant *adj*
elephant – éléphant *nm*
elephant's trunk – trompe *nf*
eleven – onze *adj inv*
eleventh – onzième *adj*
embarrassed – confus *adj*
embarrassing – gênant *adj*
embarrassment – embarras *nm*
emergency – crise *nf*
emergency – d'urgence *adj*
  in an emergency – en cas
   d'urgence
emergency aid – secours d'urgence
  nm
emergency dept – salle des urgences
  nf
emergency exit – sortie de secours
  nf
employ – employer *v reg* †
employee – employé *nm*, employée *nf*
employer – employeur *nm*,
  employeuse *nf*
empty – vide *adj*
empty – vider *v reg*
encourage – encourager *v reg* †
end – bout *nm*, fin *nf*
  at the end of the corridor –
   au bout du couloir
  at the end of – à la fin de
  in the end – en fin de compte
end – (finish) finir *v reg*,
  se terminer* *v refl*
endless – interminable *adj*
energy – énergie *nf*
engaged – (to be married) fiancé *adj*
engaged – (WC) occupé *adj*
engine – moteur *nm*
engineer – ingénieur *nm*

engineering drawing – dessin
  industriel *nm*
England – Angleterre *nf*
English – anglais *adj*
English – (language) anglais *nm*
  in English – en anglais
  English lesson – cours d'anglais
   nm
English Channel – Manche *nf*
English person – Anglais *nm*,
  Anglaise *nf*
English-speaking – anglophone *adj*
enjoy – aimer *v reg*, aimer faire *v reg*,
  s'amuser* *v refl*
  enjoy your meal! – bon appétit!
enjoyable – agréable *adj*
enormous – énorme *adj*
enough – assez *adv*
enough (of) – assez (de)
  I've had enough – j'en ai marre
enquire about – s'informer* de *v refl*
enter – entrer* *v reg*
entertainment – distraction *nf*,
  spectacle *nm*
enthusiasm – enthousiasme *nm*
entirely – entièrement *adv*
entrance – entrée *nf*
entrance ticket – billet d'entrée *nm*
envelope – enveloppe *nf*
environment – environnement *nm*
envy – envie *nf*
equal – égal *adj* (égaux *adj mpl*)
equality – égalité *nf*
equally – également *adv*
equipment – équipement *nm*,
  matériel *nm*
equivalent – équivalent *adj*
error – erreur *nf*
escalator – escalier roulant *nm*
escape – échapper à *v reg*,
  s'évader* de *v refl*
escape from – s'échapper* de *v refl*
especially – surtout, en particulier *adv*

prep - preposition	*v reg* - verb regular	*v refl* - verb reflexive	§ - see verb tables
pp - past participle	*v irreg* - verb irregular	† - see verb information	* - takes être

espresso coffee – café express *nm*
essay – rédaction *nf*
essential – essentiel, essentielle *adj*
establishment – établissement *nm*
estate agent – agence immobilière *nf*
Eurocheque – eurochèque *nm*
Europe – Europe *nf*
European – européen, européenne *adj*
European person – Européen *nm*, Europénne *nf*
European Union – Union européenne *nf*
even – même *adv*
even – (not odd) pair *adj*
even better – encore mieux *adv*
even though – quand même *conj*
evening – soir *nm*
  good evening! – bonsoir!
  see you this evening – à ce soir
evening meal – repas du soir *nm*
evenly – également *adv*
event – événement *nm*
eventually – en fin de compte *adv*
ever – jamais *adv*
ever – (at all times) toujours *adv*
ever since – depuis *prep*
every – chaque *adj*
  every time – chaque fois
every – tout, toute, tous, toutes *adj*
  everybody – tout le monde
  everyone – tout le monde
  every day – tous les jours
  every evening – tous les soirs
  every ten minutes – toutes les dix minutes
everyday – courant *adj*, usuel, usuelle *adj*
every one – chacun, chacune *indef pron*
everything – tout *pron*
everywhere – partout *adv*
evidence – preuve(s) *nf(pl)*

evil – mauvais *adj*
ex- – ancien, ancienne *adj*
exact – exact *adj*, précis *adj*
exactly – exactement, justement, précisément *adv*
examination – examen *nm*
  fail an exam – râter un examen *v reg*
  pass an exam – réussir à un examen *v reg*
  take an exam – passer un examen *v reg*
example – exemple *nm*
  for example – par exemple
excellent – excellent *adj*
except – sauf, à part *prep*
exception – exception *nf*
exchange – (swap) échanger *v reg* †
exchange – (school) échange scolaire *nm*
  go on an exchange – faire un échange *v irreg* §
exciting – passionnant *adj*
exclaim – s'écrier*, s'exclamer* *v refl*
exclamation mark (!) – point d'exclamation *nm*
excursion – excursion *nf*
excuse – excuse *nf*
  make excuses – faire des excuses *v irreg* §
excuse – excuser *v reg*
  excuse me! – excusez-moi!
exercise – exercice *nm*
exercise book – cahier *nm*
exercises – mouvements de gymnastique *nmpl*
exhausted – épuisé *adj*
exhibition – exposition *nf*
exist – exister *v reg*
exit – sortie *nf*
  emergency exit – sortie de secours *nf*
expect – attendre *v reg*

---

expel – renvoyer *v reg* †
expensive – cher, chère *adj*
experiment – expérience *nf*
explain – expliquer *v reg*
explanation – explication *nf*
explore – explorer *v reg*
explorer – explorateur *nm*
express train – rapide *nm*
expression – regard *nm*

extinguish – éteindre *v irreg* §
extra charge – supplément *nm*
   extra – en supplément
extraordinary – extraordinaire *adj*
extreme – ultra- *pref*
extremely – extrêmement *adv*
eye – œil *nm* (yeux *nmpl*)
eyebrow – sourcil *nm*
eye shadow – ombre à paupière *nf*

F

fabulous – formidable *adj*
face – figure *nf*, visage *nm*
fact – fait *nm*, réalité *nf*
   in fact – en fait, en réalité
factory – usine *nf*, fabrique *nf*
fail – échouer *v reg*
   fail an exam – rater un examen
   v reg
failed – manqué *adj*
faint – s'évanouir* *v refl*
fair – blond *adj*
fair – (amusement) foire *nf*
fair – (average) moyen, moyenne *adj*
fair – (just) juste *adj*
   it's not fair! – ce n'est pas juste!
fairly – assez *adv*
faithfully, Yours – (formal letter
   ending) Veuillez agréer, Monsieur/
   Madame, les expressions de mes
   sentiments distingués
fall – tomber* *v reg*
   fall ill – tomber* malade *v reg*
fall asleep – s'endormir* *v refl* §
false – faux, fausse *adj*
familiar – connu *adj*, familier,
   familière *adj*
family – famille *nf*

family room – (hotel) chambre
   familiale *nf*
famous – célèbre *adj*, illustre *adj*,
   renommé *adj*
fan – (supporter) fan *nmf*,
   passionné *nm*, passionnée *nf*
fancy dress – déguisement *nm*
fantastic – fantastique *adj*, génial *adj*
far away – (distant) éloigné *adj*
   far away – loin (d'ici) *adv*
   far from – loin de
   is it far? – c'est loin?
fare – (bus) prix du ticket *nm*
farm – ferme *nf*
farmer – agriculteur *nm*
   farm worker – ouvrier
   agricole *nm*
fascinating – passionnant *adj*
fashion – mode *nf*
   fashion designer – styliste *nmf*
   fashionable – à la mode *adj*
fast – (quick) rapide *adj*
fast – (quickly) vite, rapidement *adv*
   il court vite – he runs fast
fast – (watch) en avance *adv*
fast train – express *nm*
fasten – attacher *v reg*

---

fat – gros, grosse *adj*, gras, grasse *adj*

father – père *nm*

   Father Christmas – Père Noël

father-in-law – beau-père *nm*

fault – faute *nf*, tort *nm*

favourite – favori, favorite *adj*

favourite – préféré *adj*

fax – (message) fax *nm*

   fax machine – télécopieur *nm*

   fax number – numéro de télécopie *nm*

fear – peur *nf*

feather – plume *nf*

February – février *nm*

fed up – marre *adv*

   I'm fed up – j'en ai marre, j'en ai ras le bol

feed the cat – donner à manger au chat *v reg*

feel – éprouver *v reg*, sentir *v irreg* §

   feel at ease – être à l'aise *v irreg* §

   feel cold – avoir froid *v irreg* §

   feel happy – être heureux, heureuse *v irreg* §

   feel hot – avoir chaud *v irreg* §

   feel hungry – avoir faim *v irreg* §

   feel ill – mal se sentir* *v refl* §

   feel like – avoir envie de *v irreg* §

   feel sick – avoir mal au cœur *v irreg* §

   feel sleepy – avoir sommeil *v irreg* §

   feel thirsty – avoir soif *v irreg* §

   feel tired – être fatigué *v irreg* §

   feel well – bien se sentir* §

feet – *see foot*

fell – *see fall*

felt – *see feel*

felt tip pen – feutre *nm*

female – femelle *adj*

female – femelle *nf*

feminine – féminin, féminine *adj*

fence – barrière *nf*

ferret – furet *nm*

ferry – ferry *nm*

ferry terminal – gare maritime *nf*

festival – fête *nf*

fetch – aller* chercher *v irreg* §

fetch bread – ramener du pain *v reg* †

fête – (village) fête *nf*, kermesse *nf*

fever – fièvre *nf*

few – peu *nm*

   few – peu de *adj*

   a few – quelques-uns, quelques-unes *pron*

   a few – (some) quelques *adj*

   quite a few – un bon nombre de *nm coll*

fiancé(e) – fiancé *nm*, fiancée *nf*

fiddle – (violin) violon *nm*

field – champ *nm*, terrain (de sport) *nm*

fierce – féroce *adj*

fifteen – quinze *adj*

fifth – cinquième *adj*

fifty – cinquante *adj inv*

fight – se battre* *v refl*, se disputer* *v refl*

file – (computer) fichier *nm*

file – (folder, ring binder) classeur *nm*, dossier *nm*

fill – remplir *v reg*

   fill up – (petrol, diesel) faire le plein *v irreg* §

   fill in a form – (at campsite, etc) remplir une fiche *v reg*

   fill in a form – (official form) remplir un formulaire *v reg*

filling station – station de service *nf*

filling – (teeth) plombage *nm*

film – (for camera) pellicule *nf*

film – film *nm*

   detective film – film policier *nm*

   dubbed film – film doublé *nm*

   sci-fi film – film de science-fiction *nm*

film star – vedette *nf*

---

nm - noun masculine	*nmpl* - noun masculine plural	*adj* - adjective	*conj* - conjunction
nf - noun feminine	*nfpl* - noun feminine plural	*adv* - adverb	*pron* - pronoun

filter coffee – café filtre *nm*
final – final *adj*
finally – à la fin, enfin *adv*
finals – finale *nf*
   cup final – finale de la coupe *nf*
find – trouver *v reg*
find – (again) retrouver *v reg*
find out – se renseigner* *v refl*,
   découvrir *v irreg* §
fine – (delicate) fin *adj*
fine – beau, bel, belle *adj*
   be fine – (weather) faire beau
     v irreg §
   I'll be fine! – ça va aller!, ça ira!
fine – (punishment) amende *nf*
fine! – O.K!, d'accord!, entendu! *excl*
finger – doigt *nm*
finish – finir *v reg*, terminer *v reg*,
   se terminer* *v refl*
finish – (race) arriver* *v reg*
Finland – Finlande *nf*
Finnish – finlandais *adj*
Finnish person – Finlandais *nm*,
   Finlandaise *nf*
fire – feu *nm*
fire – (heater) radiateur *nm*
fire – (unplanned!) incendie *nm*
fire alarm – alarme d'incendie *nf*
fire brigade – pompiers *nmpl*
fire escape – escalier de secours *nm*
fireman – (sapeur-)pompier *nm*
fire-place – cheminée *nf*
firework – (display) feu d'artifice *nm*
firm – (solid) ferme *adj*, solide *adj*
firm – (business) entreprise *nf*,
   societé *nf*
first – premier, première *adj*
   on the first floor – au premier
     étage
at first – d'abord *adv*
first aid – premiers secours *nmpl*,
   premiers soins *nmpl*

first aid station – poste de secours
   nm
first class ticket – billet de première
   classe *nm*
first name – prénom *nm*
first of all – d'abord *adv*
first sitting – premier service *nm*
firstly – premièrement *adv*
fish – poisson *nm*
fish shop – poissonnerie *nf*
fisherman – pêcheur *nm*
fishing – pêche *nf*
   go fishing – aller* à la pêche
     v irreg §
fishing port – port de pêche *nm*
fishing rod – canne à pêche *nf*
fishmonger – poissonnier *nm*
fist – poing *nm*
fit – en forme
   be fit – être en forme *v irreg* §
   it does not fit me – ça ne me va
     pas
fitting room – cabine d'essayage *nf*
five – cinq *adj*
fix – fixer *v reg*, réparer *v reg*
fixed – fixe *adj*
fixture – (sport) match *nm*
fizzy – gazeux, gazeuse *adj*
flag – drapeau *nm*
flame – flamme *nf*
   go up in flames – brûler *v reg*
flan – tarte *nf*
   egg and cheese flan – quiche
     lorraine *nf*
flannel – gant de toilette *nm*
flash of lightning – éclair *nm*
flat – appartement *nm*
flat – plat *adj*
   flat tyre – pneu à plat *nm*
flats – (block of) immeuble *nm*
flavour – parfum *nm*
flavoured – aromatisé *adj*,
   parfumé *adj*

---

flea – puce *nf*
  flea market – marché aux puces *nm*
flight – vol *nm*
flight of stairs – escalier *nm*
fling – jeter *v reg* †
flip-flops – tongs *nfpl*
float – flotter *v reg*
flock – troupeau *nm*
flood – inondation *nf*
floor – plancher *nm*
floor – (storey) étage *nm*
  on the first floor – au premier étage
  on the next floor – à l'étage supérieur
  on the top floor – au dernier étage
floppy disk – disquette *nf*
flour – farine *nf*
flower – fleur *nf*
flower bed – parterre *nm*, plate-bande *nf*
flower vase – vase *nm*
flu – grippe *nf*
fluently – couramment *adv*
flute – flûte *nf*
  play the flute – jouer de la flûte *v reg*
fly – mouche *nf*
fly – prendre l'avion *v irreg* §, voyager en avion *v reg* †, voler *v reg*
flying – aviation *nf*
fog – brouillard *nm*
  it is foggy – il y a du brouillard *v irreg* §
fold – plier *v reg*
folder – (school) classeur *–nm*
folk music – musique folklorique *nf*
folk – gens *nmpl*
folks – parents *nmpl*
follow – suivre *v irreg* §
  followed by – suivi de

following – suivant *adj*
food – aliment *nm*, nourriture *nf*, provisions *nfpl*
  French food – cuisine française *nf*
food processor – robot de cuisine *nm*
fool – idiot *nm*, idiote *nf*
foolish – bête *adj*, sot, sotte *adj*
foot – pied *nm*
  on foot – à pied
foot – (hill, page) bas *nm*
football – football *nm*, foot *nm*
football boots – chaussures de football *nfpl*
footballer – footballeur *nm*
football field – terrain de football *nm*
football match – match de football *nm*
footpath – sentier *nm*, chemin *nm*
footstep – pas *nm*
for – car *conj*
for – pour, pendant, depuis *prep*
  for ever – pour toujours, à jamais *adv*
  for example – par exemple
  for hire – à louer
  for sale – à vendre
forbid – défendre *v reg*, interdire *v irreg* §
  forbidden – défendu *adj*, interdit *adj*
forecast – prévision *nf*
forecast – (weather) méteo *nf*
foreign – étranger *adj*
foreigner – étranger *nm*, étrangère *nf*
forest – forêt *nf*
forget – oublier *v reg*
forgive – pardonner *v reg*, excuser *v reg*
fork – fourchette *nf*
form – (class) classe *nf*
form – (paper) fiche *nf*, formulaire *nm*
former – (previous) ancien, ancienne *adj*

fortnight – quinzaine *nf*, quinze jours
  in a fortnight – dans une
    quinzaine
fortunate – heureux, heureuse *adj*
fortunately – heureusement *adv*
forty – quarante *adj*
forty-one – quarante et un *adj*
forward – en avant *adv*
  go forward – avancer *v reg* †
forward – (team) avant *nm*
fountain pen – stylo à encre *nm*
four – quatre *adj*
fourteen – quatorze *adj*
fourth – quatrième *adj*
fragile – fragile *adj*
franc – franc *nm*
France – France *nf*
frank – franc, franche *adj*
frankly – franchement *adv*
free – libre *adj*
free – (not paying) gratuit *adj*
free time – loisir *nm*, temps libre *nm*
freedom – liberté *nf*
freeze – geler *v reg* †
  it is freezing – il gèle
freezer – congélateur *nm*
French – français *adj*
  in French – en français
French – (language) français *nm*
French bean – ‡haricot vert *nm*
French fries – frites *nf*
French person – Français *nm*,
  Française *nf*
French Riviera – Côte d'Azur *nf*
French speaking countries – pays
  francophones *nmpl*
French-speaking – francophone *adj*
French version – version française
  nf
frequent – fréquent *adj*
fresh – frais, fraîche *adj*
Friday – vendredi *nm*

fridge – réfrigérateur, frigidaire® *nm,*
  frigo *nm coll*
friend – (female) amie *nf*, copine *nf*
friend – (male) ami *nm*, copain *nm*
friendly – aimable *adj*, amical *adj*
friendship – amitié *nf*
fright – peur *nf*, horreur *nf*
  be frightened – avoir peur
    v irreg §
frightened – effrayé *adj*
frightening – effrayant *adj*
fringe – frange *nf*
frog – grenouille *nf*
  frogs' legs – cuisses de grenouilles
    nfpl
from – de *prep*
from – (train coming from) en
  provenance de
from – (according to) d'après *prep*
from – (time, prices) à partir de *prep*
front – devant *nm*
  in front of – devant *prep*
front door – porte d'entrée *nf*
front wheel – roue avant *nf*
frost – gel *nm,* givre *nm*
frosty – glacial *adj*
frozen – gelé *adj*
frozen food – aliments surgelés *nmpl*,
  produits surgelés *nmpl*
fruit – fruit *nm*
fruit juice – jus de fruit *nm*
fruit machine – machine à sous *nf*
fruit tree – arbre fruitier *nm*
fruitseller – marchand de fruits *nm*
frying pan – poêle *nf*
fuel – (petrol) carburant *nm*
full – plein *adj*, complet, complète *adj*
  full of – plein de *adj*
  full time – à plein temps *adv*
full – (car park) complet
  full – (no vacancies in hotel, B&B)
    complet *adj*

---

prep - preposition	*v reg* - verb regular
pp - past participle	*v irreg* - verb irregular

v refl - verb reflexive	§ - see verb tables
† - see verb information	* - takes être

full board – pension complète *nf*
full fare – plein tarif *nm*
full stop (.) – point (final) *nm*
full speed – à toute vitesse *adv*
fun – amusement *nm*
  be fun – être chouette *v irreg coll* §
  have fun – s'amuser* *v refl*,
    rigoler *v reg*
  make fun of – se moquer* de *v refl*
fun fair – fête foraine *nf*
funny – comique *adj*, drôle *adj*,
  marrant *adj coll* rigolo,
  rigolote *adj coll*

furious – furieux, furieuse *adj*
furnished – meublé *adj*
furniture – meubles *nmpl*
further – plus loin *adv*
further education – formation
  continue *nf*
fuss – agitation *nf*
  make a fuss – faire des histoires
    v irreg §
fussy – difficile *adj*
future – avenir *nm*
future – futur *adj*
in future – à l'avenir

G

gale – tempête *nf*
gallery – galerie *nf*
  art gallery – galerie d'art *nf*,
  musée *nm*
game – jeu *nm*
  arcade game – jeu de galerie *nm*
  board game – jeu de societé *nm*
  computer game – jeu électronique
    nm
  video game – jeu vidéo *nm*
  game – (software) logiciel de
    jeu *nm*
game of tennis – partie de tennis *nf*
games room – salle de jeux *nf*
games – sport *nm*
  do games – faire du sport *v irreg* §
garage – garage *nm*
garage owner – garagiste *nm*
garden – jardin *nm*
  botanical garden – jardin des
  plantes *nm*
gardener – jardinier *nm*,
  jardinière *nf*
gardening – jardinage *nm*

  do the gardening – faire du
  jardinage *v irreg* §
garlic – ail *nm*
garment – vêtement *nm*
gas – gaz *nm*
  gas cooker – cuisinière à gaz *nf*
  gas cylinder – bouteille de gaz *nf*
gate – barrière *nf*, porte *nf*
gate crash – venir* sans invitation
  v irreg §
gather together – rassembler *v reg*
GB – Grande-Bretagne *nf*
gear – (car) vitesse *nf*
gel – (hair) gel *nm*
gender – genre *nm*
general – général *adj*
  in general – en général *adv*
generous – généreux, généreuse *adj*
Geneva – Genève
gentle – doux, douce *adj*
gentleman – monsieur *nm*
Gentlemen – Messieurs *nmpl*

---

nm - noun masculine	*nmpl* - noun masculine plural	*adj* - adjective	*conj* - conjunction
nf - noun feminine	*nfpl* - noun feminine plural	*adv* - adverb	*pron* - pronoun

gently – doucement *adv*
genuine – authentique *adj*, véritable *adj*
geography – géographie *nf*
geology – géologie *nf*
gerbil – gerbille *nf*
German – allemand *adj*
German – (language) allemand *nm*
German person – Allemand *nm*, Allemande *nf*
Germany – Allemagne *nf*
get – (become) devenir* *v irreg* §
  get – (buy) acheter *v reg* †
  get – (catch hold of) saisir *v reg*
  get – (fetch) aller* chercher *v irreg* §
  get – (find) trouver *v reg*
  get – (have) avoir *v irreg* §
  get – (obtain) obtenir *v irreg* §
  get – (understand) comprendre *v irreg* §
get a divorce – divorcer *v reg* †
get about – (travel) voyager *v reg* †, se déplacer* *v refl* †
get across – traverser *v reg*
get along – (manage) se débrouiller* *v refl*
get angry – se mettre* en colère *v refl* §, se fâcher* *v refl*
get at – (reach) parvenir* à *v irreg* §
get away – partir* *v irreg* §, s'en aller* *v irreg* §
get back – retourner* *v reg*, revenir* *v irreg* §
get bad marks – avoir de mauvaises notes *v irreg* §
get better – se remettre* *v refl* §
get down – descendre* *v reg*
get dressed – s'habiller* *v refl*
get good marks – avoir de bonnes notes *v irreg* §
get hurt – être blessé *v irreg* §

get impatient – s'impatienter* *v refl*
get in – entrer* *v reg*, arriver* *v reg*
get injured – se blesser* *v refl*
get into – monter* dans *v reg*
get into trouble – avoir des ennuis *v irreg* §
get married – se marier* *v refl*
get off the coach – descendre* du car *v reg*
get on – (succeed) réussir *v reg*
get on the train – monter* dans le train *v reg*
get on with – s'accorder* bien avec *v refl*, s'entendre* *v refl*
get out of a mess – s'en sortir* *v refl* §
get out of the car – descendre* de voiture *v reg*
get over – (illness) se remettre* *v refl* §
get ready – se préparer* *v refl*
get rid of – se débarrasser* de *v refl*
get round – (avoid) éviter *v reg*
get stung – se faire* piquer *v refl* §
get the bus – prendre l'autobus *v irreg* §
get to – arriver* à *v reg*, aller* à *v irreg* §
get to know – faire la connaissance de *v irreg* §
get used to – s'habituer* à *v refl*
get undressed – se déshabiller* *v refl*
get up – se lever* *v refl* †
ghost – fantôme *nm*
gift – cadeau *nm*
  will you gift wrap this please? – pouvez-vous en faire un paquet-cadeau, s'il vous plaît?
gifted – doué *adj*
gig – concert *nm*

giggle – ricaner *v reg*

ginger – gingembre *nm*

ginger bread – pain d'épice *nm*

girl – fille *nf,* jeune fille *nf*

girlfriend – petite amie *nf*

give – donner *v reg*

  give – (gift) offrir *v irreg* §

  give back – rendre *v reg*

  give in – se rendre* *v refl*

  give me... – donnez-moi...

  give over – (stop) cesser *v reg*

  give up – abandonner *v reg*

glad – content *adj*

gladly – volontiers *adv*

glance – regard *nm*

glass – (drinking) verre *nm*

glass – (mirror) miroir *nm*

glass – (pane of) vitre *nf*

glasses – (spectacles) lunettes *nfpl*

glass jug – carafe *nf*

gloomy – triste *adj*

glove – gant *nm*

glue – coller *v reg*

GNVQ – bac professionnel *nm*

go – aller* *v irreg* §

go – (become) devenir* *v irreg* §

go – (leave) partir* *v irreg* §

go – (function) marcher *v reg*

go – (vanish) disparaître *v irreg* §

  go along – aller* le long de
  v irreg §

  go and fetch someone – aller*
  chercher quelqu'un *v irreg* §

  go and see – (people) aller* voir
  v irreg §

  go away – s'en aller* *v refl* §,
  s'éloigner* *v refl*

  go away! – allez-vous-en! *excl*

  go babysitting – faire du
  babysitting *v irreg* §

  go back – retourner*– *v reg*

go by car – aller* en voiture
v irreg §

go boating – faire une promenade
en bateau *v irreg* §

go camping – faire du camping
v irreg §

go down – descendre* *v reg*

go downstairs – (*with avoir*)
descendre l'escalier *v reg*

go fishing – aller* à la pêche
v irreg §

go for – aller* chercher *v irreg* §

go for a bike ride – faire une
promenade à vélo *v irreg* §

go for a walk – faire une
promenade *v irreg* §

go forward – avancer *v reg* †

go home – rentrer* à la maison
v reg

go horse riding – faire de
l'équitation *v irreg* §, faire du
cheval *v irreg* §

go in (to) – entrer* dans *v reg*

go in for an exam – se présenter*
à un examen *v refl*

go jogging – faire du jogging
v irreg §

go near to – s'approcher de* *v refl*

go off – partir* *v irreg* §

go on – continuer *v reg*

go on an exchange – faire un
échange *v irreg* §

go on foot – aller* à pied *v irreg* §

go on holiday – partir* en
vacances *v irreg* §

go on, go ahead! – allez-y! *excl*

go out – sortir* *v irreg* §

go out with – fréquenter *v reg*

go out – (light) s'éteindre* *v refl* §

go over – (across) traverser *v reg*

go red – rougir *v reg*

go round the shops – courir les
magasins *v irreg* §

go round the world – faire le tour du monde *v irreg* §

go round town – faire un tour en ville *v irreg* §

go sailing – faire de la voile *v irreg* §

go shopping – faire des achats *v irreg* §, faire des commissions *v irreg* §, faire des courses *v irreg* §

go skiing – faire du ski *v irreg* §

go straight on! – allez tout droit!

go that way! – passez par là!

go through customs – passer* à la douane *v reg*

go to – aller* à *v irreg* §, se rendre* à *v refl*

go to bed – aller* au lit *v irreg* §, se coucher* *v refl*

go up – monter* *v reg*

go walking – faire des promenades *v irreg* §

go window shopping – faire du lèche-vitrines *v irreg* §

go windsurfing – faire de la planche à voile *v irreg* §

go with – accompagner *v reg*

shall we go? – si on allait?

go-kart – kart *nm*

  go-carting – karting *nm*

  to go go-carting – faire du karting *v irreg* §

goal – but *nm*

goalkeeper – gardien de but *nm*

goalless-draw – match nul *nm*

goalpost – poteau de but *nm*

goat – chèvre *nf*

goggles – lunettes protectives *nfpl*

going to – en direction de

gold – or *nm*

  made of gold – en or

  golden – (colour) doré *adj*

goldfish – poisson-rouge *nm*

golf – golf *nm*

golf course – terrain de golf *nm*

play golf – jouer au golf *v reg*

gone – *see aller** *v irreg* §

  it's all gone – il n'y en a plus

good – (well-behaved) sage *adj*

good – (well) bien *adv*

good – bon, bonne *adj*

  good evening! – bonsoir!

  good idea! – bonne idée!

  good looking – beau, bel, belle *adj*

  good luck! – bon courage! bonne chance!

  be in a good mood – être de bonne humeur *v irreg* §

  good morning! – bonjour!

  good news – bonne nouvelle *nf*

  good night! – bonne nuit!

  good-tempered – de bonne humeur *adj*

good at – fort en *adj*

good value – (of prices) intéressant *adj*, bon marché (cheap) *adj inv*

goodbye! – au revoir!

goodness – bonté *nf*

gorgeous – formidable *adj*, magnifique *adj*, splendide *adj*

got to – (must, ought to) devoir *v irreg* §

got – (have) avoir *v irreg* §

grab – saisir *v reg*

grade – note *nf*

gram – gramme *nm*

grammar – grammaire *nf*

grandchildren – petits-enfants *nmpl*

grandad – papi *nm*

granddaughter – petite-fille *nf*

grandfather – grand-père *nm*

grandmother – grand-mère *nf*

grandparents – grands-parents *nmpl*

grandson – petit-fils *nm*

granny – mamie *nf*

grapefruit – pamplemousse *nm*

grapes – raisin *nm*

---

grass – herbe *nf*

grateful – reconnaissant *adj*

grave accent (è) – accent grave *nm*

gravy – sauce *nf*

greasy – gras, grasse *adj*

great! – chouette! *excl*, fantastique! *excl*, formidable! *excl*, sensass! *excl*

great – (big) grand *adj*

great grandfather – arrière-grand-père *nm*

great grandmother – arrière-grand-mère *nf*

Great Britain – Grande Bretagne *nf*

Greece – Grèce *nf*

Greek – grec, grecque *adj*

Greek person – Grec *nm*, Grecque *nf*

greedy – gourmand *adj*

green – vert *adj*

green bean – ‡haricot vert *nm*

green pepper – poivron vert *nm*

green salad – salade verte *nf*

greengrocer – marchand de fruits et légumes *nm*

greenhouse – serre *nf*

greens – légumes verts *nmpl*

greet – saluer *v reg*

greetings card – carte de vœux *nf*

grey – gris *adj*

grin – sourire *v irreg* §

grip – saisir *v reg*, serrer *v reg*

grocer – épicier *nm*, épicière *nf*

groceries – provisions *nfpl*

grocer's shop – alimentation générale *nf*, épicerie *nf*

ground – (earth) terre *nf*
on the ground – par terre

ground – (sport) terrain *nm*

ground floor – rez-de-chaussée *nm*

group – groupe *nm*

grow – (become) devenir* *v irreg*

grow – (flowers, etc) pousser *v reg*

grow – (get bigger) grandir *v reg*

grow plants – cultiver *v reg*

grow old – vieillir *v reg*

grow up – grandir *v reg*

grown up – adulte *adj*

grumble – grogner *v reg*

grumpy – grincheur, grincheuse *adj*

guess – deviner *v reg*

guest house – pension *nf*

guide – guide *nm*

guide book – guide *nm*

guided tour – visite guidée *nf*

guilty – coupable *adj*

guinea-pig – cobaye *nm*, cochon d'Inde *nm*

guitar – guitare *nf*
play the guitar – jouer de la guitare *v reg*

guy – mec *nm sl*

gym – gymnase *nm*

gymnastics – gymnastique *nf*
do gymnastics – faire de la gymnastique *v irreg* §

---

nm - noun masculine	*nmpl* - noun masculine plural	*adj* - adjective	*conj* - conjunction
nf - noun feminine	*nfpl* - noun feminine plural	*adv* - adverb	*pron* - pronoun

H

habit – habitude *nf*
  be in the habit of – avoir
   l'habitude de *v irreg* §
  get into the habit of – prendre
   l'habitude de *v irreg* §
had – *see avoir v irreg* §
had to – *see devoir v irreg* §
hail – grêle *nf*
  it is hailing – il grêle
hair – cheveux *nmpl*
  have a haircut – se faire* couper
   les cheveux *v refl* §
hair dryer – sèche-cheveux *nm*
hairbrush – brosse à cheveux *nf*
haircut – coupe de cheveux *nf*
hairdresser – coiffeur *nm*,
  coiffeuse *nf*
hairstyle – coiffure *nf*
half – demi *adj*
  half an hour – demi-heure *nf*
  half back – (sport) demi *nm*
  half board – demi-pension *nf*
  half-brother – demi-frère *nm*
  half-price – demi-tarif *nm*
  half-sister – demi-sœur *nf*
half – mi- *pref*
  half way – à mi-chemin
  half term holiday – congé de mi-
   trimestre *nm*
half – moitié *nf*
  half price – à moitié-prix
half past – (time) et demi, et demie
  half past twelve – midi et demi
   (12.30)
  half past twelve – minuit et demi
   (00.30)
  half past two – deux heures et
   demie
hall – (entrance) vestibule *nm*
hall – (large room) salle *nf*

ham – jambon *nm*
  ham sandwich – sandwich au
   jambon *nm*
hamburger – ‡hamburger *nm*
hammer – marteau *nm*
hamster – ‡hamster *nm*
hand – main *nf*
  give s.o. a hand – donner un coup
   de main à *v reg*
handbag – sac à main *nm*
handball – ‡handball *nm*
handicapped – ‡handicapé *adj*
handkerchief – mouchoir *nm*
handle – manche *nm*
handmade – fait à la main *adj*
handsome – beau, bel, belle *adj*
handwriting – écriture *nf*
handy – commode *adj*
handyman – bricoleur *nm*
hang gliding – deltaplane *nm*
hang up – (phone) raccrocher *v reg*
happen – arriver* *v reg*,
  se passer* *v refl*
happiness – bonheur *nm*
happy – heureux, heureuse *adj*,
  content *adj*
Happy Birthday! – Bon
  anniversaire!
Happy Christmas! – Joyeux Noël!
Happy name day! – Bonne fête!
Happy New Year! – Bonne année!
happy with – satisfait *adj*
harbour – port *nm*
hard – (not easy) difficile *adj*
hard – (not soft) dur *adj*
hard disk – disque dur *nm*
hard of hearing – dur à l'oreille *adj*
hardly – à peine, ne...guère *adv*
hardware shop – droguerie *nf*,
  quincaillerie *nf*

---

hardworking – travailleur, travailleuse *adj*

harshly – durement *adv*

has – *see avoir v irreg* §

has to – *see devoir v irreg* §

hassle – difficulté *nf*, peine *nf*, mal *nm*

hassle – ‡harceler *v reg* †

haste – ‡hâte *nf*

hasten – ‡se hâter *v refl*

hasty – précipité *adj*

hat – chapeau *nm*

hate – détester *v reg*, avoir horreur de *v irreg* §

have – *see avoir v irreg* §

have a bad back – avoir mal au dos *v irreg* §

have a bath – prendre un bain *v irreg* §

have a cold – avoir un rhume *v irreg* §, être enrhumé *v irreg* §

have a detention – être collé *v irreg coll* §

have a flair for – avoir la bosse de *v irreg* §

have a good journey! – bonne route!

have a good time – s'amuser* *v refl*

have a good trip! – bon voyage!

have a good weekend! – bon week-end!

have a headache – avoir mal à la tête *v irreg* §

have a holiday – avoir des vacances *v irreg* §

have a job – travailler *v reg*

have a meal – prendre un repas *v irreg* §

have a nice day! – bonne journée!

have a nice evening! – bonne soirée!

have a problem with – avoir des ennuis avec *v irreg* §

have a raised temperature – avoir de la fièvre *v irreg* §

have a safe journey home! – bon retour!

have a sore throat – avoir mal à la gorge *v irreg* §

have a walk – faire une promenade *v irreg* §

have breakfast – prendre le petit déjeuner *v irreg* §

have difficulty in – avoir du mal à *v irreg* §

have dinner – (evening) dîner *v reg*

have free time – être libre *v irreg* §

have friends round – recevoir des amis *v irreg* §

have just done – venir de faire *v irreg* §

have lunch – déjeuner *v reg*

have something cleaned – faire nettoyer *v irreg* §

have something repaired – faire réparer *v irreg* §

have stomach ache – avoir mal au ventre *v irreg* §

have the opportunity to – avoir la possibilité de *v irreg* §

have to – devoir *v irreg* §

have to – falloir *v irreg* §

have toothache – avoir mal aux dents *v irreg* §

hay fever – rhume des foins *nm*

hazelnut – noisette *nf*

he, it – il *pers pron*

head – tête *nf*

headache – mal à la tête *nm*

heading – titre *nm*

headlight – phare *nm*

headphones – écouteurs *nmpl*

heads or tails? – pile ou face?

headscarf – foulard *nm*

---

headteacher – directeur *nm*,
  directrice *nf*, proviseur *nm*,
  principal *nm*, principale *nf*

health – santé *nf*

healthy – sain *adj*

heap – tas *nm*

hear – entendre *v reg*

hear from – recevoir des nouvelles de
  v irreg §

heart – cœur *nm*
  by heart – par cœur

heat – chaleur *nf*

heater – radiateur *nm*

heating – chauffage *nm*

heatwave – vague de chaleur *nf*

heavy – lourd *adj*

hedge – ‡haie *nf*

heel – (of shoe) talon *nm*

height – ‡hauteur *nf*

height – (person) taille *nf*

helicopter – hélicoptère *nm*

heliport – héliport *nm*

hello! – bonjour! salut!

helmet – casque *nm*

help – aide *nf*, secours *nm*
  help! – au secours!

help – aider *v reg*

help oneself – se servir* *v refl* §

hen – poule *nf*

her, it – la *pron*

her – son, sa, ses *poss adj*, à elle

herbal tea – tisane *nf*

herd – troupeau *nm*

here – ici *adv*

here are, here is – voici *prep*

hero – ‡héros *nm*

heroin – héroïne *nf*

heroine – héroïne *nf*

herself – elle-même *pron f*

hesitate – hésiter *v reg*

HGV – poids lourds *nm*

hi! – salut!

hide – cacher *v reg*
  hide o.s. – se cacher* *v refl*

hi-fi system – chaîne Hi-Fi *nf*

high – ‡haut *adj*, élevé *adj*

high speed train – train à grande
  vitesse (TGV) *nm*

high street – grand-rue *nf*

high temperature – fièvre *nf*

high tide – marée haute *nf*

high wind – tempête *nf*

highway – route nationale *nf*

highway code – code de la route *nm*

hike – randonnée *nf*
  go for a hike – faire une
  randonnée *v irreg* §

hiker – randonneur *nm*,
  randonneuse *nf*

hiking boots – chaussures de marche
  nfpl

hill – colline *nf*

him, it – le *pron*

himself – lui-même *pron*

Hindu – hindou *adj*

Hindu person – Hindou *nm*,
  Hindoue *nf*

hip – hanche *nf*

hire – louer *v reg*
  for hire – à louer

hiring – location *nf*

his – son, sa, ses *poss adj*, à lui

historic – historique *adj*

history – histoire *nf*
  ancient history – histoire
  ancienne *nf*
  modern history – histoire
  moderne *nf*

hit – frapper *v reg*

hit song – tube *nm*

hobby – passe-temps *nm*

hockey – ‡hockey *nm*

hold – tenir *v irreg* §
  hold back – retenir *v irreg* §
  hold out – tendre *v reg*

---

prep - preposition	*v reg* - verb regular	*v refl* - verb reflexive	§ - see verb tables
pp - past participle	*v irreg* - verb irregular	† - see verb information	* - takes être

hold the line please! – ne quittez pas, s'il vous plaît!

hole – trou *nm*

holiday – (public) jour férié *nm*

holiday(s) – vacances *nfpl*
  Easter holidays – vacances de Pâques *nf*
  holiday plans – projets de vacances *nmpl*
  summer holidays – grandes vacances *nfpl*
  be on holiday – être en vacances *v irreg* §
  go on holiday – partir* en vacances *v irreg* §
  on holiday – en vacances

holiday cottage – gîte *nm*

holiday maker – vacancier *nm*, vacancière *nf*

Holland – ‡Hollande *nf*

hollow – creux, creuse *adj*

holly – ‡houx *nm*

home – foyer *nm*, maison *nf*
  at home – à la maison
  at the home of – chez
  go home – rentrer* à la maison *v reg*

home address – domicile *nm*

home economics – études ménagères *nfpl*

home game – match à domicile *nm*

home-made tart – tarte maison *nf*

homework – devoirs *nmpl*
  do one's homework – faire ses devoirs *v irreg* §

honest – honnête *adj*

honey – miel *nm*

hooligan – houligan *nm*, voyou *nm*

hope – espérer *v reg* †

hope – espoir *nm*

hoping to see you soon – (letter) dans l'espoir de vous voir bientôt

horizon – horizon *nm*

on the horizon – à l'horizon

horn – (car) klaxon *nm*

horn – (music) cor *nm*

horrible – affreux, affreuse *adj*

horrifying – effroyable *adj*

horror – horreur *nf*, épouvante *nf*
  horror film – film d'épouvante *nm*
  horror story – roman d'épouvante *nm*

horse – cheval *nm* (chevaux *nmpl*)

horse riding – équitation *nf*
  go horse riding – faire de l'équitation *v irreg* §

hospital – hôpital *nm*

hostel – foyer *nm*

hostel – (youth) auberge de jeunesse *nf*

hot – chaud *adj*
  hot water – eau chaude *nf*
  I am hot – j'ai chaud
  it is hot – (weather) il fait chaud

hotel – hôtel *nm*

hour – heure *nf*

house – maison *nf*
  at my house – chez moi
  detached house – maison individuelle *nf*, pavillon *nm*
  semi-detached house – maison jumelle *nf*, maison mitoyenne *nf*

housewife – femme au foyer *nf*

housework – ménage *nm*
  do the housework – faire du ménage *v irreg* §

housing estate – lotissement *nm*

hovercraft – aéroglisseur *nm*, hovercraft *nm*

how – comment *adv*
  how about a swim? – si on allait à la piscine?
  how are things? – ça va?
  how are you? – comment allez-vous? comment vas-tu?
  how are you? – ça va?

---

how do you say ... in French?
– comment se dit ... en français?
how do you spell that? – ça
s'écrit comment?
**how long have you been
learning French?** – depuis
quand apprenez-vous le français?
how long? – combien de temps?
how many? – combien (de)? *adv*
how much? – combien (de)? *adv*
how much do I owe you? – je
vous dois combien?
how much is it? – c'est combien?
how often do you do that? –
vous faites ça souvent?
however – cependant *conj*
huge – énorme *adj*, immense *adj*
humanities – histoire-géo *nf*
humour – humour *nm*
hundred – cent *adj*
   hundreds of – des centaines de

hundredth – centième *adj*
hunger – faim *nf*
   be hungry – avoir faim *v irreg* §
   I am hungry – j'ai faim
hunt – (chase) chasser *v reg*
   hunt for – chercher *v reg*
hurdle – (sport) ‡haie *nf*
hurried – pressé *adj*
hurry – se dépêcher* *v refl*, ‡se hâter*
v refl, se précipiter* *v refl*
   hurry up! – dépêche-toi!
   dépêchez-vous!
hurry – (haste) ‡hâte *nf*
   in a hurry – à la hâte
hurt oneself – se faire* mal *v refl* §
husband – mari *nm*, époux *nm*
hydrofoil – hydroptère *nm*
hypermarket – grande surface *nf*,
hypermarché *nm*
hyphen (-) – trait d'union *nm*

I

I – je, j' *pers pron*
   I would like – j'aimerais
ice – glace *nf*
   iced – glacé *adj*
ice-cream – glace *nf*
   chocolate ice-cream – glace au
chocolat *nf*
   strawberry ice-cream – glace à
la fraise *nf*
   vanilla ice-cream – glace à la
vanille *nf*
Iceland – Islande *nf*
Icelandic – islandais *adj*
ice-rink – patinoire *nf*
ice-skating – patinage sur glace *nm*
icy – glacé *adj*, glacial *adj*

ID – pièce d'identité *nf*
idea – idée *nf*
   good idea! – bonne idée!
ideal – idéal *adj*
identify – identifier *v reg*
identity – identité *nf*
identity card – carte d'identité *nf*
idiot – imbécile *nmf*
idiotic – imbécile *adj*
if – si *conj*
ill – malade *adj*
illness – maladie *nf*
illustration – illustration *nf*
imaginary – imaginaire *adj*
imagination – imagination *nf*

imagine – imaginer *v reg*,
s'imaginer* *v refl*
immediate – immédiat *adj*
immediately – immédiatement *adv*
immense – vaste *adj*
impatience – impatience *nf*
impatient – impatient *adj*
imperfect tense – imparfait *nm*
important – important *adj*
impossibility – impossibilité *nf*
impossible – impossible *adj*
impression – effet *nm*
impressive – impressionnant *adj*
in – dans *prep*
in – en *prep* and *pron*
  in autumn – en automne
  in capital letters – en majuscules
  in case – au cas où
  in Devon – dans le Devon
  in English – en anglais
  in fact – en fait
  in fashion – à la mode
  in French – en français
  in front of – devant *prep*
  in future – désormais *adv*
  in general – en général
  in good condition – en bon état
  in green – en vert
  in London – à Londres
  in my opinion – à mon avis
  in order to – pour, afin de *prep*
  in poor condition – en mauvais
  état
  in spite of – malgré *prep*
  in spring – au printemps
  in summer – en été
  in the 20th century – au
  vingtième siècle
  in the afternoon – l'après-midi
  in the country – à la campagne
  in the east – à l'est, dans l'Est
  in the end – en fin de compte
  in the evening – le soir

  in the middle of – au centre de,
  au milieu de
  in the morning – le matin
  in the mountains – à la montagne
  in the name of – au nom de
  in the north – au nord, dans le
  Nord
  in the open air – en plein air
  in the past – autrefois *adv*
  in the process of – en train de
  in the south – au sud, dans le Sud
  in the suburbs – en banlieue
  in the west – à l'ouest, dans
  l'Ouest
  in this case – dans ce cas
  in town – en ville
  in turn – à tour de rôle
  in uniform – en uniforme
  in winter – en hiver
included – compris *adj*
  service included – service
  compris
including – y compris
incredible – incroyable *adj*
indeed – en effet, vraiment *adv*
independent – indépendant *adj*,
  autonome *adj*
independent radio – radio libre *nf*
India – Inde *nf*
Indian – indien, indienne *adj*
Indian person – Indien *nm*,
  Indienne *nf*
indicator light – clignotant *nm*
individual – individuel,
  individuelle *adj*
individual – individu *nm*
indoors – à l'intérieur *adv*
industrial – industriel,
  industrielle *adj*
industrial area – zone industrielle *nf*
industry – industrie *nf*
inform – informer *v reg*

---

nm - noun masculine   *nmpl* - noun masculine plural   *adj* - adjective   *conj* - conjunction
nf - noun feminine   *nfpl* - noun feminine plural   *adv* - adverb   *pron* - pronoun

information – renseignement *nm*
information office – agence de renseignements *nf*, bureau de renseignements *nm*
   ask for information – demander des renseignements *v reg*
   some information – un renseignement *nm*
information technology – informatique *nf*
inhabitant – habitant *nm*
injection – piqûre *nf*
injure – blesser *v reg*
injured – blessé *adj*
injury – blessure *nf*
ink jet printer – imprimante à jet d'encre *nf*
in line skates – rollers in-line *nmpl*
insect – bête *nf*, insecte *nm*
inside – intérieur *nm*
inside – dedans *adv*
inside out – à l'envers *adv*
inspect tickets – contrôler *v reg*
inspector – (tickets) contrôleur *nm*
install – installer *v reg*
instant – instant *nm*
instead of – au lieu de *prep*
instructor – moniteur *nm*
instrument – instrument *nm*
insurance – assurance *nf*
insure – assurer *v reg*
intelligence – intelligence *nf*
intelligent – intelligent *adj*
intention – intention *nf*
interest – intérêt *nm*
   be interested in – s'intéresser* à *v refl*
interesting – intéressant *adj*
international – international *adj*
internet – net *nm*, Internet *nm*
   surf the net – naviguer sur Internet *v reg*, surfer sur le Net *v reg*

interview – interviewer *v reg*
into – dans *prep*
introduce – présenter *v reg*
introduce o.s. – se présenter* *v refl*
invent – inventer *v reg*
investigate – faire une enquête *v irreg* §, enquêter sur *v reg*
invitation – invitation *nf*
invite – inviter *v reg*
Ireland – Irlande *nf*
Irish – irlandais *adj*
Irish person – Irlandais *nm*, Irlandaise *nf*
iron – fer à repasser *nm*
iron clothes – repasser *v reg*
   do the ironing – faire du repassage *v irreg* §
irritate – énerver *v reg*
irritated – énervé *adj*, irrité *adj*
is – *see* être *v irreg* §
   it is – c'est
   isn't it? – n'est-ce pas?
Islamic – islamique *adj*
island – île *nf*
isolated – isolé *adj*
IT – informatique *nf*
it – le, la, l' *pron*
it – il, elle *pron*
   it depends upon – ça dépend de
   it is cold – (weather) il fait froid
   it is a pity – c'est dommage
   it is – c'est, il est, elle est
   it was – c'était, il était, elle était
Italian – italien, italienne *adj*
Italian – (language) italien *nm*
Italian – (person) Italien *nm*, Italienne *nf*
Italy – Italie *nf*
item – article *nm*
its – son, sa, ses *poss adj*
itself – elle-même, lui-même *pron*

J

jack – (car) cric *nm*
jack – (bowls) cochonnet *nm*
jacket – veste *nf*, veston *nm*
jackpot – gros lot *nm*
jam – confiture *nf*
   jar of jam – pot de confiture *nm*
jam – (traffic) bouchon *nm*
Jamaica – Jamaïque *nf*
Jamaican – jamaïquain *adj*
January – janvier *nm*
Japan – Japon *nm*
Japanese – japonnais *adj*
Japanese person – Japonnais *nm*,
   Japonnaise *nf*
jar (of jam) – pot (de confiture) *nm*
jazz – jazz *nm*
jazz band – orchestre de jazz *nm*
jealous – jaloux, jalouse *adj*
jeans – jean bleu *nm*
   pair of jeans – jean *nm*
jelly – gelée *nf*
jet – (plane) jet *nm*
jeweller's shop – bijouterie *nf*
jewellery – bijoux *nmpl*
Jewish – juif, juive *adj*
job – emploi *nm*, poste *nm*, travail *nm*
jobs – (odd) bricolage *nm*

do odd jobs – faire du bricolage
   v irreg §
jog – faire du jogging *v irreg* §
jogging – jogging *nm*
join – joindre *v irreg* §, rejoindre
   v irreg §, devenir* membre de *v irreg* §
joke – blague *nf*, plaisanterie *nf*
jotter – cahier *nm*
journalist – journaliste *nmf*
journey – trajet *nm*, voyage *nm*
joy – joie *nf*
joy stick – manette *nf*
judge – juger *v reg* †
judo – judo *nm*
   do judo – faire du judo *v irreg* §
jug – cruche *nf*, pichet *nm*
juice – jus *nm*
   fruit juice – jus de fruit *nm*
   orange juice – jus d'orange *nm*
July – juillet *nm*
jumbo jet – avion géant *nm*
jump – sauter *v reg*
jumper – tricot *nm*
June – juin *nm*
junk room – débarras *nm*
just – (fair) juste *adj*
just – (only) ne...que
just arrived (I have) – je viens
   d'arriver

K

karate – karaté *nm*
kart – kart *nm*
kebab – brochette *nf*
keen – vif, vive *adj*

be keen on – se passionner* pour
   v refl, beaucoup aimer *v reg*
keen on sport – sportif, sportive *adj*
keep – garder *v reg*
keep an eye on – surveiller *v reg*

---

nm - noun masculine	*nmpl* - noun masculine plural	*adj* - adjective	*conj* - conjunction
nf - noun feminine	*nfpl* - noun feminine plural	*adv* - adverb	*pron* - pronoun

keep-fit – exercices physiques *nmpl*
keep to the right! – serrez la droite!
kettle – bouilloire *nf*
key – (door, car) clé *nf*
key – (on keyboard) touche *nf*
keyboard – clavier *nm*
keyhole – trou de serrure *nm*
key ring – porte-clés *nm*
kick – coup de pied *nm*
kid – gamin *nm*, gamine *nf*,
  gosse *nmf sl*
kill – tuer *v reg*
kilo(gram) – kilo(gramme) *nm*
kilometre – kilomètre *nm*
  10 kilometres from – à dix
  kilomètres de
kind – gentil, gentille *adj*
kind – sorte *nf*
  kind of – une sorte de
kindly – gentiment *adv*
kindness – gentillesse *nf*
king – roi *nm*
kiosk – kiosque *nm*

kiss – bise *nf*, bisou *nm*
kiss – embrasser *v reg*
kitchen – cuisine *nf*
kite – cerf-volant *nm*
kitten – chaton *nm*
kiwi fruit – kiwi *nm*
knee – genou *nm*
kneel – s'agenouiller* *v refl*
knickers – un slip *nm*
knife – couteau *nm*
knock – frapper *v reg*
  knock on the door – frapper à la
  porte *v reg*
knock over – renverser *v reg*
know – (fact) savoir *v irreg* §
  know how to – savoir *v irreg* §
  I don't know – je ne sais pas
  know about sthg – être au courant
  de *v irreg* §
know – (place, person, book) connaître
  v irreg §
known – connu *see* connaître *v irreg* §

L

laboratory – laboratoire *nm*
lad – garçon *nm*, gars *nm*
ladder – échelle *nf*
Ladies – Mesdames *nfpl*
Ladies – Mesdemoiselles *nfpl*
Ladies' toilets – Dames
lady – dame *nf*
  cleaning lady – femme de ménage
  nf
lady's suit – tailleur *nm*
lake – lac *nm*
lamb – agneau *nm*
lamp – lampe *nf*

land – terre *nf*
land – (plane) atterrir *v reg*
landing – (plane) atterrissage *nm*
landing – (top of stairs) palier *nm*
language – langue *nf*
  foreign language – langue
  étrangère *nf*
  modern languages – langues
  modernes *nfpl*
lantern – lanterne *nf*
laptop – (computer) portable *nm*
large – grand *adj*
laser printer – imprimante à laser *nf*

---

prep - preposition   *v reg* - verb regular   *v refl* - verb reflexive   § - see verb tables
pp - past participle   *v irreg* - verb irregular   † - see verb information   * - takes être

last – durer *v reg*
last – dernier, dernière *adj*
  last night – hier soir
  last week – la semaine dernière *nf*
  last year – l'année dernière *nf*
  at last – enfin *adv*
late – (for appointment) en retard
late – (not early) tard *adv*
later – plus tard
  see you later! – à tout à l'heure
latest – dernier, dernière *adj*
Latin – latin *nm*
laugh – rire *v irreg* §
laundrette – laverie *nf*
law – loi *nf*
lawn – gazon *nm,* pelouse *nf*
  cut (mow) lawn – tondre la
  pelouse *v reg*
lawyer – avocat *nm,* avocate *nf*
lazy – paresseux, paresseuse *adj*
le Havre – ‡le Havre
  at le Havre – au Havre
lead – mener *v reg* †
  in the lead – en tête
lead – (dog) laisse *nf*
lead – (metal) plomb *nm*
lead free – sans plomb *adj*
leader – (group) responsable *nmf*
leaf – feuille *nf*
leaflet – dépliant *nm*
lean – pencher *v reg*
lean over – se pencher* *v refl*
learn – apprendre *v irreg* §
least – le moindre, la moindre *adj*
leather – cuir *nm*
  made of leather – en cuir
leather goods – maroquinerie *nf*
leave – (go away) partir* de *v irreg* §,
  quitter *v reg*
leave – (something) laisser *v reg*
leave ... lying around – laisser
  traîner...*v reg*

leave harbour – sortir* du port
  v irreg §
leave the table – quitter la table *v reg*
left – (not right) gauche *nf*
  on the left – à gauche
left-handed – gaucher, gauchère *adj*
left luggage office – consigne *nf*
left luggage ticket – ticket de
  consigne *nm*
leg – jambe *nf*
leggings – un caleçon *nm*
leisure – loisir *nm*
leisure centre – centre de loisirs *nm*
lemon – citron *nm*
  lemon tea – thé au citron *nm*
lemonade – limonade *nf*
lend – prêter *v reg*
length – (measurement) longueur *nf*
length – (time) durée *nf*
lens – lentille *nf,* verre *nf*
  contact lenses – lentilles *nfpl*
less – moins *adv*
  less expensive – moins cher
less – moins *prep*
  less ... than – moins ... que
  less than two kilos – moins de
  deux kilos
lesson – cours *nm,* leçon *nf*
let (allow) – laisser *v reg*
  let s.o. know – informer *v reg*
  let me know – faites-moi savoir,
  prévenez-moi
let – (flat, house) louer *v reg*
  to let – à louer
letter – lettre *nf*
  letter box – boîte aux lettres *nf*
  registered letter – lettre
  recommandée *nf*
lettuce – laitue *nf,* salade *nf*
level – plat *adj*
level – niveau *nm*
  level crossing – passage à niveau *nm*
liar – menteur *nm,* menteuse *nf*

---

nm - noun masculine   *nmpl* - noun masculine plural   *adj* - adjective   *conj* - conjunction
nf - noun feminine   *nfpl* - noun feminine plural   *adv* - adverb   *pron* - pronoun

librarian – bibliothécaire *nmf*, documentaliste *nmf*

library – bibliothèque *nf*

licence – permis *nm*

lick – lécher *v reg* †

lie down –s'allonger *v refl* †, se coucher* *v refl*
  have a lie in – faire la grasse matinée *v irreg* §

life – vie *nf*
  daily life – la vie quotidienne *nf*

lifebelt – bouée de sauvetage *nf*, ceinture de sauvetage *nf*

lifeguard – maître-nageur *nm*

lift – ascenseur *nm*

lift up – lever *v reg* †

light – (not heavy) léger, légère *adj*

light –(colour) clair *adj*
  light blue – bleu clair *adj inv*

light – lumière *nf*

light – (switch on) allumer *v reg*

light bulb – ampoule *nf*

light pen – crayon optique *nm*

lighthouse – phare *nm*

lightly – légèrement *adv*

lightning – éclair *nm*

like – (similar) pareil, pareille *adj*, semblable *adj*

like – comme *prep*
  like that – comme ça, de cette façon *adv*

like – aimer *v reg*, bien aimer *v reg*
  I would like – je voudrais, j'aimerais
  like a lot – beaucoup aimer *v reg*

likely – probable *adj*

limit – limite *nf*

limit – limiter *v reg*

line – ligne *nf*

line – (queue) queue *nf*

line – (track) voie *nf*

linen – (household) linge *nm*
  dirty linen – linge sale *nm*

lion – lion *nm*

lip – lèvre *nf*
  lip-read – lire sur les lèvres *v irreg* §

lipstick – rouge à lèvres *nm*

liquid – liquide *adj*

list – liste *nf*

listen (to) – écouter *v reg*

literature – littérature *nf*

litre – litre *nm*

little – (not big) petit *adj*

little – (not much) peu *adv*
  a little more – un peu plus
  a little of – un peu de

live – (alive) vivant *adj*

live – (broadcast) en direct

live – demeurer *v reg*, habiter *v reg*, loger *v reg* †
  where do you live? – où habites-tu?

live – (be alive) vivre *v irreg* §

lively – animé *adj*, vif, vive *adj*

liver – foie *nm*

living – vivant *adj*
  earn one's living – gagner sa vie *v reg*

living room – salle de séjour *nf*

load – charger *v reg* †

loaded – chargé *adj*

loads of – un tas de, des masses de

loaf – pain *nm*

local – local *adj*, du quartier

lock – fermer à clé *v reg*

lock – verrou *nm*
  lock – (bolt) verrouiller *v reg*

locker – casier *nm*

lodge – loger *v reg* †

lodger – locataire *nmf*

lodging – hébergement *nm*

loft – grenier *nm*

lollipop – sucette *nf*

London – Londres

---

prep - preposition   *v reg* - verb regular   *v refl* - verb reflexive   § - see verb tables
pp - past participle   *v irreg* - verb irregular   † - see verb information   * - takes être

lonely – solitaire *adj*
long – long, longue *adj*
  for a long time – longtemps *adv*
long walk – randonnée *nf*
long-sighted – presbyte *adj*
longer – plus long, plus longue *adj*
  no longer – ne...plus *adv*
look – regard *nm*
look – (have the appearance of) avoir
  l'air *v irreg* §
  look after – garder *v reg*, soigner
    v reg
  look after – s'occuper* de *v refl*
  look at – regarder *v reg*
  look for – chercher *v reg*
  look forward to – attendre avec
    impatience *v reg*
  look like – ressembler à *v reg*
  look out! – attention!
  look out on to – donner sur *v reg*
lorry – camion *nm*
lorry driver – camionneur *nm*,
  routier *nm*
lose – perdre *v reg*
  lose a match – perdre un match
    v reg
  lose one's way – perdre son chemin
    v reg, se perdre* *v refl*
  lose weight – perdre du poids *v reg*
lost – perdu *adj*
  lost property – objets trouvés
    nmpl
lost property office – bureau des
  objets trouvés *nm*
lot (of) – beaucoup de *adv*
  the lot – le tout

  quite a lot – pas mal de
lottery – loterie *nf*
loud – bruyant, fort *adj*
loudly – à haute voix *adv*
loudspeaker – ‡haut-parleur *nm*
lounge – salon *nm*
lousy – infect *adj sl*, moche *adj sl*
love – amour *nm*
love – adorer *v reg*, aimer *v reg*
  I'd love to – je veux bien
  love from – (letter end) amitiés,
    bisous, grosses bises
love story – (film) film d'amour *nm*
lovely – beau, bel, belle *adj*
low – bas, basse *adj*
lower – inférieur *adj*
luck – chance *nf*
  good luck! – bonne chance!
  to be lucky – avoir de la chance
    v irreg §
  bad luck! – quel dommage!
  bad luck – malchance *nf*
luggage – bagages *nmpl*
luggage carousel – tapis à bagages
  nm
lunch – déjeuner *nm*, repas de midi *nm*
  have lunch – déjeuner *v reg*
lunch box – cantine *nf*
lunch hour – heure du déjeuner *nf*
lunch time – midi *nm*
Luxembourg – Luxembourg *nm*
Luxembourger – Luxembourgeois
  nm, Luxembourgeoise *nf*
luxurious – de luxe *adj*
lyrics – paroles *nfpl*

M

machine – machine *nf*

mad – fou, fol, folle *adj*

magazine – illustré *nm*, magazine *nm*, revue *nf*

  glossy magazine – magazine de luxe *nm*

  women's magazine – magazine féminin *nm*

magic – magie *nf*

magician – magicien *nm*

magnificent – magnifique *adj*, superbe *adj*

mail – courrier *nm*

main – principal *adj*

majestic – majestueux, majestueuse *adj*

major – (over 18) majeur *adj*

major road – RN, route nationale *nf*

make – (brand name) marque *nf*

make – faire *v irreg* §

  make a film – tourner un film *v reg*

  make a mistake – faire une erreur *v irreg* §

  make a verb agree – faire accorder un verbe *v irreg* §

  make an effort – faire un effort *v irreg* §

  make fun of – se moquer* de *v refl*

  make money – gagner de l'argent *v reg*

  make progress – faire des progrès *v irreg* §

  make the bed – faire le lit *v irreg* §

  make up one's mind – se décider à* *v refl*

make-up – maquillage *nm*

make-up bag – trousse de maquillage *nf*

  put on make-up – se maquiller* *v refl*

male – mâle, masculin *adj*

male – mâle *nm*

malicious – malin, maligne *adj*

Malta – Malte *nf*

  Maltese – maltais *adj*

man – homme *nm*

manage – se débrouiller* *v refl*

manager – directeur *nm*, directrice *nf*, gérant *nm*, gérante *nf*, patron *nm*, patronne *nf*

mango – mangue *nf*

manner – manière *nf*

mansion – château *nm*

manual – manuel, manuelle *adj*

many – nombreux, nombreuse *adj*

many – beaucoup de *adv*

map – carte *nf*, plan *nm*

March – mars *nm*

mark – marquer *v reg*

mark with a cross – mettre une croix *v irreg* §

mark – (school) note *nf*

market – marché *nm*

  covered market – marché couvert *nm*

  open air market – marché en plein air *nm*

  market square – place du marché *nf*

marmalade – confiture d'oranges *nf*

marriage – mariage *nm*

married – marié *adj*

married couple – époux *nmpl*

marry – épouser *v reg*, se marier* avec *v refl*

  get married – se marier* *v refl*

marvellous – merveilleux, merveilleuse *adj*, sensationnel, sensationnelle *adj*

mascot – mascotte *nf*

masculine – masculin *adj*

---

prep - preposition	*v reg* - verb regular	*v refl* - verb reflexive	§ - see verb tables
pp - past participle	*v irreg* - verb irregular	† - see verb information	* - takes être

mash – (potatoes) purée de pommes de terre *nf*

massive – énorme *adj*

master – maître *nm*

match – (game) match *nm*

match – (stick) allumette *nf*
  box of matches – boîte d'allumettes *nf*

materials – matériaux *nmpl*

mathematics – mathématiques *nfpl*

maths – maths *nfpl*

matron – (school) infirmière *nf*

matter – importer *v reg*
  what does it matter? – qu'importe?
  it does not matter – ça ne fait rien
  what is the matter? – qu'est-ce qu'il y a?

mattress – matelas *nm*

mauve – mauve *adj*

maximum – maximum *adj*

May – mai *nm*

may – pouvoir *v irreg* §
  may I? – puis-je?

maybe – peut-être *adv*

mayonnaise – mayonnaise *nf*

mayor – maire *nm*

me – m', me, moi *pron*

meal – repas *nm*
  evening meal – repas du soir *nm*, dîner *nm*
  midday meal – déjeuner *nm*

mean – vouloir dire *v irreg* §
  what does..mean? – que veut dire..?

mean – (unkind) méchant *adj*

mean – (with money) avare *adj*

measure – mesurer *v reg*

meat – viande *nf*

mechanic – mécanicien *nm*, mécanicienne *nf*

medal – médaille *nf*

gold medal – médaille d'or *nf*

silver medal – médaille d'argent *nf*

bronze medal – médaille de bronze *nf*

medicine – (science) médecine *nf*

medicine – (treatment) médicament *nm*

Mediterranean (Sea) – (mer) Méditerranée *nf*

medium – (steak) à point

meet – rencontrer *v reg,* se retrouver* *v refl,* se revoir* *v refl* §

meet – (be introduced to) faire la connaissance de *v irreg* §

meeting – réunion *nf*, assemblée *nf*

melon – melon *nm*

member – membre *nm*

member – (club, etc) adhérent *nm*

member's card – carte d'adhérent *nf*

memory – mémoire *nf*, souvenir *nm*

mend – réparer *v reg*

Men's toilets – Hommes

menu – menu *nm*, carte *nf*

merchandise – marchandise(s) *nf (pl)*

merit – mérite *nm*

merit – mériter *v reg*

Merry Christmas! – Joyeux Noël!

mess – désordre *nm*
  in a mess – en désordre

mess about – (in class) chahuter *v reg*

message – message *nm*, mot *nm*

messy – en désordre *adj*

metal – métal *nm*

metallic – métallique *adj*

method – méthode *nf*

metre – mètre *nm*

micro-computer – (micro-) ordinateur *nm*

microchip – puce *nf*, processeur *nm*

microphone – micro *nm*

microscope – microscope *nm*

microwave – four à micro-ondes *nm*

midday – midi *nm*

---

at midday – à midi
midday meal – repas de midi *nm*
middle – milieu *nm*
  in the middle of – au milieu de
  be in the middle of doing – être
  en train de faire *v irreg* §
middle aged – d'un certain age
midnight – minuit *nm*
  at midnight – à minuit
midnight train – train de minuit *nm*
might – pourrait
mild – doux, douce *adj*
milk – lait *nm*
milkman – laitier *nm*
milk shake – milk-shake *nm*
million – million *nm*
mince – steak haché *nm*
mind – (pay attention to) faire
  attention à *v irreg* §
  mind the step – attention à la
  marche!
  I don't mind – ça m'est égal
  would you mind? – voudriez-
  vous?
mine – à moi
  it's mine – c'est à moi
miner – mineur *nm*
mineral water – eau minérale *nf*
minibus – minibus *nm*
minimum – minimum *nm*
minor – (under 18) mineur *adj*
minor – mineur *nm*
mint – menthe *nf*
mint tea – thé à la menthe *nm*
minus – moins *prep*
minute – minute *nf*
mirror – miroir *nm*, glace *nf*
Miss – Mademoiselle, Mlle *nf*
miss – (train, etc) manquer *v reg*,
  rater *v reg*
mist – brume *nf*
mistake – erreur *nf*

make a mistake – faire une erreur
  v irreg §
misty – brumeux, brumeuse *adj*
mix – mélanger *v reg* †
mixed – mixte *adj*
mixed cold meats – assiette anglaise
  nf
mixed salad – salade composée *nf*
moan – (complain) grogner *v reg*,
  râler *v reg*
model – modèle *nm*
  scale model – maquette *nf*
  model-making – modelisme *nm*
modem – modem *nm*
moderate – modéré *adj*
modern – moderne *adj*
modern history – histoire moderne
  nf
modern languages – langues
  modernes *nfpl*
moment – instant *nm*, moment *nm*
  at this moment – à ce moment,
  actuellement
  for the moment – pour le moment
Monday – lundi *nm*
money – argent *nm*
  change money – changer de
  l'argent *v reg* †
mongrel – bâtard *nm*, chien de race
  mixte *nm*
monkey – singe *nm*
monster – monstre *nm*
month – mois *nm*
  per month – par mois
monthly – mensuel, mensuelle *adj*
monument – monument *nm*
mood – humeur *nf*
  be in a bad mood – être de
  mauvaise humeur *v irreg* §
  be in a good mood – être de
  bonne humeur *v irreg* §
moon – lune *nf*
moped – mobylette *nf*

---

prep - preposition   *v reg* - verb regular   *v refl* - verb reflexive   § - see verb tables
pp - past participle   *v irreg* - verb irregular   † - see verb information   * - takes être

more – plus, davantage, encore *adv*
  more ... than – plus...que
  more and more – de plus en plus
  more or less – plus ou moins,
   à peu près
  there is no more – il n'y en a plus
morning – matin *nm*, matinée *nf*
  next morning – le lendemain
  matin
Moroccan – marocain *adj*
Morocco – Maroc *nm*
mosque – mosquée *nf*
mosquito – moustique *nm*
most (of) – la plupart de
mother – mère *nf*
  Mothers' day – fête des Mères *nf*
mother-in-law – belle-mère *nf*
motherly – maternel, maternelle *adj*
motor boat – bateau à moteur *nm*
motor home – camping car *nm*
motorbike – moto *nf*
motorcyclist – motocycliste *nmf*,
  motard *nm*
motorised bike – vélomoteur *nm*
motorist – automobiliste *nmf*
motorway – autoroute *nf*
mountain – montagne *nf*
mountain bike – VTT (vélo tout
  terrain) *nm*
mountain climbing – alpinisme *nm*
mountaineer – alpiniste *nmf*
mouse – souris *nf*
moustache – moustache *nf*
mouth – bouche *nf*
mouthful – bouchée *nf*
move – bouger *v reg* †,
  se déplacer* *v refl* †
move forward – s'avancer* *v refl* †
move house – déménager *v reg* †

movement – mouvement *nm*
moving walkway – trottoir roulant
  nm
mow the lawn – tondre la pelouse
  v reg
Mr, Sir – Monsieur
Mrs, Ms, Madam – Mme (Madame)
much – beaucoup de *adv*
  so much – tellement *adv*
mud – boue *nf*, vase *nf*
muddy – boueux, boueuse *adj*,
  couvert de boue *adj*
mug – tasse *nf*
multi-coloured – multicolore *adj*
multiple crash – carambolage *nm*
multi-storey car park – parking
  à étages *nm*
mum(my) – maman *nf*
museum – musée *nm*
mushroom – champignon *nm*
music – musique *nf*
  pop music – musique pop *nf*
music centre – chaîne compacte *nf*
music department – rayon de
  musique *nm*
music room – salle de musique *nf*
musician – musicien *nm*,
  musicienne *nf*
Muslim – musulman *adj*
Muslim – (person) Musulman *nm*,
  Musulmane *nf*
must – *see devoir v irreg* §
mustard – moutarde *nf*
mutton – mouton *nm*
my – mon, ma, mes *poss adj*
myself – moi-même *pron*
mysterious – mystérieux, mystérieuse
  adj
mystery – mystère *nm*

N

nail – (finger) ongle *nm*
nail – (for wood) clou *nm*
naked – nu, nue *adj*
name – nom *nm*
  in the name of – au nom de
  my name is – je m'appelle †
  what is your name? – comment
  t'appelles-tu? comment vous
  appelez-vous?
name day – fête *nf*
narrow – étroit *adj*
nasty – méchant *adj*, horrible *adj*,
  vilain *adj*
nation – nation *nf*
national – national *adj*
nationalist – nationaliste *adj*
nationality – nationalité *nf*
native to – originaire de *adj*
natural – naturel, naturelle *adj*
natural history – histoire naturelle
  nf
natural sciences – sciences
  naturelles *nfpl*
naturally – naturellement *adv*
nature – nature *nf*
naughty – méchant *adj*
navy – marine *nf*
  navy blue – bleu marine *adj inv*
near (to) – près (de) *adv*
near-sighted – myope *adj*
nearby, near here – près d'ici
nearly – presque *adv*
nearly to do something – faillir
  v irreg §
  I nearly missed the train – j'ai
  failli manquer le train
neat – bien rangé *adj*
necessary – nécessaire *adj*
to be necessary – falloir *v irreg* §

it is necessary – il faut
  see *v irreg* §
it was necessary – il fallait
  v irreg §
it will be necessary – il faudra
  v irreg §
it would be necessary –
  il faudrait
neck – cou *nm*
necklace – collier *nm*
nectarine – nectarine *nf*
need – besoin *nm*
  have need of – en avoir besoin
  v irreg §
  need to – avoir besoin de *v irreg* §
needle – aiguille *nf*
needlework – couture *nf*
negative – négatif, négative *adj*
neglect – négliger *v reg* †
neglected – négligé *adj*
neighbour – voisin *nm*, voisine *nf*
neighbourhood – voisinage *nm*,
  environs *nmpl*
neighbouring – voisin *adj*
neither – non plus *conj*
neither...nor – ne...ni...ni
  I have neither brother nor
  sister – je n'ai ni frère ni sœur
nephew – neveu *nm*
nervous – nerveux, nerveuse *adj*
Netherlands – Pays Bas *nmpl*
never – jamais *adv*
never – ne...jamais *adv*
never mind – tant pis
nevertheless – néanmoins, pourtant
  adv
new – (brand new) neuf, neuve *adj*
new – nouveau, nouvel, nouvelle *adj*
  New Year – nouvel an *nm*,
  nouvelle année *nf*

---

prep - preposition   *v reg* - verb regular   *v refl* - verb reflexive   § - see verb tables
pp - past participle   *v irreg* - verb irregular   † - see verb information   * - takes être

New Year's Day – jour de l'an *nm*
New Year's Eve – la Saint-
  Sylvestre
New Zealand – Nouvelle Zélande *nf*
news – informations *nfpl*,
  nouvelles *nfpl*
news – (cinema) actualités *nfpl*
newsagent – marchand de journaux
  nm
newspaper – journal *nm*
  (journaux *pl*)
next – prochain, suivant *adj*
  next week – la semaine prochaine
    nf
  next year – l'année prochaine *nf*
next – ensuite, puis *adv*
next to – à côté de *adv*
next to – auprès de *prep*
next door – d'à côté *adj*
nice – sympathique *adj*,
  sympa *adj inv sl*
nice – (pleasant) agréable *adj*
nice – (kind) gentil, gentille *adj*
nice – (pretty) joli *adj*
nice – (sweet) mignon, mignonne *adj*
nicely – gentiment *adv*
niece – nièce *nf*
night – nuit *nf*
  good night! – bonne nuit!
  last night – hier soir *adv*
  night club – boîte de nuit *nf*
nightdress – chemise de nuit *nf*
nightmare – cauchemar *nm*
nil – zéro *nm*
nine – neuf *adj*
nineteen – dix-neuf *adj*
ninety – quatre-vingt-dix *adj*
ninety-one – quatre-vingt-onze *adj*
ninth – neuvième *adj*
no – nul, nulle *adj*
no – non
no – pas de, aucun, aucune *adj*

no entry – accès interdit, défense
  d'entrer, passage interdit
no good at – nul, nulle en *adj*
no longer – ne...plus *neg adv*
no more – ne...plus *neg adv*
no parking – défense de
  stationner, stationnement interdit
no smoking – défense de fumer
no vacancies – complet
no-one – personne *pron*
  nobody – (with verb) ne...personne,
    personne ne... *pron*
  no-one else – personne d'autre
noise – bruit *nm*
noisy – bruyant *adj*
non-drinking – non-potable *adj*
non-drinking water – eau non
  potable *nf*
non-smoking – non-fumeur *adj*
none the less – quand même *conj*
noodles – nouilles *nfpl*
noon – midi *nm*
normal – normal *adj*
normally – normalement *adv*
north – nord *nm*
North America – Amérique du Nord
  nf
North Sea – mer du Nord *nf*
Northern Ireland – Irlande du Nord
  nf
Norway – Norvège *nf*
Norwegian – norvégien,
  norvégienne *adj*
nose – nez *nm*
nosebleed – saignement de nez *nm*
  have a nosebleed – saigner du nez
    v reg
nosy – curieux, curieuse *adj*
not – ne...pas *adv*
  not allowed – interdit *adj*
  not any – aucun, aucune *adj*
  not at all – pas du tout *adv*
  not bad – pas mal *adv*

---

not expensive – pas cher *adj*
not far from here – non loin d'ici *adv*
not included – non compris *adj*
not much – pas beaucoup, peu *adv*
not one – aucun, aucune *adj*
not only – non seulement *adv*
not to know – ignorer *v reg*
not yet – pas encore *adv*
note – (short letter) mot *nm*
note – (music) note *nf*
notebook – carnet *nm*
notepad – bloc-notes *nm*
note paper – papier à lettres *nm*
nothing – rien *pron*
  nothing – (with verb) ne...rien, rien ne... *pron*
  nothing else – rien d'autre *pron*
notice – remarquer *v reg*
notice – affiche *nf*

notice board – tableau d'affichage *nm*
nought – zéro *nm*
noun – nom *nm*
novel – roman *nm*
  detective novel – roman policier *nm*
November – novembre *nm*
now – maintenant *adv*
nowadays – de nos jours *adv*
nowhere – nulle part *adv*
number – numéro *nm*, nombre *nm*
number – (figure) chiffre *nm*
number plate – plaque d'immatriculation *nf*
numerous – nombreux, nombreuse *adj*
nurse – infirmier *nm*, infirmière *nf*
nursery school – école maternelle *nf*
nut – noisette *nf,* noix *nf*
nylon – nylon *nm*
  made of nylon – en nylon

O

oak tree – chêne *nm*
obedient – obéissant *adj*
obey – obéir à *v reg*
object – objet *nm*
obliged to – obligé de
oboe – hautbois *nm*
observe – observer *v reg*
obstacle – obstacle *nm*
obstinate – obstiné, têtu *adj*
obtain – obtenir *v irreg* §
obvious – évident *adj*
occasion – occasion *nf*
occasional – occasionel, occasionelle *adj*
occupant – occupant *nm*

occupation – (job) métier *nm*, profession *nf*
occupied – (seat, etc) occupé *adj*
ocean – océan *nm*
o'clock – heure *nf*
  at six o'clock – à six heures
October – octobre *nm*
odd – bizarre *adj*
odd – (not even) impair *adj*
odd jobs – bricolage *nm*, menus travaux *nmpl*, petits boulots *nmpl coll*
  do odd jobs – faire du bricolage *v irreg* §
of – de, d' *prep*

---

prep - preposition   v reg - verb regular   v refl - verb reflexive   § - see verb tables
pp - past participle   v irreg - verb irregular   † - see verb information   * - takes être

of course – bien entendu, bien sûr,
   certainement *adv*
of it – en *pron*
of them – en *pron*
off – de *prep*
   off – (cancelled) annulé *adj*
   off – (light) éteint *adj*
   off – (tap) fermé *adj*
   day off – jour de congé *nm*
   10% off – réduction de dix pour
      cent *nf*
offence – infraction *nf*
   commit an offence – être en
      infraction *v irreg* §
offend – offenser *v reg*
offended – outragé *adj*
offer – offre *nf*
offer – offrir *v irreg* §
office – bureau *nm*
often – souvent *adv*
   how often? – tous les combien?
oil – huile *nf*
oil change – vidange *nf*
oil painting – peinture à l'huile *nf*
OK! – bien! ça va! d'accord!
old – vieux, vieil, vieille *adj*
old – (ancient) ancien, ancienne *adj*
old – (former) ancien, ancienne *adj*
old – âgé *adj*
   how old are you? – quel âge
      avez-vous?
   I am 16 years old – j'ai seize ans
old age – vieillesse *nf*
old fashioned – démodé *adj*
olive oil – huile d'olive *nf*
Olympic games – jeux olympiques
   nmpl
omelette – omelette *nf*
   omelette with herbs – omelette
      aux fines herbes *nf*
   mushroom omelette – omelette
      aux champignons *nf*
on – sur *prep*

on – (light) allumé *adj*
on – (machine) en marche *adj*
on – (tap) ouvert *adj*
on and off – de temps en temps
   adv
on behalf of – au nom de, pour,
   de la part de
on board – à bord
on foot – à pied *adv*
on Friday – vendredi
on Fridays – le vendredi
on purpose – exprès *adv*
on the ground floor – au rez-de-
   chaussée
on the left – à la gauche
on the left of – à gauche de
on the other side – de l'autre côté
on the point of – sur le point de
on the right – à droite
on the top floor – au dernier étage
on time – à l'heure
on top of – au-dessus (de)
once – une fois *adv*
once more – une fois de plus,
   de nouveau *adv*
one – un, une *indef art*
one more time – encore une fois *adv*
one-off – unique *adj*, exceptionnel,
   exceptionnelle *adj*
one-way ticket – billet simple *nm*
one-way street – sens unique *nm*
oneself – soi-même *pron*
onion – oignon *nm*
only – ne...que *adv*
only – seulement *adv*
only – unique *adj*
   only daughter – fille unique *nf*
   only son – fils unique *nm*
onwards – en avant *adv*
open – ouvert *adj*
   open – (uncovered) découvert *adj*
   in the open air – en plein air
open – ouvrir *v irreg* §

| *nm* - noun masculine | *nmpl* - noun masculine plural | *adj* - adjective | *conj* - conjunction |
| *nf* - noun feminine | *nfpl* - noun feminine plural | *adv* - adverb | *pron* - pronoun |

open on to – donner sur *v reg*

opening – ouverture *nf*
  opening hours – heures
    d'ouverture *nfpl*

opera – opéra *nm*

operation – opération *nf*
  have an operation – se faire*
    opérer *v refl* §

opinion – avis *nm*, opinion *nf*
  in my opinion – à mon avis

opinion poll – sondage *nm*

opportunity – occasion *nf*

opposite – contraire *nm*
  in the opposite direction – en
    sens contraire

opposite – en face de *prep*

opt for – opter (pour) *v reg*

optician – opticien *nm*, opticienne *nf*

optimist – optimiste *nmf*

optimistic – optimiste *adj*

optional – facultatif, facultative *adj*

or – ou *conj*

oral question – question orale *nf*

oral test – épreuve orale *nf*

orange – orange *adj*

orange – (fruit) orange *nf*

orange juice – jus d'orange *nm*

orchestra – orchestre *nm*

order – (café) commande *nf*

order – commander *v reg*

order – (sequence) ordre *nm*
  in alphabetical order – par ordre
    alphabétique
  in order of importance – par
    ordre d'importance
  in order to – pour *prep*

ordinal number – ordinal *nm*

ordinary – ordinaire *adj*

organise – arranger *v reg* †,
  organiser *v reg*

organised – organisé *adj*

orphan – orphelin *nm*, orpheline *nf*

other – autre *adj*
  the other day – l'autre jour *nm*
  otherwise – autrement *adv*

ouch! ow! – aïe! *excl*

ought – *see devoir v irreg* §

our – notre, nos *adj poss* à nous

ourselves – nous-mêmes *pron*

out – dehors *adv*
  out – (light) éteint *adj*
  out – (not at home) sorti
  out of breath – hors d'haleine
  out of date – périmé *adj*
  out of order – (broken down) en
    panne *adv*
  out of season – hors saison
  six out of ten – six sur dix
  take out of – prendre dans *v irreg* §

outfit – habit *nm*, tenue *nf*

outside – à l'extérieur, dehors *adv*

outside – extérieur *nm*

outside – hors de *prep*

oval – ovale *adj*

oven – four *nm*

over – au-dessus de *prep*

over – par-dessus *prep*

over – (across) de l'autre côté de

over – (ended) fini *adj*

over – (more than) plus de

over – (past) passé *adj*

over there – là-bas *adv*

overalls – bleu de travail *nm*

overcoat – pardessus *nm*

overseas – étranger, étrangère *adj*
  d'outre-mer *adj*

overtake – dépasser *v reg*

overturn – se renverser* *v refl*

owe – *see devoir v irreg* §

own – posséder *v reg* †

own – propre *adj*

owner – patron *nm*, patronne *nf*,
  propriétaire *nmf*

oxygen – oxygène *nm*

P

pack – (cases) faire les valises *v irreg* §
pack of cards – jeu de cartes *nm*
package – paquet *nm*
packed lunch – repas froid *nm*
pad – (writing) bloc-notes *nm*
paddock – paddock *nm*
page – feuille *nf*, page *nf*
  at the bottom of the page – au bas de la page
paid – payé *adj*
pain – douleur *nf,* mal *nm*
  be in pain – avoir mal *v irreg* §, souffrir *v irreg* §
painful – douloureux, douleureuse *adj*
paint – faire de la peinture *v irreg* §
painter – peintre *nm*
pair (of) – paire *nf*
  pair of shoes – paire de chaussures *nf*
  pair of jeans – un jean *nm*
  pair of pyjamas – un pyjama *nm*
  pair of shorts – un short *nm*
  pair of tights – un collant *nm*
  pair of trousers – un pantalon *nm*
Pakistan – Pakistan *nm*
Pakistani – pakistanais *adj*
Pakistani person – Pakistanais *nm*, Pakistanaise *nf*
palace – palais *nm*
pale – pâle *adj*
pancake – crêpe *nf*
paper – papier *nm*
paper – (newspaper) journal *nm*
paperback – livre de poche *nm*
paperclip – trombone *nm*
paragraph – paragraphe *nm*
parcel – paquet *nm*, colis *nm*
parent – parent *nm*
Paris – Paris

Parisian – parisien, parisienne *adj*
Parisian – Parisien *nm*, Parisienne *nf*
park – garer *v reg*, stationner *v reg*
park – jardin public *nm*, parc *nm*
parking – stationnement *nm*
  parking meter – parcmètre *nm*
  parking space – parking *nm*
  parking ticket – procès-verbal *nm*
parrot – perroquet *nm*
part – partie *nf*
  take part in – participer à *v reg*
  part-time – à temps partiel
part – (role) rôle *nm*
particular – particulier, particulière *adj*
  in particular – en particulier
partner – partenaire *nmf*
party – boum *nf*, fête *nf*
pass – passer* *v reg*
pass an exam – être reçu à un examen *v irreg* §, réussir à un examen *v reg*
passage – passage *nm*
passenger – passager *nm*, passagère *nf*
passenger – (train) voyageur *nm*, voyageuse *nf*
passer-by – passant *nm*, passante *nf*
Passover – Pâque juive *nf*
passport – passeport *nm*
past – passé *nm*
past – (clock time)
  five past four – quatre heures cinq
  quarter past three – trois heures et quart
  half past six – six heures et demie
pasta – pâtes *nfpl*
paste – pâte *nf*
pastime – passe-temps *nm*
pastry – pâtisserie *nf*

---

nm - noun masculine	*nmpl* - noun masculine plural	*adj* - adjective	*conj* - conjunction
nf - noun feminine	*nfpl* - noun feminine plural	*adv* - adverb	*pron* - pronoun

pastry cook – pâtissier *nm*, pâtissière *nf*

past tense – passé *nm*

pâté – pâté *nm*

path – chemin *nm*, sentier *nm*

pathetic – minable *adj*

patience – patience *nf*

patient – patient *adj*

patient – (sick person) malade *nmf*, patient *nm*, patiente *nf*

patio – terrasse *nf*

pavement – trottoir *nm*

paw – patte *nf*

pay (for) – payer *v reg* †

pay attention (to) – faire attention (à) *v irreg* §

pay a visit to – (person) aller* voir *v irreg* §

pay a visit to – (place) visiter *v reg*

pay up – régler *v reg* †

PC – (computer) ordinateur *nm*

PE – éducation physique, EPS (éducation physique et sportive) *nf*

peace – paix *nf*

peaceful – paisible *adj*, tranquille *adj*

peacefully – tranquillement *adv*

peach – pêche *nf*

peanut – cacahuète *nf*

pear – poire *nf*

peas – petits pois *nmpl*

peculiar – particulier, particulière *adj*

pedestrian – piéton *nm*

pedestrian crossing – passage clouté *nm*

pedestrian precinct – zone piétonne *nf*

pen – stylo *nm*

pencil – crayon *nm*

pencil case – trousse *nf*

pencil sharpener – taille-crayon *nm*

pen-friend – correspondant *nm*, correspondante *nf*

penknife – canif *nm*

penniless – sans le sou *adj*

pensioner – retraité *nm*, retraitée *nf*, personne du troisième âge *nf*

people – gens *nmpl*

pepper – poivre *nm*

pepper – (sweet) poivron *nm*

per – par *prep*

   per cent – pour cent

   per day – par jour

   per hour – de l'heure

   per kilo – par kilo

   per month – par mois

   per person – par personne

   per week – par semaine

percussion instrument – instrument à percussion *nm*

perfect – impeccable *adj*, parfait *adj*

perfectly – parfaitement *adv*

performance – représentation *nf*, séance *nf*, spectacle *nm*

performer – artiste *nmf*

performing arts – arts du spectacle *nmpl*, arts scéniques *nmpl*

perfume – parfum *nm*

perfume shop – parfumerie *nf*

perhaps – peut-être *adv*

period – (of time) période *nf*

period – (menstrual) règles *nfpl*

   I've got my period – j'ai mes règles

permission – autorisation *nf*, permission *nf*

permit – permis *nm*

permitted – permis *adj*

person – personne *nf*

personal – personnel, personnelle *adj*

personal stereo – baladeur *nm*

persuade – persuader *v reg*

pet – animal domestique *nm*

petrol – essence *nf*

   4-star leaded petrol – super *nm*

   unleaded petrol – essence sans plomb *nf*

---

petrol pump – pompe *nf*
petrol-pump attendant – pompiste *nm*
petrol station – station-service *nf*
pharmacy – pharmacie *nf*
phone – téléphone *nm*, appareil *nm coll*
  on the phone – à l'appareil *coll*
phone – téléphoner *v reg*, passer un coup de fil à *v reg*
phone box – cabine téléphonique *nf*
phone book – annuaire *nm*
phone call – coup de téléphone *nm*
phone card – carte téléphonique *nf*
phone number – numéro de téléphone *nm*
photo – photo *nf*
  take a photo – prendre une photo *v irreg* §
photocopy – photocopie *nf*
photocopy – photocopier *v reg*
photocopier – photocopieuse *nf*
photograph – photographier *v reg*
photographer – photographe *nmf*
photography – photographie *nf*
physical – physique *adj*
physical education – éducation physique *nf*
physics – physique *nf*
physiotherapist – kinésithérapeute *nmf*
piano – piano *nm*
  play the piano – jouer du piano *v reg*
pick – (choose) choisir *v reg*
pick – (flowers) cueillir *v irreg* §
pick up – (off the ground) ramasser *v reg*, soulever *v reg* †
pick up – (collect) prendre *v irreg* §
pick up – (child from school) récupérer *v reg* †, aller* chercher *v irreg* §

pick up – (phone) décrocher le téléphone *v reg*
picnic – pique-nique *nm*
picnic – pique-niquer *v reg*
picnic area – aire de pique-nique *nf*
picture – image *nf,* tableau *nm*
picturesque – pittoresque *adj*
piece (of) – morceau (de) *nm*
piece of information – une information *nf*
pig – cochon *nm*, porc *nm*
pile – tas *nm*
pill – comprimé *nm*
pillow – oreiller *nm*
pillowcase – taie d'oreiller *nf*
pilot – pilote *nm*
pineapple – ananas *nm*
pink – rose *adj*
pitch – terrain *nm*
pitch – (campsite) emplacement *nm*
pitch the tent – dresser la tente *v reg*
pity – pitié *nf,* dommage *nm*
  what a pity! – quel dommage!
pizza – pizza *nf*
placard – pancarte *nf*
place – endroit *nm*, lieu *nm*
  take place – avoir lieu *v irreg* §
  at my place – chez moi
place – placer *v reg* †
place – (space) place *nf*
place – (market) place du marché *nf*
place of birth – lieu de naissance *nm*
plait – natte *nf*
plan – projet *nm*
  holiday plans – projets de vacances *nmpl*
plan – avoir l'intention de faire *v irreg* §, faire des projets *v irreg* §
  as planned – comme prévu
plane – avion *nm*
  by plane – en avion
plant – plante *nf*

---

plant – planter *v reg*
plaster – (sticking) sparadrap *nm*
plastic – plastique *adj*
   made of plastic – en plastique
plate – assiette *nf*
platform – quai *nm*
platform ticket – ticket de quai *nm*
play – pièce de théâtre *nf*
play – jouer *v reg*
   play a game of tennis – faire une
   partie de tennis *v irreg* §
   play a trick on – jouer un tour à
   v reg
   play chess – jouer aux échecs *v reg*
   play football – jouer au football
   v reg
   play golf – jouer au golf *v reg*
   play the guitar – jouer de la
   guitare *v reg*
   play the piano – jouer du piano
   v reg
   play the violin – jouer du violon
   v reg
player – joueur *nm*, joueuse *nf*
playground – aire de jeu *nf*
playground – (school) cour *nf*
playing card – carte à jouer *nf*
playing field – terrain de sport *nm*
pleasant – agréable *adj*,
   sympathique *adj*
pleasantly – agréablement *adv*
please – s'il te plaît, s'il vous plaît,
   SVP
   please do not... – prière de ne
   pas...
pleased to meet you – enchanté(e)
   de faire votre connaissance
pleasure – plaisir *nm*
   with pleasure – avec plaisir,
   volontiers
plug – (bath) bonde *nf*
plug – (electric) prise de courant *nf*
plug in – brancher *v reg*

plum – prune *nf*
plumber – plombier *nm*
plural – pluriel *nm*
   in the plural – au pluriel
p.m. – de l'après-midi, du soir *adv*
pocket – poche *nf*
pocket money – argent de poche *nm*
pointed – pointu *adj*
police – police *nf*
policeman – (town) agent de police
   nm
policeman – (village, small town)
   gendarme *nm*
police station – commissariat de
   police *nm*, poste de police *nm*,
   gendarmerie *nf*
police woman – femme-agent *nf*
polite – poli *adj*
politely – poliment *adv*
politeness – politesse *nf*
polluted – pollué *adj*
pond – mare *nf*
pony – poney *nm*
pony tail – queue de cheval *nf*
poodle – caniche *nm*
pool – (man made) étang *nm*
pool – (snooker) billard américain *nm*
pool – (swimming) piscine *nf*
poor – pauvre *adj*
pop music – musique pop *nf*
popular – populaire *adj*
pork – porc *nm*
pork chop – côte de porc *nf*
port – port *nm*
Portugal – Portugal *nm*
   in Portugal – au Portugal
Portuguese – portugais *adj*
Portuguese person – Portugais *nm*,
   Portugaise *nf*
posh – chic *adj*
possess – posséder *v reg* †
possibility – possibilité *nf*

---

possible – possible *adj*
possibly – éventuellement *adv*
post – poste *nf*
  post a letter – mettre une lettre à la poste *v irreg* §, poster *v reg*
  post code – code postal *nm*
  post office – bureau de poste *nm*, P et T
postage stamp – timbre *nm*
postal order – mandat postal *nm*
postcard – carte postale *nf*
poster – affiche *nf*, poster *nm*
postman – facteur *nm*
postpone – remettre *v irreg* §
postwoman – factrice *nf*
pot – (coffee) cafetière *nf*
pot – (cooking) marmite *nf*
potato – pomme de terre *nf*
pot plant – (indoor) plante d'appartment *nf*
pottery – poterie *nf*
poultry – volaille *nf*
pound – (£) livre sterling *nf*
pound – (500 g) livre *nf*
pour (out) – verser *v reg*
powder – (washing) lessive *nf*
powerful – puissant *adj*
power point – prise de courant *nf*
practical – pratique *adj*
practical work – travaux pratiques *nmpl*
practise – (instrument) s'exercer* *v refl* †
practise – (sport) s'entraîner* *v refl*
precaution – précaution *nf*
precious – précieux, précieuse *adj*
precise – précis *adj*
prefer – mieux aimer *v reg*, préférer *v reg* †
preparations – préparatifs *nmpl*
preparatory – préparatoire *adj*
prepare – préparer *v reg*

prescription – ordonnance *nf*
presence – présence *nf*
present – (current) actuel, actuelle *adj*
  at present – à l'heure actuelle
present – cadeau *nm*
  give a present – offrir un cadeau *v irreg* §
present – (not absent) présent *adj*
  be present at – assister à *v reg*, être présent à *v irreg* §
present – (tense) présent *nm*
present – (give trophy) présenter *v reg*
press – presse *nf*
press on – (lean) appuyer sur *v reg* †
pretend – faire semblant de *v irreg* §
pretty – joli *adj*, mignon, mignonne *adj*
prevent – empêcher *v reg*
previous – ancien, ancienne *adj*
previously – auparavant *adv*
price – prix *nm*
price list – tarif *nm*
priest – (RC) curé *nm*
primary school – école primaire *nf*
primary school teacher – instituteur *nm*, institutrice *nf*
principal – principal *adj*
principle – principe *nm*
print – imprimer *v reg*
printed – imprimé *adj*
printer – (computer) imprimante *nf*
prison – prison *nf*
private – privé *adj*
private school – école privée *nf*
prize – prix *nm*
probable – probable *adj*
problem – problème *nm*
process – méthode *nf*, procédé *nm*
  be in the process of – être en train de *v irreg* §
procession – défilé *nm*

---

nm - noun masculine	*nmpl* - noun masculine plural
nf - noun feminine	*nfpl* - noun feminine plural

adj - adjective	*conj* - conjunction
adv - adverb	*pron* - pronoun

product – produit *nm*

profession – métier *nm,* profession *nf*

program – (computer) programme *nm*

programme – (TV, radio) émission *nf*

progress – progrès *nmpl*
   make progress – faire des progrès *v irreg* §

project – projet *nm*

promise – promettre *v irreg* §

pronoun – pronom *nm*

proper – correct *adj,* bon, bonne *adj*

proper noun – nom propre *nm*

propose – proposer *v reg*

protect – protéger *v reg* †

protection – protection *nf*

protest – protester *v reg*

proud – fier, fière *adj*

prove – prouver *v reg*

province – province *nf*

PSE – instruction civique *nf*

PTO – (turn over the page) TSVP (tournez, s'il vous plaît)

public – public, publique *adj*

public holiday – jour férié *nm*

public transport – transports en commun *nmpl*

publicity – publicité *nf*

pudding – dessert *nm*

pull – tirer *v reg,* traîner *v reg*

pull a face – faire une drôle de tête *v irreg* §

pullover – pull(over) *nm*

pump up tyres – gonfler les pneus *v reg*

pun – jeu de mots *nm*

punctual – ponctuel, ponctuelle *adj,* à l'heure

punctuation – ponctuation *nf*

puncture – crevaison *nf*

punctured – crevé *adj*

punish – punir *v reg*

punishment – punition *nf*

pupil – élève *nmf*
   pupil taking school lunch – demi-pensionnaire *nmf*

puppy – chiot *nm*

purple – violet, violette *adj*

purpose – but *nm*
   on purpose – exprès

purr – ronronner *v reg*

purse – porte-monnaie *nm*

push – pousser *v reg*

put – mettre *v irreg* §, placer *v reg* †
   put away – ranger *v reg* †
   put back – remettre *v irreg* §
   put down – (something) poser *v reg*
   put in the right order – mettre dans le bon ordre *v irreg* §
   put on – mettre *v irreg* §
   put on a pair of shorts – se mettre* en short *v refl* §
   put on headlights – allumer les phares *v reg*
   put on light – allumer *v reg*
   put on make-up – se maquiller* *v refl*
   put on one's shoes – se chausser* *v refl*
   put out – (light) éteindre *v irreg* §
   put out – (inconvenience) déranger *v reg* †
   put up with – supporter *v reg*

pyjamas – un pyjama *nm*

Pyrenees – Pyrénées *nfpl*

Q

quality – qualité *nf*
  good quality – de bonne qualité *adj*
  poor quality – de mauvaise qualité *adj*
quantity – quantité *nf*
quarrel – se disputer* *v refl*
quarry – carrière *nf*
quarter – quart *nm*
  quarter of a century – quart de siècle *nm*
  quarter of an hour – quart d'heure *nm*
  quarter past one – une heure et quart
  quarter to two – deux heures moins le quart
  three quarters – trois quarts *nmpl*
quarter – (district in city) quartier *nm*
queen – reine *nf*

question – question *nf*
  ask a question – poser une question *v reg*
  out of the question – hors de question
question mark (?) – point d'interrogation *nm*
question – interroger *v reg* †
question s.o. – questionner *v reg*
queue – queue *nf*
  queue – faire la queue *v irreg* §
quick – rapide *adj*
  be quick – (hurry) se dépêcher* *v refl*
quickly – rapidement, vite *adv*
quiet – calme, paisible *adj*
quilt – couette *nf*
quite – assez, tout à fait *adv*
quiz – jeu concours *nm*

R

rabbit – lapin *nm*
race – (nationality) race *nf*
race – (sport) course *nf*
racket – (tennis) raquette *nf*
radiator – radiateur *nm*
radio – radio *nf*
  be on the radio – passer* à la radio *v reg*
radio cassette player – radiocassette *nf*
railway – chemin de fer *nm*
railway carriage – voiture *nf*, wagon *nm*
railway station – gare SNCF *nf*

rain – pleuvoir *v irreg* §
  it is raining – il pleut
  it was raining – il pleuvait
  it will rain – il pleuvra
  it rained – il a plu
rain – pluie *nf*
  in the rain – sous la pluie
rainbow – arc-en-ciel *nm*
raincoat – imperméable *nm*, imper *nm*
rainy – pluvieux, pluvieuse *adj*
Ramadan – ramadan *nm*
rapid – rapide *adj*
rare – rare *adj*
rarely – rarement *adv*

---

nm - noun masculine	*nmpl* - noun masculine plural	*adj* - adjective	*conj* - conjunction
nf - noun feminine	*nfpl* - noun feminine plural	*adv* - adverb	*pron* - pronoun

raspberry – framboise *nf*
raspberry tart – tarte à la framboise *nf*
rate of exchange – cours du change *nm*, taux de change *nm*
rather – assez, plutôt *adv*
raw – cru *adj*
razor – rasoir *nm*
RE (RS) – instruction religieuse *nf*
reach – arriver* à *v reg*
read – lire *v irreg* §
    I can read – je sais lire
reader – lecteur *nm*, lectrice *nf*
reading – lecture *nf*
ready – prêt *adj*
    ready to wear – prêt-à-porter *adj*
real – véritable *adj*
realise – se rendre* compte (de) *v refl*
reality – réalité *nf*
really – vraiment *adv*
receive – recevoir *v irreg* §
recent – récent *adj*
recently – récemment, tout à l'heure *adv*
reception – réception *nf*
reception desk – bureau d'accueil *nm*
receptionist – réceptionniste *nmf*
recipe – recette *nf*
reckon – (calculate) calculer *v reg*
reckon – (judge) considérer *v reg* †
reckon – (think) penser *v reg*
recognise – reconnaître *v irreg* §
recommend – recommander *v reg*
recommended – recommandé *adj*
record – disque *nm*
    record player – électrophone *nm*
record – (on tape) enregistrer *v reg*
recorder – flûte à bec *nf*
recount – raconter *v reg*
recover – (get back) récupérer *v reg* †

recover – (get better) se remettre* *v refl* §
rectangular – rectangulaire *adj*
red – rouge *adj*
red haired – roux, rousse *adj*
red wine – vin rouge *nm*
re-do – refaire *v irreg* §
reduce – réduire *v irreg* §
reduced – réduit *adj*
reduction – réduction *nf*
reel – bobine *nf*
referee – arbitre *nm*
refill – remplir *v reg*
reflexive verbs – verbes pronominaux *nmpl*
refreshment bar – buvette *nf*
refuse – refuser *v reg*
region – région *nf*, province *nf*
registered letter – lettre recommandée *nf*
registration number – (car) numéro d'immatriculation *nm*
regret – regretter *v reg*
regular – régulier, régulière *adj*
rehearsal – répétition *nf*
relationship – rapport *nm*
relative – parent *nm*
relax – se détendre* *v refl*
relaxation – détente *nf*
relaxed – décontracté *adj*, détendu *adj*
remain – (stay) rester* *v reg*
remainder – reste *nm*
remarkable – singulier, singulière *adj*
remedy – remède *nm*
remember – se rappeler* *v refl* †, se souvenir* de *v refl* §
reminder – rappel *nm*
remote control – télécommande *nf*
remove – enlever *v reg* †
renew – remplacer *v reg* †, renouveler *v reg* †
rent – loyer *nm*

---

prep - preposition   *v reg* - verb regular   *v refl* - verb reflexive   § - see verb tables
pp - past participle   *v irreg* - verb irregular   † - see verb information   * - takes être

rent – louer *v reg*
renting – location *nf*
repair – dépannage *nm*
repair man – réparateur *nm*
repair – réparer *v reg*, dépanner *v reg*
repeat – répéter *v reg* †
repeat a year – (at school) redoubler une année *v reg*
replace – remplacer *v reg* †
reply – répondre *v reg*
report – reportage *nm*
report – (school) bulletin *nm*
represent – représenter *v reg*
representative – représentant *nm*, représentante *nf*
request – demande *nf*
rescue – sauver *v reg*
resemble – ressembler à *v reg*
reservation – réservation *nf*
reserve – réserver *v reg*
reserved – réservé *adj*
resident – habitant *nm*
resit exam – repasser un examen *v reg*
respect – respecter *v reg*
responsibility – responsabilité *nf*
rest – se reposer* *v refl*
restart – remettre en marche *v irreg* §
restaurant – restaurant *nm*
restrict – limiter *v reg*
result – résultat *nm*, bilan *nm*
retired – retraité *adj*
return – retourner* *v reg*, rentrer* *v reg*
return journey – voyage de retour *nm*
return ticket – aller-retour *nm*
reverse – reculer *v reg*
reward – récompense *nf*
rib – côte *nf*
rice – riz *nm*
rich – riche *adj*

ride – (horse) monter* à cheval *v reg*, faire de l'équitation *v irreg* §
ridiculous – ridicule *adj*
riding hat – bombe *nf*
right – droit *adj*
right – (not wrong) correct *adj*, juste *adj*
be right – avoir raison *v irreg* §
right! – bien! *excl*
right – droite *nf*
keep to the right – serrez la droite
on the right – à droite
to the right – vers la droite
right answer – la bonne réponse *nf*
right-handed – droitier, droitière *adj*
right now – tout de suite *adv*
right winger – (sport) ailier droit *nm*
ring – bague *nf*
ring – (bell) sonner *v reg*
ring the doorbell – sonner à la porte *v reg*
ring binder – classeur *nm*
ring road – périphérique *nm*
ring up – (phone) téléphoner à *v reg*
rink – patinoire *nf*
ripe – mûr *adj*
rise – monter* *v reg*, se lever* *v reg* †
risk – risque *nm*
river – fleuve *nm*, rivière *nf*
road – route *nf*
major road – RN, route nationale *nf*
road – (town) rue *nf*
road map – carte routière *nf*
road sign – panneau (de signalisation) *nm*
road user – usager de la route *nm*
roadway – chaussée *nf*
roadworks – travaux *nmpl*
roast – rôti *adj*
roast – (meat) rôti *nm*
roast chicken – poulet rôti *nm*
rock climbing – varappe *nf*

---

nm - noun masculine	*nmpl* - noun masculine plural	*adj* - adjective	*conj* - conjunction
nf - noun feminine	*nfpl* - noun feminine plural	*adv* - adverb	*pron* - pronoun

rock music – rock *nm*
role play – jeu de rôle *nm*
roll – (bread) petit pain *nm*
roller blades – rollers in-line *nmpl*
rollercoaster – montagnes russes *nfpl*
roller skate – faire du patin à roulettes *v irreg* §
roller skates – patins à roulettes *nmpl*
roof – toit *nm*
room – pièce *nf*, salle *nf*
  room with a double bed – chambre avec un grand lit *nf*
  room with twin beds – chambre à deux lits *nf*
rope – corde *nf*
rose – rose *nf*
rosé wine – vin rosé *nm*
Rosh Hashanah – Nouvel An juif *nm*
rotten – moche *adj sl*
rough book – cahier de brouillon *nm*
rough paper – papier brouillon *nm*
round – rond *adj*, circulaire *adj*
round – (slice of bread, etc) tranche *nf*, rondelle *nf*
round – autour de *prep*
  go round a corner – tourner au coin de la rue *v reg*
  go round to a friend's house – passer* chez un ami *v reg*
round about – autour de *prep*
roundabout – (fair) manège *nm*
roundabout – (traffic) rond-point *nm*
round here – par ici
route – ligne *nf*
  all routes – toutes directions
routine – routine *nf*
routine – (work) travail quotidien *nm*

row – rang *nm*
row – (boat) ramer *v reg*
royal blue – bleu roi *adj inv*
rubber – (eraser) gomme *nf*
rubber band – élastique *nm*
rubbish – ordures *nfpl*
rucksack – sac à dos *nm*
rude – impoli *adj*
rugby – rugby *nm*
rugby league – rugby à treize *nm*
rugby union – rugby à quinze *nm*
ruin – abîmer *v reg*
rule – règle *nf*
ruler – règle *nf*
run – courir *v irreg* §
run away – se sauver* *v refl*
run down – descendre* en courant *v reg*
run into – (meet) rencontrer *v reg*
run into – (hit) heurter *v reg*
run out of – (have none left) manquer de *v reg*
run out of – (building) sortir* en courant *v irreg* §
run out of petrol – tomber* en panne d'essence *v reg*
run over – écraser *v reg*
run up – monter* en courant *v reg*
runner up – (sport) second *nm*, seconde *nf*
runway – piste *nf*
rush – se dépêcher* *v refl*, se précipiter* *v refl*
  in a rush – pressé *adj*
rush hour – heure de pointe *nf*, heure d'affluence *nf*
Russia – Russie *nf*
Russian – russe *adj*
Russian person – Russe *nmf*

S

sad – triste *adj*
saddle – selle *nf*
sadly – tristement *adv*
sadness – tristesse *nf*
safe – sûr *adj*, sans danger
said – *see dire v irreg* §
sail – voile *nf*
sail – (go sailing) faire de la voile
  v irreg §
sailboard – planche à voile *nf*
sailing dinghy – dériveur *nm*
sailing ship – voilier *nm*
sailor – marin *nm*
salad – salade *nf*
salad – (green) salade verte *nf*
salad – (mixed) salade composée *nf*
salad – (tomato) salade de tomates *nf*
salami – salami *nm*
sale – vente *nf*
  for sale – à vendre
  on sale – en vente
sales – soldes *nmpl*
  in the sales – en solde
sales assistant – vendeur *nm*,
  vendeuse *nf*
salmon – saumon *nm*
salt – sel *nm*
salty – salé *adj*
same – même *adj*, pareil, pareille *adj*
  at the same time – en même
    temps
sand – sable *nm*
sandal – sandale *nf*
sand castle – château de sable *nm*
sandwich – sandwich *nm*
sanitary towel – serviette hygiénique
  nf
Santa Claus – Père Noël *nm*
sardine – sardine *nf*
satellite – satellite *nm*

satellite dish – antenne parabolique
  nf
satisfied – satisfait *adj*
satisfy – satisfaire *v irreg* §
Saturday – samedi *nm*
  see you on Saturday! – à
    samedi!
sauce – sauce *nf*
saucepan – casserole *nf*
saucer – soucoupe *nf*
sausage – saucisse *nf*
save – sauver *v reg*
  save money – économiser *v reg*,
    mettre de côté *v irreg* §
  save up – faire des économies
    v irreg §
savings – économies *nfpl*
saxophone – saxophone *nm*
say – dire *v irreg* §
scarf – (long) écharpe *nf*
scarf – (square) foulard *nm*
scary – effrayant *adj*, qui fait peur
scenery – paysage *nm*
school – école *nf*
  school – (nursery) école maternelle *nf*
  school – (primary) école primaire *nf*
  school – (secondary) collège *nm*,
    lycée *nm*
school bus – car de ramassage
  scolaire *nm*
school holidays – vacances scolaires
  nfpl
school report – bulletin scolaire *nm*
school trip – visite scolaire *nf*
school uniform – uniforme scolaire
  nm
school year – année scolaire *nf*
schoolboy – écolier *nm*
schoolgirl – écolière *nf*
science – science *nf*

---

nm - noun masculine   *nmpl* - noun masculine plural   *adj* - adjective   *conj* - conjunction
nf - noun feminine   *nfpl* - noun feminine plural   *adv* - adverb   *pron* - pronoun

science fiction – science-fiction *nf*
  science fiction film – film de science-fiction *nm*
  science fiction story – roman de science fiction *nm*
scientific – scientifique *adj*
scientist – scientifique *nmf*
scissors – ciseaux *nmpl*
scold – gronder *v reg*
scooter – scooter *nm*
score a goal – marquer un but *v reg*
score a point – marquer un point *v reg*
Scotland – Écosse *nf*
Scotsman – Écossais *nm*
Scotswoman – Ecossaise *nf*
Scottish – écossais *adj*
scream – pousser un cri *v reg*, crier *v reg*, hurler *v reg*
screen – écran *nm*
screwdriver – tournevis *nm*
scrum – (rugby) mêlée *nf*
scuba diving – plongée sous-marine *nf*
sea – mer *nf*
  at the seaside – au bord de la mer
  by the sea – au bord de la mer
seafood – fruits de mer *nmpl*
seagull – mouette *nf*
sea sickness – mal de mer *nm*
  be seasick – avoir le mal de mer *v irreg* §
search – fouiller *v reg*
seaside resort – station balnéaire *nf*
season – saison *nf*
  out of season – hors saison
season ticket – carte d'abonnement *nf*
seat – place *nf*
seat belt – ceinture de sécurité *nf*
seated – (sitting down) assis, assise *adj*
second – deuxième *adj*, second *adj*

second class – de deuxième classe *adj*
second-hand – d'occasion *adj*
secondary school – collège *nm*, lycée *nm*
secret – secret, secrète *adj*
secretary – secrétaire *nmf*
security – sécurité *nf*
see – voir *v irreg* §
  see again – revoir *v irreg* §
  see over – voir au verso
  see you later! – à tout à l'heure!
  see you on Saturday! – à samedi!
  see you soon! – à bientôt! *adv*
  see you this evening! – à ce soir!
  see you tomorrow! – à demain!
seem – apparaître *v irreg* §, avoir l'air (de) *v irreg* §, sembler *v reg*
seize – saisir *v reg*
select – selectionner *v reg*
selection – choix *nm*, sélection *nf*
selfish – égoïste *adj*
self-service restaurant – restaurant libre-service *nm*, self *nm*
self-service shop – libre-service *nm*
sell – vendre *v reg*
sellotape® – scotch® *nm*
semi-colon (;) – point-virgule *nm*
semi-detached house – maison jumelle *nf*, maison jumelée *nf*
semi-final – demi-finale *nf*
send – envoyer *v reg* †
send for the doctor – faire venir le médecin *v irreg* §
senior citizen – personne du troisième âge *nf*
sensational – sensass *adj sl*
sensible – prudent *adj*, raisonnable *adj*, sensé *adj*
sensibly – sagement *adv*
sensitive – sensible *adj*
sentence – phrase *nf*
separate – séparer *v reg*

separated – séparé *adj*
separately – séparément *adv*
separation – séparation *nf*
September – septembre *nm*
serial – (TV, radio, magazine)
  feuilleton *nm*
serious – grave *adj*, sérieux,
  sérieuse *adj*
  it's not serious – ce n'est pas
  grave
serve – servir *v irreg* §
service – service *nm*
  service (not) included – service
  (non) compris
serve oneself – se servir* *v refl* §
serviette – serviette *nf*
session – séance *nf*
set – placer *v reg* †
  set off – partir* *v irreg* §
  set off again – repartir* *v irreg* §
  set out – se mettre* en route *v refl* §
  set price menu – menu à prix fixe
  nm
  set the alarm clock – mettre le
  réveil *v irreg* §
  set the table – mettre le couvert
  v irreg §
settee – canapé *nm*
settle – (bill) régler *v reg* †
settle – (down) s'installer* *v refl*
seven – sept *adj*
seventeen – dix-sept *adj*
seventy – soixante-dix *adj*
seventy-one – soixante et onze *adj*
several – plusieurs *adj*
sew – coudre *v irreg* §
sewing – couture *nf*
sewing machine – machine à coudre
  nf
shade – ombre *nf*
  in the shade – à l'ombre
shake hands with – serrer la main à
  v reg

shall we go? – on y va?
shall we go to the cinema? – si on
  allait au cinéma?
shame – ‡honte *nf*
shameful – ‡honteux, honteuse *adj*
shampoo – shampooing *nm*
shampoo one's hair – se laver* les
  cheveux *v refl*
shape – forme *nf*
share – partager *v reg* †
sharp – aigu, aiguë *adj*
sharply – nettement *adv*
shave – se raser* *v refl*
she, it – elle *pron f*
shed – remise *nf*
sheep – mouton *nm*
sheet – drap *nm*
  sheet of paper – feuille de papier
  nf
shelf – étagère *nf,* rayon *nm*
shellfish – fruits de mer *nmpl*
shelter – abri *nm*
  sheltered from – à l'abri de
sherry – xérès *nm*
shine – briller *v reg*
shining – brillant *adj*
ship – bateau *nm,* navire *nm*
shirt – chemise *nf*
shiver – frissonner *v reg*, grelotter
  v reg
shiver – frisson *nm*, tremblement *nm*
shoe – chaussure *nf,* soulier *nm*
  pair of shoes – paire de chaussures
  nf
shoe seller – marchand de chaussures
  nm
shoe size – pointure *nf*
shooting – tir *nm*
shop – magasin *nm*
  go round the shops – faire les
  magasins *v irreg* §
shop assistant – vendeur *nm*,
  vendeuse *nf*

---

nm - noun masculine	*nmpl* - noun masculine plural	*adj* - adjective	*conj* - conjunction
nf - noun feminine	*nfpl* - noun feminine plural	*adv* - adverb	*pron* - pronoun

shopkeeper – commerçant *nm*, commerçante *nf*, marchand *nm*

shopping – achats *nmpl*, courses *nfpl*
  do the shopping – faire des achats *v irreg* §, faire des courses *v irreg* §
  go window shopping – faire du lèche-vitrines *v irreg* §

shopping bag – sac à provisions *nm*

shopping centre – centre commercial *nm*

shop window – vitrine *nf*

short – (not long) court *adj*, bref, brève *adj*

short – (not tall) petit *adj*

shortly – tout à l'heure *adv*

short-sighted – myope *adj*

shorts – short *nm*
  pair of shorts – un short *nm*

should – (ought to) devrait

shoulder – épaule *nf*

shout – cri *nm*

shout – crier *v reg*, pousser un cri *v reg*

show – (performance) spectacle *nm*

show – indiquer *v reg*, montrer *v reg*
  show a film – passer un film *v reg*

shower – douche *nf*
  have a shower – prendre une douche *v irreg* §

shower – (rain) averse *nf*
  there will be showers – il y aura des averses

showing – (film) séance *nf*

show-off – poseur *nm*, poseuse *nf*

show off – se vanter* *v refl*, faire le m'as-tu vu *v irreg coll* §

shrewd – malin, maligne *adj*

shrimp – crevette *nf*

Shrove Tuesday – mardi gras *nm*

shut – fermer *v reg*

shut in – enfermer *v reg*

shutter – volet *nm*

shy – timide *adj*

sick – (ill) malade *adj*

sick bay – infirmerie *nf*

sick person – malade *nmf*
  feel sick – avoir mal au cœur *v irreg* §

side – côté *nm*
  on the other side – de l'autre côté

side – (team) équipe *nf*

side board – buffet *nm*

sight – spectacle *nm*, vue *nf*

sightseeing – tourisme *nm*

sign – panneau *nm*, signe *nm*

sign – signer *v reg*

signal – signal *nm*

signature – signature *nf*

signpost – poteau indicateur *nm*

silence – silence *nm*

silent – silencieux, silencieuse *adj*
  be silent – se taire* *v refl* §

silently – silencieusement *adv*

silk – soie *nf*

silly – bête *adj*, idiot *adj*

silly mistake – bêtise *nf*

similar – pareil, pareille *adj*, semblable *adj*

simple – simple *adj*

simply – simplement *adv*

since – (time) depuis *prep*

since – (reason) puisque *conj*

sincere – sincère *adj*

sincerely – sincèrement *adv*

sing – chanter *v reg*

singer – chanteur *nm*, chanteuse *nf*

single – (one only) seul *adj*

single – (unmarried) célibataire *adj*

single person – célibataire *nmf*

single room – chambre à un lit *nf*

single ticket – aller simple *nm*, billet simple *nm*

singular – singulier *nm*
  in the singular – au singulier

sink – évier *nm*

---

prep - preposition	*v reg* - verb regular	*v refl* - verb reflexive	§ - see verb tables
pp - past participle	*v irreg* - verb irregular	† - see verb information	* - takes être

Sir – Monsieur *nm*
sister – sœur *nf*
sit down – s'asseoir* *v refl* §
  sit down! – (one person, informal) assieds-toi!
  sit down! – (formal, group) asseyez-vous!
  sit down at the table – se mettre* à table *v refl* §
site – emplacement *nm*
site – (building) chantier *nm*
sitting down – (seated) assis, assise *adj*
sitting room – salon *nm*
situated in – situé à *adj*
situation – cas *nm*, situation *nf*
six – six *adj*
sixteen – seize *adj*
sixteenth – seizième *adj*
sixth – sixième *adj*
sixth form college – lycée *nm*
sixty – soixante *adj*
sixty-one – soixante et un *adj*
size – grandeur *nf*
size – (clothes) taille *nf*
size – (shoes) pointure *nf*
skate – patin *nm*
skate – patiner *v reg*
skateboard – planche à roulettes *nf*
skating rink – patinoire *nf*
ski – faire du ski *v irreg* §
  cross country skiing – ski de fond *nm*
ski – ski *nm*
  ski boots – chaussures de ski *nfpl*
  ski lift – téléphérique *nm*
  ski-run – piste *nf*
skilfully – habilement *adv*
skilled – habile *adj*
skin – peau *nf*
skirt – jupe *nf*
sky – ciel *nm*

sky blue – bleu ciel *adj inv*
sledge – toboggan *nm*, luge *nf*
sleep – dormir *v irreg* §
  fall asleep – s'endormir* *v refl* §
sleep – sommeil *nm*
  be sleepy – avoir sommeil *v irreg* §
sleeper – wagon-lit *nm*
sleeping bag – sac de couchage *nm*
sleeve – manche *nf*
slice – (bread, etc) tranche *nf*
slice – (of salami) rondelle *nf*
slice – trancher *v reg*
slicing sausage – saucisson *nm*
slide – glisser *v reg*
slide – (transparency) diapositive *nf*
slightly – un peu, légèrement *adv*
slim – mince *adj*
slim – maigrir *v reg*
slip – glisser *v reg*
slipper – pantoufle *nf*
slope – pente *nf*
sloping – en pente
slot machine – distributeur automatique *nm*
slot machine – (gambling) machine à sous *nf*
slow – lent *adj*
slow down – ralentir *v reg*
slowly – lentement *adv*
slow train – omnibus *nm*
small – petit *adj*
small ad – petite annonce *nf*
small change – petite monnaie *nf*
small scale – réduit *adj*
small shop – boutique *nf*
smart – (clever) débrouillard *adj coll*, intelligent *adj*
smart – (fashionable) chic *adj inv*
smart card – carte à mémoire *nf*
smell – odeur *nf*
smell – sentir *v irreg* §
smelly – malodorant *adj*

smile – sourire *nm*
smile – sourire *v irreg* §
smoke – fumée *nf*
smoke – fumer *v reg*
smoker – fumeur *nm*, fumeuse *nf*
  smoking – fumeur
  non smoking – non-fumeur
smooth – lisse *adj*
snack – casse-croûte *nm*
snack bar – buvette *nf*
snail – escargot *nm*
sneeze – éternuer *v reg*
snobbish – snob *adj*
snooker – jeu de billard *nm*
snow – neiger *v reg* †
snow – neige *nf*
  snowball – boule de neige *nf*
  snowfall – chute de neige *nf*
  snowman – bonhomme de neige
  nm
  snowstorm – tempête de neige *nf*
so – (therefore) donc *conj*
  so much – tant (de), tellement *adv*
  so much the better – tant mieux
  adv
  so much, many – autant de *adv*
  so what! – bof! *excl*
  so what? – et alors?
soak – tremper *v reg*
soaked – mouillé *adj*, trempé *adj*
  soaked to the skin – mouillé
  jusqu'aux os *adj*
soap – savon *nm*
soap opera – feuilleton *nm*
soccer – football *nm*
society – société *nf*
sock – chaussette *nf*
socket – prise de courant *nf*
sofa – canapé *nm*
soft – doux, douce *adj*, mou, mol,
  molle *adj*
software – logiciel *nm*

sold – vendu *adj*
soldier – militaire *nm*
solemn – solennel, solennelle *adj*
solicitor – avoué *nm*, notaire *nm*
solid – solide *adj*
solution – solution *nf*
solve – résoudre *v irreg* §
some – du, de la, de l', des *art*
some – quelque, quelques *adj*
  some ideas – quelques idées *nfpl*
some – en *pron*
some – quelques-uns, quelques-unes
  pron
  somebody – quelqu'un *pron*
  someone else – quelqu'un d'autre
  pron
  something – quelque chose *pron*
  something bad – quelque chose
  de mauvais
  something else – quelque chose
  d'autre
  something good – quelque chose
  de bon
sometime – un de ces jours,
  un jour *adv*
sometimes – parfois, quelquefois *adv*
somewhere – quelque part *adv*
somewhere else – ailleurs, autre part
  adv
son – fils *nm*
son-in-law – gendre *nm*
song – chanson *nf*
soon – bientôt *adv*
sore throat – avoir mal à la gorge
  v irreg §, avoir une angine *v irreg* §
sorry! – je suis désolé!, pardon! *excl*
  be sorry – présenter ses excuses
  v reg
  I'm sorry! – pardonnez-moi!,
  excusez-moi!
sort – sorte *nf*
sort of – sorte de *nf*
  what sort of...? – quel genre de...?

sound – son *nm*

soup – potage *nm,* soupe *nf*

south – sud *nm*

South Africa – Afrique du Sud *nf*

South America – Amérique du Sud *nf*

South of France – Midi *nm*

souvenir – souvenir *nm*

soya – soja *nm*

space – espace *nm*

space – (room) place *nf*
  is there any room? – il y a de la place?

spade – pelle *nf*

spaghetti – spaghetti *nmpl*

Spain – Espagne *nf*

Spaniard – Espagnol *nm,* Espagnole *nf*

Spanish – espagnol *adj*

Spanish – (language) espagnol *nm*

spare part – pièce de rechange *nf*

spare time – loisirs *nmpl*

spare wheel – roue de secours *nf*

sparkling – (wine) mousseux, mousseuse *adj*

sparkling – (water) pétillant *adj*

speak – parler *v reg*
  speak French – parler français *v reg*
  speak French fluently – parler français couramment *v reg*
  speak French badly – parler français comme une vache espagnole *v reg*
  speak loudly – parler fort *v reg*

speak to – s'adresser à* *v refl*

special – particulier, particulière *adj,* spécial *adj*

speciality – spécialité *nf*

special offer – promotion *nf*

spectacle – (show) spectacle *nm*

spectacles – (glasses) lunettes *nfpl*

spectacular – spectaculaire *adj*

spectator – spectateur *nm,* spectatrice *nf*

speech – parole *nf*

speech marks ("-") – guillemets *nmpl*

speed – vitesse *nf,* rapidité *nf*
  at top speed – à toute vitesse

speedboat – vedette *nf*

spell – épeler *v reg* †
  how do you spell that? – ça s'écrit comment?

spelling – orthographe *nf*

spend – (money) dépenser *v reg*

spend – (time) passer *v reg*
  spend one's holiday – passer les vacances *v reg*

spider – araignée *nf*

spider's web – toile d'araignée *nf*

spinach – épinards *nmpl*

spiteful – méchant *adj*

splendid – épatant *adj,* splendide *adj,* magnifique *adj*

spoil – abîmer *v reg,* gâter *v reg*

spoiled – abîmé *adj,* manqué *adj*

sponge – éponge *nf*

spoon – cuillère *nf*

spoonful – cuillerée *nf*

sport – sport *nm*

sports car – voiture de sport *nf*

sports centre – centre sportif *nm*

sports ground – terrain de sport *nm*

sporty – sportif, sportive *adj*

spot – (place) endroit *nm*

spot – (zit) bouton *nm,* pustule *nf*

spotted – (fabric) à pois *adj*

sprain one's ankle – se fouler* la cheville *v refl*

spray – arroser *v reg*

spread – (with butter, jam, etc) tartiner *v reg*

spring – printemps *nm*
  in spring – au printemps

springboard – tremplin *nm*

---

sprout – chou de Bruxelles *nm*

spy – espion *nm*, espionne *nf*

spying – espionnage *nm*

  spy film – film d'espionnage *nm*

  spy story – roman d'espionnage *nm*

square – (in town) place *nf*

square – (on paper) case *nf*

square – (shape) carré *adj*

square – (shape) carré *nm*

squash – (drink)sirop *nm*

squash – (sport) squash *nm*

squeeze – serrer *v reg*

stable – écurie *nf*

stadium – stade *nm*

staff room – salle des professeurs *nf*

stage – scène *nf*

  be on stage – être en scène
    v irreg §

stain – tache *nf*

stain – tacher *v reg*

stairs, staircase – escalier *nm*

stall – kiosque *nm*

stalls – (theatre) orchestre *nm*

stamp – timbre *nm*

  book of stamps – carnet de
    timbres *nm*

  collect stamps – collectionner des
    timbres *v reg*

stand – (on feet) se tenir* *v refl* §

  standing up – debout *adv*

  stand up – se lever* *v refl* †

stand – (put up with) supporter *v reg*

staple – agrafe *nf*

stapler – agrafeuse *nf*

star – (show business) vedette *nf*

star – (sky) étoile *nf*

start – commencer *v reg* †

start – (beginning) début *nm*

  at the start – au début de

start of school year – rentrée *nf*

start – (vehicle) démarrer *v reg*

start up – mettre en marche *v irreg* §

starter – (food) hors d'œuvre *nmpl*

state – état *nm*

stately home – château *nm*,
  manoir *nm*

station – gare *nf*

stationer's shop – papeterie *nf*

stay – rester* *v reg*, séjourner *v reg*

stay at a hotel – descendre* dans un
  hôtel *v reg*

stay at home – rester* à la maison
  v reg

stay – séjour *nm*

steady – régulier, régulière *adj*

steak – steak *nm*

  steak and chips – steak-frites *nm*

steal – voler *v reg*

steam – vapeur *nf*

steering wheel – volant *nm*

step – pas *nm*

step – (on stairs) marche *nf*

stepbrother – demi-frère *nm*

stepdaughter – belle-fille *nf*

stepfather – beau-père *nm*

stepmother – belle-mère *nf*

stepsister – demi-sœur *nf*

stepson – beau-fils *nm*

stereo – chaîne-stéréo *nf*

  personal stereo – baladeur *nm*

stewardess – hôtesse *nf*

stick – (glue) coller *v reg*

stick of bread – baguette *nf*

sticker – autocollant *nm*

sticky tape – scotch® *nm*

stiff – raide *adj*

still – (not moving) immobile *adj*

still – (yet) encore, toujours *adv*

sting – piqûre *nf*

sting – piquer *v reg*

stocking – bas *nm*

stocky – costaud *adj*

stomach – estomac *nm*, ventre *nm*

stomach ache – mal à l'estomac *nm*, mal au ventre *nm*
stone – pierre *nf*
  built of stone – en pierre
stool – tabouret *nm*
stop – arrêt *nm*
  bus stop – arrêt d'autobus *nm*
stop – (doing sthg) arrêter (de faire) *v reg*
stop – (halt) stopper *v reg*
stop (o.s.) – s'arrêter*(de) *v refl*
  stop smoking – s'arrêter* de fumer *v refl*
stop – (prevent) empêcher *v reg*
storey – étage *nm*
storm – tempête *nf,* orage *nm*
stormy – orageux, orageuse *adj*
story – histoire *nf*, récit *nm*
  horror story – roman d'épouvante *nm*
  science fiction story – roman de science fiction *nm*
storyteller – raconteur *nm*, raconteuse *nf*
stove – poêle *nm*
stove – (cooker) cuisinière *nf*
straight – droit, raide *adj*
straight away – aussitôt, tout de suite *adv*
straight on – tout droit, directement *adv*
strange – curieux, curieuse *adj*
strange – étrange *adj*
stranger – étranger *nm*, étrangère *nf*
strawberry – fraise *nf*
stream – ruisseau *nm*
street – rue *nf*
  at the corner of street – au coin de la rue
stressed out – stressé *adj*
strict – sévère *adj*
strike – (hit) frapper *v reg*
strike – (walk-out) grève *nf*

on strike – en grève
strike – faire la grève *v irreg* §
striker – (football) buteur *nm*
string – ficelle *nf*
string orchestra – orchestre de cordes *nm*
striped – rayé *adj*, à rayures
stroll – flâner *v reg*
strong – fort *adj*
stubborn – entêté *adj*, têtu *adj*, obstiné *adj*
student – étudiant *nm*, étudiante *nf*
student at lycée – lycéen *nm*, lycéenne *nf*
studies – études *nfpl*
studio – atelier *nm*, studio *nm*
studious – studieux, studieuse *adj*
study – étudier *v reg*, faire ses études *v irreg* §
study – (room) bureau *nm*, cabinet de travail *nm*
stupid – bête *adj*, idiot *adj*, stupide *adj*
  do something stupid – faire une bêtise *v irreg* §
sturdy – solide *adj*
style – style *nm*
subject – (school) matière *nf*
subscription – abonnement *nm*, souscription *nf*
subtitled – sous-titré *adj*
suburb – banlieue *nf*
  in the suburbs – en banlieue
subway – passage souterrain *nm*
succeed – réussir *v reg*
success – succès *nm*
such a – tel, telle *adj*
sudden – brusque *adj*, subit *adj*
suddenly – brusquement, soudain, tout à coup *adv*
suffer – souffrir *v irreg* §
sugar – sucre *nm*
suggest – suggérer *v reg* †

---

nm - noun masculine   *nmpl* - noun masculine plural   *adj* - adjective   *conj* - conjunction
nf - noun feminine   *nfpl* - noun feminine plural   *adv* - adverb   *pron* - pronoun

suit – (man's) complet *nm*
suit – (woman's) tailleur *nm*
suitable – convenable *adj*
suitcase – valise *nf*
sulk – bouder *v reg*
sum – (arithmetic) calcul *nm*
summer – été *nm*
  in summer – en été
summer camp – colonie de vacances *nf*
summer holidays – grandes vacances *nfpl*
summit – sommet *nm*
sun – soleil *nm*
sunbathe – se bronzer* *v refl*, prendre un bain de soleil *v irreg* §
sunburn – coup de soleil *nm*
sun cream – crème solaire *nf*
sun-glasses – lunettes de soleil *nfpl*
sun-stroke – insolation *nf*
sun-tanned – bronzé *adj*
Sunday – dimanche *nm*
sunny – ensoleillé *adj*
sunrise – lever du soleil *nm*
sunset – coucher de soleil *nm*
sunshade – parasol *nm*
super – formidable *adj*
super unleaded petrol – super sans plomb *nm*
superior – supérieur *adj*
supermarket – supermarché *nm*
supervise – surveiller *v reg*
supper – souper *nm*
support – soutenir *v irreg* §
sure – sûr *adj*
surely – certainement, sûrement *adv*
surf – faire du surf *v irreg* §
surfboard – planche de surf *nf*
surfing – surf *nm*
surf the net – naviguer sur Internet *v reg*, surfer sur le Net *v reg*

surgery – cabinet de consultation *nm*, salle de consultation *nf*
surname – nom de famille *nm*
surprise – surprise *nf*
surprise – surprendre *v irreg* §
surprised – surpris *adj*
surprising – étonnant *adj*, surprenant *adj*
surrounded by – entouré de *adj*
surroundings – environs *nmpl*
survey – enquête *nf*, sondage *nm*
suspect – se douter de* *v refl*, soupçonner *v reg*
suspicion – soupçon *nm*
swallow – avaler *v reg*
swallow – (bird) hirondelle *nf*
swap – échanger *v reg* †
sweater – pullover *nm*
sweatshirt – sweat-shirt *nm*
Sweden – Suède *nf*
Swedish – suédois *adj*
Swedish person – Suédois *nm*, Suédoise *nf*
sweep – balayer *v reg* †
sweet – bonbon *nm*
sweet – (nice) doux, douce *adj*, mignon, mignonne *adj*
sweet – (tasting) sucré *adj*
sweet shop – confiserie *nf*
sweet-smelling – parfumé *adj*
swiftness – rapidité *nf*
swim – nager *v reg* †
  I can swim – je sais nager *v reg* †
swimming – natation *nf*
swimming pool – piscine *nf*
swimsuit – maillot de bain *nm*
swing – balancer *v reg* †
swing – (child's) balançoire *nf*
Swiss – suisse *adj*
Swiss person – Suisse *nmf*
switch on – (gas, light) ouvrir *v irreg* §
switch on – (the radio) allumer *v reg*

Switzerland – Suisse *nf*
swollen – gonflé *adj*
swot – bosser *v reg sl*, bûcher *v reg sl*

synagogue – synagogue *nf*
syrup – sirop *nm*
system – système *nm*

T

T-shirt – tee-shirt *nm*
table – table *nf*
  to lay the table – mettre le couvert *v irreg* §
table-cloth – nappe *nf*
table tennis – ping pong *nm*
table wine – vin ordinaire *nf*
tablet – cachet *nm*, comprimé *nm*
tail – queue *nf*
  heads or tails? – pile ou face?
tailor – tailleur *nm*
take – prendre *v irreg* §
take – (person) emmener *v reg* †
  take away – emporter *v reg*
  take away again – remporter *v reg*
  take back – reprendre *v irreg* §
  take drugs – se droguer* *v refl*
  take exam – passer un examen *v reg*
  take hold of – saisir *v reg*, s'emparer* de *v refl*
  take notes – prendre des notes *v irreg* §
  take off – (aircraft) décoller *v reg*
  take off – (coat, etc) ôter *v reg*
  take one's driving test – passer le permis *v reg*
  take one's place – se placer* *v refl* †
  take part in – participer à *v reg*
  take photos – faire des photos *v irreg* §
  take place – avoir lieu *v irreg* §

take the dog for a walk – promener le chien *v reg* †
take the first on the left – prenez la première à gauche
take the first on the right – prenez la première à droite
take-away – à emporter
  take-away meals – plats à emporter *nmpl*
talk – parler *v reg*
talkative – bavard *adj*
tall – grand *adj*, haut *adj*, de haute taille
tanned – bronzé *adj*
tap – robinet *nm*
tape – bande *nf*
tape – enregistrer *v reg*
tape recorder – magnétophone *nm*
tart – (apple) tarte (aux pommes) *nf*
task – tâche *nf*
taste – goût *nm*
taste – goûter *v reg*
tax – impôt *nm*, taxe *nf*
taxi – taxi *nm*
tea – (drink) thé *nm*
  tea with milk – thé au lait *nm*
  tea without milk – thé nature *nm*
tea – (meal) goûter *nm*
teach – enseigner *v reg*
teacher – enseignant *nm*, enseignante *nf*
teacher – (primary) instituteur *nm*, institutrice *nf*
teacher – (secondary) professeur *nm*

teaching – enseignement *nm*

tea cup – tasse à thé *nf*

team – équipe *nf*

teapot – théière *nf*

tease – taquiner *v reg*

teaspoon – cuillère à café *nf*

tea towel – torchon *nm*

technical secondary school – CET (collège d'enseignement technique) *nm*

technician – technicien *nm*, technicienne *nf*

technology – technologie *nf*

teddy bear – nounours *nm*

teenager – adolescent *nm*, adolescente *nf*, jeune *nmf*

telephone – téléphone *nm*

telephone – téléphoner *v reg*

telephone box – cabine téléphonique *nf*

telephone directory – annuaire *nm*

telephone number – numéro de téléphone *nm*

television – télévision *nf*
   on television – à la télévision

television set – téléviseur *nm*

tell – dire *v irreg* §, raconter *v reg*

tell lies – mentir *v irreg* §

tell off – gronder *v reg*

telly – télé *nf*

temperature – température *nf*
   have a high temperature – avoir de la fièvre *v irreg* §

ten – dix *adj*
   ten out of ten – dix sur dix

tenant – locataire *nmf*

tender – tendre *adj*

tennis – tennis *nm*
   game of tennis – partie de tennis *nf*
   tennis ball – balle de tennis *nf*
   tennis court – court *nm*
   tennis shoes – tennis *nfpl*

tense – nerveux, nerveuse *adj*

tense – temps *nm*
   in the present tense – au présent

tent – tente *nf*
   pitch tent – dresser une tente *v reg*

tenth – dixième *adj*

term – (school) trimestre *nm*
   half-term – congé de mi-trimestre *nm*

terrace – terrasse *nf*

terrible – épouvantable *adj*, terrible *adj*

terrific – fantastique *adj*, formidable *adj*, super *adj*

terrify – terrifier *v reg*
   be terrified – avoir très peur *v irreg* §

test – épreuve *nf*
   driving test – épreuve du permis de conduire *nm*

text book – manuel (scolaire) *nm*

Thames – Tamise *nf*

than – que, qu' *conj*
   less ... than – moins ... que
   more ... than – plus...que

thank – remercier *v reg*

thank you – merci
   thank you very much – merci beaucoup

thanks to – grâce à

that – ça, cela *pron*
   that, those – ce, cet, cette, ces ...là *adj*
   that – que *conj*
   that comes to ten francs – ça fait dix francs en tout
   that depends – ça dépend
   that is to say – c'est à dire
   that's all – c'est tout
   that's better – ça va mieux
   that's enough – ça suffit
   that's it! – ça y est!

thatched roof – toit de chaume *nm*

---

prep - preposition	*v reg* - verb regular	*v refl* - verb reflexive	§ - see verb tables
pp - past participle	*v irreg* - verb irregular	† - see verb information	* - takes être

that one – celui-là *m*,
   celle-là *f dem pron*
the – le, la, l', les *art*
theatre – théâtre *nm*
theft – vol *nm*
their – leur, leurs *poss adj*,
   à eux, à elles
theirs – le leur, la leur,
   les leurs *poss pron*
them – les *pron*
themselves – eux-mêmes,
   elles-mêmes *pron*
then – alors, ensuite, puis *adv*
there – là *adv*
   there are, there is – voilà *prep*
there – (with verb) y *adv*
   I am going there – j'y vais
there are – il y a
   there are not – il n'y a pas de
therefore – donc *conj*
there is – il y a
   there is not – il n'y a pas de
there was, there were – il y avait
there will be – il y aura
there would be – il y aurait
thermometer – thermomètre *nm*
they – ils, elles *pers pron*
they – (people in general) on *pers pron*
thick – (not thin) épais, épaisse *adj*
thickness – épaisseur *nf*
thief – voleur *nm*, voleuse *nf*
thigh – cuisse *nf*
thin – maigre *adj*, mince *adj*
thing – chose *nf*
thingummyjig – truc *nm*
think – réfléchir *v reg*, songer *v reg* †
think about – penser à *v reg*
think of – (have opinion about)
   penser de *v reg*
third – (fraction) tiers *adj*
third – (in order) troisième *adj*
thirst – soif *nf*

be thirsty – avoir soif *v irreg* §
   I am thirsty – j'ai soif
thirteen – treize *adj*
thirtieth – trentième *adj*
thirty – trente *adj*
this, these – ce, cet, cette, ces *dem adj*
   this is Anne speaking – c'est
      Anne à l'appareil
this way – par ici
those – ceux-là, celles-là *pl dem pron*
thought – pensée *nf*
thousand – mille *adj inv*, *nm*
   thousands of – des milliers de
threaten – menacer *v reg* †
three – trois *adj*
throat – gorge *nf*
   have a sore throat – avoir mal à
      la gorge *v irreg* §, avoir une angine
      v irreg §
throat pastille – pastille pour la
   gorge *nf*
through – à travers *adv*
   through train – train direct *nm*
throw – jeter *v reg* †, lancer *v reg* †
thumb – pouce *nm*
thunder – tonnerre *nm*
thunder – tonner *v reg*
thunderstorm – orage *nm*
   there will be thunderstorms –
      il y aura des orages
Thursday – jeudi *nm*
tick (✓) – cocher *v reg*
ticket – billet *nm*, ticket *nm*
   book of tickets – carnet de tickets
      nm
   return ticket – aller-retour *nm*
   single ticket – billet simple *nm*
ticket inspector – contrôleur de
   billets *nm*
ticket machine – distributeur de
   billets *nm*
ticket office – guichet *nm*
tide – marée *nf*

---

high tide – marée haute *nf*
low tide – marée basse *nf*
tidy – bien rangé *adj*, net, nette *adj*
tidy – ranger *v reg* †
  tidy up – ranger ses affaires *v reg* †
tie – cravate *nf*
tie – attacher *v reg*
tight – étroit *adj*
tights – un collant *nm*
till – caisse *nf*
till – (until) jusqu'à *prep*
tilt – pencher *v reg*
time – (occasion) fois *nf*
  every time – chaque fois
  the first time – la première fois
  the last time – la dernière fois
time – temps *nm*
  a long time ago – il y a longtemps
    adv
  for a long time – longtemps *adv*
  free time – temps libre *nm*
  from time to time – de temps en
    temps
  on time – à temps, à l'heure
time – (by clock) heure *nf*
  at what time? – à quelle heure?
  dinner time – heure du déjeuner *nf*
  what time is it? – quelle heure
    est-il?
time off – congé *nm*
timetable – horaire *nm*
timetable – (school) emploi du temps
  nm
timpani – timbales *nfpl*
tin – boîte *nf*
tin opener – ouvre-boîte *nm*
tiny – tout petit *adj*, minuscule *adj*
tip – (money) pourboire *nm*
tip – (end) bout *nm*
tip – (summit) sommet *nm*
tired – fatigué *adj*
tiring – fatigant *adj*

tissue – mouchoir en papier *nm*
title – titre *nm*
to – (in order to) pour *prep*
to, at – à *prep*
  to Paris – à Paris
  to the cinema – au cinéma *nm*
  to the church – à l'église *nf*
  to the hotel – à l'hôtel *nm*
  to the post office – à la poste *nf*
  to the shops – aux magasins *nmpl*
  to the school – aux écoles *nfpl*
toast – pain grillé *nm*
tobacconist – (bureau de) tabac *nm*,
  café-tabac *nm*
today – aujourd'hui *adv*
toe – doigt de pied *nm*
together – ensemble *adv*
toilet – toilette *nf*, waters *nmpl*,
  WC *nmpl*
toilet block – bloc sanitaire *nm*
toilets – les cabinets *nmpl*
token – jeton *nm*
told – *see dire v irreg* §
tolerate – tolérer *v reg* †
toll – péage *nm*
tomato – tomate *nf*
tomorrow – demain *adv*
  day after tomorrow – après-
    demain *nm*
  from tomorrow – à partir de
    demain
tomorrow evening – demain soir
tomorrow morning – demain matin
ton – tonne *nf*
tone – ton *nm*
tone – (on phone) tonalité *nf*
tongue – langue *nf*
tonight – ce soir *nm*, cette nuit *nf*
too – (as well) aussi *adv*
  too bad – tant pis
  too many – trop *adv*
  too many people – trop de monde
  too much – trop *adv*

---

tool – outil *nm*
tooth – dent *nf*
toothache – mal aux dents *nm*
  have toothache – avoir mal aux
    dents *v irreg* §
toothbrush – brosse à dents *nf*
toothpaste – dentifrice *nm*,
  pâte dentifrice *nf*
top – ‡haut *nm*
  at the top – dans le haut
  at the top of – en haut de
torch – lampe de poche *nf*,
  lampe électrique *nf*
torn – déchiré *adj*
tortoise – tortue *nf*
toss a coin – tirer à pile ou face *v reg*
total – total *nm*
totally – totalement, tout à fait *adv*
touch – toucher *v reg*
tough – robuste *adj*, solide *adj*
  tough luck! – tant pis pour toi!
tour – tour *nm*
tourism – tourisme *nm*
tourist – touriste *nmf*
tourist centre – ville touristique *nf*
tourist information office –
  syndicat d'initiative *nm*
tourist office – office de tourisme *nm*
tournament – tournoi *nm*
tow – remorquer *v reg*
towards – (time, place) vers *prep*
  towards midday – vers midi
towards – (in relation to) envers *prep*
towel – serviette de bain *nf*
tower – tour *nf*
tower block – tour d'habitation *nf*
town – ville *nf*
  in town – en ville
  in the town centre – au centre de
    la ville
town centre – centre-ville *nm*
town hall – hôtel de ville *nm*,
  mairie *nf*

town plan – plan de la ville *nm*
toy – jouet *nm*
track – piste *nf*
tracksuit – survêtement *nm*
tractor – tracteur *nm*
trade – (business) commerce *nm*
trade – (profession) métier *nm*
tradition – tradition *nf*
traditional – traditionnel,
  traditionnelle *adj*
traffic – (drugs) trafic *nm*
traffic – (vehicles) circulation *nf*
traffic island – îlot directionel *nm*
traffic jam – embouteillage *nm*,
  bouchon *nm*
traffic lights – feux *nmpl*
trailer – remorque *nf*
train – train *nm*
  by train – par le train
  catch the train – prendre le train
    v irreg §
  get on the train – monter* dans le
    train *v reg*
  through train – train direct *nm*
train – (sport) s'entraîner* *v refl*
trainer – (coach) entraîneur *nm*
trainers – baskets *nmpl*, tennis *nfpl*,
  chaussures de sport *nfpl*
train – (animal) dresser (un animal)
training – (vocational) formation *nf*
tram – tramway *nm*
trampoline – trampoline *nm*
  trampoline – faire du trampoline
    v irreg §
transform – transformer (en) *v reg*
transistor – (radio) transistor *nm*
translate – traduire *v irreg* §
translation – traduction *nf*
transport – transport *nm*
travel – se déplacer* *v refl* †,
  voyager *v reg* †
  travel by bus – voyager en
    autobus *v reg* †

nm - noun masculine	*nmpl* - noun masculine plural	*adj* - adjective	*conj* - conjunction
nf - noun feminine	*nfpl* - noun feminine plural	*adv* - adverb	*pron* - pronoun

travel by car – voyager en voiture
v reg †

travel by coach – voyager en,
par le car *v reg* †

travel by train – voyager par le,
en train *v reg* †

travel agency – agence de voyages
nf

traveller – voyageur *nm*,
voyageuse *nf*

travellers' cheque – chèque de
voyage *nm*

tray – plateau *nm*

treasure – trésor *nm*

treat – (medical) traiter *v reg*

treat – (present) cadeau *nm*

treatment – traitement *nm*

tree – arbre *nm*
fruit tree – arbre fruitier *nm*

tremble – trembler *v reg*

trembling – tremblant *adj*

tremendously – énormément *adv*

trendy – branché *adj*

triangle – triangle *nm*

trip – (outing) excursion *nf*

trip – (journey) voyage *nm*

trip up – trébucher *v reg*

trolley – (supermarket) chariot *nm*,
caddie® *nm*

trombone – trombone *nm*

trouble – peine *nf*
be in trouble – avoir des ennuis
v irreg §

trousers – (pair of) pantalon *nm*

trout – truite *nf*

truant – faire l'école buissonnière
v irreg §

true – vrai *adj*

trumpet – trompette *nf*

trunk road – route nationale *nf*

trunks – (swimming) slip de bain *nm*,
maillot de bain *nm*

truth – vérité *nf*

try – essayer *v reg* †
try on clothes – essayer *v reg* †

try to – essayer de *v reg* †,
tâcher de *v reg*

tube – tube *nm*

tube station – station de métro *nf*

tuck shop – (school) boutique à
provisions *nf*

Tuesday – mardi *nm*

tuna – thon *nm*

tune – (music) air *nm*

tune – (instrument) accorder *v reg*

tunnel – tunnel *nm*

turkey – dinde *nf*

turn – tourner *v reg*

turn – tour *nm*

turn off – (light) éteindre *v irreg* §

turn off – (tap) fermer le robinet *v reg*

turn on – (light) allumer *v reg*

turn on – (tap) ouvrir le robinet
v irreg §

turn pale – pâlir *v reg*

turn round – se retourner* *v refl*

TV news – téléjournal *nm*

twelfth – douzième *adj*

twelve – douze *adj*

twelve o'clock – midi *nm*, minuit *nm*

twentieth – vingtième *adj*

twenty – vingt *adj*

twenty one – vingt et un *adj*

twenty-first – vingt et unième *adj*

twice – deux fois *adv*

twins – jumeaux *nmpl*, jumelles *nfpl*

twist an ankle – se tordre* la
cheville *v refl*

two – deux *adj*

type – genre *nm*, type *nm*, sorte *nf*

type – taper à la machine *v reg*

typewriter – machine à écrire *nf*

typical – typique *adj*

typist – dactylo *nf*

tyre – pneu *nm*

---

flat tyre – pneu à plat *nm*
punctured tyre – pneu crevé *nm*
tyre pressure – pression des pneus *nf*

check the tyre pressure –
vérifier la pression des pneus *v reg*

U

ugly – laid *adj*, vilain *adj*,
moche *adj sl*
UK – Royaume-Uni *nm*
umbrella – parapluie *nm*
unaccustomed – inaccoutumé *adj*
unaware of – ignorant de *adj*
be unaware of – ignorer *v reg*
unbearable – insupportable *adj*
unbelievable – incroyable *adj*
uncle – oncle *nm*
uncomfortable – peu confortable
adj, désagréable *adj*
under – sous, en-dessous de *prep*
underclothes – vêtements de dessous
nmpl
underground – métro *nm*
underground station – station de
métro *nf*
underground ticket – ticket de
métro *nm*
underline – souligner *v reg*
underneath – au-dessous (de),
par-dessous *prep*
underpants – caleçon *nm*, slip *nm*
understand – comprendre *v irreg* §
understood – compris *see
comprendre v irreg* §
underwater – sous-marin
underwear – sous-vêtements *nmpl*
undress – se déshabiller* *v refl*
unemployed – au chômage
unemployed person – chômeur *nm*,
chômeuse *nf*
unemployment – chômage *nm*

uneven – inégal (inégaux *mpl*) *adj*
unexpected – inattendu *adj*
unfair – injuste *adj*
unfavourable – défavorable *adj*
unfold – déplier *v reg*
unforgettable – inoubliable *adj*
unfortunate – malheureux,
malheureuse *adj*
unfortunately – malheureusement
adv
ungrateful – ingrat *adj*
unhappy – triste *adj*, malheureux,
malheureuse *adj*
unhurt – sauf, sauve *adj*
uniform – uniforme *nm*
unify – unifier *v reg*
unit – unité *nf*
United Kingdom – Royaume-Uni
nm
universal – universel, universelle *adj*
universe – univers *nm*
university – université *nf*
unjust – injuste *adj*
unknown – inconnu *adj*
unleaded petrol – essence sans
plomb *nf*
unlucky – malchanceux,
malchanceuse *adj*
unpleasant – désagréable, pénible *adj*
untidy – en désordre *adj*
until – jusque *prep*
until Sunday – jusqu'à dimanche
untruthful – menteur, menteuse *adj*
unwell – indisposé *adj*, souffrant *adj*

---

nm - noun masculine	*nmpl* - noun masculine plural	*adj* - adjective	*conj* - conjunction
nf - noun feminine	*nfpl* - noun feminine plural	*adv* - adverb	*pron* - pronoun

up – en haut, en l'air *adv*
  be up – (out of bed) être levé
  v irreg §, être debout *v irreg* §
  up there – là-haut
upon – sur *prep*
upper – supérieur *adj*
upside down – sens dessous dessus,
  à l'envers
upstairs – à l'étage, en haut
up there – là-haut *adv*
urban – urbain *adj*
urgency – urgence *nf*
urgent – urgent *adj*
us – nous *pron*
USA – Etats-Unis *nmpl*

use – employer *v reg* †, utiliser *v reg*,
  se servir* de *v refl* §
use – usage *nm*
useful – utile *adj*
useless – incapable *adj*, inutile *adj*
user – usager *nm*
usherette – ouvreuse *nf*
usual – ordinaire *adj*
usual – habituel, habituelle *adj*
  as usual – comme d'habitude
usual – normal *adj*
usually – d'habitude, en général,
  généralement *adv*
utensil – ustensile *nm*

V

(no) vacancies – complet
vacuum cleaner – aspirateur *nm*
vacuum – passer l'aspirateur *v reg*
vague – vague *adj*
vain – (conceited) vaniteux,
  vaniteuse *adj*
valid – valable *adj*
valley – vallée *nf*
value – valeur *nf*
van – camionnette *nf*
vanilla – vanille *nf*
vanilla ice cream – glace à la
  vanille *nf*
vanity – (conceit) vanité *nf*
varied – varié *adj*
vary – varier *v reg*
VAT – TVA
  (taxe à la valeur ajoutée) *nf*
VCR – magnétoscope *nm*
veal – veau *nm*
vegan – végétalien *nm*, végétalienne *nf*

vegetable – légume *nm*
vegetarian – végétarien, végétarienne
  adj
vegetarian – végétarien *nm*,
  végétarienne *nf*
vehicle – véhicule *nm*
veil – voile *nm*
velvet – velours *nm*
verb – verbe *nm*
version – version *nf*
  in the original version – en
  version originale
very – très *adv*
very close – tout près
veterinary surgeon – vétérinaire *nm*
vicar – (Protestant) pasteur *nm*
victim – victime *nf*
victorious – victorieux,
  victorieuse *adj*
victory – victoire *nf*
video – vidéo *adj*

---

video camera – caméscope *nm*
video cassette – cassette vidéo *nf*
video game – jeu vidéo *nm*
video recorder – magnétoscope *nm*
video – enregistrer (au magnétoscope)
    v reg
view – vue *nf*
viewer – téléspectateur *nm*,
    téléspectatrice *nf*
vigorous – vigoureux, vigoureuse *adj*
vile – ignoble *adj*
village – village *nm*
vine – vigne *nf*
vinegar – vinaigre *nm*
vine grower – vigneron *nm*
vineyard – vignoble *nm*
viola – alto *nm*
violence – violence *nf*

violent – brutal *adj*
violently – brutalement *adv*
violin – violon *nm*
visibility – visibilité *nf*
visible – visible *adj*
visit – visite *nf*
visit – (a place) visiter *v reg*
visit – (people) aller* voir *v irreg* §,
    rendre visite à *v reg*
visitor – invité *nm*, invitée *nf*,
    visiteur *nm*, visiteuse *nf*
visual – visuel, visuelle *adj*
vital – indispensable *adj*
vocabulary – vocabulaire *nm*
voice – voix *nf*
volleyball – volley(-ball) *nm*
vomit – vomir *v reg*

W

waffle – gaufre *nf*
wages – salaire *nm*
waist – taille *nf*
  waist measurement – tour de
    taille *nm*
waistcoat – gilet *nm*
wait – patienter *v reg*
  ask him to wait – faites-le
    patienter
wait (for) – attendre *v reg*
waiter – garçon (de café), serveur *nm*
waiting room – salle d'attente *nf*
waitress – serveuse *nf*
wake up – se réveiller* *v refl*
Wales – Pays de Galles *nm*
walk – marcher *v reg*,
    aller* à pied *v irreg* §
walk – (stroll) promenade *nf*

walk – se promener* *v refl* †
walk the dog – promener le chien
    v reg †
go for a walk – faire une
    promenade *v irreg* §
walkman® – baladeur *nm*
wall – mur *nm*
wallet – portefeuille *nm*
wallpaper – tapisser *v reg*
want – désirer *v reg*
want – (to) vouloir *v irreg* §,
    avoir envie de *v irreg* §
war – guerre *nf*
warden – (youth hostel) mère
    aubergiste *nf*, père aubergiste *nm*
warden – (traffic) contractuel *nm*,
    contractuelle *nf*
wardrobe – armoire *nf*, penderie *nf*
warm – (assez) chaud *adj*

| nm - noun masculine | nmpl - noun masculine plural | adj - adjective | conj - conjunction |
| nf - noun feminine | nfpl - noun feminine plural | adv - adverb | pron - pronoun |

be warm – (person) avoir chaud *v irreg* §

be warm – (weather) faire chaud *v irreg* §

warm up – échauffement *nm*
   warm up – échauffer *v reg*

warn – prévenir *v irreg* §

warning – avertissement *nm*

was – était *see* être *v irreg* §
   it was – c'était

was able to – pouvait *see* pouvoir *v irreg* §

was obliged to – devait *see* devoir *v irreg* §

wash – (clothes etc) laver *v reg*

wash basin – lavabo *nm*

wash o.s. – se laver* *v refl*

wash one's hair – se laver* la tête *v refl*

washing – (clothes) lessive *nf*
   do the washing – faire la lessive *v irreg* §

washing machine – lave-linge *nm*

washing up – vaisselle *nf*
   do the washing up – faire la vaisselle *v irreg* §

wasp – guêpe *nf*

waste – (money) gaspiller *v reg*

waste – (time) perdre *v reg*

wasted – inutile *adj*, perdu *adj*, vain *adj*

watch – montre *nf*

watch – regarder *v reg*

water – eau *nf*

water – (plants) arroser *v reg*

water sports – sports nautiques *nmpl*
   water skiing – ski nautique *nm*
   water-ski – faire du ski nautique *v irreg* §
   do watersports – faire des sports nautiques *v irreg* §

wave – (hand) faire signe (de la main) *v irreg* §

wave – (sea) vague *nf*

way – chemin *nm*, route *nf*, voie *nf*
   on the way – en route
   right way – la bonne route *nf*

way in – entrée *nf*, accès *nm*

way out – sortie *nf*

we – nous *pron*

we'll (we will) – *see future tenses*

weak – faible *adj*

wear – (clothes) porter *v reg*

wear out – user *v reg*

weather – temps *nm*
   in bad weather – par mauvais temps
   in good weather – par beau temps

weather forecast – bulletin météo(rologique) *nm*, méteo *nf*

wedding – noce *nf*

wedding dress – robe de mariée *nf*

Wednesday – mercredi *nm*

weeds – les mauvaises herbes *nfpl*

week – semaine *nf*
   during the week – pendant la semaine
   last week – la semaine dernière
   next week – la semaine prochaine
   per week – par semaine

weekend – weekend *nm*

weekly – hebdomadaire *adj*

weep – pleurer *v reg*

weigh – peser *v reg* †

weight – poids *nm*

welcome – bienvenu *adj*
   welcome! – soyez le bienvenu! vous êtes la bienvenue!

welcome – accueillir *v irreg* §

welcoming – accueillant *adj*

well – bien *adv*
   all is well – tout va bien
   as well – aussi *adv*
   I am well – je vais bien
   to be well – bien aller* *v irreg* §
   well-behaved – sage *adj*

---

prep - preposition   *v reg* - verb regular   *v refl* - verb reflexive   § - see verb tables
pp - past participle   *v irreg* - verb irregular   † - see verb information   * - takes être

well-built – (person) costaud *adj*
well-cooked – bien cuit *adj*
well-done! – bravo!
well-known – bien connu *adj*
well-paid – bien payé *adj*
well – (for water) puits *nm*
Welsh – gallois *adj*
Welsh – (language) gallois *nm*
Welsh – (person) Gallois *nm,* Galloise *nf*
went – allé *see aller* *v irreg* §
west – ouest *nm*
  in the west – à l'ouest
western – (film) western *nm*
West Indian – antillais *adj*
West Indian – (person) Antillais *nm,* Antillaise *nf*
West Indies – Antilles *nfpl*
wet – mouillé *adj*
wet paint – peinture fraîche *nf*
wet through – trempé jusqu'aux os *adj*
what? – hein? *excl*
what – (which) ce qui, ce que *rel pron*
what? – comment?
  what is ...like? – comment est ...?
  what is your name? – comment t'appelles tu? comment vous appelez-vous?
what? – que?
  what did you say? – que dites-vous?
  what has become of him? – qu'est-il devenu?
  what does... mean? – que veut dire...?
what? – (which?) quel, quelle? *adj*
  what a pity! – quel dommage!
  what colour? – de quelle couleur?
  what is the time? – quelle heure est-il?
what? – qu'est-ce que?
  what is it? – qu'est-ce que c'est?

what is it in French? – qu'est-ce que c'est en français?
what? – qu'est-ce qui?
  what's going on? – qu'est-ce qui se passe?
  what's the matter? – qu'est-ce qui ne va pas?
what? – quoi? *pron*
  what else? – quoi encore?
  what is it about? – de quoi s'agit-il?
  what's new? – quoi de neuf?
what is the way to..? – pour aller à..?
whatsit – truc *nm,* machin *nm*
wheel – roue *nf*
wheelbarrow – brouette *nf*
wheelchair – fauteuil roulant *nm*
when – lorsque *conj*
when – quand *adv*
when? – quand? *adv*
where – où *adv*
  I see where he is – je vois où il est
where? – où? *adv*
  where do you come from? – d'où venez-vous?
whether – si *conj*
which – que, qui *pron*
which? – quel, quelle? *adj*
while – pendant que, tandis que *conj*
whilst – alors que
whisky – scotch *nm*
whisper – chuchoter *v reg*
white – blanc, blanche *adj*
white wine – vin blanc *nm*
white coffee – café crème *nm*
who? – qui? *pron*
  who is coming in? – qui entre?
  who(m) did you see? – qui as-tu vu?
  whose book is this? – à qui est ce livre?
whole – entier, entière *adj,* intégral *adj*

wholemeal bread – pain complet *nm*
why? – pourquoi? *conj*
wide – large *adj*
widely – largement *adv*
widen – élargir *v reg*
widow – veuve *nf*
widowed – veuf, veuve *adj*
widower – veuf *nm*
width – largeur *nf*
wife – femme *nf,* épouse *nf*
wild – sauvage *adj*
  wild animal – animal sauvage *nm*
will – *see future tenses* §
will – (want to) vouloir *v irreg* §
win – gagner *v reg,* vaincre *v irreg* §
wind – vent *nm*
  it is windy – il fait du vent
window – fenêtre *nf*
window – (shop) vitrine *nf*
  window shopping – faire du
    lèche-vitrines *v irreg* §
windscreen – pare-brise *nm*
windsurf – faire de la planche à voile
  v irreg §
wine – vin *nm*
winger – (sport) ailier *nm*
winner – vainqueur *nm*
winter – hiver *nm*
  in winter – en hiver
  winter sports – sports d'hiver
    nmpl
wipe – essuyer *v reg* †
wise – sage *adj*
wish – désir *nm,* envie *nf*
wish – souhaiter *v reg*
wish – vœu *nm*
  best wishes – meilleurs vœux *nmpl*
wish (to) – vouloir *v irreg* §,
  avoir envie de *v irreg* §
with – avec, auprès de *prep*
  with best wishes from – (letter)
    amicalement

with pleasure – avec plaisir
with success – avec succès
without – sans *prep*
  without doubt – sans doute
witness – témoin *nm*
woman – femme *nf*
wonder – se demander* *v refl*
wonderful – magnifique *adj,*
  merveilleux, merveilleuse *adj*
wood – bois *nm*
  wooden – en bois
wool – laine *nf*
  woollen – en laine
word – mot *nm,* parole *nf*
word processing – traitement de
  texte *nm*
word processor – machine de
  traitement de texte *nf*
work – travail *nm*
  part-time work – travail à
    mi-temps *nm*
work – travailler *v reg*
  work hard – travailler dur *v reg*
  work part-time – travailler à
    mi-temps *v reg*
work – (clock etc) marcher *v reg*
work – (machine) fonctionner *v reg*
worker – ouvrier *nm,* ouvrière *nf*
workshop – atelier *nm*
world – mondial *adj*
world – monde *nm*
worm – ver de terre *nm*
worn out – usé *adj*
worried – troublé *adj,* anxieux,
  anxieuse *adj*
worry – s'inquiéter* *v refl* †
  don't worry! – ne t'inquiète pas!
    ne vous inquiétez pas!
worse – pire *adj*
  so much the worse for them –
    tant pis pour eux
worth – valeur *nf*
  be worth – valoir *v irreg* §

---

it's not worth it – ça ne vaut pas la peine

wrap up – envelopper *v reg*

wrist – poignet *nm*

wrist watch – montre *nf*

write – écrire *v irreg* §

write back – répondre *v reg*

write down – noter *v reg*

writer – écrivain *nm*

writing paper – papier à lettres *nm*

written test – épreuve écrite *nf*

wrong – faux, fausse *adj*

  be wrong – avoir tort *v irreg* §

  I am wrong – j'ai tort

wrong number – mauvais numéro *nm*

wrong side – envers *nm*

  wrong way round – à l'envers

X

Xmas – Noël *nm*

X-ray – rayon X *nm*

Y

yacht – yacht *nm*

  yacht marina – port de plaisance *nm*

yard – cour *nf*, jardin *nm*

yawn – bâiller *v reg*

year – an *nm,* année *nf*

  be... years old – avoir... ans *v irreg* §

  be in Year 7 – être en sixième *v irreg* §

  be in Year 8 – être en cinquième *v irreg* §

  be in Year 9 – être en quatrième *v irreg* §

  be in Year 10 – être en troisième *v irreg* §

  be in Year 11 – être en seconde *v irreg* §

  be in Year 12 – être en première *v irreg* §

  be in Year 13 – être en terminale *v irreg* §

  last year – l'année dernière *nf*

  next year – l'année prochaine *nf*

  school year – année scolaire *nf*

yearly – annuel, annuelle *adj*

yell – hurler *v reg*

yellow – jaune *adj*

yes – oui *adv*

  yes I am! – mais si!

yesterday – hier *adv*

  yesterday evening – hier soir

yet – encore, déjà, pourtant *adv*

  not yet – pas encore

yoga – yoga *nm*

yoghurt – yaourt *nm*

you – tu *pron*, vous *pron*

young – jeune *adj*, petit *adj*

  young people – jeunesse *nf*

younger – plus jeune *adj*

---

nm - noun masculine	*nmpl* - noun masculine plural	*adj* - adjective	*conj* - conjunction
nf - noun feminine	*nfpl* - noun feminine plural	*adv* - adverb	*pron* - pronoun

youngest – cadet, cadette *adj*
your – ton, ta, tes *poss adj*
your – votre, vos *poss adj*
yours – à toi, à vous
yourself – toi-même, vous-même *pron*
Yours faithfully – Veuillez agréer, Monsieur/Madame, les expressions de mes sentiments distingués

Yours sincerely – (formal) Je vous prie de croire en l'expression de mes sentiments les meilleurs
Yours sincerely – (informal) cordialement à vous, bien à vous
youth – jeunesse *nf*
youth club – club des jeunes *nm*, foyer des jeunes *nm*, maison des jeunes *nf*
youth hostel – auberge de jeunesse *nf*

Z

zap – (computer game) enlever *v reg* †
zap – (channel hopping) zapper *v reg*
zebra – zèbre *nm*
zebra crossing – passage clouté *nm*
zero – zéro *nm*
zip – fermeture éclair *nf*
zit – pustule *nf*, bouton *nm*

zone – zone *nf*
  pedestrian zone – zone piétonne *nf*
  industrial zone – zone industrielle *nf*
zoo – jardin zoologique *nm*, zoo *nm*

Infinitif/Impératif Infinitive/Imperative	Présent Present	Imparfait Imperfect	Passé Composé Perfect	Futur Future	Passé Simple Past Historic
accueillir *to welcome*	*see cueillir*				
aller* *to go* va! (vas-y!) allons! allez!	je vais tu vas il/elle va nous allons vous allez ils/elles vont	j'allais tu allais il/elle allait nous allions vous alliez ils/elles allaient	je suis allé(e) tu es allé(e) il est allé elle est allée nous sommes allé(e)s vous êtes allé(e) allé(e)s ils sont allés elles sont allées	j'irai tu iras il/elle ira nous irons vous irez ils/elles iront	il/elle alla ils/elles allèrent
(s'*)apercevoir *to notice*	*see recevoir*				
apparaître *to appear*	*see paraître*				
appartenir *to belong to*	*see tenir*				
apprendre *to learn*	*see prendre*				
s'asseoir* *to sit down* assieds-toi! asseyons-nous! asseyez-vous!	je m'assieds tu t'assieds il/elle s'assied nous nous asseyons vous vous asseyez ils/elles s'asseyent	je m'asseyais tu t'asseyais il/elle s'asseyait nous nous asseyions vous vous asseyiez ils/elles s'asseyaient	je me suis assis(e) tu t'es assis(e) il s'est assis elle s'est assise nous nous sommes assis(es) vous vous êtes assis(e)(es) ils se sont assis elles se sont assises	je m'assiérai tu t'assiéras il/elle s'assiéra nous nous assiérons vous vous assiérez ils/elles s'assiéront	il/elle s'assit ils/elles s'assirent
atteindre *to reach*	*see joindre*				
avoir *to have* aie! ayons! ayez!	j'ai tu as il/elle a nous avons vous avez ils/elles ont	j'avais tu avais il/elle avait nous avions vous aviez ils/elles avaient	j'ai eu tu as eu il/elle a eu nous avons eu vous avez eu ils/elles ont eu	j'aurai tu auras il/elle aura nous aurons vous aurez ils/elles auront	il/elle eut ils/elles eurent

Infinitif/Impératif Infinitive/Imperative	Présent Present	Imparfait Imperfect	Passé Composé Perfect	Futur Future	Passé Simple Past Historic
boire *to drink*	je bois	je buvais	j'ai bu	je boirai	il/elle but
	tu bois	tu buvais	tu as bu	tu boiras	
bois!	il/elle boit	il/elle buvait	il/elle a bu	il/elle boira	ils/elles burent
buvons!	nous buvons	nous buvions	nous avons bu	nous boirons	
buvez!	vous buvez	vous buviez	vous avez bu	vous boirez	
	ils/elles boivent	ils/elles buvaient	ils/elles ont bu	ils/elles boiront	
bouillir *to boil*	je bous	je bouillais	j'ai bouilli	je bouillirai	il/elle bouillit
	tu bous	tu bouillais	tu as bouilli	tu bouilliras	
bous!	il/elle bout	il/elle bouillait	il/elle a bouilli	il/elle bouillira	ils/elles bouillirent
bouillons!	nous bouillons	nous bouillions	nous avons bouilli	nous bouillirons	
bouillez!	vous bouillez	vous bouilliez	vous avez bouilli	vous bouillirez	
	ils/elles bouillent	ils/elles bouillaient	ils/elles ont bouilli	ils/elles bouilliront	
comprendre *to understand*	*see prendre*				
conduire *to drive*	je conduis	je conduisais	j'ai conduit	je conduirai	il/elle conduisit
	tu conduis	tu conduisais	tu as conduit	tu conduiras	
conduis!	il/elle conduit	il/elle conduisait	il/elle a conduit	il/elle conduira	ils/elles conduisirent
conduisons!	nous conduisons	nous conduisions	nous avons conduit	nous conduirons	
conduisez!	vous conduisez	vous conduisiez	vous avez conduit	vous conduirez	
	ils/elles conduisent	ils/elles conduisaient	ils/elles ont conduit	ils/elles conduiront	
connaître *to know* (a person, place, book, film)	je connais	je connaissais	j'ai connu	je connaîtrai	il/elle connut
	tu connais	tu connaissais	tu as connu	tu connaîtras	
connais!	il/elle connaît	il/elle connaissait	il/elle a connu	il/elle connaîtra	ils/elles connurent
connaissons!	nous connaissons	nous connaissions	nous avons connu	nous connaîtrons	
connaissez!	vous connaissez	vous connaissiez	vous avez connu	vous connaîtrez	
	ils/elles connaissent	ils/elles connaissaient	ils/elles ont connu	ils/elles connaîtront	

Infinitif/Impératif Infinitive/Imperative	Présent Present	Imparfait Imperfect	Passé Composé Perfect	Futur Future	Passé Simple Past Historic
construire *to build* construis! construisons! construisez!	je construis tu construis il/elle construit nous construisons vous construisez ils/elles construisent	je construisais tu construisais il construisait nous construisions vous construisiez ils/elles construisaient	j'ai construit tu as construit il/elle a construit nous avons construit vous avez construit ils/elles ont construit	je construirai tu construiras il/elle construira nous construirons vous construirez ils/elles construiront	il/elle construisit ils/elles construisirent
contenir *to contain* *see tenir*					
coudre *to sew* couds! cousons! cousez!	je couds tu couds il/elle coud nous cousons vous cousez ils/elles cousent	je cousais tu cousais il/elle cousait nous cousions vous cousiez ils/elles cousaient	j'ai cousu tu as cousu il/elle a cousu nous avons cousu vous avez cousu ils/elles ont cousu	je coudrai tu coudras il/elle coudra nous coudrons vous coudrez ils/elles coudront	il/elle cousit ils/elles cousirent
courir *to run* cours! courons! courez!	je cours tu cours il/elle court nous courons vous courez ils/elles courent	je courais tu courais il/elle courait nous courions vous couriez ils/elles couraient	j'ai couru tu as couru il/elle a couru nous avons couru vous avez couru ils/elles ont couru	je courrai tu courras il/elle courra nous courrons vous courrez ils/elles courront	il/elle courut ils/elles coururent
couvrir *to cover* couvre! couvrons! couvrez!	je couvre tu couvres il/elle couvre nous couvrons vous couvrez ils/elles couvrent	je couvrais tu couvrais il/elle couvrait nous couvrions vous couvriez ils/elles couvraient	j'ai couvert tu as couvert il/elle a couvert nous avons couvert vous avez couvert ils/elles ont couvert	je couvrirai tu couvriras il/elle couvrira nous couvrirons vous couvrirez ils/elles couvriront	il/elle couvrit ils/elles couvrirent

Infinitif/Impératif Infinitive/Imperative	Présent Present	Imparfait Imperfect	Passé Composé Perfect	Futur Future	Passé Simple Past Historic
craindre *to fear,* *be afraid* crains! craignons! craignez!	je crains tu crains il/elle craint nous craignons vous craignez ils/elles craignent	je craignais tu craignais il/elle craignait nous craignions vous craigniez ils/elles craignaient	j'ai craint tu as craint il/elle a craint nous avons craint vous avez craint ils/elles ont craint	je craindrai tu craindras il/elle craindra nous craindrons vous craindrez ils/elles craindront	il/elle craignit ils/elles craignirent
croire *to believe,* *think* crois! croyons! croyez!	je crois tu crois il/elle croit nous croyons vous croyez ils/elles croient	je croyais tu croyais il/elle croyait nous croyions vous croyiez ils/elles croyaient	j'ai cru tu as cru il/elle a cru nous avons cru vous avez cru ils/elles ont cru	je croirai tu croiras il/elle croira nous croirons vous croirez ils/elles croiront	il/elle crut ils/elles crurent
cueillir *to pick* cueille cueillons cueillez	je cueille tu cueilles il/elle cueille nous cueillons vous cueillez ils/elles cueillent	je cueillais tu cueillais il/elle cueillait nous cueillions vous cueilliez ils/elles cueillaient	j'ai cueilli tu as cueilli il/elle a cueilli nous avons cueilli vous avez cueilli ils/elles ont cueilli	je cueillerai tu cueilleras il/elle cueillera nous cueillerons vous cueillerez ils/elles cueilleront	il/elle cueillit ils/elles cueillirent
cuire *to cook*	see conduire				
découvrir *to discover*	see couvrir				
décrire *to describe*	see écrire				
détruire *to destroy* détruis! détruisons! détruisez!	je détruis tu détruis il/elle détruit nous détruisons vous détruisez ils/elles détruisent	je détruisais tu détruisais il/elle détruisait nous détruisions vous détruisiez ils/elles détruisaient	j'ai détruit tu as détruit il/elle a détruit nous avons détruit vous avez détruit ils/elles ont détruit	je détruirai tu détruiras il/elle détruira nous détruirons vous détruirez ils/elles détruiront	il/elle détruisit ils/elles détruisirent
devenir* *to become*	see venir*				

Infinitif/Impératif Infinitive/Imperative	Présent Present	Imparfait Imperfect	Passé Composé Perfect	Futur Future	Passé Simple Past Historic
devoir *to have to*	je dois	je devais	j'ai dû	je devrai	il/elle dut
	tu dois	tu devais	tu as dû	tu devras	
dois!	il/elle doit	il/elle devait	il/elle a dû	il/elle devra	ils/elles durent
devons!	nous devons	nous devions	nous avons dû	nous devrons	
devez!	vous devez	vous deviez	vous avez dû	vous devrez	
	ils/elles doivent	ils/elles devaient	ils/elles ont dû	ils/elles devront	
dire *to say, tell*	je dis	je disais	j'ai dit	je dirai	il/elle dit
	tu dis	tu disais	tu as dit	tu diras	
dis!	il/elle dit	il/elle disait	il/elle a dit	il/elle dira	ils/elles dirent
disons!	nous disons	nous disions	nous avons dit	nous dirons	
dites!	vous dites	vous disiez	vous avez dit	vous direz	
	ils/elles disent	ils/elles disaient	ils/elles ont dit	ils/elles diront	
dissoudre *to dissolve*	je dissous	je dissolvais	j'ai dissous	je dissoudrai	
	tu dissous	tu dissolvais	tu as dissous	tu dissoudras	
dissous!	il/elle dissout	il/elle dissolvait	il/elle a dissous	il/elle dissoudra	
dissolvons!	nous dissolvons	nous dissolvions	nous avons dissous	nous dissoudrons	
dissolvez!	vous dissolvez	vous dissolviez	vous avez dissous	vous dissoudrez	
	ils/elles dissolvent	ils/elles dissolvaient	ils/elles ont dissous	ils/elles dissoudront	
disparaître *to disappear*	*see* paraître				
dormir *to sleep*	je dors	je dormais	j'ai dormi	je dormirai	il/elle dormit
	tu dors	tu dormais	tu as dormi	tu dormiras	
dors!	il/elle dort	il/elle dormait	il/elle a dormi	il/elle dormira	ils/elles dormirent
dormons!	nous dormons	nous dormions	nous avons dormi	nous dormirons	
dormez!	vous dormez	vous dormiez	vous avez dormi	vous dormirez	
	ils/elles dorment	ils/elles dormaient	ils/elles ont dormi	ils/elles dormiront	

Infinitif/Impératif Infinitive/Imperative	Présent Present	Imparfait Imperfect	Passé Composé Perfect	Futur Future	Passé Simple Past Historic
écrire to write écris! écrivons! écrivez!	j'écris tu écris il/elle écrit nous écrivons vous écrivez ils/elles écrivent	j'écrivais tu écrivais il/elle écrivait nous écrivions vous écriviez ils/elles écrivaient	j'ai écrit tu as écrit il/elle a écrit nous avons écrit vous avez écrit ils/elles ont écrit	j'écrirai tu écriras il/elle écrira nous écrirons vous écrirez ils/elles écriront	il/elle écrivit ils/elles écrivirent

s'endormir*
  to go to sleep,
  fall asleep
 	
endors-toi!
endormons-nous!
endormez-vous!
	je m'endors
	tu t'endors
	il/elle s'endort
	nous nous
	  endormons
	vous vous endormez
	ils/elles s'endorment
		je m'endormais
		tu t'endormais
		il/elle s'endormait
		nous nous endormions
		vous vous endormiez
		ils/elles s'endormaient
			je me suis endormi(e)
			tu t'es endormi(e)
			il s'est endormi
			elle s'est endormie
			nous nous sommes endormi(e)s
			vous vous êtes endormi(e)(s)
			ils se sont endormis
			elles se sont endormies
				je m'endormirai
				tu t'endormiras
				il/elle s'endormira
				nous nous endormirons
				vous vous endormirez
				ils/elles s'endormiront
					il/elle
					  s'endormit
					
					ils/elles
					  s'endormirent

entretenir to maintain	see tenir				

éteindre
  to extinguish,
  switch off
 	
éteins!
éteignons!
éteignez!
	j'éteins
	tu éteins
	il/elle éteint
	nous éteignons
	vous éteignez
	ils/elles éteignent
		j'éteignais
		tu éteignais
		il/elle éteignait
		nous éteignions
		vous éteigniez
		ils/elles éteignaient
			j'ai éteint
			tu as éteint
			il/elle a éteint
			nous avons éteint
			vous avez éteint
			ils/elles ont éteint
				j'éteindrai
				tu éteindras
				il/elle éteindra
				nous éteindrons
				vous éteindrez
				ils/elles éteindront
					il/elle éteignit
					
					ils/elles
					  éteignirent

être to be sois! soyons! soyez!	je suis tu es il/elle est nous sommes vous êtes ils/elles sont	j'étais tu étais il/elle était nous étions vous étiez ils/elles étaient	j'ai été tu as été il/elle a été nous avons été vous avez été ils/elles ont été	je serai tu seras il/elle sera nous serons vous serez ils/elles seront	il/elle fut ils/elles furent

Infinitif/Impératif Infinitive/Imperative	Présent Present	Imparfait Imperfect	Passé Composé Perfect	Futur Future	Passé Simple Past Historic
faire to do, make	je fais tu fais il/elle fait nous faisons vous faites ils/elles font	je faisais tu faisais il/elle faisait nous faisions vous faisiez ils/elles faisaient	j'ai fait tu as fait il/elle a fait nous avons fait vous avez fait ils/elles ont fait	je ferai tu feras il/elle fera nous ferons vous ferez ils/elles feront	il/elle fit ils/elles firent
fais! faisons! faites!					
falloir to have to	il faut	il fallait	il a fallu	il faudra	il fallut
fuir to flee	je fuis tu fuis il/elle fuit nous fuyons vous fuyez ils/elles fuient	je fuyais tu fuyais il/elle fuyait nous fuyions vous fuyiez ils/elles fuyaient	j'ai fui tu as fui il/elle a fui nous avons fui vous avez fui ils/elles ont fui	je fuirai tu fuiras il/elle fuira nous fuirons vous fuirez ils/elles fuiront	il/elle fuit ils/elles fuirent
fuis! fuyons! fuyez!					
inscrire to inscribe	see écrire				
instruire to instruct	see construire				
interdire to forbid	see dire				
interrompre to interrupt	see rompre				
introduire to introduce	see construire				
joindre to join	je joins tu joins il/elle joint nous joignons vous joignez ils/elles joignent	je joignais tu joignais il/elle joignait nous joignions vous joigniez ils/elles joignaient	j'ai joint tu as joint il/elle a joint nous avons joint vous avez joint ils/elles ont joint	je joindrai tu joindras il/elle joindra nous joindrons vous joindrez ils/elles joindront	il/elle joignit ils/elles joignirent
joins! joignons! joignez!					

Infinitif/Impératif Infinitive/Imperative	Présent Present	Imparfait Imperfect	Passé Composé Perfect	Futur Future	Passé Simple Past Historic
lire to read lis! lisons! lisez!	je lis tu lis il/elle lit nous lisons vous lisez ils/elles lisent	je lisais tu lisais il/elle lisait nous lisions vous lisiez ils/elles lisaient	j'ai lu tu as lu il/elle a lu nous avons lu vous avez lu ils/elles ont lu	je lirai tu liras il/elle lira nous lirons vous lirez ils/elles liront	il/elle lut ils/elles lurent
maintenir to maintain	see tenir				
mentir to lie mens! mentons! mentez!	je mens tu mens il/elle ment nous mentons vous mentez ils/elles mentent	je mentais tu mentais il/elle mentait nous mentions vous mentiez ils/elles mentaient	j'ai menti tu as menti il/elle a menti nous avons menti vous avez menti ils/elles ont menti	je mentirai tu mentiras il/elle mentira nous mentirons vous mentirez ils/elles mentiront	il/elle mentit ils/elles mentirent
mettre to put mets! mettons! mettez!	je mets tu mets il/elle met nous mettons vous mettez ils/elles mettent	je mettais tu mettais il/elle mettait nous mettions vous mettiez ils/elles mettaient	j'ai mis tu as mis il/elle a mis nous avons mis vous avez mis ils/elles ont mis	je mettrai tu mettras il/elle mettra nous mettrons vous mettrez ils/elles mettront	il/elle mit ils/elles mirent
mourir* to die meurs! mourons! mourez!	je meurs tu meurs il/elle meurt nous mourons vous mourez ils/elles meurent	je mourais tu mourais il/elle mourait nous mourions vous mouriez ils/elles mouraient	je suis mort(e) tu es mort(e) il est mort elle est morte nous sommes mort(e)s vous êtes mort(e)(s) ils sont morts elles sont mortes	je mourrai tu mourras il/elle mourra nous mourrons vous mourrez ils/elles mourront	il/elle mourut ils/elles moururent

Infinitif/Impératif Infinitive/Imperative	Présent Present	Imparfait Imperfect	Passé Composé Perfect	Futur Future	Passé Simple Past Historic
naître* to be born	je nais	je naissais	je suis né(e)	je naîtrai	il/elle naquit
	tu nais	tu naissais	tu es né(e)	tu naîtras	
	il/elle naît	il/elle naissait	il est né	il/elle naîtra	
nais!	nous naissons	nous naissions	elle est née	nous naîtrons	ils/elles naquirent
naissons!	vous naissez	vous naissiez	nous sommes né(e)s	vous naîtrez	
naissez!	ils/elles naissent	ils/elles naissaient	vous êtes né(e)(s)	ils/elles naîtront	
			ils sont nés		
			elles sont nées		
obtenir to obtain	see tenir				
offrir to offer	j'offre	j'offrais	j'ai offert	j'offrirai	il/elle offrit
	tu offres	tu offrais	tu as offert	tu offriras	
	il/elle offre	il/elle offrait	il/elle a offert	il/elle offrira	
offre!	nous offrons	nous offrions	nous avons offert	nous offrirons	ils/elles offrirent
offrons!	vous offrez	vous offriez	vous avez offert	vous offrirez	
offrez!	ils/elles offrent	ils/elles offraient	ils/elles ont offert	ils/elles offriront	
ouvrir to open	j'ouvre	j'ouvrais	j'ai ouvert	j'ouvrirai	il/elle ouvrit
	tu ouvres	tu ouvrais	tu as ouvert	tu ouvriras	
	il/elle ouvre	il/elle ouvrait	il/elle a ouvert	il/elle ouvrira	
ouvre!	nous ouvrons	nous ouvrions	nous avons ouvert	nous ouvrirons	ils/elles ouvrirent
ouvrons!	vous ouvrez	vous ouvriez	vous avez ouvert	vous ouvrirez	
ouvrez!	ils/elles ouvrent	ils/elles ouvraient	ils/elles ont ouvert	ils/elles ouvriront	
paraître to appear, seem	je parais	je paraissais	j'ai paru	je paraîtrai	il/elle parut
	tu parais	tu paraissais	tu as paru	tu paraîtras	
	il/elle paraît	il/elle paraissait	il/elle a paru	il/elle paraîtra	
parais!	nous paraissons	nous paraissions	nous avons paru	nous paraîtrons	ils/elles parurent
paraissons!	vous paraissez	vous paraissiez	vous avez paru	vous paraîtrez	
paraissez!	ils/elles paraissent	ils/elles paraissaient	ils/elles ont paru	ils/elles paraîtront	
parcourir to run along	see courir				

Infinitif/Impératif Infinitive/Imperative	Présent Present	Imparfait Imperfect	Passé Composé Perfect	Futur Future	Passé Simple Past Historic
partir* to leave, go away pars! partons! partez!	je pars tu pars il/elle part nous partons vous partez ils/elles partent	je partais tu partais il/elle partait nous partions vous partiez ils/elles partaient	je suis parti(e) tu es parti(e) il est parti elle est partie nous sommes parti(e)s vous êtes parti(e)(s) ils sont partis elles sont parties	je partirai tu partiras il/elle partira nous partirons vous partirez ils/elles partiront	il/elle partit ils/elles partirent
parvenir* to manage, get to, reach, succeed parviens! parvenons! parvenez!	je parviens tu parviens il/elle parvient nous parvenons vous parvenez ils/elles parviennent	je parvenais tu parvenais il/elle parvenait nous parvenions vous parveniez ils/elles parvenaient	je suis parvenu(e) tu es parvenu(e) il est parvenu elle est parvenue nous sommes parvenu(e)s vous êtes parvenu(e)(s) ils sont parvenus elles sont parvenues	je parviendrai tu parviendras il/elle parviendra nous parviendrons vous parviendrez ils/elles parviendront	il/elle parvint ils/elle parvinrent
peindre to paint peins! peignons! peignez!	je peins tu peins il/elle peint nous peignons vous peignez ils/elles peignent	je peignais tu peignais il/elle peignait nous peignions vous peigniez ils/elles peignaient	j'ai peint tu as peint il/elle a peint nous avons peint vous avez peint ils/elles ont peint	je peindrai tu peindras il/elle peindra nous peindrons vous peindrez ils/elles peindront	il/elle peignit ils/elles peignirent
permettre to permit	see mettre				

Infinitif/Impératif Infinitive/Imperative	Présent Present	Imparfait Imperfect	Passé Composé Perfect	Futur Future	Passé Simple Past Historic
se plaindre* to complain plains-toi! plaignons-nous! plaignez-vous!	je me plains tu te plains il/elle se plaint nous nous plaignons vous vous plaignez ils/elles se plaignent	je me plaignais tu te plaignais il/elle se plaignait nous nous plaignions vous vous plaigniez ils/elles se plaignaient	je me suis plaint(e) tu t'es plaint(e) il s'est plaint elle s'est plainte nous nous sommes plaint(e)s vous vous êtes plaint(e)(s) ils se sont plaints elles se sont plaintes	je me plaindrai tu te plaindras il/elle se plaindra nous nous plaindrons vous vous plaindrez ils/elles se plaindront	il/elle se plaignit ils/elles se plaignirent
plaire to please plais! plaisons! plaisez!	je plais tu plais il/elle plaît nous plaisons vous plaisez ils/elles plaisent	je plaisais tu plaisais il/elle plaisait nous plaisions vous plaisiez ils/elles plaisaient	j'ai plu tu as plu il/elle a plu nous avons plu vous avez plu ils/elles ont plu	je plairai tu plairas il/elle plaira nous plairons vous plairez ils/elles plairont	il/elle plut ils/elles plurent
pleuvoir to rain	il pleut	il pleuvait	il a plu	il pleuvra	il plut
poursuivre to pursue	see suivre				
pouvoir to be able to, can	je peux (puis-je?) tu peux il/elle peut nous pouvons vous pouvez ils/elles peuvent	je pouvais tu pouvais il/elle pouvait nous pouvions vous pouviez ils/elles pouvaient	j'ai pu tu as pu il/elle a pu nous avons pu vous avez pu ils/elles ont pu	je pourrai tu pourras il/elle pourra nous pourrons vous pourrez ils/elles pourront	il/elle put ils/elles purent
prendre to take prends! prenons! prenez!	je prends tu prends il/elle prend nous prenons vous prenez ils/elles prennent	je prenais tu prenais il/elle prenait nous prenions vous preniez ils/elles prenaient	j'ai pris tu as pris il/elle a pris nous avons pris vous avez pris ils/elles ont pris	je prendrai tu prendras il/elle prendra nous prendrons vous prendrez ils/elles prendront	il/elle prit ils/elles prirent
prescrire to prescribe	see écrire				

Infinitif/Impératif Infinitive/Imperative	Présent Present	Imparfait Imperfect	Passé Composé Perfect	Futur Future	Passé Simple Past Historic
prévenir *to warn, inform*	je préviens tu préviens il/elle prévient nous prévenons vous prévenez ils/elles préviennent	je prévenais tu prévenais il/elle prévenait nous prévenions vous préveniez ils/elles prévenaient	j'ai prévenu tu as prévenu il/elle a prévenu nous avons prévenu vous avez prévenu ils/elles ont prévenu	je préviendrai tu préviendras il/elle préviendra nous préviendrons vous préviendrez ils/elles préviendront	il/elle prévint ils/elles prévinrent
préviens! prévenons! prévenez!					
prévoir *to foresee*	*see* voir				
produire *to produce*	*see* construire				
promettre *to promise*	*see* mettre				
recevoir *to receive*	je reçois tu reçois il/elle reçoit nous recevons vous recevez ils/elles reçoivent	je recevais tu recevais il/elle recevait nous recevions vous receviez ils/elles recevaient	j'ai reçu tu as reçu il/elle a reçu nous avons reçu vous avez reçu ils/elles ont reçu	je recevrai tu recevras il/elle recevra nous recevrons vous recevrez ils/elles recevront	il/elle reçut ils/elles reçurent
reçois! recevons! recevez!					
reconnaître *to recognise*	je reconnais tu reconnais il/elle reconnaît nous reconnaissons vous reconnaissez ils/elles reconnaissent	je reconnaissais tu reconnaissais il/elle reconnaissait nous reconnaissions vous reconnaissiez ils/elles reconnaissaient	j'ai reconnu tu as reconnu il/elle a reconnu nous avons reconnu vous avez reconnu ils/elles ont reconnu	je reconnaîtrai tu reconnaîtras il/elle reconnaîtra nous reconnaîtrons vous reconnaîtrez ils/elles reconnaîtront	il/elle reconnut ils/elles reconnurent
reconnais! reconnaissons! reconnaissez!					
recouvrir *to cover, recover*	*see* couvrir				
réduire *to reduce*	je réduis tu réduis il/elle réduit nous réduisons vous réduisez ils/elles réduisent	je réduisais tu réduisais il/elle réduisait nous réduisions vous réduisiez ils/elles réduisaient	j'ai réduit tu as réduit il/elle a réduit nous avons réduit vous avez réduit ils/elles ont réduit	je réduirai tu réduiras il/elle réduira nous réduirons vous réduirez ils/elles réduiront	il/elle réduit ils/elles réduirent
réduis! réduisons! réduisez!					

Infinitif/Impératif Infinitive/Imperative	Présent Present	Imparfait Imperfect	Passé Composé Perfect	Futur Future	Passé Simple Past Historic
refaire *to re-do, re-make*	see faire				
rejoindre *to re-join*	see joindre				
relire *to re-read*	see lire				
reluire *to shine*	see conduire				
remettre *to replace, remit, put back on, postpone*	see mettre				
repartir* *to leave again*	see partir*				
reprendre *to take, get back, resume*	see prendre				
résoudre *to solve*	je résous to résous il/elle résout nous résolvons vous résolvez ils/elles résolvent	je résolvais tu résolvais il/elle résolvait nous résolvions vous résolviez ils/elles résolvaient	j'ai résolu tu as résolu il/elle a résolu nous avons résolu vous avez résolu ils/elles ont résolu	je résoudrai tu résoudras il/elle résoudra nous résoudrons vous résoudrez ils/elles résoudront	il/elle résolut ils/elles résolurent
ressentir *to feel, experience*	see sentir				
retenir *to hold back, keep*	see tenir				
revenir* *to come back, return*	see venir*				
revoir *to see again*	see voir				
rire *to laugh* ris! rions! riez!	je ris tu ris il/elle rit nous rions vous riez ils/elles rient	je riais tu riais il/elle riait nous riions vous riiez ils/elles riaient	j'ai ri tu as ri il/elle a ri nous avons ri vous avez ri ils/elles ont ri	je rirai tu riras il/elle rira nous rirons vous rirez ils/elles riront	il/elle rit ils/elles rirent

Infinitif/Impératif Infinitive/Imperative	Présent Present	Imparfait Imperfect	Passé Composé Perfect	Futur Future	Passé Simple Past Historic
rompre to break romps! rompons! rompez!	je romps tu romps il/elle rompt nous rompons vous rompez ils/elles rompent	je rompais tu rompais il/elle rompait nous rompions vous rompiez ils/elles rompaient	j'ai rompu tu as rompu il/elle a rompu nous avons rompu vous avez rompu ils/elles ont rompu	je romprai tu rompras il/elle rompra nous romprons vous romprez ils/elles rompront	il/elle rompit ils/elles rompirent
satisfaire to satisfy	see faire				
savoir to know (a fact, or how to do something) sache! sachons! sachez!	je sais tu sais il/elle sait nous savons vous savez ils/elles savent	je savais tu savais il/elle savait nous savions vous saviez ils/elles savaient	j'ai su tu as su il/elle a su nous avons su vous avez su ils/elles ont su	je saurai tu sauras il/elle saura nous saurons vous saurez ils/elles sauront	il/elle sut ils surent
sentir to smell, feel, sense sens! sentons! sentez!	je sens tu sens il/elle sent nous sentons vous sentez ils/elles sentent	je sentais tu sentais il/elle sentait nous sentions vous sentiez ils/elles sentaient	j'ai senti tu as senti il/elle a senti nous avons senti vous avez senti ils/elles ont senti	je sentirai tu sentiras il/elle sentira nous sentirons vous sentirez ils/elles sentiront	il/elle sentit ils/elles sentirent
se sentir* to feel (ill, well, etc) sens-toi! sentons-nous! sentez-vous!	je me sens tu te sens il/elle se sent nous nous sentons vous vous sentez ils/elles se sentent	je me sentais tu te sentais il/elle se sentait nous nous sentions vous vous sentiez ils/elles se sentaient	je me suis senti(e) tu t'es senti(e) il s'est senti elle s'est sentie nous nous sommes senti(e)(s) vous vous êtes senti(e)(s) ils se sont sentis elles se sont senties	je me sentirai tu te sentiras il/elle se sentira nous nous sentirons vous vous sentirez ils/elles se sentiront	il/elle se sentit ils/elles se sentirent

Infinitif/Impératif / Infinitive/Imperative	Présent / Present	Imparfait / Imperfect	Passé Composé / Perfect	Futur / Future	Passé Simple / Past Historic
servir *to serve* sers! servons! servez!	je sers tu sers il/elle sert nous servons vous servez ils/elles servent	je servais tu servais il/elle servait nous servions vous serviez ils/elles servaient	j'ai servi tu as servi il/elle a servi nous avons servi vous avez servi ils/elles ont servi	je servirai tu serviras il/elle servira nous servirons vous servirez ils/elles serviront	il/elle servit ils/elles servirent
se servir* (de) *to use* sers-toi! servons-nous! servez-vous!	je me sers tu te sers il/elle se sert nous nous servons vous vous servez ils/elles se servent	je me servais tu te servais il/elle se servait nous nous servions vous vous serviez ils/elles se servaient	je me suis servi(e) tu t'es servi(e) il s'est servi elle s'est servie nous nous sommes servi(e)s vous vous êtes servi(e)(s) ils se sont servis elles se sont servies	je me servirai tu te serviras il/elle se servira nous nous servirons vous vous servirez ils/elles se serviront	il/elle se servit ils/elles se servirent
sortir* *to go out* sors! sortons! sortez!	je sors tu sors il/elle sort nous sortons vous sortez ils/elles sortent	je sortais tu sortais il/elle sortait nous sortions vous sortiez ils/elles sortaient	je suis sorti(e) ** tu es sorti(e) il est sorti elle est sortie nous sommes sorti(e)s vous êtes sorti(e)(s) ils sont sortis elles sont sorties	je sortirai tu sortiras il/elle sortira nous sortirons vous sortirez ils/elles sortiront	il/elle sortit ils/elles sortirent
souffrir *to suffer* souffre! souffrons! souffrez!	je souffre tu souffres il/elle souffre nous souffrons vous souffrez ils/elles souffrent	je souffrais tu souffrais il/elle souffrait nous souffrions vous souffriez ils/elles souffraient	j'ai souffert tu as souffert il/elle a souffert nous avons souffert vous avez souffert ils/elles ont souffert	je souffrirai tu souffriras il/elle souffrira nous souffrirons vous souffrirez ils/elles souffriront	il/elle souffrit ils/elles souffrirent

*** use avoir as the auxiliary if there is a direct object, e.g. j'ai sorti mon mouchoir*

Infinitif/Impératif Infinitive/Imperative	Présent Present	Imparfait Imperfect	Passé Composé Perfect	Futur Future	Passé Simple Past Historic
soumettre to submit	see mettre				
sourire to smile souris! sourions! souriez!	je souris tu souris il/elle sourit nous sourions vous souriez ils/elles sourient	je souriais tu souriais il/elle souriait nous sourions vous souriez ils/elles souriaient	j'ai souri tu as souri il/elle a souri nous avons souri vous avez souri ils/elles ont souri	je sourirai tu souriras il/elle sourira nous sourirons vous sourirez ils/elles souriront	il/elle sourit ils/elles sourirent
soutenir to support	see tenir				
se souvenir* de to remember	see venir*				
suffire to suffice suffis! suffisons! suffisez!	je suffis tu suffis il/elle suffit nous suffisons vous suffisez ils/elles suffissent	je suffisais tu suffisais il/elle suffisait nous suffisions vous suffisiez ils/elles suffissaient	j'ai suffi tu as suffi il/elle a suffi nous avons.suffi vous avez suffi ils/elles ont suffi	je suffirai tu suffiras il/elle suffira nous suffirons vous suffirez ils/elles suffiront	il/elle suffit ils/elles suffirent
suivre to follow suis! suivons! suivez!	je suis tu suis il/elle suit nous suivons vous suivez ils/elles suivent	je suivais tu suivais il/elle suivait nous suivions vous suiviez ils/elles suivaient	j'ai suivi tu as suivi il/elle a suivi nous avons suivi vous avez suivi ils/elles ont suivi	je suivrai tu suivras il/elle suivra nous suivrons vous suivrez ils/elles suivront	il/elle suivit ils/elles suivirent
surprendre to surprise	see prendre				
survenir* to take place	see venir*				
survivre to survive	see vivre				

Infinitif/Impératif Infinitive/Imperative	Présent Present	Imparfait Imperfect	Passé Composé Perfect	Futur Future	Passé Simple Past Historic
se taire* *to be silent* tais-toi! taisons-nous! taisez -vous!	je me tais tu te tais il/elle se tait nous nous taisons vous vous taisez ils/elles se taisent	je me taisais tu te taisais il/elle se taisait nous nous taisions vous vous taisiez ils/elles se taisaient	je me suis tu(e) tu t'es tu(e) il s'est tu elle s'est tu(e) nous nous sommes tu(e)s vous vous êtes tu(e)(s) ils se sont tus elle se sont tues	je me tairai tu te tairas il/elle se taira nous nous tairons vous vous tairez ils/elles se tairont	il/elle se tut ils/elles se turent
tenir *to hold* tiens! tenons! tenez!	je tiens tu tiens il/elle tient nous tenons vous tenez ils/elles tiennent	je tenais tu tenais il/elle tenait nous tenions vous teniez ils/elles tenaient	j'ai tenu tu as tenu il/elle a tenu nous avons tenu vous avez tenu ils/elles ont tenu	je tiendrai tu tiendras il/elle tiendra nous tiendrons vous tiendrez ils/elles tiendront	il/elle tint ils/elles tinrent
se tenir* *to stand* tiens-toi! tenons-nous! tenez-vous!	je me tiens tu te tiens il/elle se tient nous nous tenons vous vous tenez ils/elles se tiennent	je me tenais tu te tenais il/elle se tenait nous nous tenions vous vous teniez ils/elles se tenaient	je me suis tenu(e) tu t'es tenu(e) il s'est tenu elle s'est tenue nous nous sommes tenu(e)s vous vous êtes tenu(e)(s) ils se sont tenus elles se sont tenues	je me tiendrai tu te tiendras il/elle se tiendra nous nous tiendrons vous vous tiendrez ils/elles se tiendront	il/elle se tint ils/elles se tinrent
traduire *to translate*	see conduire				
transmettre *to transmit*	see mettre				

Infinitif/Impératif Infinitive/Imperative	Présent Present	Imparfait Imperfect	Passé Composé Perfect	Futur Future	Passé Simple Past Historic
vaincre *to defeat* vaincs! vainquons! vainquez!	je vaincs tu vaincs il/elle vainc nous vainquons vous vainquez ils/elles vainquent	je vainquais tu vainquais il/elle vainquait nous vainquions vous vainquiez ils/elles vainquaient	j'ai vaincu tu as vaincu il/elle a vaincu nous avons vaincu vous avez vaincu ils/elles ont vaincu	je vaincrai tu vaincras il/elle vaincra nous vaincrons vous vaincrez ils/elles vaincront	il/elle vainquit ils/elles vainquirent
valoir *to be worth*	je vaux tu vaux il/elle vaut nous valons vous valez ils/elles valent	je valais tu valais il/elle valait nous valions vous valiez ils/elles valaient	j'ai valu tu as valu il/elle a valu nous avons valu vous avez valu ils/elles ont valu	je vaudrai tu vaudras il/elle vaudra nous vaudrons vous vaudrez ils/elles vaudront	il/elle valut ils/elles valurent
venir* *to come* viens! venons! venez!	je viens tu viens il/elle vient nous venons vous venez ils/elles viennent	je venais tu venais il/elle venait nous venions vous veniez ils/elles venaient	je suis venu(e) tu es venu(e) il est venu elle est venue nous sommes venu(e)s vous êtes venu(e)(s) ils sont venus elles sont venues	je viendrai tu viendras il/elle viendra nous viendrons vous viendrez ils/elles viendront	il/elle vint ils/elles vinrent
vivre *to live, be alive* vis! vivons! vivez!	je vis tu vis il/elle vit nous vivons vous vivez ils/elles vivent	je vivais tu vivais il/elle vivait nous vivions vous viviez ils/elles vivaient	j'ai vécu tu as vécu il/elle a vécu nous avons vécu vous avez vécu ils/elles ont vécu	je vivrai tu vivras il/elle vivra nous vivrons vous vivrez ils/elles vivront	il/elle vécut ils/elles vécurent

Infinitif/Impératif Infinitive/Imperative	Présent Present	Imparfait Imperfect	Passé Composé Perfect	Futur Future	Passé Simple Past Historic
voir *to see*	je vois	je voyais	j'ai vu	je verrai	il/elle vit
	tu vois	tu voyais	tu as vu	tu verras	
vois!	il/elle voit	il/elle voyait	il/elle a vu	il/elle verra	
voyons!	nous voyons	nous voyions	nous avons vu	nous verrons	
voyez!	vous voyez	vous voyiez	vous avez vu	vous verrez	
	ils/elles voient	ils/elles voyaient	ils/elles ont vu	ils/elles verront	ils elles virent
vouloir *to wish, want*	je veux	je voulais	j'ai voulu	je voudrai	il/elle voulut
	tu veux	tu voulais	tu as voulu	tu voudras	
	il/elle veut	il/elle voulait	il/elle a voulu	il/elle voudra	
veuille!	nous voulons	nous voulions	nous avons voulu	nous voudrons	
veuillons!	vous voulez	vous vouliez	vous avez voulu	vous voudrez	
veuillez!	ils/elles veulent	ils/elles voulaient	ils/elles ont voulu	ils/elles voudront	ils/elles voulurent

If you are looking for a reflexive verb and do not find it in the table, look for it without se or s'
Example: se mettre* en colère   *see* mettre
Do remember that all reflexive verbs take être in the Perfect Tense even when the non-reflexive verb takes avoir!

GRAMMAR INFORMATION

ARTICLES

the

French nouns are grammatically either masculine or feminine.
Masculine nouns use **le** for *the*. Feminine nouns use **la** for *the*.
Both masculine and feminine nouns use **l'** for *the* in front of nouns which begin
with a vowel or a silent **h**. Other nouns beginning with **h** need a full **le** or **la**.
     Example: *hedge*   ‡haie *nf*   is **la** haie
Both masculine and feminine nouns use **les** for *the* in front of plural nouns.

a, an, some

Masculine nouns use **un** for *a* or *an*. Feminine nouns use **une** for *a* or *an*.
Both masculine and feminine nouns use des for *some* in front of plural nouns.

Du, de la, de l', des, de

There are five different ways of expressing the ideas of **some, any** or **no**:

masculine singular:	Il mange **du** pain	*He eats some bread*
feminine singular:	Il mange **de la** viande	*He eats some meat*
any noun starting with a vowel	Je bois **de l'**eau	*I drink some water*
any noun starting with a silent h	J'achète **de l'**huile	*I buy some oil*
any plural noun	J'achète **des** pommes	*I buy some apples*

If the sentence is negative, use **de** for all nouns (singular and plural) starting with a
consonant, and **d'** for all nouns (singular and plural) starting with a vowel or a
silent h.

Je n'ai pas **de** pain	*I have no bread*
Je n'ai pas **de** monnaie	*I haven't any change*
Je n'ai pas **d'**argent	*I have no money*
Je n'ai pas **de** pommes	*I haven't any apples*

POSSESSION

French has no equivalent of the apostrophe **s** which is used in English to signify
ownership, so the words **du, de la, de l'** and **des** are also used for this purpose:

le sac **du** garçon	*the boy's bag (one bag, one boy)*
le sac **de la** fille	*the girl's bag (one girl, one bag)*
le sac **de l'**enfant	*the child's bag (one child, one bag)*
le sac **des** garçons	*the boys' bag (one bag, more than one boy)*
les sacs **des** garçons	*the boys' bags*
	(more than one bag, more than one boy)
le sac **d'**Anne et **de** Paul	*Anne and Paul's bag*

Possessive Adjectives

The words expressing the ideas of ownership are adjectives and therefore they must match their noun. They match the gender of the thing owned, not the sex of the owner!

"C'est **mon** pullover, c'est **ma** chemise, ce sont **mes** chaussures." dit Luc. "Ils sont **à moi!**"

*"It's **my** pullover, it's **my** shirt, they're **my** shoes!" says Luke. "They are **mine!**"*

	MS	FS	Plural (M&F)		Meaning
	1 person/thing		2+ persons/things		
1 owner	**mon** père	**ma** mère	**mes** frères	**mes** sœurs	*my*
	ton père	**ta** mère	**tes** frères	**tes** sœurs	*your*
	son père	**sa** mère	**ses** frères	**ses** sœurs	*his*
	son père	**sa** mère	**ses** frères	**ses** sœurs	*her*
2+ owners	**notre** père	**notre** mère	**nos** frères	**nos** sœurs	*our*
	votre père	**votre** mère	**vos** frères	**vos** sœurs	*your*
	leur père	**leur** mère	**leurs** frères	**leurs** sœurs	*their*

DEMONSTRATIVE ADJECTIVES

There are four words for **this/that** and **these/those**

masculine singular	Je préfère **ce** pullover	*I prefer this pullover*
masculine singular noun with vowel	Je préfère **cet** anorak	*I prefer this anorak*
masculine noun with silent h	Je préfère **cet** hôtel	*I prefer this hotel*
feminine singular	Je préfère **cette** chemise	*I prefer this shirt*
any plural noun	Je préfère **ces** chaussettes	*I prefer these socks*

To emphasise the words *this* and *that*, the suffixes **-ci** and **-là** are added to the noun:

Example:	ce pullover-**ci**	*this pullover*
	ce pullover-**là**	*that pullover*

NEGATIVES

Two words are usually required in French to turn a positive statement into a negative one. The first one is always **ne** or **n'**. The second one gives the exact meaning.

Je réponds	+ **ne... pas**	becomes	Je **ne** réponds **pas**
I answer			*I don't answer*
Je réponds	+ **ne... jamais**	becomes	Je **ne** réponds **jamais**
I answer			*I never answer*
Je dis	+ **ne... rien**	becomes	Je **ne** dis **rien**
I say			*I say nothing*
Je vois	+ **ne... personne**	becomes	Je **ne** vois **personne**
I see			*I see no-one, I can't see anybody*

REGULAR VERBS

There are three families or groups of verbs which form the patterns for other verbs to follow.

Each one is known by the last two letters of the infinitive, **-er**, **-ir**, or **-re**.

The largest group of regular verbs is the **-er** group. These behave like **regarder**.

Infinitif Infinitive	Présent Present	Passé Composé Perfect	Impératif Imperative
regarder *to look at, watch*	je regarde tu regardes il/elle regarde nous regardons vous regardez ils/elles regardent	j'ai regardé tu as regardé il/elle a regardé nous avons regardé vous avez regardé ils/elles ont regardé	 regarde regardons regardez
	Imparfait **Imperfect**	**Futur** **Future**	**Passé Simple** **Past Historic**
	je regardais tu regardais il/elle regardait nous regardions vous regardiez ils/elles regardaient	je regarderai tu regarderas il/elle regardera nous regarderons vous regarderez ils/elles regarderont	 il/elle regarda ils/elles regardèrent

Commonly used regular -er verbs include:

accepter, accompagner, accrocher, aider, aimer, arriver*, chercher, compter, danser, déjeuner, désirer, dessiner, détester, donner, durer, éclater, écouter, entrer*, frapper, fréquenter, fumer, gagner, indiquer, inviter, jouer, laver, louer, marcher, monter*, montrer, oublier, parler, penser, pleurer, porter, poser, pousser, préparer, quitter, raconter, rencontrer, rentrer*, réparer, réserver, rester*, retourner*, rouler, sauter, sonner, téléphoner, tomber*, toucher, tourner, traverser, trouver, verser, visiter, voler

Verbs marked * take **être** in the *passé composé.*

Example: Elle est montée au dernier étage   *She went up to the top floor*
Il est rentré à 7 heures   *He came home at 7 o'clock*

However, **monter** and **rentrer** will take **avoir** if they have a direct object:

Example: Elle a monté sa valise   *She took her case upstairs*
Il a rentré les provisions dans la maison *He brought the groceries in*

A smaller family is the **-ir** group These verbs behave like **finir**.

Infinitif Infinitive	Présent Present	Passé Composé Perfect	Impératif Imperative
finir *to finish*	je finis tu finis il/elle finit nous finissons vous finissez ils/elles finissent	j'ai fini tu as fini il/elle a fini nous avons fini vous avez fini ils/elles ont fini	finis finissons finissez
	Imparfait Imperfect	**Futur Future**	**Passé Simple Past Historic**
	je finissais tu finissais il/elle finissait nous finissions vous finissiez ils/elles finissaient	je finirai tu finiras il/elle finira nous finirons vous finirez ils/elles finiront	il/elle finit ils/elles finirent

Commonly used regular -ir verbs include: choisir, remplir, rougir, saisir.

The third family is the **-re** group. These verbs behave like **répondre.**

Infinitif Infinitive	Présent Present	Passé Composé Perfect	Impératif Imperative
répondre *to answer, reply*	je réponds tu réponds il/elle répond nous répondons vous répondez ils/elles répondent	j'ai répondu tu as répondu il/elle a répondu nous avons répondu vous avez répondu ils/elles ont répondu	réponds répondons répondez
	Imparfait Imperfect	**Futur Future**	**Passé Simple Past Historic**
	je répondais tu répondais il/elle répondait nous répondions vous répondiez ils/elles répondaient	je répondrai tu répondras il/elle répondra nous répondrons vous répondrez ils/elles répondront	il/elle répondit ils/elles répondirent

Commonly used regular -re verbs include: attendre, descendre*, entendre, rendre, vendre. Verbs marked * take **être** in the passé composé.

    Example: Nous sommes descendus de bonne heure *We came downstairs early*
However, **descendre** will take **avoir** when it has a direct object.

    Example: Elle a descendu sa valise   *She brought her case downstairs*

REFLEXIVE VERBS

These are verbs which describe actions such as washing and getting dressed which people do for themselves. They have an extra pronoun.
There are some verbs which are reflexive in French but not in English.
These include *s'arrêter* and *se sentir*.
All reflexive verbs behave like *se laver*.
The vast majority of them are -er verbs, but the more common irregular reflexive verbs can be found in the irregular verb table. They are marked *v refl* §.

	Présent Present	Passé Composé Perfect	Impératif Command
se laver *to wash* (*oneself*)	je me lave tu te laves il/elle se lave nous nous lavons vous vous lavez ils/elles se lavent	je me suis lavé(e) tu t'es lavé(e) il s'est lavé elle s'est lavée nous nous sommes lavé(e)s vous vous êtes lavé(e)/lavé(e)s ils se sont lavés elles se sont lavées	lave-toi lavons-nous lavez-vous
	Imparfait **Imperfect**	**Futur** **Future**	**Passé Simple** **Past Historic**
	je me lavais tu te lavais il/elle se lavait nous nous lavions vous vous laviez ils/elles se lavaient	je me laverai tu te laveras il/elle se lavera nous nous laverons vous vous laverez ils/elles se laveront	il/elle se lava ils/elles se lavèrent

Commonly used reflexive verbs include:

s'amuser, s'arrêter, se baigner, se coucher, se dépêcher, se déshabiller, s'habiller, se laver, se trouver (*v refl*)

s'allonger, s'appeler, se déplacer, s'engager, s'ennuyer, s'exercer, s'inquiéter, s'intéresser à, se lever, se noyer, se placer, se promener, se rappeler, se succéder, se venger (*v refl* †) (See pages 232-233)

s'apercevoir, s'asseoir, se sentir, se souvenir de (*v refl* §) (See pages 208-226)

Reflexive verbs all take **être** in the *passé composé* and are marked *.

ER VERBS WITH VARIATIONS

Some of the frequently used -er verbs have variations from the usual present tense pattern. These are marked *v reg* †.

- **Manger** and other verbs ending in -ger need an extra -e- in the **nous** form:

  Example: je mange   tu manges   il/elle mange

  nous mangeons   vous mangez   ils/elles mangent

Commonly used verbs of this type include: allonger, aménager, arranger, bouger, changer, charger, corriger, déranger, échanger, engager, exiger, interroger, juger, loger, longer, mélanger, nager, négliger, neiger, obliger, partager, piger, plonger, prolonger, protéger, rager, rallonger, ranger, rédiger, ronger, songer, soulager, venger, voyager

- **Commencer** and other verbs ending in -cer need a cedilla in the **nous** form:

  Example: je commence   tu commences   il/elle commence

  nous commençons   vous commencez   ils/elles commencent

Commonly used verbs of this type include: agacer, annoncer, avancer, balancer, coincer, déplacer, divorcer, effacer, enfoncer, exercer, froncer, glacer, grincer, lancer, menacer, percer, pincer, placer, prononcer, recommencer, remplacer, renforcer, renoncer, sucer, tracer

- **S'appeler** doubles the l where the ending is silent:

  Example: je m'appelle   tu t'appelles   il/elle s'appelle

  nous nous appelons   vous vous appelez ils/elles s'appellent

Commonly used verbs of this type include: appeler, grommeler, peler, rappeler, renouveler

- **Jeter** doubles the t where the ending is silent:

  Example: je jette   tu jettes   il/elle jette

  nous jetons   vous jetez   ils/elles jettent

- Verbs like **lever** add accents where the ending is silent:

  Example: je lève   tu lèves   il/elle lève

  nous levons   vous levez   ils/elles lèvent

Commonly used verbs of this type include: acheter, amener, crever, élever, emmener, enlever, épeler, geler, haleter, marteler, mener, peser, ramener, semer, soulever

- Verbs like **préférer** change the final accent from **é** to **è** for a silent ending:

  Example: je préfère   tu préfères   il/elle préfère

            nous préférons   vous préférez   ils/elles préfèrent

Commonly used verbs of this type include: accélérer, céder, compléter, digérer, espérer, interpréter, lécher, oblitérer, pécher, pénétrer, précéder, posséder, récupérer, régler, régner, répéter, révéler, sécher, succéder, suggérer, tolérer, transférer, vociférer

Note: **protéger** behaves like this group, but also has an extra **e** in the **nous** form:

  Example: il protège   nous protégeons

- **Envoyer** and other verbs ending in **-yer** change the **y** to **i** with a silent ending:

  Example: j'envoie   tu envoies   il/elle envoie

            nous envoyons   vous envoyez   ils/elles envoient

Commonly used verbs of this type include: aboyer, appuyer, balayer, effrayer, employer, ennuyer, essayer, essuyer, nettoyer, renvoyer, tournoyer

In the present tense **payer** can be either **je paie** or **je paye**
In the future tense it can be either: **je paierai** or **je payerai**
Note that the irregularities in the present tense of these verbs affect other tenses.

IRREGULAR VERBS

There are many irregular verbs in French. These are listed in the verb table on pages 208-226.

PERFECT TENSE

This is the tense which is used in **conversation** and in **letters** to describe:
- an action in the past which has been completed
- an action in the past which happened on one occasion only

The *passé composé* has two parts:
- the auxiliary verb, which is the present tense of either **avoir** or **être**
- and the past participle

Perfect tense with avoir

To form the past participles of **regular verbs**, remove the final two letters
(**-er, -ir, -re**) from the infinitive and add **-é**, **-i** or **-u** to the remaining stem:

  regarder becomes **regardé**   **finir** becomes **fini**   **répondre** becomes **répondu**

The past participles of **irregular verbs** have to be looked up in the verb table, then learnt. Past participles are marked *pp* when they are listed in this dictionary.

Perfect tense with être

Not all verbs take **avoir**. There are 16 common verbs which form the perfect tense with **être** as the auxiliary. These are marked * in this dictionary. Most of them can be remembered in groups which are opposite (or nearly opposite) in meaning.

arriver*	descendre*	venir*	entrer*	naître*	tomber*
partir*	monter*	revenir*	rentrer*	mourir*	rester*
		aller*	sortir*		retourner*

When they are arranged in this order, the initial letters of the first verb in each group spell the word **a d v e n t** - it might help in remembering them!

The important point with the verbs which take être is that the past participle must agree with the subject:

	Masculine	**Feminine**
je suis	venu	venue
tu es	venu	venue
il est	venu	
elle est		venue
on est	venu	
Chris est	venu **(boy)**	venue **(girl)**
nous sommes	venus	venues
vous êtes	venu(s)**	venue(s)**
ils sont	venus	
elles sont		venues
les enfants sont	venus	

** depending on whether *vous* is masculine or feminine, singular or plural

Three of the sixteen verbs which take **être** are also commonly found with **avoir** when they have a direct object.
    Examples:

J'ai monté les valises	*I took the cases upstairs*
J'ai descendu les bagages	*I brought the luggage down*
Elle a sorti son mouchoir	*She took out her handkerchief*

PRONOUNS

- **Tu** is used when speaking to **one** person you know well, to a member of the family, to a child or to a pet.

- **Vous** is used when speaking to **two** or more people, either good friends or strangers.
  Vous is also used when speaking to **one adult** you do not know very well.

- **Il** and **elle** can mean **it** when referring to masculine or feminine nouns.

- **On** has a variety of meanings: **we, one, they, you, people, someone.**

- **Ils** is used for **they** when **all** the nouns referred to are masculine or when there is a group of nouns, **one** of which is masculine.

- **Elles** is used for **they** when speaking of 2+ girls or women or when **all** the nouns in a list are feminine.

WRITING LETTERS AND POSTCARDS

In the GCSE (and many other examinations) candidates are often asked to write a letter or a postcard in French. In examinations, it is particularly important to **carry out the tasks set in the question.** In other words, you should not write a pre-prepared letter which has only a vague resemblance to the question on the exam paper.

Postcards are nearly always to friends. Letters can be to friends and family (informal letters) or to businesses, hotels or public offices (formal letters).

Informal letters and postcards

Letter envelope:
When you write an envelope or a card to an address in France:-
> The surname is written first, often in capitals.
> The word **rue** is written with a small **r.**
> There is a 5-figure postcode. It is written
> before the name of the town, on the same line.
> The town is written in capital letters.

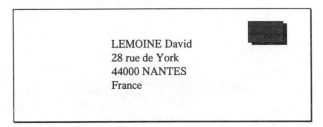

The name and address of the sender are normally written on the back of the envelope, after the word *Expéditeur:* or *Exp:* (Sender).

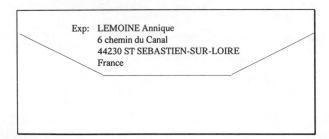

Informal Letters:

Town and date: It is usual just to write the name of the town and the date.
                     Put this information in the **top right-hand corner** of the page.

Dear ...   Cher Robert,   (male)
                     Chère Anne,   (female)
                     Cher Robert, chère Anne,   (more than one person)
                     Chers amis,   (plural, all male, male and female)
                     Chères amies,   (plural, all female)

Tu or vous?   Informal letters and postcards to one person are usually written
                     in the **tu** form.
                     Check that **tu** is used consistently, and if you need to say
                     "please..." remember to use "...s'il **te** plaît"

Closing   Useful phrases include:

                     C'est tout pour aujourd'hui   *That's all for today*
                     Maintenant je vais faire mes   *Now I'm going to do*
                     devoirs   *my homework*
                     En attendant de tes nouvelles   *I'm looking forward to*
                                                      hearing from you
                     Ecris-moi bientôt   *Write soon*
                     A bientôt   *See you soon*

Signing off   This list becomes more friendly as you read on.
                     Just use one of these phrases:

                     Amicalement
                     Amitiés
                     Ton ami   (if you are male)
                     Ton amie   (if you are female)
                     Ton correspondant   (if you are male)
                     Ta correspondante   (if you are female)
                     Grosses bises

                     Finally, sign your name.

Formal letters

Your address	In the **top left-hand corner** of the page write your own name and address. French people often write their surname first in capital letters and their first name in upper and lower case letters. (Example: *LEMOINE David*)
Date:	In the **top right-hand corner** of the page write the date.

Recipient's Address

In the **top right-hand corner** of the page under the date put the address you are writing to.

Dear ...	Monsieur,	*Dear Sir*
	Madame,	*Dear Madam*
	Messieurs,	*Dear Sirs*

Tu or vous?	Formal letters are always written in the **vous** form.
Signing off	Business letters in French usually end with a *formule* which is the equivalent of *Yours sincerely* or *Yours faithfully*. There are many variations of the *formule*. The two versions suggested here are often used.

Veuillez agréer, Monsieur, l'expression de mes sentiments distingués.

Je vous prie d'agréer, Madame, l'expression de mes sentiments distingués.

Remember to change *Monsieur* to *Madame* or *Messieurs* to match the gender and number of the person or people who will receive the letter.

Finally, sign your name.

The envelope:	Your name and address are normally written on the back of the envelope, after Expéditeur/Exp. (See page 236).

Sample formal letter

> *le 6 juin 1998*
>
> *WHITE John*   *Syndicat d'initiative*
> *32 New Street*   *2 place du marché*
> *OLDTOWN*   *23310 BAINVILLE*
> *OT6 7XY*   *France*
> *GB*
>
> *Messieurs,*
>
> *Je vous écris pour savoir.......*
>
>
>
> *Veuillez agréer, Messieurs, l'expression de mes sentiments distingués.*
>
> *John White*

Sample informal letter

> *Malvern, le 6 juin 1998*
>
> *Chère Béatrice,*
>
> *Je t'écris pour savoir.......*
>
>
>
> *En attendant de tes nouvelles*
> *Amitiés*
>
> *John*

INSTRUCTIONS

Note: These instructions have been given in the **vous** form, which is the one used by most text books and exam boards. Versions of the most frequently used command words in the **tu** form can be found at the end of this section on page 244.

All four skills: Listening, Reading, Speaking, Writing

Sequence words

d'abord	*first*
maintenant	*now*
puis	*then*

Questions

à quelle heure?	*at what time?*
c'est combien?	*how much is it?*
combien coûte...?	*how much does ... cost?*
comment?	*how?*
comment est-il?	*what is he/it like?*
lequel préférez-vous?	*which one do you prefer?*
où?	*where?*
où est?	*where is?*
où sont?	*where are?*
pourquoi?	*why?*
quand?	*when?*
qu'est-ce que?	*what?*
que veut dire...?	*what does ... mean?*
qui a raison?	*who is right?*

Information

à votre avis	*in your opinion*
elle parle au sujet de	*she is talking about*
elle parle avec...	*she is speaking to ...*
en anglais	*in English*
en chiffres	*in numbers*
en français	*in French*
entre deux personnes	*between two people*
faux	*false, wrong*
il parle au sujet de	*he is talking about*
il y aura deux pauses pendant l'annonce	*there will be two pauses in the announcement*
il y aura deux pauses pendant l'extrait	*there will be two pauses in the extract*

les réponses suivantes	*the following answers*
pour chaque client	*for each customer*
pour chaque personne	*for each person*
pour chaque question	*for each question*
quelques phrases	*some sentences*
quelques questions	*some questions*
tournez la page	*turn over the page*
voici un exemple	*here is an example*
vous n'aurez pas besoin de toutes les lettres	*you will not need all the letters*
vrai	*true*

Listening and Reading

arrangez les mots correctement	*arrange the words in the correct order*
choisissez la description qui correspond le mieux	*choose the description which best fits*
choisissez la réponse correcte	*choose the correct answer*
cochez la case	*tick the box*
cochez la phrase appropriée	*tick the appropriate sentence*
cochez les cases (appropriées)	*tick the (appropriate) boxes*
cochez seulement 5 cases	*tick 5 boxes only*
complétez le tableau	*complete the table*
complétez la grille	*complete the grid*
complétez la liste	*complete the list*
complétez les comparaisons	*complete the comparisons*
complétez les détails	*complete the details*
complétez les phrases	*complete the sentences*
corrigez l'affirmation	*correct the statement*
corrigez les erreurs	*correct the mistakes*
corrigez les fautes	*correct the mistakes*
décidez	*decide*
dessinez une flèche pour montrer quelle illustration va avec quel panneau	*draw an arrow to show which picture goes with which sign*
écrivez dans la case le numéro de l'illustration	*write the number of the illustration in the box*
écrivez l'équivalent en anglais	*write the equivalent in English*
écrivez le mot qui ne va pas avec les autres	*write the odd word out*
écrivez le numéro	*write the number*
écrivez les détails	*write the details*
écrivez la lettre	*write the letter*
écrivez la lettre qui correspond	*write the letter which matches*
écrivez les numéros qui correspondent	*write the numbers which match*
écrivez les réponses	*write the answers*

écoutez attentivement	*listen carefully*
écoutez bien	*listen carefully*
écoutez l'exemple	*listen to the example*
encerclez oui ou non	*circle yes or no*
est-ce que les phrases sont vraies ou fausses?	*are the sentences true or false?*
expliquez comment	*explain how*
expliquez pourquoi	*explain why*
faites correspondre	*match up*
faites des notes	*make notes*
indiquez sur le plan	*mark on the plan/map*
indiquez sur la carte	*mark on the map*
lisez attentivement	*read carefully*
lisez l'article, le texte, l'histoire	*read the article, the text, the story*
lisez la lettre	*read the letter*
lisez la liste	*read the list*
lisez les annonces	*read the adverts*
lisez les informations	*read the information*
lisez les instructions	*read the instructions*
lisez les phrases suivantes	*read the following sentences*
lisez les questions	*read the questions*
lisez un extrait d'un journal	*read the extract from a newspaper*
mettez la bonne lettre dans la case	*put the correct letter in the box*
mettez les images dans le bon ordre	*put the pictures into the correct order*
notez les détails	*note down the details*
prenez des notes	*make notes*
regardez la grille	*look at the grid*
regardez les dessins	*look at the drawings*
regardez les notes	*look at the notes*
remplissez la grille	*fill in the grid*
remplissez les blancs	*fill in the blanks*
répondez à toutes les questions	*answer all the questions*
répondez aux questions	*answer the questions*
répondez en français	*answer in French*
répondez en français ou cochez les cases	*answer in French or tick the boxes*
si l'affirmation est vraie, cochez la case **vrai**	*if the statement is true, tick the **true** box*
si la phrase est vraie, cochez la case **vrai**	*if the sentence is true, tick the **true** box*
si la remarque est fausse,	*if the statement is incorrect,*
écrivez une remarque correcte	* write a correct one*
soulignez	*underline*
tournez la page	*turn the page, turn over*
trouvez la bonne réponse à chaque question	*choose the right answer to each question*

trouvez la phrase qui correspond à chaque photo	*find the sentence which matches each photo*
trouvez l'erreur	*find the mistake*
trouvez le symbole qui correspond au mot	*find the symbol which matches the word*
trouvez le texte qui correspond à chaque image/dessin/titre	*find the text which matches each picture/drawing/title*
trouvez les mots, les phrases	*find the words, the phrases*
trouvez X sur le plan	*find X on the plan*
vous allez entendre deux fois une série de petites conversations	*you will hear twice a series of short conversations*
vous allez entendre un message/une conversation/un dialogue/une émission/ un programme/un reportage à la radio/ une interview à la télévision	*you are going to hear a message/ a conversation/a dialogue/ a programme/a programme/ a radio report/a TV interview*
vous pouvez utiliser un dictionnaire si vous voulez	*you may use a dictionary if you wish*
vous trouverez des informations sur....	*you will find information on...*

Speaking

décrivez l'image	*describe the picture*
demandez les informations suivantes	*ask for the following information*
finissez poliment la conversation	*end the conversation politely*
parlez	*speak*
posez des questions	*ask questions*
racontez les choses que vous avez faites	*say what you did*
regardez les images, les photos	*look at the pictures, the photos*
remerciez le commerçant	*thank the shopkeeper*
saluez l'examinateur	*greet the examiner*
utilisez ces symboles pour faire un dialogue	*use the symbols to make up a dialogue*
vous allez répondre à quelques questions	*you are going to reply to some questions*

Writing

choisissez le thème 1 ou le thème 2	*choose title 1 or title 2*
dans votre lettre vous devez....	*in your letter you should...*
demandez des conseils	*ask for advice*
demandez les détails suivants	*ask for the following details*
donnez les renseignements	*give information*
écrivez environ 100 mots	*write about 100 words*
écrivez les détails	*write the details*
écrivez un article	*write an article*
écrivez une carte postale	*write a postcard*
écrivez une lettre	*write a letter*

écrivez une réponse	*write a reply*
écrivez votre avis avec les raisons	*write your opinion and the reasons for it*
expliquez comment	*explain how*
expliquez pourquoi	*explain why*
faites une comparaison	*make a comparison*
faites une description	*describe/write a description of*
faites une liste	*write a list*
faites un résumé	*summarise*
imaginez que...	*imagine that...*
mentionnez	*mention*
modifiez	*change*
préparez les tâches suivantes en français	*prepare the following tasks in French*
préparez un dépliant, un poster	*prepare a brochure, a poster*
présentez-vous	*introduce yourself*
racontez ce que vous avez fait	*say what you did*
racontez les choses que vous avez faites	*say what you did*
racontez vos impressions	*give your impressions*
remplissez la fiche	*fill in the form*
remplissez le formulaire	*fill in the form*
répondez à la lettre	*reply to the letter*
répondez aux questions posées dans la lettre	*answer the questions asked in the letter*
vous pouvez utiliser un dictionnaire	*you can use a dictionary*

Common commands in the tu form

arrange	*arrange*	lis	*read*
choisis	*choose*	mentionne	*mention*
coche	*tick*	mets	*put*
complète	*complete*	note	*note*
corrige	*correct*	parle	*speak (about)*
décide	*decide*	pose	*ask (questions)*
décris	*describe*	prépare	*prepare*
demande	*ask*	raconte	*tell (a story)*
dessine	*draw*	regarde	*look at*
donne	*give*	remplis	*fill in*
écoute	*listen to*	réponds	*reply*
écris	*write*	salue	*greet*
encercle	*circle*	souligne	*underline*
explique	*explain*	tourne	*turn*
fais	*make*	trouve	*find*
finis	*finish*	tu peux	*you can*
imagine	*imagine*	utilise	*use*
indique	*indicate*		